# Into the Wilderness Dream

# Into the Wilderness Dream

## Exploration Narratives of the
## American West 1500–1805

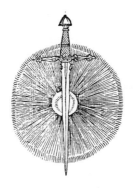

Edited by Donald A. Barclay,
James H. Maguire, and Peter Wild

University of Utah Press
Salt Lake City

See page 387 for permissions.

**Library of Congress Cataloging-in-Publication Data**

Into the wilderness dream : exploration narratives of the American
   West, 1500–1805 / edited by Donald A. Barclay, James H. Maguire, and
   Peter Wild.
     p.  cm.
   Includes bibliographical references and index.
   ISBN 0-87480-443-4. — ISBN 0-87480-444-2 (pbk.)
   1. West (U.S.) — Discovery and exploration.  2. West (U.S.)—
Description and travel—Early works to 1800.  I. Barclay, Donald
A., 1958–   .  II. Maguire, James H.  III. Wild, Peter, 1940–   .
F592.I68   1994
978'.01—dc20                              93-34275

# Contents

# Acknowledgments

The editors appreciate the help of historian Darlis Miller, anthropologist Marilyn Saul, and the faculties and staffs of the University of Arizona Library, the Boise State University Library, and the New Mexico State University Library.

For the fine translation of Montalvo's *Las Sergas de Esplandián* appearing below, we thank Professor Richard Kinkade of the University of Arizona's Department of Spanish and Portuguese. While offering readers accessible English, Professor Kinkade's rendition preserves the flavor of the sixteenth-century Spanish.

# Introduction

Centuries before there was an America or a 1492 or a Christopher Columbus, peoples such as the ancient Greeks imagined fabulous lands lying westward, out in the Atlantic, beyond the Gates of Hercules. Such notions seem endemic to cultures, regardless of the slim evidence to substantiate the dreams, for, whatever else humans are, they are dreaming animals, given to transcending reality on the wings of fancy. And there's usually a sufficient supply of travelers' rumors, of tales spun by daydreamers, and of outright liars to feed such dreams, until they achieve the status of reality. Indeed the power of wish fulfillment avidly builds on the slightest evidence. Hadn't the great traveler Herodotus himself seen a Pygmy cavalry mounted on cranes, as well as other, even more wondrous marvels? The miraculous lies out there in a misty territory just beyond the known. If medieval peasants believed in monstrous Wild Men and Wild Women lurking in the gloom of their own forests, it's not much of a step in fact from that to belief in eupeptic Isles of Flowers and Isles of Angels—so short a step in fact that early cartographers drew such islands on maps, as their fancies moved them.

So during the Age of Discovery, when the prows of European ships were slicing into the beaches of unknown lands—lands with strange animals and stranger peoples, lands that seemed to go on forever and whose vastness surely harbored riches—the explorers simply had chanced upon the physical confirmations of what had already existed for centuries in peoples' fertile minds. Within this context, that people would plunge off into jungles bent on finding cities of gold or fountains of youth is hardly as preposterous as some schoolbooks make out. As he skimmed the Venezuelan coast, past the mouth of the Orinoco, Columbus declared that up that river "... I believe in my soul... the earthly paradise is situated" (Jones 1964, 8). The Great Navigator must have felt the excitement of being close to what people always have craved: Heaven on Earth.

It should not be supposed, however, that the oneiric urge was the sole factor pulling Europeans toward the new lands. We're perhaps overly fixated on the flashy exploits of Columbus and De Soto, and as a result we tend to forget that a host of figures made significant forays into the unknown for any number of combined motives. Much of this surely was economic, if not a matter of survival. People are divided by schisms and move on, seek alternatives to depleted soils, or follow their cravings and look elsewhere for the luxuries and necessities their homelands don't provide. Civilizations as far apart in chronology, geography, and culture as the ancient Egyptians and the Hopi Indians of the American Southwest may appear to be relatively stable, as they stayed close to the Nile River or remained secure in their mesa-top aeries. But such peoples weren't exclusively stay-at-homes. They participated in systems of trade routes often hundreds if not thousands of miles long. To varying degrees historians emphasize economic factors behind travel and exploration, yet we'd also suggest that if humans are dreamers, they're also traveling animals, compelled to have a look at the other side of the mountain, if for no other reason than to see what's there. In short, humans are footloose creatures.

As to the New World, other, ever more complex dimensions would evolve as the process of discovery erupted into a royal fracas among nations, a free-for-all beginning the greatest mass migration in human history. First of all, if this *was* the "earthly paradise," who would possess it? Ecumenicalism was hardly the watchword. There was some talk, though not especially heeded talk, about protecting the rights of natives to their homelands. More practically European powers got down to the business of squabbling among themselves. Spain had gotten an early jump in the New World, but Portugal wanted her slice. Ever suspicious of its old enemy—Roman Catholic Spain—Protestant England leapt into the fray, sending forth not only explorers to stake out chunks of an unmapped continent, but privateers such as Sir Francis Drake, to prey on the gold-fat Spanish galleons. For a while history became a barroom brawl, with Spain, Portugal, England, France, and other European countries going at it tooth and nail. Even the pope got involved now and then. Cloak-and-dagger intrigues within each country added to the confusion, as adventurers jockeyed for power in games of one-upmanship with their rivals. Given the atmosphere of jealousies and betrayals among and within nations, it's little wonder that Columbus eventually came home in chains, or that Cortez's rivals manipulated the conqueror of Mexico's mind-boggling wealth to the sidelines, where he ended his life in poverty.

But if this is shot and powder for cynics, there's a positive side to the mass commotion spun by the ancient dream. Peering across the foggy sea from England, the seventeenth-century philosopher John Locke put it this way: "In the beginning all the world was *America*." That is, the New World was, or was perceived to be, humanity's last hope, a pristine place of freedom and abundance, where a humanity gone sorely wrong had one more chance to work out the botched attempts at building a decent civilization.

Perhaps in our present affluence of goods and freedoms we don't appreciate how gloomy a place Europe was when the New World suddenly appeared glittering over the western horizon. Peasants doggedly tilled the land for their masters, often living in huts along with their pigs and cows. Chances of brighter prospects, of escaping their iron drudgery, hardly were to be considered. Meanwhile the privileged few entertained themselves by striving for power in wars that tore back and forth across the earth in a progress of rape, pillage, and burning. It was just such endless turmoil and human misery that later led Thomas Jefferson to declare Europe "a great mad-house."

Then bright America hoves into view—free land, free timber, silver, gold, pearls—amazing riches all there for the taking. In a word—hope. No wonder peasants gawked at the marvelous prospects and, as would their descendants a couple of hundred years later in their manic rush for California, simply abandoned their plows, their churches, their masters for the promise of a radical improvement of their lot across the ocean.

And not only their physical lot. Converging with the dazzling opportunities (or maybe because of them), new concepts were budding in Europe about the individual's potential place in the world, new ideas about religious choice, personal development, and political freedoms; in short, ideas about the shedding of the old repressions and economic slavery that led in a direct line to the hopeful documents of the *Declaration of Independence* and the *Constitution*—to the very attitudes about what society should and can be that move us in our sometimes desperate "Pursuit of Happiness."

In brief the explorers before Lewis and Clark who probed the new continent in a sense were new men who had peeled off their restrictive clothing. But they also arrived in pursuit of ancient dreams now about to be fulfilled. Or so they thought. Such ebullient expectations shaped what they saw, how they saw, and how they reacted. And it is precisely this complex of attitudes and aspirations that the following pages in part document for the North American continent. Attitudes and aspirations that, one might add, sometimes for the better and sometimes for the worse, continue to drive us. In this sense such a book as this is an exploration of our origins, an expansion of our own concepts of who we are today.

It is also a comment on the flexuous relationship between the imagination and reality, between events and the literature that springs out of them. We've commented earlier about the human propensity both to dream and be footloose. Travel literature combines the two urges, and not only concerning satisfaction on the part of armchair writers and readers. The oldest extant works of European literature, the *Iliad* and the *Odyssey*, spring from the expeditions involved in the tale of Troy. Thereafter, down through European literature, the travel motif has been strong. For whether or not one leaves home and braves the hazards of the open road and the open sea, the very idea of it flings open the doors of the imagination on what lies beyond everyday affairs. The wonder in Shakespeare's *Tempest* no doubt owes much to contemporary tales of shipwreck on strange shores, and whether we're considering Chaucer or Herman Melville, Jonathan Swift, Ernest Hemingway, or the host of nature and science-fiction writers currently popular, we're dealing with people testing the unknown with language. How much more powerful the urge must have been in the American West, when human beings believed they might still plunge off into the wilderness and find a rumored lost tribe of Welsh Indians or the prehistoric mammoths President Jefferson thought might exist in the unknown wilds beyond the Mississippi River. In a sense the explorers appearing in the following pages undid the mythical possibilities. Slowly they came to realize that the hills were *not* full of gold, that California was *not* an island ruled by a beautiful queen named Calafia. Slowly they had to admit that the longed-for Northwest Passage, as so many other things, simply did not exist. But while disproving illusions, such explorers also opened the door on realities not imagined, and in some cases they have proved far more complex and unyielding than illusions projected by the mind. And it's this new reality we're living with—in essence, the awareness of our relationships with each other and the land—that while proving far more intractable of solution also is a large part of the explorers' legacy to us.

Having said that, we should make clear that we are not promoting the Great-Man Theory of History, popular in centuries past. On the one hand, the explorers we present were bright and able achievers indeed, and some perhaps belong in the category of genius. No doubt each gave a singular twist to history, left us with an individually stamped legacy, as did, in other fields, Galileo and Beethoven. Yet on the other hand, though such people often appear on the cutting edge of the thinking and accomplishments of their times, they also were products of a context, of a *Zeitgeist*. Given the long developments in Europe leading to the explorations of the Portuguese and such technological breakthroughs as the use of the compass, it would be as silly to argue that if Columbus had not discovered the New World no one else would have, as it would be to suppose that only Beethoven could have broken the conventions of classical music.

And neither do we subscribe to the currently fashionable Devil Theory of History; that is, the view that if Europeans had stayed out of the New World, today it would remain a pristine land of native peoples living in harmony with nature. Such a notion has romantic appeal, but it also ignores reality and is an insult to the diversity of indigenous peoples, who were not always "at one" with nature or with each other, contrary to what some industrialized people would like to imagine. Survival for the Indians depended on exploiting the environment—and each other—as best they could. And that they sometimes did so to their own demise is borne out by those irrigation cultures of the American Southwest whose bones now lie beneath the desert sands, in part because their own successes eventually did them in. They, variously, overcut their forests, depleted their soils, and caused the siltation of their own irrigation ditches, until their civilizations collapsed. In this we are dealing with the impact of technology on the land, and if anything can be generalized about the subject it is in fact this. The Europeans prevailed because they were better at technology than the peoples they conquered. The Europeans only accelerated an ages-old process, and the problem remains: How can humans create a sustainable relationship with the earth?

Along similar lines it would be easy to turn self-righteous and brand piratical Sir Francis Drake or mogul of the fur trade Sir Alexander Mackenzie as aggressive men bent on exploiting their fellows and fleecing a continent. There is some truth to the view, but not enough. In geopolitical terms, Drake, Mackenzie, and other explorers were figures in a complex of dynamic forces beyond any individual's control. Working themselves out through the centuries, the forces resulted in the settlement of vast geographical areas of the western United States and Canada. In the larger view, then, we are not dealing with questions of personal morality but with historical processes, processes that can be just as brutal, just as "red in tooth and claw" when it comes to history as when it comes to nature. Despite our personal wishes, violence is all around us, all around the world, in all cultures, and, sadly, it seems a persistent human trait. One need not turn to the well-known example of the Aztecs' vicious treatment of the neighboring tribes they conquered and the human sacrifice of Aztec captives. As the Spanish wanderer Cabeza de Vaca could attest from his own cruel experience, at times the Indians took slaves and otherwise brutalized their fellows, both white and Indian, a fact about human nature that deserves to be faced head-on rather than ignored in preference for gauzy, self-serving vagaries about Noble Savages.

Sentimentalized or not, the truth is that the Indians, in the course of invading an uninhabited New World, can lay the first claim to exploring North America. Unfortunately, however, they left no pre–Lewis-and-Clark record of the process, at least not in the European sense of printed maps and published accounts. Nonetheless, as seen in the cases of Cabeza de Vaca, La Vérendrye, Mackenzie, and most of the European adventurers, the information Indians supplied was important, and at times crucial, to the slow process of piecing together geography. On the other hand, sometimes playfully and at other times because of their own misunderstanding of geography, Indians could mislead their eager European auditors, and this illustrates a universal truth: that all humanity shares a similar set of human foibles.

This does not mean that narratives from a wider spectrum of humanity than is represented in these pages would not be desirable. The impressions of the Indian men and women who encountered European explorers, the impressions of the European women who participated in the later explorations, the impressions of the forgotten groundlings who labored for the leaders of the explorations are either too few or entirely lacking. These peoples have not been excluded from this anthology by the editors, but rather by a history that placed the power of literacy and the power of the press in the hands of an elite few. Had history been different, this anthology would be more representative; because the record cannot be changed, this anthology is what it is—a sampling of the existent narratives.

For all that, the early explorations were, in one way of looking at them, part of a long process that made the future triumph of Lewis and Clark possible. Their trip during 1804–6 was a culmination, for it found a route over the continent by crossing the Louisiana Purchase and the lands beyond to the Pacific Ocean. Furthermore by strengthening the United States' claims to the Pacific Northwest, the expedition began the final stage of knitting the Republic into a transcontinental nation. Yet as essential as this and other explorations were in shaping the United States and Canada, that story has often been told and told well. The following excerpts, together with their introductions, take a somewhat different tack into a less-known aspect of the matter.

If the records of most explorers tend to be dry, bare-bones recitations of the facts—"Went thirty leagues today. Many pine trees. The water in the spring tastes salty."—to our delight we've found others calculated for effect. To varying degrees they draw on the spectrum of verbal devices, such as imagery, sarcasm, and humor. They are, in brief, literature, or, in some cases, works approaching literature; for in one way or another, they manipulate language and the imagination behind it for purposes other than the simple transfer of information. Surely, as will be seen, this is manifestly true of a Cabeza de Vaca shaping his account in hopes of softening his king's heart and changing the policies of Spain, as it is, for quite different ends, of the acerb Georg Wilhelm Steller. Still other selections do not reach the full bloom of literature in the strictest sense. Instead they are prototypical, stating themes that grow into major elements of western American writing. Thus Castañeda's early comment on the land's beauty grows over the centuries into Edward Abbey's lament for a West gone wrong. It's an old theme in the region, one illustrating how history works its way into literature.

With this in mind, we offer the following exploration accounts, selections from a much larger body of writings that rightly deserve to take their places among more widely recognized works of western American literature.

The centuries-long gropings into the mists of the unknown to discover the shape of a continent have so fascinated the human imagination that scholars in pursuit of the process have left a mass of enlightening comment. This could generate an impressive list of works that would go on for many pages and still fall far short of completeness. As an alternative, for each chapter the editors risk oversimplification by mentioning several volumes that may prove helpful as a beginning for readers seeking a more detailed view of the explorers and the context of their accomplishments. Bernard DeVoto's *The Course of Empire* often appears here. Though somewhat dated, the book nonetheless offers gracious yet succinct introductions to many figures of the American West.

We ask that readers keep in mind the key difference between DeVoto's book and this anthology: whereas *The Course of Empire* is a history, *Into the Wilderness Dream* collects literary and protoliterary excerpts from narratives that tell the story of the encounter between ancient dreams and an even more ancient reality. To help readers experience that encounter as the explorers experienced it, we have refrained from providing maps and footnotes that explain exactly where the explorers were and what they were seeing. People whose appetites for history are whetted by this anthology can satisfy their hunger for more historical information by consulting the sources of our selections, which provide maps and footnotes sufficient to satisfy most people's curiosity. We have tried to follow not the feet but the imaginations of our authors.

To reiterate—as we must in order to avoid misperceptions—not all pre–Lewis-and-Clark exploration narratives give evidence of the imagination at work or play. For every exciting or artfully crafted page we've read in compiling this book, we've had to plow through dozens of others devoid of anything but the driest of details and the barest of facts. What we have assembled rises above those dusty pages and sparkles with the force of literature: we see—feelingly—what it was like for explorers to enter the unknown lands of the American West, lands dreamed about for centuries. We also find familiar stories, patterns of narrative, and types and archetypes. We recognize them because either by direct influence or because the western environment repeatedly shapes a certain pattern of experience, transformations of these literary designs have reappeared in the more recent literature of the nineteenth- and twentieth-century West. The western prairie, for example, evoked similar responses from explorers and early travelers; and in *The Great Prairie Fact and Literary Imagination*, Robert Thacker defines and then traces "the processes—recorded in literary texts—by which Europeans and their descendants came to understand the imaginative demands of prairie space and to incorporate them into esthetic conventions" (1989, 2). David Wyatt's *The Fall into Eden* (1986) offers a similar study of the interaction between California landscapes and literature.

Perhaps of even more relevance to the West at the dawn of the twenty-first century, these narratives show us how diverse this region always has been—diverse in people and landforms, wildlife and climate, history and myth. Although *Into the Wilderness Dream* is not a history, we hope that it will encourage an exploration similar to the one outlined by the historian Patricia Nelson Limerick at the conclusion of *The Legacy of Conquest* (1987, 349), her study of the dynamics of western history: "Indians, Hispanics, Asians, blacks, Anglos, businesspeople, workers, politicians, bureaucrats, natives, and newcomers, we share the same region and its history, but we wait to be introduced. The serious exploration of the historical process that made us neighbors provides that introduction."

Besides hoping that readers will undertake the serious exploration Limerick recommends, we also want them to enjoy this collection and accept our invitation to travel imaginatively with us into the dream of the New World.

## Selected Bibliography

Burpee, Lawrence J. *The Search for the Western Sea: The Story of the Exploration of North-Western America.* [1907]. 2 vols. New York: Macmillan, 1936.

Clissold, Stephen. *The Seven Cities of Cíbola.* New York: Potter, 1962.

DeVoto, Bernard. *The Course of Empire.* Boston: Houghton Mifflin, 1952.

Jones, Howard Mumford. *O Strange New World.* New York: Viking, 1964.

Limerick, Patricia Nelson. *The Legacy of Conquest: The Unbroken Past of the American West.* New York: Norton, 1987.

Lyon, Thomas J., ed. *This Incomperable Lande: A Book of American Nature Writing.* Boston: Houghton Mifflin, 1989.

Morison, Samuel Eliot. *The Great Explorers: The European Discovery of America.* New York: Oxford University Press, 1978.

Thacker, Robert. *The Great Prairie Fact and Literary Imagination.* Albuquerque: University of New Mexico Press, 1989.

Wyatt, David. *The Fall into Eden.* Cambridge, New York: Cambridge University Press, 1986.

# CHAPTER 1

# Two Views of the Mists

*Throughout, this book emphasizes the dreams about the New World that combined with other factors to lead Europeans swarming over a continent. Yet for thousands of years, native peoples had been dreaming about the lands they occupied. Fantasizing is universal, necessary to stimulate the mind and to create ways of dealing with stark reality. However, differences between cultural attitudes, especially those as far apart as the European and the American Indian, can be so wide that they defy bridging. To take one major aspect of cultures, the concept of time, for an example; Europeans and Indians share so little in this respect that the two approaches resist neat analysis and comparison. To say that the European tends to think of himself as moving forward through time and the Indian as sitting still while events move past him is to illustrate one large gap with a metaphor that pictures but does not fully explain the two concepts. Yet despite the possibility that this and other differences never will be satisfactorily clarified, perhaps the most important thing to realize is that there were vast gulfs in European and Indian approaches, and the differences helped determine how the two groups thought about the land. To hazard a generalization, Europeans tended to confuse their expectations with everyday reality, while Indians tended to keep the two separate.*

*Isles of the Blest, mountains that glow through the night, gold and pearls for the taking—we've already seen that Europeans could get wildly ebullient in their imaginings about the new regions across the sea, then act on their delusions, thus creating their own misfortunes. Yet there was a counterforce to their flights. One of the ancient Greeks' lasting contributions to western civilization is the idea of discovering truth, of scientifically measuring and plotting and intellectually weighing evidence, in order to arrive at objective knowledge. Whatever the bizarre qualities, even, one could argue, the madness, of Europeans' mental processes, there was an opposite tug: to part the mists of fantasy and determine what "really" lay out there, what the land was like and what it meant in rational terms. The process of finding out was*

1

*long and uneven, full of twists and turns, but the dreams bent and eventually succumbed. Despite their mental leapings, explorers slowly pieced together geography and determined the shape of western North America. Slowly the dreams that they had acted upon yielded to sobriety.*

*Much was gained and much was lost. Sailors trying to reach what now is called Alaska can give thanks for the charts that prevent them from blindly tacking off into the vastness of the Pacific Ocean, as sometimes happened to their less fortunate fellows of a couple of centuries ago. On the other hand, romantics can wonder, "What good is a map without blank spaces on it, without unknown regions to stir the imagination?" The lack of myth and wayward sentiment can lead to terrible ironies, to scientists who impale a butterfly on a pin and think they've thereby captured truth. And worse than that, to larger destruction. Proud of their scientific rectitude, convinced that science provided them with all the answers, engineering types beaming over their yardage have given us choked freeways, asphalted cities, and devastated forests. However beneficial science can be, the world is so complex that science never can give all the answers, but only one set of answers, a narrow paradigm that hardly satisfies our cravings for the mystical. To believe otherwise is to indulge in the self-deception of hubris, the lack of humility and the delusion of godlike power that the Greeks, for all their rationality, constantly warned about.*

*A popular error holds that Indians took the opposite approach. Yet Native Americans did not exist in a dreamy state, happy mooncalves spinning charming myths while they drifted through the harmony of nature. Nature indeed was their context, but it was a demanding one. Native people struggled against subzero cold, waterless deserts, starvation, and hordes of mosquitoes. Lacking the European technology that allows humans to overcome nature, Indians either adjusted their ways or perished. Practicality was the key to Indian survival.*

*It's a point often missed. In a complex ceremony accompanied by poetry and music, Yaqui dancers, for instance, pretend they are deer. Our vision made rosy by romantic longings, it's easy to see the dance as a charming cultural efflorescence. This it is, but it's also a hunting rite. The original purpose of the Deer Dance was to call on supernatural powers to control nature and entice a deer so that it could be killed. The dance, so it was believed, improved one's chances in the live-or-die business of getting enough to eat.*

*Not all features of Indian culture can be traced to specific ends. No doubt Indians often sang and danced and told stories, as other peoples do, for sheer entertainment. Yet whatever the case, the result was a parallel system quite different from the warring, European dichotomy of dream contending with* reality. An Indian tale about animals or spirits could have its own emotional, soul-satisfying validity without interfering with the tenets of daily life. Some Indians dance for rain and may believe that the ceremony is essential to bring the storms that will assure good harvests, yet in practical terms the same Indians have developed traditional forms of agriculture that make the most of precipitation, even when little of it falls; they don't let the dream get in the way of reality. This contrasts with the European settlers who met with disaster on the arid High Plains of western North America because they acted out their madcap delusions that "Rain follows the plow."

As to exploration, Indians moved about for any number of reasons—for food, trade, and out of curiosity. The following is from a long tale that is part of the Navajo Mountain Chant, a lengthy ceremony used variously for curing or assuring abundant crops. Here a young hunter travels unwillingly, as a captive of the Ute tribe, who lived to the north of the Navajos. Once he escapes, the man's problem is how to survive in hostile territory and get back home; the tale takes on an Alice-in-Wonderland quality as spirits and magic come to his assistance. Yet as can be seen in the specific place names mentioned elsewhere in the adventure, places readily identifiable today, it also is a story of exploration, about the practicality of learning about one's surrounding territory in order to survive.

### Selected Bibliography

Matthews, Washington. "The Mountain Chant: A Navajo Ceremony." Pp. 397–400 in *Fifth Annual Report of the Bureau of Ethnology: 1883–1884.* Ed. by John Wesley Powell. Washington, D.C.: U.S. Government Printing Office, 1887.

ANONYMOUS

# Two Views of the Mists

Now HE FEARED more than ever for his safety; he felt sure that his captors contemplated his death by torture. The pipes were lit and the council began. The talking in the strange tongue that he could not understand had lasted long into the night, when he fancied that he heard the voice of the Yèbitcai (Anglicized, Yày-bi-chy or Gay-bi-chy) above the din of human voices, saying "hu'hu'hu'hu" in the far distance. He strained his attention and listened well, and after a while he felt certain that he heard the voice again nearer and louder. It was not long until the cry was repeated for the third time, and soon after the captive heard it once more, loudly and distinctly, immediately to the west of the lodge. Then there was a sound as of footsteps at the door, and the white lightning entered through the smoke-hole and circled around the lodge, hanging over the heads of the council. But the Ute heard not the voice which the Navajo heard and saw not the vision he beheld. Soon the Yàybichy (Qastcèëlçi) entered the lodge and standing on the white lightning, said: "What is the matter with you, my grandchild? You take no thought about anything. Something you must do for yourself, or else, in the morning you will be whipped to death—that is what the council has decided. Pull out four pegs from the bottom of the tent, push it open there, and then you can shove things through." The Navajo answered, "How shall I do it? See the way I am tied! I am poor! See how I am wound up!" But Qastcèëlçi again said: "When you leave, take with you those bags filled with embroideries and take with you tobacco from the pouches near the fire." Scarcely had Qastcèëlçi disappeared when the Navajo heard a voice overhead, and a bird named quocçòɨi flew down through the smoke-hole, hovered four times around the lodge over the heads of the Ute, and departed by the way it had entered. In a moment after it had disappeared a few of the Ute began to nod and close their eyes; soon the others showed signs of drowsiness; some stretched themselves out on the ground overpowered with sleep; others rose and departed from time to time, singly and in little groups, to seek their lodges and repose there. The last to drop asleep were the old man and the old woman who sat at the door; but at length their chins fell upon their bosoms. Then the Navajo, fearing no watchers, went to work and loosened the cords that bound him; he lifted, from the inside, some of the pegs which held the edge of the tent, and shoved out the two bags of embroideries which Qastcèëlçi had told him to take. Passing out through the door of the lodge, where he found both the watch-dogs sound asleep, and taking with him the cords with which he had been tied and some of the tobacco, he went round to the back of the lodge, where he had put the bags; these he tied with the cords in such a manner that they would make an easily balanced double bundle. He shouldered his bundle and was all ready to start.

At this moment he heard, at a little distance to the south of where he stood, the hoot of an owl. Instantly recollecting the words of the owl-like form which he had encountered at the spring at nightfall, he set off in the direction from which the call proceeded. He had not walked far until he came to a precipitous bluff formed by two branching cañons, and it seemed at first impossible for him to proceed farther. Soon, however, he noticed a tall spruce tree, which grew beside the precipice from the foot to the summit, for the day had now begun to dawn and he could see objects more clearly. At this juncture Qastcèëlçi again appeared to him and said: "How is it, my grandchild, that you are still here? Get on the top of that spruce tree and go down into the cañon on it." The Navajo stretched out his hand to seize the top of the tree, but it swayed away from his grasp. "See, my grandfather," he said to Qastcèëlçi, "it moves away from me; I cannot reach it." Then Qastcèëlçi flung the white lightning around the top of the tree, as an Indian flings his lasso around the neck of a horse, and drew it in to the edge of the cliff. "Descend," he commanded the Indian, "and when you reach the bottom take four sprays from the tree, each from a different part. You may need them in the future." So the Navajo went down, took the four sprays as he was bidden and put them under his robe.

At the base of the bluff he again met Qastcèëlçi, and at this moment he heard a noise, as of a great and distant tumult, which seemed to come from above and from beyond the edge of the cliff whence they had descended. From moment to moment it grew louder and came nearer, and soon the sounds of angry voices could be distinguished. The Ute had discovered the flight of their captive and were in hot pursuit. "Your enemies are coming for you," said the divine one; "but yonder small holes on the opposite side of the cañon are the doors of my dwelling, where you may hide. The bottom of the cañon is strewn with large rocks and fallen trees; it would take you much time and hard labor to get over these if I did not help you; but I will do something to make your way easy." As he said this he blew a strong breath, and instantly a great white rainbow spanned the cañon. The Navajo tried to step on this in order to cross, but it was so soft that his feet went through; he could not step on it. Qastcèëlçi stood beside him and laughed at his fruitless attempts to get on the rainbow. After he had enjoyed this sport sufficiently the ye (Anglicized, gay or yay) blew another strong breath, when at once the rainbow became as hard as ice and they both crossed it with ease. When they reached the opposite wall of the cañon Qastcèëlçi pointed to a very small hole in the cliff and said, "This is the door of my lodge; enter!" By this time the shouts of the Ute sounded very loud in the ears of the terrified fugitive and it seemed to him that his pursuers must have reached the edge of the opposite cliff, where they would not be long before they would see him; still, hard as he tried to enter the cave, he could not succeed; the hole was not big enough for him to put his head in. The Yàbichy roared with laughter and slapped his hands together as he witnessed the abject fear and the fruitless efforts of the Navajo. When he had laughed enough he blew on the little hole and it spread instantly into a large orifice, through which they both entered with ease. They passed through three rooms and stopped in the fourth. Here Qastcèëlçi took the bags from the back of the Navajo, opened them, and drew from them some beautifully garnished clothing—a pair of moccasins, a pair of long-fringed leggings, and a shirt. He arrayed himself in these and went out, leaving the Navajo in the cave. As soon as his rescuer was gone the fugitive heard loud noises without and the sound of many angry voices, which continued for a long, long time. At last they died away and were heard no more. The Ute had tracked him to the edge of the cliff where he got on the tree; but there they lost his trail and searched all the neighborhood to see if they could regain it; hence the noises. When all was silent Qastcèëlçi returned and said, "Your enemies have departed; you can leave in safety." So, taking a tanned elk skin to cover his back and a pair of new moccasins to protect his feet, the Navajo set out from the cave.

It was nightfall when he emerged. He turned his face in the direction of his home and walked rapidly all the night. As day dawned he began to feel hopeful; but, ere the sun rose, distant sounds, which grew louder and louder, reached his ear. He knew them to be the voices of his pursuers and again he became sorely afraid. He hurried on and came near the foot of a high isolated pinnacle of rock, whose top appeared to be inaccessible. Glancing to the summit, however, he beheld standing there a black mountain sheep. Thinking that this singular vision was sent to him as a sign from the yays (gods) and boded well for him, he came to the base of the rock, when the sheep addressed him, saying: "My grandson, come around to the other side of the rock and you will find a place where you may ascend." He went around as he was bidden and saw the cleft in the rock, but it was too narrow for him to climb in it. Then the sheep blew into the cleft and it spread out so wide that he entered it easily and clambered to the summit. Here he found the sheep standing in four tracks, marked or sunken in the rock, one hoof in each track, and under the center of his body was a small hole in the rock. Into this hole the sheep bade him enter; but he replied that the hole was too small. Then the sheep blew on the hole and it spread so wide open that both the man and the sheep entered easily and descended into the heart of the rock. Here there were again four apartments; two of them were blue and two were black; rainbows extended in all directions through them. In the fourth room, which was black, the sheep left the Navajo to rest, and departed. Soon the fugitive heard, as on the previous day, when he lay hidden in the cave of Qastcèëlçi, the voices of the angry Ute calling and haranguing all around the rock, and he continued to hear them for a very long time. Soon after the clamor ceased the sheep returned to him to notify him that his enemies had withdrawn and that he could set out on his journey again without fear.

He journey homeward all the night, and when daylight began to appear he found himself on the banks of the stream where the Ute slept the night before they reached their tents, when they bore him home a captive. Here again he heard in the distance the voices of his pursuers and he hastened his steps. Presently he met a little old man sitting on the ground and cleaning cactus fruit. The old man had a sharp nose, little bright eyes, and a small moustache growing on each side of his upper lip. At once the Navajo recognized him as the Bush rat (*Neotoma mexicana*). The latter asked the traveler where he came from. "Oh, I am just roaming around here," was the answer. But the rat, not satisfied, repeated his question three times, in a manner which gave the Navajo to understand that his answer was not credited. So at last he answered truthfully that he was a Navajo who had been captured by the Ute, and that he was fleeing homeward from his captors, who were at that moment close behind him in pursuit. "It is well," said the rat, "that you have told me this, for I think I can save you. On yonder hillside there is a flat rock, and round about it are piled many little sticks and stones. It is my home, and I will guide you thither." He led the Indian to the rock and, showing him a small hole under it, bade him stoop low and place his head near the hole. As the Navajo obeyed the rat blew a strong breath on the hole, which at once opened wide enough to let the visitor in. The rat followed immediately behind him as he entered. Inside of the den there were an old woman, two young men, and two young women. These constituted the family of the Bush rat, who left the den as soon as the stranger was safely housed.

# CHAPTER 2

# Queen Calafia, Griffins, and the Naming of the Golden State (1500)

*Someone once noted that the United States has two capitals, one of politics, the other of fantasy. These capitals are, of course, Washington, D.C., and Hollywood, California. Ironically the national psyche finds the latter vastly more satisfying than the former. And not only Hollywood, but the dreamland the movie-making capital represents. California is a modern Lotus Land, where the warm tide of the young heart brims with satisfaction at the endless beaches and buoyant hopes. This involves a bright curiosity. In a nation whose written history is short, the sunny attitude has been around for well over four hundred years. And what's more, the state's very name is traceable to the fantastic dreams of Europeans. Traceable to a writer who never saw California or any other part of the New World.*

*The precise year when the name California was first applied to the state is uncertain. The speculations of scholars have ranged from explorers such as Hernando Cortez and Fortún Jiménez and on to various geographers. However, one thing is certain. Around the middle of the sixteenth century, California begins appearing on Spanish maps of the New World. The how and why of it is simple enough to explain. Yet, more intricately, the circumstances illustrate how what people read may influence what they later find, half a planet away. In brief, some Spaniard chose California as a place-name because the land reminded him of a marvelous tale in a book, and the label has stuck, resonating with the stuff of fantasy ever since (Gudde 1960, 46–47).*

*This brings us to a brief dip into Spanish literary history. In the early years of the sixteenth century, Garcí Ordóñez (or Rodríguez) de Montalvo published* Las Sergas de Esplandián (The Adventures of Esplandian). *This was a continuation of what generally is known as the* Amadis de Gaule, *a chivalric romance that had gone through several hands and been popular in Europe for at least two hundred years. The wildly ranging adventure tale takes the reader to many fantastic places around the world and is chock-full of fair damsels, monsters, giants, and enchantresses.*

*Spinning the story from his imagination, Montalvo reported a fabulous "island called California," a place lying close to the very West Indies the Spaniards were then exploring, inhabited by beautiful black women who indulged in some rather bizarre behavior. It should be remembered that the early explorers possessed a mind-set that often confused fact and fiction, dream and reality. When they first bumped into the present California, they thought they'd found a large island exactly where Montalvo said it would be, "to the right of the Indies." Naturally enough, the newcomers dubbed the place California. It would take another few hundred years for people to realize that Montalvo was uncannily right on yet another score: California's wealth in gold.*

*The following translates two chapters from Montalvo's Las Sergas concerning Queen Calafia. The pieces illustrate how strange a world the explorers thought they might enter with each step around the next bend. While shooting for accuracy, the English version also attempts to preserve some of the fluidity of the Spanish prose of the period. It might help the reader through the wild ride ahead to be prepared for the unexpected and keep in mind the basic situation in this portion of the romance. The Christians are defending the city of Constantinople from a siege by the pagan Turks. In the circumstances at hand, the Turks are being assisted in their attack by Queen Calafia and her troops, who have come all the way from California to help them.*

### Selected Bibliography

Gudde, Erwin G., ed. *California Place Names: The Origins and Etymology of Current Geographical Names.* Berkeley: University of California Press, 1960.

Montalvo, Garcí Ordóñez (or Rodríguez) de. Pp. 539–41 in *Las Sergas de Esplandián.* [1500?]. Ed. by Pascual de Gayangos. Biblioteca de Autores Españoles 40. Madrid: Imprenta de los Sucesores de Hernando, 1919.

O'Connor, John J. *Amadis de Gaule and Its Influence on Elizabethan Literature.* New Brunswick, N.J.: Rutgers University Press, 1970.

Polk, Dora Beale. *The Island of California: A History of the Myth.* Spokane, Wash.: Arthur H. Clark, 1991.

GARCI ORDÓÑEZ DE MONTALVO

# Queen Calafia, Griffins, and the Naming of the Golden State

### Of the fearful and unexpected succor which Queen Calafia brought in support of the Turks at the port of Constantinople.

AND NOW I WOULD LIKE to tell you about one of the strangest things ever to be found either in writing or the memory of mankind, where on the following day the city was on the verge of being lost, and how from whence came its danger there also came its salvation. Know that to the right of the Indies there was an island called California, very near the Earthly Paradise, which was inhabited by black women without a single man among them, and there they lived much as Amazons. These women were powerful of body, valiant, ardent of heart, and endowed with great strength; the island itself was made up of great cliffs and rugged mountains, more so than any other place on earth; and their arms were all of gold—as were the harnesses of the wild beasts which they tamed and rode—since there was on this island no other metal. They lived in well-wrought caves and had many ships in which they set out for other parts to pillage and plunder, and those men whom they seized, they carried off with them, slaying them cruelly as you shall now hear. And at times, when they had made peace with their enemies, they would mix with them freely and unite with them carnally, from whence many of them would become pregnant, and if they gave birth to a female child, they would keep it, and if they gave birth to a male child, straight away they would slay it. The cause of this, as you shall see, was because in their own minds they were firmly determined to reduce all men to such a small number that they might easily overcome them together with all their lands, keeping only those whom they considered useful for the purpose of procreation that their species might not perish.

On this island called California there were many griffins which, due to the ruggedness of the terrain and the infinite number of wild beasts which inhabited it, could be found in no other place on earth; and at that season of the year when the griffins gave birth to their young, these women, covered all over with thick leather, would catch them with great artfulness and bring them to their caves and there would raise them. And when they had shed their down for feathers, they would feed them the flesh of those men and the male children which they had birthed, and with such art and so often that the griffins came to know these women well and would do them no harm. Any man who ventured onto the island they would straightway kill and eat; and even though they might be sated, they would still not hesitate to snatch them up, flying through the air, and when they tired of carrying them, they would let them fall to their death. At the time, then, when those great men among the pagans had set sail with their grand flotillas, as the story has already informed you, there reigned on that island of California a queen of great stature, quite beautiful for one of their kind, in the flower of her youth, desirous in her mind of achieving great things, possessed of great strength, courage and cunning, and brave of heart, more so than any other of those queens who had reigned before her. And having learned of how the greater part of the world had now mobilized against the Christians, and knowing not who they were, nor having knowledge of any other lands other than those which were her neighbors, desiring to see the world and its diverse generations, believing that with her great strength and that of her subjects they might gain with good will or force the better part, spoke now with all those who were skilled in war, that it would be good to embark in their great flotillas, that they also might undertake that adventure which those great princes and other leaders had now undertaken; encouraging them and exhorting them, placing before them the very great honor and profit which such an undertaking would bring them, and above all the very great renown which would be theirs throughout the world, while remaining on that island, doing no other thing save that which their ancestors had done, was but to live as if buried alive, like the living dead, spending their days without fame, without glory, even as dumb animals.

So many things did that great queen tell them that they were moved not only to consent to such an undertaking, but with such great desire to spread their fame throughout the world that they urged her to set out on the sea at once that they might find themselves in battle together with those great men. Observing the will of her subjects, the Queen commanded her great fleet to be provisioned with food and arms all of gold without delay and indeed with every other thing which might be necessary, and commanded that the greatest of her vessels be modified in such a way that it appeared to be a great cage made of thick spars, and in it she place five hundred griffins who, as you have been told, had been raised since they were small to feed on the flesh of men; and having placed there, too, those beasts on which they rode, which were of diverse types, together with the most select and best-armed women in the fleet, leaving the island well guarded and secure, she set out to sea; and such was her haste that she arrived at the fleet of the pagans that same night of the battle which I have already recounted; and her arrival was very well received by these men, such that she was at once visited by those great lords eager to pay her homage. She wished to know their current state of affairs, begging them to tell her in great detail, and having heard their story, said: "You have attacked this city with your great armies and were unable to take it; now I with my army, if it please you, will attempt to see if my forces may prevail tomorrow, if you wish to follow my counsel." All of these great lords told her that however she might design it, so also would they command that her will be done. "Well, then, have all of your captains command straight away that under no circumstances should they nor any of their men stir from their quarters until I shall command it and you will witness the strangest battle that you have yet to see nor have yet heard of." This was straight away communicated to the great Sultan of Liquia and the Sultan of Halapa, who were in charge of all the hosts that were in that land, and they thus commanded all their people, wondering greatly at that which the queen had in mind to do.

### How the griffins carried off those whom they spied upon the ramparts and, these having been killed, they returned for more; the fiercest hunt ever witnessed; and how the Turks who quit their quarters, received the same treatment, how they who had expected help from the griffins, by the griffins were cruelly slain.

The night passed and the following morning Queen Calafia came on shore with her women armed all in gold and studded with precious gems which on the island of California were found as abundantly as stones, and they rode astride their wild beasts, harnessed as you have heard; and she ordered a portal of the vessel to be opened from whence the griffins might emerge. When they saw that the portals were opened, the griffins came rushing out, greatly pleased to be able to fly through the air, and they soon spied the large number of people on top of the ramparts. As they were hungry and entirely without fear, each one snatched as many as he might in his claws and, taking wing, commenced to eat them. Many arrows were spent against them and many great blows were given with lances and with swords, but their plumage was so thick and rough that no blow reached their flesh. This was, then, the most beautiful and agreeable hunt the Turks had ever witnessed up until then, and as they watched the griffins rise in the air with their enemies, they gave great shouts and cries of joy that pierced the heavens; and it was the saddest and most bitter spectacle ever seen by those within the city who saw the griffins snatch up father and son, brother and relative. And such was their plaint and to such a degree their rage that one was driven to compassion at the sight.

After the griffins had roamed for a time through the air, and having let go their prey, some in the sea, others on land, they returned at last and with no fear at all seized as many more victims again, at which the Turks were doubly pleased and the Christians that much more afflicted. What more can I say? So great was the fright of those on the ramparts that had not some of them sought refuge in the towers, there to save themselves, the ramparts had been completely abandoned with none remaining there to defend them. When Queen Calafia saw this, she shouted to the sultans in a loud voice to have their men scale the walls, since the city had been taken. Then all rushed out at once and, setting their ladders, climbed over the walls. The griffins, who had already let loose their prey, seeing them thus and having no knowledge of who they were, snatched them up in the same manner as they had dealt with the Christians and, flying through the air, carried them off, letting them fall in places from which none could escape their death. Here pleasure turned to tribulation, and those without the walls, taking great pity on them, wept; and those within, thinking themselves vanquished when they saw their enemies clambering over the walls, were now greatly consoled. At this point, while those who had stormed the bastions feared for their lives, expecting to die like their companions, the Christians who had taken refuge in the towers now emerged and quickly slew many of the Turks who had reached the ramparts, and the others they forced to leap down, and they then returned to their towers because they saw the griffins approaching.

When Queen Calafia had seen all this, she was greatly saddened and said: "My idols, whom I adore and in whom I believe, what has happened that my arrival should thus be as favorable to my enemies as to my friends? For I believed your aid and my stalwart troops and equipment were enough to assure defeat. But surely it shall not be so." Then she commanded her troops to scale the walls with their ladders and to at-

# A Dream Revised:
# The New World Odyssey of
# Cabeza de Vaca (1528)

*About the time Columbus was first setting foot on a Caribbean island, an infant named Alvar Núñez Cabeza de Vaca was taking his first steps on the legs that would eventually take him across the North American continent. As an adult Cabeza de Vaca would come to learn more about the New World than Columbus ever did, yet just as surely as Columbus's dream of sailing west to reach Asia colored his interpretation of the things he saw on his voyages, Cabeza de Vaca's own New World dreams would color his interpretation of the things he saw during his long walk through Texas, New Mexico, Arizona, and northern Mexico.*

*Born into a family of the fighting Spanish gentry, Cabeza de Vaca was raised in a house staffed by Guanche servants, enslaved when his grandfather ruthlessly conquered the Canary Islands (Bishop [1933?], 7). After seeing military service in Spain and Italy, in 1527, Cabeza de Vaca was appointed royal treasurer and second-in-command of an expedition bent on plundering the unknown region called La Florida. Lead and financed by Pánfilo de Narváez, a one-eyed veteran of bloody campaigns in Mexico and Cuba, this expedition would meet with nothing but disaster.*

*As soon as Narváez's ships made landfall in the New World, more than 140 of those who had made the voyage from Spain took the opportunity to desert. Soon after, a hurricane destroyed two ships, drowning 60 men and 20 horses. Recalling the hurricane as a supernatural event, Cabeza de Vaca (1983, 29) wrote in his* Relación *that "from midnight on, we heard a great roaring and the sound of many voices, of little bells, also flutes, tambourines, and other instruments . . ."*

*After the expedition landed near Tampa Bay, Narváez proposed to lead 300 foot soldiers and cavalry on an inland march in search of Apalachen, a city rumored to be rich with gold. Cabeza de Vaca protested this plan to separate the bulk of the force from the ships, but Narváez—inflamed by the discovery of a small gold rattle in a coastal village and anxious to loot a treasure possibly exceeding that of Mexico—insisted on carrying out his plan.*

*Narváez's land force was quickly done in by hunger, swamps, and Indian ambushes. After discovering that Apalachen was no more than a small farming settlement, the Spaniards, unable to regain contact with their ships, sacrificed their metal weapons, spare clothes, and even their horses, to build five makeshift barges in which they intended to reach settlements in Mexico. Exhausted and emaciated, the Spaniards somehow managed to sail north and west along the Gulf Coast, there encountering hostile natives, the Mississippi Delta, and a storm that finally separated the overloaded barges.*

*Driven ashore by the storm, those aboard Cabeza de Vaca's barge found themselves stranded on a coastal island (probably Galveston Island) without food, weapons, or clothes. Although Cabeza de Vaca's party (as well as the survivors of a second barge driven ashore nearby) were at first aided by local Indians, the coastal natives were too poor to care for their unexpected guests through the entire winter. Hunger, cold, and despair rapidly killed off the miserable castaways.*

*Those few Spaniards who did manage to survive their initial hardships came to have reason to wish they had not, for they were soon reduced to the status of slaves. When Cabeza de Vaca describes his marginal existence on the Texas coast, it is impossible to miss the irony of a proud would-be conquistador reduced to laboring in the service of half-starved natives:*

> My life had become unbearable. In addition to much other work, I had to grub roots in the water or from underground canebrakes. My fingers got so raw that if a straw touched them they would bleed. The broken canes often slashed my flesh; I had to work amidst them without benefit of clothes.

*Cabeza de Vaca spent some six years along the Texas coast, during that time improving his lot by becoming a trader who wandered from tribe to tribe. During this period he also first practiced faith healing, a profession that would play a pivotal role in seeing him safely across the continent. Always desiring to return to civilization, Cabeza de Vaca eventually made his escape from the coast, joining up with the three remaining survivors of the 300 who had marched into Florida: Estevánico (Estebán), a Moorish slave; Andrés*

Dorantes, an officer of the expedition; and Alonso del Castillo, another officer.

The four made their way inland, often aided and guided by natives, who are portrayed as being increasingly in awe of the strangers' miraculous healing powers. Soon Cabeza de Vaca's story of mere survival is transformed into an epic of peaceful conquest. Marching inland in an increasingly glorious procession, Cabeza de Vaca and company are neither slaves nor conquistadors, but rather "Children of the Sun," worshipped beings who can cure all afflictions with a word and a touch. Adoring throngs of natives begin escorting the Sun Children every step of the way, showering them with gifts and submitting to their every command.

Besides marking a change from failure to triumph, the story of the westward procession of the Sun Children also marks a change in Cabeza de Vaca's New World dream. His former dream of the New World as a land ripe for plunder is replaced by a dream of the New World as a second Eden, populated by "instinctive Christians" (DeVoto 1983, 40) who can be won to the cross and the crown through kindness more easily than through war.

Because the land becomes more edenic as the Sun Children move westward—food is more abundant, the natives are more civilized, signs of great mineral wealth abound—Cabeza de Vaca takes his place as an early promoter of the idea that the American continent gets better the further one travels into the sunset. So convincing, in fact, is Cabeza de Vaca's promotion of the lands he saw in the West—and of those undoubtedly even-better lands just beyond his sight—that his narrative directly inspired the westering expeditions of De Soto, Marcos de Niza, and Coronado.

Cabeza de Vaca's change of dream (so appealing to modern sensibilities) distinguishes him from Columbus and others whose idées fixes about the New World never varied, despite all evidence to the contrary. Still Cabeza de Vaca's change remains "the story of one illusion traded for another" (Wild 1991, 26). The dream of a simple and harmonious conversion of Indians and their lands to European values and systems would never come to pass.

The new dream is compelling, though, and as it unfolds the narrative itself becomes ever more dreamy, loosening its hold on strict reportage. Bernard DeVoto has noted this change, pointing out that Cabeza de Vaca's westward procession is a march into the land of myth, into a territory where the author becomes "majestically unregardful of landmarks and geography" (1983, 18). And, DeVoto might have added, unregardful of human nature and anthropology.

While such a flight into myth and dream may seem weak and regrettable to some, it is understandable in light of the psychological and social pressures at work on Cabeza de Vaca. The authorities may well have suspected the returned adventurer of cowardice, incompetence, or even heresy, so one function of the narrative is to defend its author against such suspicions. And what better way to downplay the failure to find treasure in Florida than to overstate the value of the people and resources found in the West? Another function of the narrative is to argue for kinder treatment of native people, a task it accomplishes through subtle eloquence and carefully crafted structure—stylistic elements that may well have come at the expense of historical truth.

History's loss is literature's gain. Myth-bound, complex, and dramatic, Cabeza de Vaca's narrative is literature that can be read and enjoyed for itself, regardless of its considerable value as a historical document.

The first account of the Cabeza de Vaca saga was the "Joint Report" written for the Audiencia of Española by Cabeza de Vaca, Castillo, and Dorantes upon their return to Mexico City. The earliest existing version of this report dates from 1539 and was reprinted in volume 3, book 35 of Gonzalo Fernando Oviedo y Valdés's Historia General y Natural de las Indias. Cabeza de Vaca's own narrative, La Relación, was first published in 1542 at Zamora. A second edition with the running title of Naufragios ("Shipwrecks") was published in 1555 at Valladolid. In its entirety and in fragments, La Relación has been published in various European languages under a number of titles. The translation reprinted here was made by Cyclone Covey. The comments in brackets that appear throughout the text are Covey's; the comments in braces are the editors' of this volume.

## Selected Bibliography

Cabeza de Vaca, Alvar Nunez. *Cabeza de Vaca's Adventures in the Unknown Interior of America*. Trans. by Cyclone Covey. Albuquerque: University of New Mexico Press, 1983.

Bishop, Morris. *The Odyssey of Cabeza de Vaca*. New York: Century, [1933?].

De Voto, Bernard. *The Course of Empire*. Lincoln: University of Nebraska Press, 1983.

Wild, Peter. *Alvar Núñez Cabeza de Vaca*. Boise, Id.: Boise State University, 1991.

CABEZA DE VACA

# A Dream Revised: The New World Odyssey of Cabeza de Vaca (1528)

## Our Escape

THE SECOND DAY after our juncture with the Anagados [i.e., on 22 September 1534], we commended ourselves to God our Lord and made our break. Although the season was late and the prickly pears nearly gone, we still hoped to travel a long distance on acorns which we might find in the woods.

Hurrying along that day in dread of being overtaken, we spied some smoke billows and headed in their direction. We reached them after vespers, to find one Indian. He fled when he saw us coming. We sent the Negro after him, and the Indian stopped when he saw only a lone pursuer. The Negro told him we were seeking the people who made those fires. He said their houses were nearby and he would guide us. We followed as he ran on to announce us.

We saw the houses at sunset. Two crossbow shots before reaching them, we found four Indians waiting to welcome us. . . . Right away they brought us a lot of prickly pears having heard of us and the wonders our Lord worked by us. If there had been nothing but these cures, they were enough to open ways for us through a poor region like this, find us guides for often uninhabited wastes, and lead us through immediate dangers, not letting us be killed, sustaining us through great want, and instilling in those nations the heart of kindness, as we shall see.

## Our Success with Some of the Afflicted and My Narrow Escape

The very evening of our arrival, some Indians came to Castillo begging him to cure them of terrible headaches. When he had made the sign of the cross over them and commended them to God, they instantly said that all pain had vanished and went to their houses to get us prickly pears and chunks of venison, something we had tasted of precious little.

We returned many thanks to God, Whose compassion and gifts day by day increased. After the sick had been tended, the Indians danced and sang in festivity till sunrise. The celebration of our coming extended to three days. . . .

## More Cures

A crowd of Indians came to Castillo next morning bringing five sick persons who had cramps. Each of the five offered his bow and arrows, and Castillo accepted them. At sunset he blessed them and commended them to God our Lord. We all prayed the best we could for their health; we knew that only through Him would these people help us so we might emerge from this unhappy existence. And He bestowed health so bountifully that every patient got up the morning following as sound and strong as if he had never had an illness.

This caused great admiration and moved us to further gratitude to our Lord, Whose demonstrated mercy gave us a conviction that He would liberate us and bring us to a place where we might serve Him. I can say for myself that I had always trusted His providence and that He would lead me out of my captivity; I constantly expressed this to my companions. . . .

Since the Indians all through the region talked only of the wonders which God our Lord worked through us, individuals sought us from many parts in hopes of healing. The evening of the second day after our arrival at these thickets, some of the Susolas came to us and pressed Castillo to go treat their ailing kinsmen—one wounded, the others sick and, among them, a fellow very near his end. Castillo happened to be a timid practitioner—the more so, the more serious and dangerous the case—feeling that his sins would weigh and some day impede his performing cures. The Indians urged me to go heal them. They liked me, remembering I had ministered to them in the grove where they gave us nuts and skins when I first reunited with the Christians.

So I had to go with them. Dorantes brought Estevánico and accompanied me. As we drew near the huts of the afflicted, I saw that the man we hoped to save was dead: many mourners were weeping around him, and his house was already down—sure signs that the inhabitant was no more. I found his eyes rolled up, his pulse gone, and every appearance of death, as Dorantes agreed. Taking off the mat that covered him, I supplicated our Lord in his behalf and in behalf of the rest who ailed, as fervently as I could. After my blessing and breathing on him many times, they brought me his bow and a basket of pounded prickly pears.

The [local] natives then took me to treat many others, who had fallen into a stupor, and gave me two more baskets of prickly pears. I, in turn, gave these to the [Susola] Indians who accompanied us. We returned to our lodgings, while the Indians whom we had given the fruit waited till evening to return.

When they got back that evening, they brought the tidings that the "dead" man I had treated had got up whole and walked; he had eaten and spoken with these Sosulas, who further reported that all I had ministered to had recovered and were glad. Throughout the land the effect was a profound wonder and fear. People talked of nothing else, and wherever the fame of it reached, people set out to find us so we should cure them and bless their children. . . .

Up to now, Dorantes and his Negro had not attempted to practice; but under the soliciting pressure of these pilgrims from diverse places, we all became physicians, of whom I was the boldest and most venturous in trying to cure anything. With no exceptions, every patient told us he had been made well. Confidence in our ministrations as infallible extended to a belief that none could die while we remained among them.

## The Story of the Visitation of Mr. Badthing

The Avavares and the tribes we had left behind related an extraordinary experience which, in our equivalent of their vague way of counting, seemed to have occurred fifteen or sixteen years before.

They said that a little man wandered through the region whom they called Badthing [*Mala Cosa*]. He had a beard and they never saw his features distinctly. When he came to a house, the inhabitants trembled and their hair stood on end. A blazing brand would suddenly shine at the door as he rushed in and seized whom he chose, deeply gashing him in the side with a very sharp flint two palms long and a hand wide. He would thrust his hand through the gashes, draw out the entrails, cut a palm's length from one, and throw it on the embers. Then he would gash an arm three times, the second cut on the inside of the elbow, and would sever the limb. A little later he would begin to rejoin it, and the touch of his hands would instantly heal the wounds.

They said that frequently during the dance he appeared in their midst, sometimes in the dress of a woman, at other times in that of a man. When he liked, he would take a *buhío* up into the air and come crashing down with it. They said they offered him victuals many times but he never ate. They asked him where he came from and where his home was. He pointed to a crevice in the ground and said his home was there below.

We laughed and scoffed. Indignant at our disbelief, they brought us many whom they said had been so seized, and we saw the gash marks in the right places. We told them he was an evil one and, as best we could, taught them that if they would believe in God our Lord and become Christians like us, they need never fear him, nor would he dare come and inflict those wounds; they could be certain he would not appear while we remained in the land. This delighted them and they lost much of their dread. . . .

## Four Fresh Receptions

At sunset we reached a village of a hundred huts. All the people who lived in them were awaiting us at the village outskirts with terrific yelling and violent slapping of their hands against their thighs. They had with them their precious perforated gourd rattles (pebbles inside) which they produce only at such important occasions as the dance or a medical ceremony and which no one but the owner dares touch. They say there is a virtue in them and that, since they do not grow in that area, they obviously come from heaven. All they know is that the rivers bring them when they flood.

This people hysterically crowded upon us, everyone competing to touch us first; we were nearly killed in the crush. Without letting our feet touch ground, they carried us to the huts they had made for us. We took refuge in them and absolutely refused to be feasted that night. They themselves, however, sang and danced the whole night through. In the morning they brought every single inhabitant of the village for us to touch and bless as they had heard we had done elsewhere. After our performance, they presented many arrows to the women of the other village who had accompanied theirs.

When we left next day, all the people of the place went with us and the next people received us as well as the last, giving us of what they had to eat, including the deer they had killed that day. Here we saw a new custom. Members of the tribe would take the bows and arrows, shoes and beads (if they wore any) from individuals who came to get cured and lay them before us as inducement. As soon as the sick were treated, they went away glad, saying they were sound.

We left these Indians and went on to others, who also welcomed us and brought us their sick who, when blessed, declared themselves sound. If anyone did not actually recover, he still contended he would. What they who did recover related caused general rejoicing and dancing; so we got no sleep.

## A Strange New Development

Leaving these Indians, we proceeded to the next village, where another novel custom commenced: Those who accompanied us plundered our hospitable new hosts and ransacked their huts, leaving nothing. We watched this with deep concern but were in no position to do anything about it; so for the present had to bear with it until such time as we might gain greater authority. Those who had lost their possessions, seeing our dejection, tried to console us. They said they were so honored to have us that their property was well bestowed—and that they would get repaid by others farther on, who were very rich.

All through the day's travel we had been badly hampered by the hordes of Indians following us. We could not have escaped if we had tried, they pursued so closely just to touch us. Their insistence on this privilege cost us three hours in going through them so they might depart. Next day, all the inhabitants of the newly reached village came before us. The majority had one clouded eye and others were completely blind, to our astonishment. They are a people of fine forms, pleasant features, and whiter than any of the nations we had so far seen.

Here we began to see mountains. They seemed to sweep in succession from the North Sea and, from what the Indians told us, we believe they rise fifteen leagues from the sea. . . .

## My Famous Operation in the Mountain Country

They fetched me a man who, they said, had long since been shot in the shoulder through the back and that the arrowhead had lodged above his heart. He said it was very painful and kept him sick. I probed the wound and discovered the arrowhead had passed through the cartilage. With a flint knife I opened the fellow's chest until I could see that the point was sideways and would be difficult to extract. But I cut on and, at last, inserting my knife-point deep, was able to work the arrowhead out with great effort. It was huge. With a deer bone, I further demonstrated my surgical skill with two stitches while blood drenched me, and stanched the flow with hair from a hide. The villagers asked me for the arrowhead, which I gave them. The whole population came to look at it, and they sent it into the back country so the people there could see it.

They celebrated this operation with their customary dances and festivities. Next day, I cut the stitches and the patient was well. My incision appeared only like a crease in the palm of the hand. He said he felt no pain or sensitivity there at all.

Now this cure so inflated our fame all over the region that we could control whatever the inhabitants cherished.

We showed them the copper rattle we had recently been given, and they told us that many layers of this material were buried in the place whence it came, that this [metal] was highly valued, and that the people who made it lived in fixed dwellings. We conceived the country they spoke of to be on the South Sea, which we had always understood was richer in mineral resources than that of the North.

## The Severe Month's March to the Great River

From here the manner of receiving us changed, in that those who came out to greet us with presents did not get despoiled or their houses rifled; rather, when we got to their houses, they themselves offered us everything they had, including the houses, and we turned the things over to the chief personages in our escort to distribute. The people who had relinquished their property always, of course, followed us to the next large village to recoup. They would warn the villagers among whom we came to be sure to hold back nothing, since we knew all and could cause them to die; the sun revealed everything to us. For the first few days a new group walked with us they would continually tremble and dared not speak or even look up to the heavens. . . .

We told our new hosts that we wished to go where the sun sets; but they said people in that direction were remote. We commanded them to send and make known our coming anyway. They stalled and made various excuses, because the people to the west were their enemies, whom they wanted to avoid. Not daring to disobey, however, they sent two women—one of their own and the other a captive from the "remote" enemy people—for women can deal as neutrals anywhere, even during war. We followed them to a stopping place where we agreed to wait, and waited five days. The Indians who stayed with us concluded the women could not have found anybody.

We told them, then, to conduct us northward. They answered as before: there were no people in that direction for a very long distance, nothing to eat, and no water. When we remained adamant, they still excused themselves as best they could, and our gorge rose. One night I went to sleep in the woods apart from them, but they shortly came to me and stayed awake all night telling me of their terror and pleading with me to be angry no longer, that they would lead us where we would though it meant their death. We still feigned displeasure in order to keep the upper hand, and a singular circumstance strengthened that hand mightily.

That very day, many of the Indians had fallen ill, and the next day eight men died. All over that area, wherever this became known, the natives panicked; they seemed to think they would die at sight of us. They supplicated us to kill no more of them in our wrath, for they believed we caused their death by merely willing it. The truth is, we could hardly have felt more distressed—at their loss and also at the possibility that they would either all die off or abandon us in fright and that other tribes ever after would flee from us. We prayed to God our Lord to restore them and, from that moment, the sick began to mend. . . .

Three days had passed since we came to this stopping place, and the sick had recovered. Now the women we had sent out returned. They said they found few people, nearly all having gone for cattle [buffalo], it being the season. . . .

So next morning the able-bodied set forth with us. At the end of three *jornadas* we held up while Alonso del Castillo went ahead with Estevánico, the Negro, taking the two women for guides. The captive one led them to a river [the Río Grande] which ran between mountains where her father's town lay. The dwellings of this town [just below El Paso] were the first to be seen which looked like real houses.

After Castillo and Estevánico got there and talked with the residents, Castillo, with five or six of them, returned at the end of three days to the spot we had held up. He reported finding permanent houses where the people ate beans and melons [squash] and that he had seen corn. Overjoyed at this news, we gave boundless thanks to our Lord. . . .

## The Long Swing-Around

After the two days of indecision, we concluded that our destiny lay toward the sunset and so took the trail north only as far as we had to in order to reach the westward one, and then swung down until eventually we came out at the South Sea. The seventeen *jornadas* of hunger the Cow People warned us of, and which proved to be just as bad as they said, could not deter us. . . .

One day as the sun went down out on the plains between massive mountains, we came upon people who for a third of the year eat nothing but powdered straw and, that being the season we passed through, we had to eat it ourselves until at last, at the end of the seventeen *jornadas*, we got to the [Ópata] people of permanent houses who had plenty of corn.

They gave us a great quantity of corn, cornmeal, calabashes, beans, and cotton blankets, all of which we loaded onto the guides who had led us here, and they went back the happiest people on earth. We gave many thanks to God our Lord for bringing us to this land of abundance.

Some of the houses here are made of earth, the rest of cane mats. We marched more than a hundred leagues through continuously inhabited country of such domiciles, where corn and beans remained plentiful. The people gave us innumerable deerhide and cotton blankets, the latter better than those of New Spain, beads made of coral from the South Sea, fine turquoises from the north—in fact, everything they had, including a special gift to me of five emerald [probably malachite] arrowheads such as they use in their singing and dancing. These looked quite valuable. I asked where they came from. They said from lofty mountains to the north, where there were towns of great population and great houses, and that the arrowheads had been purchased with feather bushes and parrot plumes.

Among this people, women are better treated than in any part of the Indies we had come through. They wear knee-length cotton shirts and, over them, half-sleeved skirts of scraped deerskin that reach to the ground and that are laced together in front with leather strips. The women soap this outer garment with a certain root which cleanses well and keeps the deerskin becoming. And they wear shoes. . . .

These Indians ever stayed with us until they safely delivered us to others. They were all convinced that we came from Heaven. (Anything that is new to them or beyond their comprehension is explained as coming from Heaven.) We Christians traveled all day without food, eating only at night—and then so little as to astonish our escort. We never felt tired, being so inured to hardship, which increased our enormous influence over them. To maintain this authority the better, we seldom talked with them directly, but made the Negro our intermediary. He was constantly in conversation, finding out about routes, towns, and other matters we wished to know.

We passed from one strange tongue to another, but God our Lord always enabled each new people to understand us and we them. You would have thought, from the questions and answers in signs, that they spoke our language and we theirs. We did know six Indian languages, but could not always avail ourselves of them; there are a thousand dialectical differences.

Through all these nations, the people who were at war quickly made up so they could come meet us with everything they possessed. Thus we left all the land in peace. And we taught all the people by signs, which they understood, that in Heaven was a Man we called God, who had created the heavens and the earth; that all good came from Him and that we worshipped and obeyed Him and called Him our Lord; and that if they would do the same, all would be well with them. They apprehended so readily that, if we had had enough command of their language to make ourselves perfectly understood, we would have left them all Christians.

We told them what we could and, from then on, at sunrise, they would raise their arms to the sky with a glad cry, then run their hands down the length of their bodies. They repeated this ritual at sunset.

They are a substantial people with a capacity for unlimited development.

## The Buckle and the Horseshoe Nail

A few days farther on we came to another town where rain was falling so heavily that we could not cross the swollen [Yaqui] river and had to wait fifteen days.

In this time Castillo happened to see an Indian wearing around his neck a little sword-belt buckle with a horseshoe nail stitched to it.

He took the amulet, and we asked the Indian what it was. He said it came from Heaven. But who had brought it? He and the Indians with him said that some bearded men like us had come to that river from Heaven, with horses, lances, and swords, and had lanced two natives.

Casually we inquired what had become of those men. They had gone to sea, said the Indians. They had put their lances into the water, got into the water themselves, and finally were seen moving on top of the water into the sunset.

We gave many thanks to God our Lord. Having almost despaired of finding Christians again, we could hardly restrain our excitement. Yet we anxiously suspected that these men were explorers who had merely made a flying visit on their voyage of discovery. But having at last some exact information to go on, we quickened our pace, and, as we went, heard more and more of Christians. We told the natives we were going after those men to order them to stop killing, enslaving, and dispossessing the Indians; which made our friends very glad.

We hastened through a vast territory, which we found vacant, the inhabitants having fled to the mountains in fear of the Christians. With heavy hearts we looked out over the lavishly watered, fertile, and beautiful land, now abandoned and burned and the people thin and weak, scattering or hiding in fright. Not having planted, they were reduced to eating roots and bark; and we shared their famine the whole way. Those who did receive us could provide hardly anything. They themselves looked as if they would willingly die. They brought us blankets they had concealed from the other Christians and told us how the latter had come through razing the towns and carrying off half the men and all the women and boys; those who had escaped were wandering about as fugitives. We found the survivors too alarmed to stay anywhere very long, unable or unwilling to till, preferring death to a repetition of their recent horror. While they seemed delighted with our company, we grew apprehensive that the Indians resisting farther on at the frontier would avenge themselves on us.

When we got there, however, they received us with the same awe and respect the others had—even more, which amazed us. Clearly, to bring all these people to Christianity and subjection to Your Imperial Majesty, they must be won by kindness, the only certain way.

They took us to a village on the crest of a range of mountains; it was a difficult ascent. The many people who had taken refuge there from the Christians received us well, giving us all they had: over 2,000 backloads of corn, which we distributed to the distressed, pathetic beings who had guided us to that place. . . .

All along the way we could see the tracks of the Christians and traces of their camps. We met our messengers at noon. They had been unable to contact any Indians, who roved the woods out of sight, eluding the Christians. The night before, our heralds had spied on the Christians from behind trees and seen them marching many Indians in chains.

This intelligence terrified our escort, some of whom ran to spread the news that the Christians were coming, and many more would have followed if we had not managed to forbid them and to palliate their fright. We had with us [Pima] Indians from a hundred leagues back whom we could not at this time discharge with the recompense due them.

For further reassurance to our escort, we held up where we were for the night. The following day we slept on the trail at the end of the *jornada*. The day after that, our heralds guided us to the place they had watched the Christians. We got there that afternoon and saw at once they had told the truth. We noted by the stakes the horses had been tied to that the men were mounted. . . .

Throughout this region, wherever we encountered mountains, we saw undeniable indications of gold, antimony, iron, copper, and other metals. . . .

## The First Confrontation

I overtook four of them {Christians} on their horses. They were dumbfounded at the sight of me, strangely undressed and in company with Indians. They just stood staring for a long time, not thinking to hail me or come closer to ask questions.

"Take me to your captain," I at last requested; and we went together half a league to a place [near Ocoroni on the Sinaloa] where we found their captain, Diego de Alcaraz.

When we had talked awhile, he confessed to me that he was completely undone, having been unable to catch any Indians in a long time; he did not know which way to turn; his men were getting too hungry and exhausted. I told him of Castillo and Dorantes ten leagues away with an escorting multitude. He immediately dispatched three of his horsemen to them, along with fifty of his Indian allies. The Negro went, too, as a guide; I stayed behind. . . .

## The Falling-Out with Our Countrymen

After five days, Andrés Dorantes and Alonso del Castillo arrived with those who had gone for them; and they brought more than 600 natives of the vicinity whom the Indians who had been escorting us drew out of the woods and took to the mounted Christians, who thereupon dismissed their own escort.

When they arrived, Alcaraz begged us to order the villagers of this river out of the woods in the same way to get us food. It would be unnecessary to command them to bring food, if they came at all; for the Indians were always diligent to bring us all they could.

We sent our heralds to call them, and presently there came 600 Indians with all the corn they possessed. They brought it in clay-sealed earthen pots which had been buried. They also brought whatever else they had; but we wished only a meal, so gave the rest to the Christians to divide among themselves.

After this we had a hot argument with them, for they meant to make slaves of the Indians in our train. We got so angry that we went off forgetting the many Turkish-shaped bows, the many pouches, and the five emerald arrowheads, etc., which we thus lost. And to think we had given these Christians a supply of cowhides and other things that our retainers had carried a long distance!

It proved difficult to persuade our escorting Indians to go back to their homes, to feel apprehensive no longer, and to plant their corn. But they did not want to do anything until they had first delivered us into the hands of other Indians, as custom bound them. They feared they would die if they returned without fulfilling this obligation whereas, with us, they said they feared neither Christians nor lances.

This sentiment roused our countrymen's jealousy. Alcaraz bade his interpreter tell the Indians that we were members of his race who had been long lost; that his group were the lords of the land who must be obeyed and served, while we were inconsequential. The Indians paid no attention to this. Conferring among themselves, they replied that the Christians lied: We had come from the sunrise, they from the sunset; we healed the sick, they killed the sound; we came naked and barefoot, they clothed, horsed, and lanced; we coveted nothing but gave whatever we were given, while they robbed whomever they found and bestowed nothing on anyone. . . .

To the last I could not convince the Indians that we were of the same people as the Christian slavers. Only with the greatest effort were we able to induce them to go back home. We ordered them to fear no more, reestablish their towns, and farm.

Already the countryside had grown rank from neglect. This is, no doubt, the most prolific land in all these Indies. It produces three crops a year; the trees bear a great variety of fruit; and beautiful rivers and brimming springs abound throughout. There are gold- and silver-bearing ores. The people are well disposed, serving such Christians as are their friends with great good will. They are comely, much more so than the

Mexicans ["Mexicans" evidently meaning any Indians south of the Pima family]. This land, in short, lacks nothing to be regarded as blest.

When the Indians took their leave of us they said they would do as we commanded and rebuild their towns, if the Christians let them. And I solemnly swear that if they have not done so it is the fault of the Christians.

After we had dismissed the Indians in peace and thanked them for their toil in our behalf, the Christians subtly sent us on our way [under arrest] in the charge of an *alcalde* named Cebreros, attended by two horsemen [and a number of Indian allies]. They took us through forests and wastes so we would not communicate with the natives and would neither see nor learn of their crafty scheme afoot. Thus we often misjudge the motives of men; we thought we had effected the Indians' liberty, when the Christians were but poising to pounce....

## The Great Transformation

As soon as these Indians got home, all the inhabitants of that province who were friendly to the Christians and had heard of us, came to visit, bearing beads and feathers. We commanded them to build churches with crosses; up to that time none had been erected. We also bade them bring their principal men to be baptized.

Then the Captain made a solemn covenant with God not to invade or consent to invasion, or enslave any of that region we had guaranteed safety; to enforce and defend this sacred contract until Your Majesty and Governor Nuño de Guzmán, or the Viceroy in your name, should direct further as to the service of God and Your Highness.

Indians came to us shortly with tidings that many people had descended from the mountains and were living again in the valleys; that they had erected churches with crosses, and were doing everything we required. Each day we heard further to the same effect.

Fifteen days after our taking up residence in this town, Alcaraz got back with his cohorts. They reported to the Captain the way the Indians had come down and repopulated the plain; how they would issue from their formerly deserted villages carrying crosses, take the visitors to their houses and give of what they had. The Christians even slept among these hosts overnight! They could not comprehend such a novelty. Since the natives said their safety had been officially assured, the Christians decided to depart quietly.

We are thankful to our merciful God that it should be in the days of

Your Majesty's dominion that these nations might all come voluntarily to Him who created and redeemed us. We are convinced that Your Majesty is destined to do this much and that it is entirely within reason to accomplish. For in the 2,000 leagues we sojourned by land and sea, including ten months' ceaseless travel after escaping captivity, we found no sacrifices and no idolatry.

In that period, we crossed from sea to sea. The data we took great pains to collect indicate that the width of the continent, at its widest, may be 200 leagues; and that pearls and great riches are to be found on the coast of the South Sea, near which the best and most opulent of all nations flourishes.

# CHAPTER 4

# A Violent Pursuit of the Dream: The Gentleman of Elvas's Account of the de Soto Expedition (1539)

*La Leyenda Negra, the Black Myth of Spanish cruelty, was largely the propaganda creation of Protestant Englishmen, who had little right to consider themselves the moral superiors to any nationality when it came to meting out cruelty. Nevertheless there were Spanish conquistadors who fit the bloodthirsty stereotypes the myth promoted. One such conquistador was Hernando de Soto.*

*Born into a family of modest means, the young de Soto went adventuring in the New World to seek his fortune. He found it in the treasure rooms of the Inca empire, returning home from Peru a rich man. De Soto must not have been rich beyond his wildest dreams, however, for he used part of his Inca loot to finance a 1539 gold-hunting expedition to La Florida—the terra incognita that included all lands north of Mexico.*

*De Soto's desire to explore La Florida was fired in part by the Relación of Cabeza De Vaca, whom de Soto asked to serve as second in command on his expedition. De Vaca declined the honor, perhaps out of a personal ambition to lead his own expedition, perhaps because he realized that de Soto was unsympathetic to his idea that Indians should be treated kindly and fairly. If that was de Vaca's assumption, it was a good one, for as soon as de Soto and his army hit the Florida coast, they commenced a campaign of terror from which the natives of the region never recovered. Besides stealing food and enchaining slaves as they went along, de Soto's Europeans quashed native resistance with every killing technology at their disposal: Indians were shot, stabbed, hanged, burnt, quartered, run down with horses, and torn apart by war dogs. Even worse de Soto's army unknowingly emitted a cloud of Euro-pean diseases that cut down Indian populations with an efficiency that no arquebus shot or crossbow bolt could match. In some of the areas de Soto's army visited, the death rate from disease may have reached 85 to 100 percent (Dye 1989, 31). The only bit of justice in the whole business was that de Soto himself succumbed to fever, dying on the banks of the Mississippi before the expedition's survivors managed to straggle back to Mexico in 1543, half-dead and empty-handed. Their dreamed-of cities of gold, as well as a shortcut to the western sea, had eluded them.*

*Though the de Soto expedition is probably most remembered for having explored the southeastern United States and for reaching the Mississippi River, the expedition also penetrated into Oklahoma and Texas. The con-quistadors came as far west as they did in hopes of traveling overland to Mexico; but discouraged by the lack of food, the small, impoverished native populations, and the general aridness of the West, they disappointedly turned back to the Mississippi, to build barges and sail to Mexico.*

*The story of the de Soto expedition is told, among other places, in the narrative of the Gentleman of Elvas, a Portuguese knight who served in de Soto's army. Though the Gentleman of Elvas keeps himself so far out of his narrative that his exact identity is today unknown, his presence is felt as his text struggles with perhaps the greatest paradox of the conquest of the New World: How could people who marched under the banner of Christianity in-flict such cruelty on Native Americans? At times the Gentleman of Elvas tries to justify European cruelty by conventionally portraying the Indians as sneaky and rebellious beings, mere obstacles in the path of the great de Soto, the bringer of the Word. Yet at other times the author rails against the cru-elty of the Europeans, and throughout the text he makes it clear that it is the desire to find cities of gold, not the desire to save souls, that draws the greedy conquistadors further and further west. Also the Gentleman of Elvas fre-quently ennobles Indians, usually through the use of impossibly eloquent, highly fictionalized speeches given by Indian chiefs to their white van-quishers—a literary device that would carry down to the time of the Nez Percé Chief Joseph and beyond.*

*As in the narrative of Cabeza de Vaca, the narrative of the Gentleman of Elvas depicts a dream of the West ending in misery and failure. Unlike de Vaca, however, the Gentleman of Elvas does not recast the dream in order to create a new justification for westward exploration. Having failed to find gold, he finds no pat answer for why the great unexplored lands exist or how native peoples and those of Europe will ever manage to coexist. In failing to find an answer, Elvas puts himself in distinguished company, for the ques-*

*tions he raises, however naively and indirectly, are the questions that four hundred years of American thinking have been unable to answer.*

*There exist four first-hand accounts of the de Soto expedition, the oldest of which is the one written by the Gentleman of Elvas (Milanich 1991, xv–xvi). Originally published in 1557 at Evora, Portugal, the Elvas narrative was first published in English by Richard Hakluyt, who issued it in 1609 under the title* Virginia Richly Valued by the Description of the Mainland of Florida. *The portion of the Gentleman of Elvas's narrative that is reprinted here was translated from the Portuguese by Buckingham Smith in 1866. The notes in brackets have been inserted by the editors of this volume.*

### Selected Bibliography

Dye, David H. "Death March of Hernando de Soto." *Archaeology* 42(3) (1989):27–31.

Lewis, Theodore H., ed. "The Narrative of the Expedition of Hernando de Soto by the Gentleman of Elvas," in *Spanish Explorers in the Southern United States, 1528–1543.* New York: Scribners, 1925.

Milanich, Jerald T. "Introduction." *Spanish Borderlands Sourcebooks,* vol. 11. Ed. by David Hurst Thomas. New York: Garland, 1991.

HERNANDO DE SOTO

# A Violent Pursuit of the Dream: The Gentleman of Elvas's Account of the de Soto Expedition (1539)

### How the Governor went from Aquixo to Casqui, and thence to Pacaha; and how this country differs from the other.

THE RIO GRANDE being crossed, the Governor marched a league and a half, to a large town of Aquixo, which was abandoned before his arrival. Over a plain thirty Indians were seen to draw nigh, sent by the cacique to discover what the Christians intended to do, but who fled directly as they saw them. The cavalry pursued, killed ten, and captured fifteen. As the town toward which the Governor marched was near the river, he sent a captain, with the force he thought sufficient, to take the piraguas up the stream. As they frequently wound about through the country, having to go round the bays that swell out of the river, the Indians had opportunity to attack those in the piraguas, placing them in great peril, being shot at with bows from the ravines, while they dared not leave the shore, because of the swiftness of the current; so that, as soon as the Governor got to the town, he directly sent crossbowmen to them down the stream, for their protection. When the piraguas arrived, he ordered them to be taken to pieces, and the spikes kept for making others, when they should be needed.

The Governor slept at the town one night, and the day following he went in quest of a province called Pacaha, which he had been informed was nigh Chisca, where the Indians said there was gold. He passed through large towns in Aquixo, which the people had left for fear of the Christians. From some Indians that were taken, he heard that three days' journey thence resided a great cacique, called Casqui. He came to a small river, over which a bridge was made, whereby he crossed. All that day, until sunset, he marched through water, in places coming to the knees; in others, as high as the waist. They were greatly rejoiced on reaching the dry land; because it had appeared to them that they should travel about, lost, all night in the water. At mid-day they came to the first town of Casqui, where they found the Indians off their guard, never having heard of them. Many men and women were taken, much clothing, blankets, and skins; such they likewise took in another town in sight of the first, half a league off in the field, whither the horsemen had run.

This land is higher, drier, and more level than any other along the river that had been seen until then. In the fields were many walnut-trees, bearing tender-shelled nuts in the shape of acorns, many being found stored in the houses. The tree did not differ in any thing from that of Spain, nor from the one seen before, except the leaf was smaller. There were many mulberry-trees, and trees of plums (persimmons), having fruit of vermilion hue, like one of Spain, while others were gray, differing, but far better. All the trees, the year round, were as green as if they stood in orchards, and the woods were open.

The Governor marched two days through the country of Casqui, before coming to the town where the cacique was, the greater part of the way lying through fields thickly set with great towns, two or three of them to be seen from one. He sent word by an Indian to the cacique, that he was coming to obtain his friendship and to consider him as a brother; to which he received for answer, that he would be welcomed; that he would be received with special good-will, and all that his lordship required of him should be done; and the chief sent him on the road a present of skins, shawls, and fish. After these gifts were made, all the towns into which the Governor came were found occupied; and the inhabitants awaited him in peace, offering him skins, shawls, and fish.

Accompanied by many persons, the cacique came half a league on the road from the town where he dwelt to receive the Governor, and, drawing nigh to him, thus spoke:

> Very High, Powerful, and Renowned Master:
>
> I greet your coming. So soon as I had notice of you, your power and perfections, although you entered my territory capturing and killing the dwellers upon it, who are my vassals, I determined to conform my wishes to your will, and hold as right all that you might do, believing that it should be so for a good reason, providing against some future event, to you perceptible but from me concealed; since an evil may well be permitted to avoid another greater, that good can arise, which I trust will be so; for from so excellent a prince, no bad motive is to be suspected. My ability is so small to serve you, according to your great merit, that though you should consider even my abundant will and humility in proffering you all manner of services, I must still deserve little in your sight. If this ability can with reason be valued, I pray you receive it, and with it my country and my vassals, of me and them disposing at your pleasure; for though you were lord of the earth, with no more good-will would you be received, served, and obeyed.

The Governor responded appropriately in a few words which satisfied the chief. Directly they fell to making each other great proffers, using much courtesy, the cacique inviting the Governor to go and take lodging in his houses. He excused himself, the better to preserve peace, saying that he wished to lie in the field; and, because the heat was excessive, he pitched the camp among some trees, quarter of a league from the town. The cacique went to his town, and returned with many Indians singing, who, when they had come to where the Governor was, all prostrated themselves. Among them were two blind men. The cacique made an address, of which, as it was long, I will give the substance in a few words. He said, that inasmuch as the Governor was son of the Sun, he begged him to restore sight to those Indians: whereupon the blind men arose, and they very earnestly entreated him to do so. Soto answered them, that in the heavens above there was One who had the power to make them whole, and do whatever they could ask of Him, whose servant he was; that this great Lord made the sky and the earth, and man after His image; that He had suffered on the tree of the true cross to save the human race, and risen from the grave on the third day,—what of man there was of Him dying, what of divinity being immortal; and that, having ascended into heaven, He was there with open arms to receive all that would be converted to Him. He then directed a lofty cross of wood to be made and set up in the highest part of the town, declaring to the cacique that the Christians worshipped that, in the form and memory of the one on which Christ suffered. He placed himself with his people before it, on their knees, which the Indians did likewise; and he told them that from that time thenceforth they should thus worship the Lord, of whom he had spoken to them, that was in the skies, asking Him for whatsoever they stood in need of.

. . . The night of the day the Governor left, he slept at a town of Casqui; and the next day he passed in sight of two other towns, and arrived at the lake, which was half a crossbow-shot over, of great depth and swiftness of current. The Indians had just got the bridge done as he came up. It was built of wood, in the manner of timber thrown across from tree to tree; on one side there being a rail of poles, higher than the rest, as a support for those who should pass. The cacique of Casqui having come with his people, the Governor sent word by an Indian to the cacique of Pacaha, that though he might be at enmity with him of Casqui, and that chief be present, he should receive neither injury nor insult, provided that he attended in peace and desired his friendship, for as a brother would he treat him. The Indian went as he was bid, and returned, stating that the cacique took no notice of the message, but that he fled out of the town, from the back part, with all his people. Then the Governor entered there, and with the cavalry charged in the direction the Indians were running, and at another town, a quarter of a league off, many were taken. As fast as they were captured, the horsemen delivered them to the Indians of Casqui, who, from being their enemies, brought them with great heed and pleasure to the town where the Christians were, greatly regretting that they had not the liberty to kill them. Many shawls, deer-skins, lion and bear-skins, and many cat-skins were found in the town. Numbers who had been a long time badly covered, there clothed themselves. Of the shawls they made mantles and cassocks; some made gowns and lined them with cat-skins, as they also did the cassocks. Of the deer-skins were made jerkins, shirts, stockings, and shoes; and from the bear-skins they made very good cloaks, such as no water could get through. They found shields of raw cowhide out of which armor was made for the horses.

### The message sent to Quigaltam, and the answer brought back to the Governor, and what occurred the while.

... The Governor sank into a deep despondency at sight of the difficulties that presented themselves to his reaching the sea; and, what was worse, from the way in which the men and horses were diminishing in numbers, he could not sustain himself in the country without succor. Of that reflection he pined: but, before he took to his pallet, he sent a messenger to the cacique of Quigaltam, to say that he was the child of the Sun, and whence he came all obeyed him, rendering their tribute; that he besought him to value his friendship, and to come where he was; that he would be rejoiced to see him; and in token of love and his obedience, he must bring him something from his country that was in most esteem there. By the same Indian, the chief returned this answer:

> As to what you say of your being the son of the Sun, if you will cause him to dry up the great river, I will believe you: as to the rest, it is not my custom to visit any one, but rather all, of whom I have ever heard, have come to visit me, to serve and obey me, and pay me tribute, either voluntarily or by force. If you desire to see me, come where I am; if for peace, I will receive you with special good-will; if for war, I will await you in my town; but neither for you, nor for any man, will I set back one foot.

When the messenger returned, the Governor was already low, being very ill of fevers. He grieved that he was not in a state to cross the river at once, and go in quest of the cacique, to see if he could not abate that pride; though the stream was already flowing very powerfully, was nearly half a league broad, sixteen fathoms in depth, rushing by in furious torrent, and on either shore were many Indians; nor was his power any longer so great that he might disregard advantages, relying on his strength alone.

Every day the Indians of Guachoya brought fish, until they came to be in such plenty that the town was covered with them. . . .

That the Indians might stand in terror of them, the Governor determined to send a captain to Nilco, which the people of Guachoya had told him was inhabited, and, treating the inhabitants there severely, neither town would dare to attack him: so he commanded Captain Nuño de Tobar to march thither with fifteen horsemen, and Captain Juan de Guzman, with his company of foot, to ascend the river by water in canoes. The cacique of Guachoya ordered canoes to be brought, and many warriors to come, who went with the Christians. Two leagues from Nilco, the cavalry, having first arrived, waited for the foot, and thence together they crossed the river in the night. At dawn, in sight of the town, they came upon a scout, who, directly as he saw the Christians, set up loud yells, and fled to carry the news to those in the place. Nuño de Tobar, and those with him, hastened on so rapidly, that they were upon the inhabitants before they could all get out of town. The ground was open field; the part of it covered by the houses, which might be a quarter of a league in extent, contained five or six thousand souls. Coming out of them, the Indians ran from one to another habitation, numbers collecting in all parts, so that there was not a man on horseback who did not find himself amidst many; and when the captain ordered that the life of no male should be spared, the surprise was such, that there was not a man among them in readiness to draw a bow. The cries of the women and children were such as to deafen those who pursued them. About one hundred men were slain; many were allowed to get away badly wounded, that they might strike terror into those who were absent.

Some persons were so cruel and butcher-like that they killed all before them, young and old, not one having resisted little nor much; while those who felt it their duty to be wherever there might be resistance, and were esteemed brave, broke through the crowds of Indians, bearing down many with their stirrups and the breasts of their horses, giving some a thrust and letting them go, but encountering a child or a woman would take and deliver it over to the footmen. To the ferocious and bloodthirsty, God permitted that their sin should rise up against them in the presence of all—when there was occasion for fighting showing extreme cowardice, and in the end paying for it with their lives. . . .

## How the Governor Luys de Moscoso left Guachoya and went to Chaguete, and from thence to Aguacay.

Some were glad of the death of Don Hernando de Soto, holding it certain that Luys de Moscoso, who was given to leading a gay life, preferred to see himself at ease in a land of Christians, rather than continue the toils of war, discovering and subduing, which the people had come to hate, finding the little recompense that followed. The [new] Governor ordered that the captains and principal personages should come together, to consult and determine upon what they would do; and, informed of the population there was on all sides, he found that towards the west the country was most inhabited, and that descending the stream, after passing Quigaltam, it was desert and had little subsistence. He besought them all to give him their opinion in writing, signed with their names, that, having the views of every one, he might determine whether to follow down the river or enter the land.

To every one it appeared well to march westwardly, because in that direction was New Spain, the voyage by sea being held more hazardous and of doubtful accomplishment, as a vessel of sufficient strength to weather a storm could not be built, nor was there captain nor pilot, needle nor chart, nor was it known how distant might be the sea; neither had they any tidings of it, or if the river did not take some great turn through the land, or might not have some fall over rocks where they might be lost. Some, who had seen the sea-card, found that by the shore, from the place where they were to New Spain, there should be about five hundred leagues; and they said that by land, though they might have to go round about sometimes, in looking for a peopled country, unless some great impassable wilderness should intervene, they could not be hindered from going forward that summer; and, finding provision for support in some peopled country where they might stop, the following summer they should arrive in a land of Christians; and that, going by land, it might be they should discover some rich country which would avail them. Moscoso, although it was his desire to get out of the land of Florida in the shortest time, seeing the difficulties that lay before him in a voyage by sea, determined to undertake that which should appear to be the best of all. . . .

### How the Governor marched from Nondacao to Soacatino and Guasco, passing through a wilderness, whence, for want of a guide and interpreter, he retired to Nilco.

The Governor set out from Nondacao for Soacatino, and on the fifth day came to a province called Aays. The inhabitants had never heard of the Christians. So soon as they observed them entering the territory the people were called out, who, as fast as they could get together, came by fifties and hundreds on the road, to give battle. While some encountered us, others fell upon our rear; and when we followed up those, these pursued us. The attack continued during the greater part of the day, until we arrived at their town. Some men were injured, and some horses, but nothing so as to hinder travel, there being not one dangerous wound among all. The Indians suffered great slaughter.

The day on which the Governor departed, the guide told him he had heard it said in Nondacao, that the Indians of Soacatino had seen other Christians; at which we were all delighted, thinking it might be true, and that they could have come by the way of New Spain; for if it were so, finding nothing in Florida of value, we should be able to go out of it, there being fear we might perish in some wilderness. The Governor, having been led for two days out of the way, ordered that the Indian be put to the torture, when he confessed that his master, the cacique of Nondacao, had ordered him to take them in that manner, we being his enemies, and he, as his vassal, was bound to obey him. He was commanded to be cast to the dogs, and another Indian guided us to Soacatino, where we came the following day.

The country was very poor, and the want of maize was greatly felt. The natives being asked if they had any knowledge of other Christians, said they had heard that near there, towards the south, such men were moving about. For twenty days the march was through a very thinly peopled country, where great privation and toil were endured; the little maize there was, the Indians having buried in the scrub, where the Christians, at the close of the day's march, when they were well weary, went trailing, to seek for what they needed of it to eat.

Arrived at a province called Guasco, they found maize, with which they loaded the horses and the Indians; thence they went to another settlement, called Naquiscoça, the inhabitants of which said that they had no knowledge of any other Christians. The Governor ordered them put to torture, when they stated that farther on, in the territories of another chief, called Naçacahoz, the Christians had arrived, and gone back toward the west, whence they came. He reached there in two days, and took some women, among whom was one who said that she had seen Christians, and, having been in their hands, had made her escape from them. The Governor sent a captain with fifteen cavalry to where she said they were seen, to discover if there were any marks of horses, or signs of any Christians having been there; and after travelling three or four leagues, she who was the guide declared that all she had said was false; and so it was deemed of everything else the Indians had told of having seen Christians in Florida.

As the region thereabout was scarce of maize, and no information could be got of any inhabited country to the west, the Governor went back to Guasco. The residents stated, that ten days' journey from there, toward the sunset, was a river called Daycao, whither they sometimes went to drive and kill deer, and whence they had seen persons on the other bank, but without knowing what people they were. The Christians took as much maize as they could find, to carry with them; and journeying ten days through a wilderness, they arrived at the river of which the Indians had spoken. Ten horsemen sent in advance by the Governor had crossed; and, following a road leading up from the bank, they came upon an encampment of Indians living in very small huts, who, directly as they saw the Christians, took to flight, leaving what they had, indications only of poverty and misery. So wretched was the country, that what was found everywhere, put together, was not half an alqueire [a peck] of maize. Taking two natives, they went back to the river, where the Governor waited; and on coming to question the captives, to ascertain what towns there might be to the west, no Indian was found in the camp who knew their language.

The Governor commanded the captains and principal personages to be called together that he might determine now by their opinions what was best to do. The majority declared it their judgment to return to the River Grande of Guachoya, because in Anilco and thereabout was much maize; that during the winter they would build brigantines, and the following spring go down the river in them in quest of the sea, where having arrived, they would follow the coast thence along to New Spain,—an enterprise which, although it appeared to be one difficult to accomplish, yet from their experience it offered the only course to be pursued. They could not travel by land, for want of an interpreter; and they considered the country farther on, beyond the River Daycao, on which they were, to be that which Cabeça de Vaca had said in his narrative should have to be traversed, where the Indians wandered like Arabs, having no settled place of residence, living on prickly pears, the roots of plants, and game; and that if this should be so, and they, entering upon that tract, found no provision for sustenance during winter, they must inevitably perish, it being already the beginning of October; and if they remained any longer where they were, what with rains and snow, they should neither be able to fall back, nor, in a land so poor as that, to subsist.

The Governor, who longed to be again where he could get his full measure of sleep, rather than govern and go conquering a country so beset for him with hardships, directly returned, getting back from whence he came.

CHAPTER 5

# Exploring the Myth:
# Fray Marcos de Niza's Discovery
# of a City of Cíbola (1539)

*When Cabeza de Vaca and his companions stumbled back to New Spain, the
story of their miraculous return set off a flurry of interest in the lands to the
north of the Spanish New World settlements. Numbered among the inter-
ested was Viceroy Antonio de Mendoza, who authorized Fray Marcos de
Niza to go north and verify the rumors of cities and riches swirling in the
wake of Cabeza de Vaca's return from the void.*

*Marcos set out in March of 1539, guided by Estebán, the Moor who had
crossed the continent with Cabeza de Vaca. The expedition was not a success.
According to Marcos's narrative, advance-scout Estebán was killed by the natives of the southernmost of the legendary Seven Cities of Cíbola. (In fact
Esteban was killed at the small pueblo of Hawikuh, located southwest of
present-day Zuni, New Mexico) (Thrapp 1988, 940). After claiming the city
for his king, but without daring to set foot in it, Marcos turned tail and
headed for home "with much more fear than food" ([1926], 30).*

*From such ignominious circumstances comes the narrative of Marcos, a
work of reportage and wish fulfillment that freely mixes descriptions of sights
he claimed to have seen (but may not have) with stories he claimed to have
heard from natives. And though it is hard to see how such an implausible,
unsubstantiated narrative could have launched the large and costly Coronado expedition, it is easy to see how the narrative fit the needs of people who
were desperate to believe that the land of their dreams lay to the northwest.
Tantalizingly the narrative offers the footloose Esteban, always a frustrating
day or two ahead of the narrator (and the reader), continuously marking his
progress with a trail of ever-bigger crosses that imply increasing riches while,*

*at the same time, neatly symbolize the twin economic and religious impetuses of exploration. Along with Estebán the narrative presents Marcos himself, a pious padre who nonetheless tempts his readers with a distant, sparkling glimpse of a city "bigger than the city of Mexico" ([1926], 29).*

*For Marcos's eager-to-believe audience, the possibilities suggested by the narrative's vague hints of wealthy cities must have been more convincing than any tangible proofs the author could have produced. But the allure of the narrative comes not just from hints of gold to be gained and souls to be saved; along with these tangible commodities, Marcos is selling the powerful substance of myth. Specifically he is selling the myth of the Seven Cities, a legend that has been identified as having its origins in medieval Spain (Hallenbeck 1949, 1). According to this myth, seven Spanish bishops and their followers sailed west to establish new cities after being displaced by Moorish invaders. The nebulous location of the Seven Cities drifted westward as the Spanish empire expanded, always remaining just beyond the fringe of the known world.*

*It cannot be claimed that this myth alone was enough to inspire Coronado and his gold-hungry followers to set off to the north. All that can be said is that the myth was powerful enough that for many years the Spanish sought the Seven Cities as fervently as they sought the mythical Strait of Anian. And propelled by parallel myths, later generations of explorers would scour the North American wilderness for mythical bands of blue-eyed Welsh Indians and lost tribes of Israelites. Even in the late twentieth century, there are those who continue to explore the wilderness of history in search of Native American utopias that never were. Aware of the power of myth, Fray Marcos incorporates the legend of the Seven Cities to pump vitality into a narrative that would be nothing more than another vague rumor of gold without its attractive mythical element.*

*Fray Marcos's story earned him a spot on the Coronado Expedition, but when his wonderful city turned out to be no more than an adobe pueblo inhabited by a few hundred farmers, the good father turned back to Mexico rather than remain with an army of disgruntled gold-seekers. He died in a monastery near Mexico City in 1558.*

*The translation presented here was made by Percy M. Baldwin and was first published in 1926. Baldwin made his translation from a printed version of the narrative found in the* Documentos Inéditos del Archivo de Indias, *vol. 3 (Baldwin [1926], 3). The comments in brackets have been added by the editors of this volume.*

## Selected Bibliography

Baldwin, M. "Foreword." In *Discovery of the Seven Cities of Cíbola, by Marco da Niza*. Albuquerque: El Palacio Press, [1926].

Bandelier, Adolph F. *Adolph F. Bandelier's The Discovery of New Mexico by the Franciscan Monk, Friar Marcos de Niza in 1539*. Ed. and trans. by Madeleine Turrell Rodack. Tucson: University of Arizona Press, 1981.

Hallenbeck, Cleve. "Historical Background." *Journey of Fray Marcos de Niza*. Dallas: University Press, 1949.

da Niza, Marcos. *Discovery of the Seven Cities of Cíbola*. Ed. and trans. by Percy M. Baldwin. Albuquerque: El Palacio Press, [1926].

Thrapp, Dan L. *Encyclopedia of Frontier Biography*. 3 vols. Glendale, Cal.: Arthur H. Clark, 1988.

FRAY MARCOS DE NIZA

# Exploring the Myth: Fray Marcos de Niza's Discovery of a City of Cíbola (1539)

## Relation

WITH THE AID and favor of the most holy Virgin Mary, our Lady, and of our seraphic father, St. Francis, I, Fray Marcos de Niza, a professed religious of the order of St. Francis, in fulfillment of the instructions above given of the most illustrious lord, Don Antonio de Mendoza, viceroy and governor for H. M. of New Spain, left the town of San Miguel, in the province of Culiacan, on Friday, March 7th, 1539. I took with me as companion Friar Honoratus and also Stephen of Dorantes [Estebán], a negro, and certain Indians, which the said Lord Viceroy bought for the purpose and set at liberty. . . .

I was received everywhere I went with much hospitality and rejoicing and with triumphal arches. The inhabitants also gave me what food they had, which was little, because they said it had not rained for three years, and because the Indians of that territory think more of hiding than of growing crops, for fear of the Christians of the town of San Miguel, who up to that time were accustomed to make war upon and enslave them. . . .

I took my way over a desert for four days, and at the end of the desert I found some other Indians, who were astonished to see me, as they had no news of Christians, having no traffic with the people on the other side of the desert. These Indians made me very welcome, giving me plenty of food, and they endeavored to touch my clothes, calling me *Sayota*, which means in their language, "man from heaven." I made them understand, the best I could by my interpreters, the content of my instructions, namely, the knowledge of Our Lord in heaven and of H. M. on earth. And always, by all the means that I could, I sought to learn about a country with numerous towns and a people of a higher culture than those I was encountering, but I had no news except that they told me that in the country beyond, four or five days' journey thence, where the chains of mountains ended, there was an extensive and level open tract, in which they told me there were many and very large towns inhabited by a people clothed with cotton. When I showed them some metals which I was carrying, in order to take account of the metals of the country, they took a piece of gold and told me that there were vessels of it among the people of the region and that they wear certain articles of that metal suspended from their noses and ears, and that they had some little blades of it, with which they scrape and relieve themselves of sweat. . . .

I sent Indian messengers to the sea, by three ways, whom I charged to bring back to me people from the coast and from some of the islands, that I might inform myself concerning them. In another direction I sent Stephen Dorantes, the negro, whom I instructed to take the route toward the north for fifty or sixty leagues to see if by that way he might obtain an account of any important thing such as we were seeking. I agreed with him that if he had any news of a populous, rich and important country he should not continue further but should return in person or send me Indians with a certain signal which we arranged, namely, that if it were something of medium importance, he should send me a white cross of a hand's breadth, if it were something of great importance, he should send me one of two hands' breadth, while if it were bigger and better than New Spain, he should send me a great cross. . . .

In four days' time there came messengers from Stephen with a very great cross, as high as a man, and they told me on Stephen's behalf that I should immediately come and follow him, because he had met people who gave him an account of the greatest country in the world, and that he had Indians who had been there, of whom he sent me one. This man told me so many wonderful things about the country, that I forebore to believe them until I should have seen them, or should have more certitude of the matter. He told me that it was thirty days' journey from where Stephen was staying to the first city of the country, which was named Cíbola. As it appears to me to be worth while to put in this paper what this Indian, whom Stephen sent me, said concerning the country, I will do so. He asserted that in the first province there were seven very great cities, all under one lord, that the houses, constructed of stone and lime, were large, that the smallest were of one story with a terrace above, that there were others of two and three stories, whilst that of the lord had four, and all were joined under his rule. He said that the doorways of the principal houses were much ornamented with turquoises, of which there was a great abundance, and that the people of those cities went very well clothed. He told me many other particulars, not only of the seven cities but of other provinces beyond them, each one of which he said was much bigger than that of the seven cities. That I might understand the matter as he knew it, we had many questions and answers and I found him very intelligent.

. . . I left Vacapa on the second day of the Easter festival, taking the same road that Stephen had followed. I had received from him more messengers, with another big cross as big as the first which he sent, urging me to hurry and stating that the country in question was the best and greatest of which he had ever heard. These messengers gave me, individually, the same story as the first, except that they told me much more and gave me a clearer account. So for that day, the second of Easter, and for two more days I followed the same stages of the route as Stephen had; at the end of which I met the people who had given him news of the seven cities and of the county beyond. They told me that from there it was thirty days' journey to the city of Cíbola, which is the first of the seven. I had an account not from one only, but from many, and they told me in great detail the size of the houses and the manner of them, just as the first ones had. They told me that beyond these seven cities there were other kingdoms named Marata, Acus and Totonteac. I desired very much to know for what they went so far from their homes and they told me that they went for turquoises, cowhides and other things, that there was a quantity of these things in that town. Likewise I asked what they exchanged for such articles and they told me the sweat of their brows and the service of their persons, that they went to the first city, which is called Cíbola, where they served in digging the ground and performing other work, for which work they are given oxhides of the kind produced in that country, and turquoises. The people of this town all wear good and beautiful turquoises hanging from their ears and noses and they say that these jewels are worked into the principal doors of Cíbola. They told me that the fashion of clothing worn in Cíbola is a cotton shirt reaching to the instep, with a button at the throat and a long cord hanging down, the sleeves of the shirts being the same width throughout their length; it seems to me this would resemble the Bohemian style. They say that those people go girt with belts of turquoises and that over these shirts some wear excellent cloaks and others very well dressed cowhides, which are considered the best clothing, and of which they say there is a great quantity in that country. The women likewise go clothed and covered to the feet in the same manner.

These Indians received me very well and took great care to learn the day of my departure from Vacapa, so that they might furnish me on the way with victuals and lodgings. They brought me sick persons that I might cure them and they tried to touch my clothes; I recited the Gospel over them. They gave me some cowhides so well tanned and dressed that they seemed to have been prepared by some highly civilized people, and they all said that they came from Cíbola.

. . . I arrived at another settlement, where I was very well received by its people, who also endeavored to touch my clothing. They gave me information concerning the country whither I was bound as much in detail as those I had met before, and they told me that some persons had gone from there with Stephen Dorantes, four or five days previously. Here I found a great cross which Stephen had left for me, as a sign that the news of the good country continually increased, and he had left word for me to hurry and that he would wait for me at the end of the first desert. Here I set up two crosses and took possession, according to my instructions, because that country appeared to me better than that which I had already passed and hence it was fitting to perform the acts of possession.

In this manner I traveled five days, always finding people, who gave me a very hospitable reception, many turquoises and cowhides and the same account of the country. They all spoke to me right away of Cíbola and that province as people who knew that I was going in search of it. They told me how Stephen was going forward, and I received from him messengers who were inhabitants of that town and who had been some distance with him. He spoke more and more enthusiastically of the greatness of the country and he urged me to hurry. Here I learned that two days' journey thence I would encounter a desert of four days' journey, in which there was no provision except what was supplied by making shelters for me and carrying food. I hurried forward, expecting to meet Stephen at the end of it, because he had sent me word that he would await me there.

Before arriving at the desert, I came to a green, well watered settlement, where there came to meet me a crowd of people, men and women, clothed in cotton and some covered with cowhides, which in general they consider a better dress material than cotton. All the people of this town wear turquoises hanging from their noses and ears; these ornaments are called *cacona*. Among them came the chief of the town and his two brothers, very well dressed in cotton, *encaconados*, and each with a necklace of turquoises around his neck. They brought to me a quantity of game—venison, rabbits and quail—also maize and meal, all in great abundance. They offered me many turquoises, cowhides, very pretty cups and other things, of which I accepted none, for such was my custom since entering the country where we were not known. And here I had the same account as before of the seven cities and the kingdoms and provinces as I have related above. I was wearing a garment of dark woolen cloth, of the kind called *Saragossa*, which was given to me by Francisco Vazquez de Coronado, governor of New Galicia. The chief of the village and other Indians touched it with their hands and told me that there was plenty of that fabric in Totonteac, and that the natives of that place were clothed with it. At this I laughed and said it could not be so, that it must be garments of cotton which those people wore. Then they said to me: "Do you think that we do not know that what you wear and what we wear is different? Know that in Cíbola the houses are full of that material which we are wearing, but in Totonteac there are some small animals from which they obtain that with which they make a fabric like yours." This astonished me, as I had not heard of any such thing previously, and I desired to inform myself more particularly about it. They told me that the animals are of the size of the Castilian greyhounds which Stephen had with him; they said there were many of them in Totonteac. I could not guess what species of animals they might be. . . .

Continuing our journey, at a day's march from Cíbola, we met two other Indians, of those who had gone with Stephen, who appeared bloody and with many wounds. At this meeting, they and those that were with me set up such a crying, that out of pity and fear they also made me cry. So great was the noise that I could not ask about Stephen nor of what had happened to them, so I begged them to be quiet that we might learn what had passed. They said to me: "How can we be quiet, when we know that our fathers, sons, and brothers who were with Stephen, to the number of more than three hundred men, are dead? And we no more dare go to Cíbola, as we have been accustomed." Nevertheless, as well as I could, I endeavored to pacify them and to put off their fear, although I myself was not without need of someone to calm me. I asked the wounded Indians concerning Stephen and as to what had happened. They remained a short time without speaking a word, weeping along with those of their towns. A last they told me that when Stephen arrived at a day's journey from Cíbola, he sent his messengers with his calabash to the lord of Cíbola to announce his arrival and that he was coming peacefully and to cure them. When the messengers gave him the calabash and he saw the rattles, he flung it furiously on the floor and said: "I know these people; these rattles are not of our style of workmanship; tell them to go back immediately or not a man of them will remain alive." Thus he remained very angry. The messengers went back sad, and hardly dared to tell Stephen of the reception they had met. Nevertheless they told him and he said that they should not fear, that he desired to go on, because, although they answered him badly, they would receive him well. So he went and arrived at the city of Cíbola just before sunset, with all his company, which would be more than three hundred men, besides many women. The inhabitants would not permit them to enter the city, but put them in a large and commodious house outside the city. They at once took away from Stephen all that he carried, telling him that the lord so ordered. "All that night," said the Indians, "they gave us nothing to eat nor drink. The next day, when the sun was a lance-length high, Stephen went out of the house and some of the chiefs with him. Straightway many people came out of the city and, as soon as he saw them, he began to flee and we with him. Then they gave us these arrowstrokes and cuts and we fell and some dead men fell on top of us. Thus we lay till nightfall, without daring to stir. We heard loud voices in the city and we saw many men and women watching on the terraces. We saw no more of Stephen and we concluded that they had shot him with arrows as they had the rest that were with him, of whom there escaped only us."

In view of what the Indians had related and the bad outlook for continuing my journey as I desired, I could not help but feel their loss and mine. God is witness of how much I desired to have someone of whom I could take counsel, for I confess I was at a loss what to do. I told them that Our Lord would chastize Cíbola and that when the Emperor knew what had happened he would send many Christians to punish its people. They did not believe me, because they say that no one can withstand the power of Cíbola. I begged them to be comforted and not to weep and consoled them with the best words I could muster, which would be too long to set down here. With this I left them and withdrew a stone's throw or two apart, to commend myself to God, and remained thus an hour and a half. When I went back to them, I found one of my Indians, named Mark, who had come from Mexico, and he said to me: "Father, these men have plotted to kill you, because they say that on account of you and Stephen their kinsfolk have been murdered, and that there will not remain a man or woman among them all who will not be killed." I then divided among them all that remained of dry stuffs and other articles, in order to pacify them. I told them to observe that if they killed me they would do me no harm, because I would die a Christian and would go to heaven, and that those who killed me would suffer for it, because the Christians would come in search of me, and, against my will, would kill them all. With these and many other words I pacified them somewhat, although there was still high feeling on account of the people killed. I asked that some of them should go to Cíbola, to see if any other Indian had escaped and to obtain some news of Stephen, but I could not persuade them to do so. Seeing this, I told them that, in any case, I must see the city of Cíbola, and they said that no one would go with me. Finally, seeing me determined, two chiefs said that they would go with me.

With these and with my own Indians and interpreters, I continued my journey till I came within sight of Cíbola. It is situated on a level stretch on the brow of a roundish hill. It appears to be a very beautiful city, the best that I have seen in these parts; the houses are of the type that the Indians described to me, all of stone, with their stories, and terraces, as it appeared to me from a hill whence I could see it. The town is bigger than the city of Mexico. At times I was tempted to go to it, because I knew that I risked nothing but my life, which I had offered to God the day I commenced the journey; finally I feared to do so, considering my danger and that if I died, I would not be able to give an account of this country, which seems to me to be the greatest and best of the discoveries. When I said to the chiefs who were with me, how beautiful Cíbola appeared to me, they told me that it was the least of the seven cities, and that Totonteac is much bigger and better than all the seven, and that it has so many houses and people that there is no end to it. Viewing the situation of the city, it occurred to me to call that country the new kingdom of St. Francis, and there, with the aid of the Indians, I made a big heap of stones and on top of it I placed a small slender cross, not having the materials to construct a bigger one. I declared that I placed that cross and landmark in the name of Don Antonio de Mendoza, viceroy and governor of New Spain for the Emperor, our lord, in sign of possession, in conformity with my instructions. I declared that I took possession there of all the seven cities and of the kingdoms of Totonteac and Acus and Marata, and that I did not go to them, in order that I might return to give an account of what I had done and seen.

Then I started back, with much more fear than food, and went to meet the people whom I had left behind, with the greatest haste I could make. I overtook them after two days' march and went with them till we had passed the desert and arrived at their home. Here I was not made welcome, as previously, because the men, as well as the women, indulged in much weeping for the persons killed at Cíbola.

# CHAPTER 6

# Deceived by the Dream: Pedro de Castañeda's Long Look Back at the Coronado Expedition (1540)

*Pedro de Castañeda was no doubt a hopeful young man when he marched north as a common soldier in Coronado's army of treasure hunters. Aware of the stories of Cabeza de Vaca and Fray Marcos de Niza, exposed to the tempting golden rumors spread by the Spaniards' Indian allies, Castañeda, along with the rest of the army, set out with the conviction that glittering fortunes were waiting to be picked up in the North.*

*Filled with such optimistic confidence, the Coronado expedition left Compostela, Mexico, in February 1540 and spent nearly three years wandering generally northward, penetrating as far north as present-day Kansas (Thrapp 1988, 326). The years of futile wandering must have taken their toll on optimism, for when Castañeda got around to recording his account of the Coronado expedition some twenty years after the fact, he writes as a disappointed old man who has indelibly learned "the difference between the report which told about vast treasures, and the places where nothing like this was either found or known" (Hodge 1925, 343).*

*Castañeda's disappointment is more wistful than bitter, however, for time has made him understand that what he and his companions lost by abandoning the lands of their youth—lands he calls "the marrow of the land in these western parts" (Hodge 1925, 283)—was not the fabled riches of gold and silver but the genuine "good country they had in their hands" (Hodge 1925, 284). This sense of the West as a land of lost youth and lost opportunity marks Castañeda's narrative as the first work to treat the West with the kind of nostalgia that was to become a hallmark of western writing from the age of James Fenimore Cooper to that of Wallace Stegner.*

*Castañeda's narrative also has the distinction of being one of the first ac-*

*counts of the West that was not written by a gentleman or a cleric. In keeping with the author's station, many of the situations described—such as the experience of getting lost on the open plains or the feelings of the ordinary soldiers toward their leaders—seem to come from a writer looking up from the bottom ranks. Similarly the author's habit of referring to key Indian figures by mocking nicknames such as "Whiskers" and "the Turk" suggests that he is writing in the voice of a rough-and-ready soldier.*

*This is not to say that Castañeda is an incompetent writer. His descriptions of buffalo herds, open prairies, and pueblo life ring truer and are more economical than what most better-educated writers could produce. He also has enough writing talent to build his narrative around a powerful irony. To the young Castañeda, the climax of the story is the realization that the army has been deceived by its Indian guide, the Turk, who has led the soldiers to the buffalo plains only to admit that his tales about cities of gold and silver were lies. To the old Castañeda, however, the story climaxes with his slow-in-coming realization that he and his companions deceived themselves: it was their own false dreams of gold and silver, not the lies of the Turk, that caused them to let the good land slip through their hands. In light of this irony, it is easy to appreciate the regret that inspires the final chapter of Castañeda's narrative—a desperate attempt to shape the geography of myth and fact into a route that leads back to the lost land of youth.*

*The translation of Castañeda reprinted here was made by George Parker Winship and was first published in 1896. Because Castañeda's original three-part manuscript long ago disappeared, Winship's translation is based on a copy of the manuscript executed in Seville in 1596 (Hodge 1925, 277). The portion of the text reprinted here begins with Castañeda's introduction and then jumps to Coronado's siege of Tiguex Pueblo (located near the site of present-day Bernalillo, New Mexico). The comments in brackets were added by Winship; the comments in braces were added by the editors of this volume.*

### Selected Bibliography

Bolton, Herbert E. *Coronado: Knight of Pueblos and Plains*. Albuquerque: University of New Mexico Press, 1964.

Day, A. Grove. *Coronado's Quest*. Berkeley: University of California Press, 1964.

Hodge, Frederick W., ed. "The Narrative of the Expedition of Coronado, by Pedro de Castañeda." In *Spanish Explorers in the Southern United States, 1528–1534*. New York: Scribners, 1925.

Thrapp, Dan L. *Encyclopedia of Frontier Biography*. 3 vols. Glendale, Cal.: Arthur H. Clark, 1988.

PEDRO DE CASTAÑEDA

# Deceived by the Dream: Pedro de Castañeda's (1540) Long Look Back at the Coronado Expedition

**Account of the Expedition to Cíbola which took place in the year 1540, in which all those settlements, their ceremonies and customs, are described. Written by Pedro de Castañeda, of Najera.**

TO ME IT SEEMS very certain, my very noble lord, that it is a worthy ambition for great men to desire to know and wish to preserve for posterity correct information concerning the things that have happened in distant parts, about which little is known. I do not blame those inquisitive persons who, perchance with good intentions, have many times troubled me not a little with their requests that I clear up for them some doubts which they have had about different things that have been commonly related concerning the events and occurrences that took place during the expedition to Cíbola, or the New Land, which the good viceroy—may he be with God in His glory—Don Antonio de Mendoza {First Viceroy of New Spain (Mexico)}, ordered and arranged, and on which he sent Francisco Vazquez de Coronado as captain general. In truth, they have reason for wishing to know the truth, because most people very often make things of which they have heard, and about which they have perchance no knowledge, appear either greater or less than they are. They make nothing of those things that amount to something, and those that do not they make so remarkable that they appear to be something impossible to believe. This may very well have been caused by the fact that, as that country was not permanently occupied, there has not been any one who was willing to spend his time in writing about its peculiarities, because all knowledge was lost of that which it was not the pleasure of God—

He alone knows the reason—that they should enjoy. In truth, he who wishes to employ himself thus in writing out the things that happened on the expedition, and the things that were seen in those lands, and the ceremonies and customs of the natives, will have matter enough to test his judgment, and I believe that the result can not fail to be an account which, describing only the truth, will be so remarkable that it will seem incredible.

And besides, I think that the twenty years and more since that expedition took place have been the cause of some stories which are related. For example, some make it an uninhabitable country, others have it bordering on Florida, and still others on Greater India, which does not appear to be a slight difference. They are unable to give any basis upon which to found their statements. There are those who tell about some very peculiar animals, who are contradicted by others who were on the expedition, declaring that there was nothing of the sort seen. Others differ as to the limits of the provinces and even in regard to the ceremonies and customs, attributing what pertains to one people to others. All this has had a large part, my very noble lord, in making me wish to give now, although somewhat late, a short general account for all those who pride themselves on this noble curiosity, and to save myself the time taken up by these solicitations. Things enough will certainly be found here which are hard to believe. All or the most of these were seen with my own eyes, and the rest is from reliable information obtained by inquiry of the natives themselves. Understanding as I do that this little work would be nothing in itself, lacking authority, unless it were favored and protected by a person whose authority would protect it from the boldness of those who, without reverence, give their murmuring tongues liberty, and knowing as I do how great are the obligations under which I have always been, and am, to your grace, I humbly beg to submit this little work to your protection. . . .

May it please our Lord to so favor me that with my slight knowledge and small abilities I may be able by relating the truth to make my little work pleasing to the learned and wise readers, when it has been accepted by your grace. For my intention is not to gain the fame of a good composer or rhetorician, but I desire to give a faithful account and to do this slight service to your grace, who will, I hope, receive it as from a faithful servant and soldier, who took part in it. Although not in a polished style, I write that which happened—that which I heard, experienced, saw, and did.

I always notice, and it is a fact, that for the most part when we have something valuable in our hands, and deal with it without hindrance, we do not value or prize it so highly as if we understood how much we should miss it after we had lost it, and the longer we continue to have it the less we value it; but after we have lost it and miss the advantages of it, we have a great pain in the heart, and we are all the time imagining and trying to find ways and means by which to get it back again. It seems to me that this has happened to all or most of those who went on the expedition which, in the year of our Savior Jesus Christ 1540, Francisco Vazquez Coronado led in search of the Seven Cities {of Cíbola}. Granted that they did not find the riches of which they had been told, they found a place in which to search for them and the beginning of a good country to settle in, so as to go on farther from there. Since they came back from the country which they conquered and abandoned, time has given them a chance to understand the direction and locality in which they were, and the borders of the good country they had in their hands, and their hearts weep for having lost so favorable an opportunity. Just as men see more at the bullfight when they are upon the seats than when they are around in the ring, now when they know and understand the direction and situation in which they were, and see, indeed, that they can not enjoy it nor recover it, now when it is too late they enjoy telling about what they saw, and even of what they realize that they lost, especially those who are now as poor as when they went there. They have never ceased their labors and have spent their time to no advantage. I say this because I have known several of those who came back from there who amuse themselves now by talking of how it would be to go back and proceed to recover that which is lost, while others enjoy trying to find the reason why it was discovered at all. . . .

## Of why Tiguex revolted, and how they were punished, without being to blame for it.

It has been related how the general reached Tiguex, where he found Don Garcia Lopez de Cardenas and Hernando de Alvarado, and how he sent the latter back to Cicuye, where he took the captain Whiskers and the governor of the village, who was an old man, prisoners. The people of Tiguex did not feel well about this seizure. In addition to this, the general wished to obtain some clothing to divide among his soldiers, and for this purpose he summoned one of the chief Indians of Tiguex, with whom he had already had much intercourse and with whom he was on good terms, who was called Juan Aleman by our men, after a Juan Aleman who lived in Mexico, whom he was said to resemble. The general told him that he must furnish about three hundred or more pieces of cloth, which he needed to give his people. He said that he was not able to do this, but that it pertained to the governors; and that besides this, they would have to consult together and divide it among the villages, and that it was necessary to make the demand of each town separately. The general did this, and ordered certain of the gentlemen who were with him to go and make the demand; and as there were twelve villages, some of them went on one side of the river and some on the other. As they were in very great need, they did not give the natives a chance to consult about it, but when they came to a village they demanded what they had to give, so that they could proceed at once. Thus these people could do nothing except take off their own cloaks and give them to make up the number demanded of them. And some of the soldiers who were in these parties, when the collectors gave them some blankets or cloaks which were not such as they wanted, if they saw any Indian with a better one on, they exchanged with him without more ado, not stopping to find out the rank of the man they were stripping, which caused not a little hard feeling.

Besides what I have just said, one whom I will not name, out of regard for him, left the village where the camp was and went to another village about a league distant, and seeing a pretty woman there he called her husband down to hold his horse by the bridle while he went up; and as the village was entered by the upper story, the Indian supposed he was going to some other part of it. While he was there the Indian heard some slight noise, and then the Spaniard came down, took his horse, and went away. The Indian went up and learned that he had violated, or tried to violate, his wife, and so he came with the important men of the town to complain that a man had violated his wife, and he told how it happened. When the general made all the soldiers and the persons who were with him come together, the Indian did not recognize the man, either because he had changed his clothes or for whatever other reason there may have been, but he said that he could tell the horse, because he had held his bridle, and so he was taken to the stables, and found the horse, and said that the master of the horse must be the man. He denied doing it, seeing that he had not been recognized, and it may be that the Indian was mistaken in the horse; anyway, he went off without getting any satisfaction. The next day one of the Indians, who was guarding the horses of the army, came running in, saying that a companion of his had been killed, and that the Indians of the country were driving off the horses toward their villages. The Spaniards tried to collect the horses again, but many were lost, besides seven of the general's mules.

The next day Don Garcia Lopez de Cardenas went to see the villages and talk with the natives. He found the villages closed by palisades and a great noise inside, the horses being chased as in a bull fight and shot with arrows. They were all ready for fighting. Nothing could be done, because they would not come down on to the plain and the villages are so strong that the Spaniards could not dislodge them. The general then ordered Don Garcia Lopez de Cardenas to go and surround one village with all the rest of the force. This village was the one where the greatest injury had been done and where the affair with the Indian woman occurred. Several captains who had gone on in advance with the general, Juan de Saldivar and Barrionuevo and Diego Lopez and Melgosa, took the Indians so much by surprise that they gained the upper story, with great danger, for they wounded many of our men from within the houses. Our men were on top of the houses in great danger for a day and a night and part of the next day, and they made some good shots with their crossbows and muskets. The horsemen on the plain with many of the Indian allies from New Spain smoked them out from the cellars into which they had broken, so that they begged for peace. Pablo de Melgosa and Diego Lopez, the alderman from Seville, were left on the roof and answered the Indians with the same signs they were making for peace, which was to make a cross. They then put down their arms and received pardon. They were taken to the tent of Don Garcia, who, according to what he said, did not know about the peace and thought that they had given themselves up of their own accord because they had been conquered. As he had been ordered by the general not to take them alive, but to make an example of them so that the other natives would fear the Spaniards, he ordered two hundred stakes to be prepared at once to burn them alive. Nobody told him about the peace that had been granted them, for the soldiers knew as little as he, and those who should have told him about it remained silent, not thinking that it was any of their business. Then when the enemies saw that the Spaniards were binding them and beginning to roast them, about a hundred men who were in the tent began to struggle and defend themselves with what there was there and with the stakes they could seize. Our men who were on foot attacked the tent on all sides, so that there was great confusion around it, and then the horsemen chased those who escaped. As the country was level, not a man of them remained alive, unless it was some who remained hidden in the village and escaped that night to spread throughout the country the news that the strangers did not respect the peace they had made, which afterward proved a great misfortune. After this was over, it began to snow, and they abandoned the village and returned to the camp just as the army came from Cíbola.

## Of how they besieged Tiguex and took it and of what happened during the siege.

As I have already related, it began to snow in that country just after they captured the village, and it snowed so much that for the next two months it was impossible to do anything except to go along the roads to advise them to make peace and tell them that they would be pardoned and might consider themselves safe, to which they replied that they did not trust those who did not know how to keep good faith after they had once given it, and that the Spaniards should remember that they were keeping Whiskers prisoner and that they did not keep their word when they burned those who surrendered in the village. Don Garcia Lopez de Cardenas was one of those who went to give this notice. He started out with about thirty companions and went to the village of Tiguex to talk with Juan Aleman. Although they were hostile, they talked with him and said that if he wished to talk with them he must dismount and they would come out and talk with him about a peace, and that if he would send away the horsemen and make his men keep away, Juan Aleman and another captain would come out of the village and meet him. Everything was done as they required, and then when they approached they said that they had no arms and that he must take his off. Don Garcia Lopez did this in order to give them confidence, on account of his great desire to get them to make peace. When he met them, Juan Aleman approached and embraced him vigorously, while the other two who had come with him drew two mallets which they had hidden behind their backs and gave him two such blows over his helmet that they almost knocked him senseless. Two of the soldiers on horseback had been unwilling to go very far off, even when he ordered them, and so they were near by and rode up so quickly that they rescued him from their hands, although they were unable to catch the enemies because the meeting was so near the village that of the great shower of arrows which were shot at them one arrow hit a horse and went through his nose. The horsemen all rode up together and hurriedly carried off their captain, without being able to harm the enemy, while many of our men were dangerously wounded. They then withdrew, leaving a number of men to continue the attack. Don Garcia Lopez de

Cardenas went on with a part of the force to another village about half a league distant, because almost all the people in this region had collected into these two villages. As they paid no attention to the demands made on them except by shooting arrows from the upper stories with loud yells, and would not hear of peace, he returned to his companions whom he had left to keep up the attack on Tiguex. A large number of those in the village came out and our men rode off slowly, pretending to flee, so that they drew the enemy on to the plain, and then turned on them and caught several of their leaders. The rest collected on the roofs of the village and the captain returned to his camp.

After this affair the general ordered the army to go and surround the village. He set out with his men in good order, one day, with several scaling ladders. When he reached the village, he encamped his force near by, and then began the siege; but as the enemy had had several days to provide themselves with stores, they threw down such quantities of rocks upon our men that many of them were laid out, and they wounded nearly a hundred with arrows, several of whom afterward died on account of the bad treatment by an unskillful surgeon who was with the army. The siege lasted fifty days, during which time several assaults were made. The lack of water was what troubled the Indians most. They dug a very deep well inside the village, but were not able to get water, and while they were making it, it fell in and killed thirty persons. Two hundred of the besieged died in the fights. One day when there was a hard fight, they killed Francisco de Obando, a captain who had been army-master all the time that Don Garcia Lopez de Cardenas was away making the discoveries already described, and also Francisco Pobares, a fine gentleman. Our men were unable to prevent them from carrying Francisco de Obando inside the village, which was regretted not a little, because he was a distinguished person, besides being honored on his own account, affable and much beloved, which was noticeable. One day, before the capture was completed, they asked to speak to us, and said that, since they knew we would not harm the women and children, they wished to surrender their women and sons, because they were using up their water. It was impossible to persuade them to make peace, as they said that the Spaniards would not keep an agreement made with them. So they gave up about a hundred persons, women and boys, who did not want to leave them. Don Lope de Urrea rode up in front of the town without his helmet and received the boys and girls in his arms, and when all of these had been surrendered, Don Lope begged them to make peace, giving them the strongest promises for their safety. They told him to go away, as they did not wish to trust themselves to people who had no regard for friendship or their own word which they had pledged. As he seemed unwilling to go away, one of them put an arrow in his bow ready to shoot, and threatened to shoot him with it unless he went off, and they warned him to put on his helmet, but he was unwilling to do so, saying that they would not hurt him as long as he stayed there. When the Indian saw that he did not want to go away, he shot and planted his arrow between the fore feet of the horse, and then put another arrow in his bow and repeated that if he did not go away he would really shoot him. Don Lope put on his helmet and slowly rode back to where the horsemen were, without receiving any harm from them. When they saw that he was really in safety, they began to shoot arrows in showers, with loud yells and cries. The general did not want to make an assault that day, in order to see if they could be brought in some way to make peace, which they would not consider.

Fifteen days later they decided to leave the village one night, and did so, taking the women in their midst. They started about the fourth watch, in the very early morning, on the side where the cavalry was. The alarm was given by those in the camp of Don Rodrigo Maldonado. The enemy attacked them and killed one Spaniard and a horse and wounded others, but they were driven back with great slaughter until they came to the river [Rio Grande] where the water flowed swiftly and very cold. They threw themselves into this, and as the men had come quickly from the whole camp to assist the cavalry, there were few who escaped being killed or wounded. Some men from the camp went across the river next day and found many of them who had been overcome by the great cold. They brought these back, cured them, and made servants of them. This ended that siege, and the town was captured, although there were a few who remained in one part of the town and were captured a few days later.

Two captains, Don Diego de Guevara and Juan de Saldivar, had captured the other large village after a siege. Having started out very early one morning to make an ambuscade in which to catch some warriors who used to come out every morning to try to frighten our camp, the spies, who had been placed where they could see when they were coming, saw the people come out and proceed toward the country. The soldiers left the ambuscade and went to the village and saw the people fleeing. They pursued and killed large numbers of them. At the same time those in the camp were ordered to go over the town, and they plundered it, making prisoners of all the people who were found in it, amounting to about a hundred women and children. This siege ended the last of March, in the year '42 [1541].

### Of how the general managed to leave the country in peace so as to go in search of Quivira, where the Turk said there was the most wealth.

. . . And when the river, which for almost four months had been frozen over so that they crossed the ice on horseback, had thawed out, orders were given for the start for Quivira, where the Turk said there was some gold and silver, although not so much as in Arche and the Guaes. There were already some in the army who suspected the Turk, because a Spaniard named Cervantes, who had charge of him during the siege, solemnly swore that he had seen the Turk talking with the devil in a pitcher of water, and also that while he had him under lock so that no one could speak to him, the Turk had asked him what Christians had been killed by the people at Tiguex. He told him "nobody," and then the Turk answered: "You lie; five Christians are dead, including a captain." And as Cervantes knew that he told the truth, he confessed it so as to find out who had told him about it, and the Turk said he knew it all by himself and that he did not need to have anyone tell him in order to know it. And it was on account of this that he watched him and saw him speaking to the devil in the pitcher, as I have said. . . .

The army left Tiguex on the fifth of May and returned to Cicuye, which, as I have said, is twenty-five marches, which means leagues, from there, taking Whiskers with them. . . .

The governor and Whiskers gave the general a young fellow called Xabe, a native of Quivira, who could give them information about the country. This fellow said that there was gold and silver, but not so much of it as the Turk had said. The Turk, however, continued to declare that it was as he had said. He went as a guide, and thus the army started off from here.

### Of how they started in search of Quivira and of what happened on the way.

The army started from Cicuye, leaving the village at peace and, as it seemed, contented, and under obligations to maintain the friendship because their governor and captain had been restored to them. . . .

After ten days more they came to some settlements of people who lived like Arabs and who are called Querechos {Apaches} in that region. They had seen the cows {buffalo} for two days. These folks live in tents made of the tanned skins of the cows. They travel around near the cows, killing them for food. They did nothing unusual when they saw our army, except to come out of their tents to look at us, after which they came to talk with the advance guard, and asked who we were. The general talked with them, but as they had already talked with the Turk, who was with the advance guard, they agreed with what he had said. That they were very intelligent is evident from the fact that although they conversed by means of signs they made themselves understood so well that there was no need of an interpreter. They said that there was a very large river over toward where the sun came from, and that one could go along this river through an inhabited region for ninety days without a break from settlement to settlement. They said that the first of these settlements was called Haxa, and that the river was more than a league wide and that there were many canoes on it. These folks started off from here next day with a lot of dogs which dragged their possessions. For two days, during which the army marched in the same direction as that in which they had come from the settlements—that is, between north and east, but more toward the north—they saw other roaming Querechos and such great numbers of cows that it already seemed something incredible.

These people gave a great deal of information about settlements, all toward the east from where we were. Here Don Garcia broke his arm and a Spaniard got lost who went off hunting so far that he was unable to return to the camp, because the country is very level. The Turk said it was one or two days to Haya (Haxa). The general sent Captain Diego Lopez with ten companions lightly equipped and a guide to go at full speed toward the sunrise for two days and discover Haxa, and then return to meet the army, which set out in the same direction next day. They came across so many animals that those who were on the advance guard killed a large number of bulls. As these fled they trampled one another in their haste until they came to a ravine. So many of the animals fell into this that they filled it up, and the rest went across on top of them. The men who were chasing them on horseback fell in among the animals without noticing where they were going. Three of the horses that fell in among the cows, all saddled and bridled, were lost sight of completely.

As it seemed to the general that Diego Lopez ought to be on his way back, he sent six of his companions to follow up the banks of the little river, and as many more down the banks, to look for traces of the horses at the trails to and from the river. It was impossible to find tracks in this country, because the grass straightened up again as soon as it was trodden down. They were found by some Indians from the army who had gone to look for fruit. These got track of them a good league off, and soon came up with them. They followed the river down to the camp, and told the general that in the twenty leagues they had been over they had seen nothing but cows and the sky. There was another native of Quivira with the army, a painted Indian named Ysopete. This Indian had always declared that the Turk was lying, and on account of this the army paid no attention to him, and even now, although he said that the Querechos had consulted with him, Ysopete was not believed.

The general sent Don Rodrigo Maldonado, with his company, forward from here. He travelled four days and reached a large ravine like those of Colima, in the bottom of which he found a large settlement of people. Cabeza de Vaca and Dorantes had passed through this place, so that they presented Don Rodrigo with a pile of tanned skins and other things, and a tent as big as a house, which he directed them to keep until the army came up. He sent some of his companions to guide the army to that place, so that they should not get lost, although he had been making piles of stones and cow-dung for the army to follow. This was the way in which the army was guided by the advance guard.

When the general came up with the army and saw the great quantity of skins, he thought he would divide them among the men, and placed guards so that they could look at them. But when the men arrived and saw that the general was sending some of his companions with orders for the guards to give them some of the skins, and that these were going to select the best, they were angry because they were not going to be divided evenly, and made a rush, and in less than a quarter of an hour nothing was left but the empty ground.

The natives who happened to see this also took a hand in it. The women and some others were left crying, because they thought that the strangers were not going to take anything, but would bless them as Cabeza de Vaca and Dorantes had done when they passed through here. They found an Indian girl here who was as white as a Castilian lady, except that she had her chin painted like a Moorish woman. In general they all paint themselves in this way here, and they decorate their eyes.

### Of how great stones fell in the camp, and how they discovered another ravine, where the army was divided into two parts.

While the army was resting in this ravine, as we have related, a tempest came up one afternoon with a very high wind and hail, and in a very short space of time a great quantity of hailstones, as big as bowls, or bigger, fell as thick as raindrops, so that in places they covered the ground two or three spans or more deep. . . .

From here the general sent out to explore the country, and they found another settlement four days from there. . . . The country was well inhabited, and they had plenty of kidney beans and prunes like those of Castile, and tall vineyards. These village settlements extended for three days. This was called Cona. Some Teyas, as these people are called, went with the army from here and travelled as far as the end of the other settlements with their packs of dogs and women and children, and then they gave them guides to proceed to a large ravine where the army was. They did not let these guides speak with the Turk, and did not receive the same statements from these as they had from the others. These said that Quivira was toward the north, and that we should not find any good road thither. After this they began to believe Ysopete. . . .

The army rested several days in this ravine and explored the country. Up to this point they had made thirty-seven days' marches, travelling six or seven leagues a day. It had been the duty of one man to measure and count his steps.

They found that it was 250 leagues to the settlements {the Tiguex villages}. When the general Francisco Vazquez realized this, and saw that they had been deceived by the Turk heretofore, and as the provisions were giving out and there was no country around here where they could procure more, he called the captains and ensigns together to decide on what they thought ought to be done. They all agreed that the general should go in search of Quivira with thirty horsemen and half a dozen foot soldiers, and that Don Tristan de Arellano should go back to Tiguex with all the army. When the men in the army learned of this decision, they begged their general not to leave them to conduct the further search, but declared that they all wanted to die with him and did not want to go back. This did not do any good, although the general agreed to send messengers to them within eight days saying whether it was best for them to follow him or not, and with this he set off with the guides he had and with Ysopete. The Turk was taken along in chains.

### Of how the army returned to Tiguex and the general reached Quivira.

The general started from the ravine with the guides that the Teyas had given him. He appointed the alderman Diego Lopez his army-master, and took with him the men who seemed to him to be most efficient, and the best horses. The army still had some hope that the general would send for them, and sent two horsemen, lightly equipped and riding post, to repeat their petition.

. . . The army waited for its messengers and spent a fortnight here, preparing jerked beef to take with them. It was estimated that during this fortnight they killed 500 bulls. The number of these that were without any cows was something incredible. Many fellows were lost at this time who went out hunting and did not get back to the army for two or three days, wandering about the country as if they were crazy, in one direction or another, not knowing how to get back where they started from, although this ravine extended in either direction so that they could find it. Every night they took account of who was missing, fired guns and blew trumpets and beat drums and built great fires, but yet some of them went off so far and wandered about so much that all this did not give them any help, although it helped others. The only way was to go back where they had killed an animal and start from there in one direction and another until they struck the ravine or fell in with somebody who could put them on the right road. It is worth noting that the country there is so level that at midday, after one has wandered about in one direction and another in pursuit of game, the only thing to do is to stay near the game quietly until sunset, so as to see where it goes down, and even then they have to be men who are practised to do it. Those who are not, had to trust themselves to others.

The general followed his guides until he reached Quivira, which took forty-eight days' marching, on account of the great detour they had made toward Florida {to the southeast}. He was received peacefully on account of the guides whom he had. They asked the Turk why he had lied and had guided them so far out of their way. He said that his country was in that direction and that, besides this, the people at Cicuye had asked him to lead them off on to the plains and lose them, so that the horses would die when their provisions gave out, and they would be so weak if they ever returned that they could be killed without any trouble, and thus they could take revenge for what had been done to them. This was the reason why he had led them astray, supposing that they did not know how to hunt or to live without corn, while as for the gold, he did not know where there was any of it. He said this like one who had given up hope and who found that he was being persecuted, since they had begun to believe Ysopete, who had guided them better than he had, and fearing lest those who were there might give some advice by which some harm would come to him. They garroted him, which pleased Ysopete very much, because he had always said that Ysopete was a rascal and that he did not know what he was talking about and had always hindered his talking with anybody. Neither gold nor silver nor any trace of either was found among these people. Their lord wore a copper plate on his neck and prized it highly.

The messengers whom the army had sent to the general returned, as I said, and then, as they brought no news except what the alderman had delivered, the army left the ravine and returned to the Teyas, where they took guides who led them back by a more direct road. They readily furnished these, because these people are always roaming over this country in pursuit of the animals and so know it thoroughly. They keep their road in this way: In the morning they notice where the sun rises and observe the direction they are going to take, and then shoot an arrow in this direction. Before reaching this they shoot another over it, and in this way they go all day toward the water where they are to end the day. In this way they covered in twenty-five days what had taken them thirty-seven days going, besides stopping to hunt cows on the way. They found many salt lakes on this road, and there was a great quantity of salt. There were thick pieces of it on top of the water bigger than tables, as thick as four or five fingers. Two or three spans down under water there was salt which tasted better than that in the floating pieces, because this was rather bitter.

. . . A painted Indian woman ran away from Juan de Saldibar and hid in the ravines about this time, because she recognized the country of Tiguex where she had been a slave. She fell into the hands of some Spaniards who had entered the country from Florida to explore it in this direction. After I got back to New Spain I heard them say that the Indian told them that she had run away from other men like them nine days, and that she gave the names of some captains; from which we ought to believe that we were not far from the region they discovered, although they said they were more than 200 leagues inland. I believe the land at that point is more than 600 leagues across from sea to sea. . . .

## Of how the general returned from Quivira and of other expeditions toward the North. . . .

Another captain went down the river in search of the settlements which the people at Tutahaco had said were several days distant from there. This captain went down eighty leagues and found four large villages which he left at peace. He proceeded until he found that the river sank into the earth, like the Guadiana in Estremadura. He did not go on to where the Indians said that it came out much larger, because his commission did not extend for more than eighty leagues' march. After this captain got back Don Tristan selected forty companions and, leaving the army to Francisco de Barrionuevo, he started with them in search of the general. When he reached Cicuye the people came out of the village to fight, which detained him there four days, while he punished them, which he did by firing some volleys into the village. These killed several men, so that they did not come out against the army, since two of their principal men had been killed on the first day. Just then word was brought that the general was coming, and so Don Tristan had to stay there on this account also, to keep the road open. Everybody welcomed the general on his arrival, with great joy. The Indian Xabe, who was the young fellow who had been given to the general at Cicuye when he started off in search of Quivira, was with Don Tristan de Arellano and when he learned that the general was coming he acted as if he was greatly pleased, and said, "Now when the general comes, you will see that there are gold and silver in Quivira, although not so much as the Turk said." When the general arrived, and Xabe saw that they had not found anything, he was sad and silent, and kept declaring that there was some. He made many believe that it was so, because the general had not dared to enter into the country on account of its being thickly settled and his force not very strong, and that he had returned to lead his army there after the rains, because it had begun to rain there already, as it was early in August when he left. It took him forty days to return, travelling lightly equipped. The Turk had said when they left Tiguex that they ought not to load the horses with too much provisions, which would tire them so that they could not afterward carry the gold and silver, from which it is very evident that he was deceiving them. . . .

### Of how they live at Tiguex, and of the province of Tiguex and its neighborhood.

Tiguex is a province with twelve villages on the banks of a large, mighty river {Rio Grande}, some villages on one side and some on the other. It is a spacious valley two leagues wide, and a very high, rough, snow-covered mountain chain lies east of it. There are seven villages in the ridges at the foot of this—four on the plain and three situated on the skirts of the mountain.

There are seven villages seven leagues to the north, at Quirix, and the seven villages of the province of Hemes are forty leagues northeast [northwest]. It is forty leagues north or east to Acha, and four leagues southeast to Tutahaco, a province with eight villages. In general, these villages all have the same habits and customs, although some have some things in particular which the others have not. They are governed by the opinions of the elders. They all work together to build the villages, the women being engaged in making the mixture and the walls, while the men bring the wood and put it in place. They have no lime, but they make a mixture of ashes, coals, and dirt which is almost as good as mortar, for when the house is to have four stories, they do not make the walls more than half a yard thick. They gather a great pile of twigs of thyme [sagebrush] and sedge grass and set it afire, and when it is half coals and ashes they throw a quantity of dirt and water on it and mix it all together. They make round balls of this, which they use instead of stones after they are dry, fixing them with the same mixture, which comes to be like a stiff clay. Before they are married the young men serve the whole village in general, and fetch the wood that is needed for use, putting it in a pile in the courtyard of the villages, from which the women take it to carry to their houses.

The young men live in the estufas, which are in the yards of the village. They are underground, square or round, with pine pillars. Some were seen with twelve pillars and with four in the centre as large as two men could stretch around. They usually had three or four pillars. The floor was made of large, smooth stones, like the baths which they have in Europe. They have a hearth made like the binnacle or compass box of a ship, in which they burn a handful of thyme at a time to keep up the heat, and they can stay in there just as in a bath. The top was on a level with the ground. Some that were seen were large enough for a game of ball. When any man wishes to marry, it has to be arranged by those who govern. The man has to spin and weave a blanket and place it before the woman, who covers herself with it and becomes his wife. The houses belong to the women, the estufas to the men. If a man repudiates his woman, he has to go to the estufa. It is forbidden for women to sleep in the estufas, or to enter these for any purpose except to give their husbands or sons something to eat. The men spin and weave. The women bring up the children and prepare the food. The country is so fertile that they do not have to break up the ground the year round, but only have to sow the seed, which is presently covered by the fall of snow, and the ears come up under the snow. In one year they gather enough for seven. A very large number of cranes and wild geese and crows and starlings live on what is sown, and for all this, when they come to sow for another year, the fields are covered with corn which they have not been able to finish gathering.

There are a great many native fowl in these provinces, and cocks with great hanging chins. When dead, these keep for sixty days, and longer in winter, without losing their feathers or opening, and without any bad smell, and the same is true of dead men.

The villages are free from nuisances, because they go outside to excrete, and they pass their water into clay vessels, which they empty at a distance from the village. They keep the separate houses where they prepare the food for eating and where they grind the meal, very clean. This is a separate room or closet, where they have a trough with three stones fixed in stiff clay. Three women go in here, each one having a stone, with which one of them breaks the corn, the next grinds it, and the third grinds it again. They take off their shoes, do up their hair, shake their clothes, and cover their heads before they enter the door. A man sits at the door playing on a fife while they grind, moving the stones to the music and singing together. They grind a large quantity at one time, because they make all their bread of meal soaked in warm water, like wafers. They gather a great quantity of brushwood and dry it to use for cooking all through the year. There are no fruits good to eat in the country, except the pine nuts. They have their preachers. Sodomy is not found among them. They do not eat human flesh nor make sacrifices of it. The people are not cruel, for they had Francisco de Ovando in Tiguex about forty days, after he was dead, and when the village was captured, he was found among their dead, whole and without any other wound except the one which killed him, white as snow, without any bad smell. I found out several things about them from one of our Indians, who had been a captive among them for a whole year. I asked him especially for the reason why the young women in that province went entirely naked, however cold it might be, and he told me that the virgins had to go around this way until they took a husband, and that they covered themselves after they had known man. The men here wear little shirts of tanned deerskin and their long robes over this. In all these provinces they have earthenware glazed with antimony and jars of extraordinary labor and workmanship, which were worth seeing.

## Which treats of the plains that were crossed, of the cows, and of the people who inhabit them.

We have spoken of the settlements of high houses which are situated in what seems to be the most level and open part of the mountains, since it is 150 leagues across before entering the level country between the two mountain chains which I said were near the North Sea and the South Sea, which might better be called the Western Sea along this coast. This mountain series is the one which is near the South Sea. In order to show that the settlements are in the middle of the mountains, I will state that it is eighty leagues from Chichilticalli, where we began to cross this country, to Cíbola; from Cíbola, which is the first village, to Cicuye, which is the last on the way across, is seventy leagues; it is thirty leagues from Cicuye to where the plains begin. It may be we went across in an indirect or roundabout way, which would make it seem as if there was more country than if it had been crossed in a direct line, and it may be more difficult and rougher. This can not be known certainly, because the mountains change their direction above the bay at the mouth of the Firebrand (Tizon) River.

Now we will speak of the plains. The country is spacious and level, and is more than 400 leagues wide in the part between the two mountain ranges—one, that which Francisco Vazquez Coronado crossed, and the other that which the force under Don Fernando de Soto crossed, near the North Sea, entering the country from Florida. No settlements were seen anywhere on these plains.

In traversing 250 leagues, the other mountain range was not seen, nor a hill nor a hillock which was three times as high as a man. Several lakes were found at intervals; they were round as plates, a stone's throw or more across, some fresh and some salt. The grass grows tall near these lakes; away from them it is very short, a span or less. The country is like a bowl, so that when a man sits down, the horizon surrounds him all around at the distance of a musket shot. There are no groves of trees except at the rivers, which flow at the bottom of some ravines where the trees grow so thick that they were not noticed until one was right on the edge of them. They are of dead earth. There are paths down into these, made by the cows when they go to the water, which is essential throughout these plains. As I have related in the first part, people follow the cows, hunting them and tanning the skins to take to the settlements in the winter to sell, since they go there to pass the winter, each company going to those which are nearest, some to the settlements at Cicuye, others toward Quivira, and others to the settlements which are situated in the direction of Florida. These people are called Querechos and Teyas. They described some large settlements, and judging from what was seen of these people and from the accounts they gave of other places, there are a good many more of these people than there are of those at the settlements. They have better figures, are better warriors, and are more feared. They travel like the Arabs, with their tents and troops of dogs loaded with poles and having Moorish pack-saddles with girths. When the load gets disarranged, the dogs howl, calling some one to fix them right. These people eat raw flesh and drink blood. They do not eat human flesh. They are a kind people and not cruel. They are faithful friends. They are able to make themselves very well understood by means of signs. They dry the flesh in the sun, cutting it thin like a leaf, and when dry they grind it like meal to keep it and make a sort of pea soup of it to eat. A handful thrown into a pot swells up so as to increase very much. They season it with fat, which they always try to secure when they kill a cow. They empty a large gut and fill it with blood, and carry this around the neck to drink when they are thirsty. When they open the belly of a cow, they squeeze out the chewed grass and drink the juice that remains behind, because they say that this contains the essence of the stomach. They cut the hide open at the back and pull it off at the joints, using a flint as large as a finger, tied to a little stick, with as much ease as if working with a good iron tool. They give it an edge with their own teeth. The quickness with which they do this is something worth seeing and noting.

There are very great numbers of wolves on these plains, which go around with the cows. They have white skins. The deer are pied with white. Their skin is loose, so that when they are killed it can be pulled off with the hand while warm, coming off like pigskin. The rabbits, which are very numerous, are so foolish that those on horseback killed them with their lances. This is when they are mounted among the cows. They fly from a person on foot.

## Which treats of the direction which the army took, and of how another more direct way might be found, if anyone was to return to that country.

I very much wish that I possessed some knowledge of cosmography or geography, so as to render what I wish to say intelligible, and so that I could reckon up or measure the advantage those people who might go in search of that country would have if they went directly through the centre of the country, instead of following the road the army took. However, with the help of the favor of the Lord, I will state it as well as I can, making it as plain as possible.

It is, I think, already understood that the Portuguese, Campo, was the soldier who escaped when Friar Juan de Padilla was killed at Quivira, and that he finally reached New Spain from Panuco, having travelled across the plains country until he came to cross the North Sea mountain chain, keeping the country that Don Hernando de Soto discovered all the time on his left hand, since he did not see the river of the Holy Spirit (Espiritu Santo) at all. After he had crossed the North Sea mountains, he found that he was in Panuco, so that if he had not tried to go to the North Sea, he would have come out in the neighborhood of the border land, or the country of the Sacatecas, of which we now have some knowledge.

This way would be somewhat better and more direct for anyone going back there in search of Quivira, since some of those who came with the Portuguese are still in New Spain to serve as guides. Nevertheless, I think it would be best to go through the country of the Guachichules, keeping near the South Sea mountains all the time, for there are more settlements and a food supply, for it would be suicide to launch out on to the plains country, because it is so vast and is barren of anything to eat, although, it is true, there would not be much need of this after coming to the cows. This is only when one goes in search of Quivira, and of the villages which were described by the Indian called Turk, for the army of Francisco Vazquez Coronado went the very farthest way round to get there, since they started from Mexico and went 110 leagues to the west, and then 100 leagues to the northeast, and 250 to the north, and all this brought them as far as the ravines where the cows were, and after travelling 850 leagues they were not more than 400 leagues distant from Mexico by a direct route. If one desires to go to the country of Tiguex, so as to turn from there toward the west in search of the country of India, he ought to follow the road taken by the army, for there is no other, even if one wished to go by a different way, because the arm of the sea which reaches into this coast toward the north does not leave room for any. But what might be done is to have a fleet and cross this gulf and disembark in the neighborhood of the Island of Negroes and enter the country from there, crossing the mountain chains in search of the country from which the people at Tiguex came, or other peoples of the same sort. As for entering from the country of Florida and from the North Sea, it has already been observed that the many expeditions which have been undertaken from that side have been unfortunate and not very successful, because that part of the country is full of bogs and poisonous fruits, barren, and the very worst country that is warmed by the sun. But they might disembark after passing the river of the Holy Spirit, as Don Hernando de Soto did. Nevertheless, despite the fact that I underwent much labor, I still think that the way I went to that country is the best. There ought to be river courses, because the necessary supplies can be carried on these more easily in large quantities. Horses are the most necessary things in the new countries, and they frighten the enemy most. . . . Artillery is also much feared by those who do not know how to use it. A piece of heavy artillery would be very good for settlements like those which Francisco Vazquez Coronado discovered, in order to knock them down, because he had nothing but some small machines for slinging and nobody skilful enough to make a catapult or some other machine which would frighten them, which is very necessary.

I say, then, that with what we now know about the trend of the coast of the South Sea, which has been followed by the ships which explored the western part, and what is known of the North Sea toward Norway, the coast of which extends up from Florida, those who now go to discover the country which Francisco Vazquez entered, and reach the country of Cíbola or of Tiguex, will know the direction in which they ought to go in order to discover the true direction of the country which the Marquis of the Valley, Don Hernando Cortes, tried to find, following the direction of the gulf of the Firebrand (Tizon) River {Gulf of California, Colorado River}.

This will suffice for the conclusion of our narrative. Everything else rests on the powerful Lord of all things, God Omnipotent, who knows how and when these lands will be discovered and for whom He has guarded this good fortune.

# CHAPTER 7

# Sir Francis Drake and the Brass Plate (1579)

*The lot of the historian is not always a happy one. Unlike the fictionist, who weaves the stuff of reality into a story in hopes of delighting an audience, the scholar of the past does something of the opposite. The scholar penetrates the myths surrounding a subject, working backwards in hopes of finding what "really" happened, and what the scholar discovers may not be pleasing to readers. This is particularly true when it comes to a nation's heroes.*

*All cultures have figures larger than life, who embody the qualities the culture most admires. It's a truism also that the public generally, and almost all of us as individuals, crave and perhaps need such figures—models who succeed where the rest of us daily fail and thus give us hope. They serve as patterns telling us who we are, and they lure us toward achieving larger possibilities despite our stumblings in an imperfect world. Yet as the national scandals of recent years have borne out, under the harsh glare of scrutiny few flesh-and-blood heroes live up to the idealized images we in our needs have unfairly created for them. In such cases historians, charged with focusing all the objectivity they can muster on a subject, often find themselves in a troubling role, as iconoclasts of what gives the public sustenance.*

*Happily, then, as a measure of our yearnings, we all but stand up and cheer when coming upon the rare example of a hero who promises not to let us down—who was strong-willed but considerate, deeply religious but not humorless, dashingly bold yet intelligent, who rose from humble origins to stand at the helm of critical situations and bring them across the shoals, and half a globe away left his bold mark on the opening of the New World. Who, in short, pretty well spans the assorted qualities of herodom. And two other things. He almost changed, at least we can speculate that he might have, the sad course of relations between the American Indians and their European invaders (Sugden 1990, 137). And one other particular: he left behind a brass plate, the* sine qua non *of a physical detail that has turned into the sort of fetching mystery that continues to titillate those of us who enjoy the stuff of poetry along with the mandated, if somewhat onerous, burden of historical objectivity.*

*Francis Drake was born in southwestern England, the son of a farmer who was also a devout lay preacher. Driven to sea by the family's poverty, the youthful Drake learned the ropes of sailing in the tempestuous waters of the North Sea. Family connections set him on the course to fame by placing him on the first of several voyages to the New World's West Indies. At the time they were colonies of Roman Catholic Spain, arch rival of Protestant England. On his early adventures, Drake gained wide sailing experience and an equally important taste for revenge against the Spanish, who on his second voyage attacked and killed a number of Drake's fellow seamen.*

*This background led to the next stage of his career. Queen Elizabeth noted her young subject's abilities and panache and in 1572 granted Drake a privateering commission. In effect this was a license to prey on enemy Spain, especially the shipping that funneled Spain's riches from the New World back to the homeland. Leading an expedition of two small ships, Drake boldly sailed into the port of Nombre de Dios, Panama, then, after a sharp battle in which he was wounded, quickly sailed out again loaded with plunder. The event became the basis both of his fortune and of his still larger fame, and it illustrates the unnerving tactics he would use to great effect thereafter: swift attacks on the Spanish in unexpected places, followed by rapid escapes back into the wilderness of the sea. So bold was Drake, that he sailed into the great harbor of Valparaiso, Chile, and, speaking Spanish, got himself invited onto one of the ships at anchor. Once aboard, he and his crew locked up the Spaniards, plundered the town, and made a speedy getaway. But though they robbed their national enemy wherever they could, taking bars of silver and gold, heaps of emeralds and pearls, and the casks of Chilean wine for which they'd developed a taste, Drake's men avoided unnecessary violence. Drake became so known for his courtesy to his victims that he often won their admiration—much to the ire of the Spanish authorities (Morison 1978, 691–96). Such is the stuff of which heroes are made.*

*To his nation's delight, Drake piled coup upon coup. He concluded his extended plundering voyage of 1577–80 by becoming the first Englishman to circumnavigate the world. Though his resulting fame caused jealousies in England, Drake's star continued to rise. As vice admiral of the fleet defending England, in 1588 he sailed out to do battle with his usual dash, helping to rout the Spanish Armada then threatening England's shores. Hailed by poems, songs, and broadsheets, condemned by the Spaniards, who felt his sting as "the master-thief of the unknown world," he died in 1596 of a fever, on his last foray to the West Indies.*

*The following pages are excerpted from* The World Encompassed by Sir Francis Drake, *an account by Francis Fletcher (dates unknown), Drake's chaplain on the world-circling voyage. We discover Drake in medias res, in the year of 1579, stripping Guatulco, Mexico, the last port of the New World raided on the prolonged plundering adventure. Note Fletcher's flippancy in the first paragraph, as the English thieves relieve the Spanish of their valuables.*

*Thereafter the tone becomes more serious, for Drake's success had left him in something of a pickle. The basic problem was how to get back safely to England. To the south, the ports were wasps' nests already poked by Drake's pirate stick, buzzing with anger at his rude depredations. Spanish warships were sure to be laying for him, waiting for the Englishman to try a run back around the tip of South America, in a reversal of the route whence he came. Yet* The Golden Hind, *a small vessel to begin with, rode low in the water, made slow and less maneuverable from her load of gold and silver bars. Eliminating the dangerous return-route option left the captain with two choices, both of them challenging in their own ways. He could sail westward out into the Pacific, toward the South Seas and Africa. That would be the long way home, one that might mean an encounter with Spanish ships plying between South America and the Philippine Islands. Or, the less obvious choice, he could sail north, into the uncharted waters of unknown realms.*

*Once again, Drake took the unexpected tack. He sailed north. Though his motives aren't entirely clear, several factors likely came into play in reaching the decision. His ship not only was overloaded, it was leaking badly and in need of repairs. He needed to resupply his stores and rest his men before undertaking any long voyage. Perhaps such ends could be accomplished in peace on the shores of the unexplored lands to the north, where there were no Spaniards. And by choosing the alternative, he might find the fabled Northwest Passage, a rumored waterway linking the Pacific with the Atlantic Ocean and providing a shortcut back to England.*

*As we'll see, the biting cold of the northern latitudes discouraged the men, who had been acclimated to tropical heat. Also the coastline trended to the west, showing no sign of an eastern bend leading to a passage existing in rumor only. Wisely Drake knew when to back out of a plan. He turned south and landed on the wild coast of northern California, likely in what is still known as Drake's Bay, about thirty-six miles north of San Francisco. The bulk of the following text details the events of the next five weeks and Drake's relations with the Indians today called the Coast Miwok, before a repaired and restocked* Golden Hind *headed for home across the Pacific.*

*The ship had to be dragged up on the beach and turned on its side in order to be serviced. This called for a second wise decision, the construction of a temporary fort, in case the inhabitants of the wild place proved hostile. Beyond that precaution, the account shows kindness and concern and curiosity toward the natives, in contrast to the far less fortuitous developments between them and Europeans elsewhere. However, it should be said that the meetings between two widely different cultures anywhere are not often marked by prolonged amiability, though it is tempting to speculate what might have evolved if men of Drake's abilities and tolerance had been in charge of future colonies. Still even this good will between two groups may have been more apparent than real. It may well have been that the wailing and self-mutilations on the part of the Indians were not signs of respect for them as gods, as the English supposed. Some anthropologists think that the Indians were frightened at what they thought were spirits returned from the dead (Sugden 1990, 136).*

*In any case another first for Drake. His claim to the surrounding country by nailing up a decree on "a plate of brasse" marks the first English possession of land in what is now North America. Little did Drake know what he had done, what a thrill he was creating for some historians and titters for others. For years Professor Herbert E. Bolton pleaded with his students at the University of California at Berkeley to keep their eyes open for Drake's lost plate. Then in 1936 a man named Beryle Shinn found it under a rock and delivered the relic into the hands of a rejoicing Bolton. A remarkable discovery, claim enthusiasts of a plate now displayed in Berkeley's august Bancroft Library. A prank by one of the good professor's waggish students, say skeptics (Morison 1978, 713–16; The Plate of Brass Reexamined). Yet another example of Drake's long reach through the centuries and his ability to keep the blood of his admirers coursing.*

## Selected Bibliography

Fletcher, Francis. *The World Encompassed by Sir Francis Drake.* [1628]. Ed. by W. S. Vaux. Pp. 113–14, 118–34. London: Hakluyt Society, 1854.

Morison, Samuel Eliot. *The Great Explorers: The European Discovery of America.* New York: Oxford University Press, 1978.

*The Plate of Brass Reexamined.* Berkeley: Bancroft Library, 1977.

Sugden, John. *Sir Francis Drake.* London: Barrie and Jenkins, 1990.

SIR FRANCIS DRAKE

# Sir Francis Drake and the Brass Plate (1579)

## Drake sacks Guatulco, then heads north, and anchors off the coast of California on June 17, 1579

THE NEXT HARBOR therefore which we chanced with on *April* 15, in 15 deg., 40 min. was *Guatulco*, so named of the Spaniards who inhabited it, with whom we had some entercourse, to the supply of many things which we desired, and chiefely bread, etc. And now hauing reasonably, as wee thought, prouided ourselues, we departed from the coast of America for the present; but not forgetting, before we gate a-shipboard, to take with vs also a certaine pot (of about a bushell in bignesse) full of ryalls of plate, which we found in the towne, together with a chaine of gold, and some other iewells, which we intreated a gentleman Spaniard to leaue behinde him, as he was flying out of towne.

From *Guatulco* we departed the day following, viz., *Aprill* 16, setting our course directly into the sea, whereon we sayled 500 leagues in longitude, to get a winde and betweene that and *June* 3, 1400 leagues in all, till we came into 42 deg. of North latitude, where in the night following we found such alteration of heate, into extreame and nipping cold, that our men in generall did grieuously complaine thereof, some of them feeling their healths much impaired thereby; neither was it that this chanced in the night alone, but the day following carried with it not onely the markes, but the stings and force of the night going before, to the great admiration of vs all; for besides that the pinching and biting aire was nothing altered, the very roapes of our ship were stiffe, and the raine which fell was an vnnatural congealed and frozen substance, so that we seemed rather to be in the frozen Zone then any way so neere vnto the sun, or these hotter climates. . . .

And also from these reasons we coniecture, that either there is no passage at all through these Northerne coasts (which is most likely), or if there be, that yet it is vnnauigable. Adde hereunto, that though we searched the coast diligently, euen vnto the 48 deg., yet found we not the land to trend so much as one point in any place towards the East, but rather running on continually North-west, as if it went directly to meet with Asia; and euen in that height, when we had a franke wind to haue carried vs through, had there beene a passage, yet we had a smooth and calme sea, with ordinary flowing and reflowing, which could not haue beene had there beene a frete; of which we rather infallibly concluded, then coniectured, that there was none. But to returne.

The next day, after our comming to anchor in the aforesaid harbour, the people of the countrey shewed themselues, sending off a man with great expedition to vs in a canow. Who being yet but a little from the shoare, and a great way from our ship, spake to vs continually as he came rowing on. And at last at a reasonable distance staying himselfe, he began more solemnely a long and tedious oration, after his manner: vsing in the deliuerie thereof many gestures and signes, mouing his hands, turning his head and body many wayes; and after his oration ended, with great shew of reuerence and submission returned backe to shoare againe. He shortly came againe the second time in like manner, and so the third time, when he brought with him (as a present from the rest) a bunch of feathers, much like the feathers of a blacke crow, very neatly and artificially gathered vpon a string, and drawne together into a round bundle; being verie cleane and finely cut, and bearing in length an equall proportion one with another; a speciall cognizance (as wee afterwards obserued) which they that guard their kings person weare on their heads. With this also he brought a little basket made of rushes, and filled with an herbe which they called *Tabáh*. Both which being tyed to a short rodde, he cast into our boate. Our Generall intended to haue recompenced him immediatly with many good things he would haue bestowed on him; but entring into the boate to deliuer the same, he could not be drawne to receiue them by any meanes, saue one hat, which being cast into the water out of the ship, he tooke vp (refusing vtterly to meddle with any other thing, though it were vpon a board put off vnto him) and so presently made his returne. After which time our boate could row no way, but wondring at vs as at gods, they would follow the same with admiration.

The 3 day following, uiz., the 21, our ship hauing receiued a leake at sea, was brought to anchor neerer the shoare, that, her goods being landed, she might be repaired; but for that we were to preuent any danger that might chance against our safety, our Generall first of all landed his men, with all necessary prouision, to build tents and make a fort for the defence of our selues and goods: and that wee might vnder the shelter of it with more safety (what euer should befall) end our businesse; which when the people of the countrey perceiued vs doing, as men set on fire to war in defence of their countrie, in great hast and companies, with such weapons as they had, they came downe vnto vs, and yet with no hostile meaning or intent to hurt vs: standing, when they drew neere, as men rauished in their mindes, with the sight of such things as they neuer had seene or heard of before that time: their errand being rather with submission and feare to worship vs as Gods, then to haue any warre with vs as with mortall men. Which thing, as it did partly shew itselfe at that instant, so did it more and more manifest itself afterwards, during the whole time of our abode amongst them. At this time, being willed by signes to lay from them their bowes and arrowes, they did as they were directed, and so did all the rest, as they came more and more by companies vnto them, growing in a little while to a great number, both of men and women.

To the intent, therefore, that this peace which they themselues so willingly sought might, without any cause of the breach thereof on our part given, be continued, and that wee might with more safety and expedition end our businesses in quiet, our Generall, with all his company, vsed all meanes possible gently to intreate them, bestowing vpon each of them liberally good and necessary things to couer their nakednesse; withall signifying vnto them we were no Gods, but men, and had neede of such things to couer our owne shame; teaching them to vse them to the same ends, for which cause also wee did eate and drinke in their presence, giuing them to vnderstand that without that wee could not liue, and therefore were but men as well as they.

Notwithstanding nothing could perswade them, nor remoue that opinion which they had conceiued of vs, that wee should be Gods.

In recompence of those things which they had receiued of vs, as shirts, linnen cloth, etc., they bestowed vpon our Generall, and diuerse of our company, diuerse things, as feathers, cawles of networke, the quiuers of their arrowes, made of fawne skins, and the very skins of beasts that their women wore vpon their bodies. Hauing thus had their fill of this times visiting and beholding of vs, they departed with ioy to their houses, which houses are digged round within the earth, and haue from the vppermost brimmes of the circle clefts of wood set vp, and ioyned close together at the top, like our spires on the steeple of a Church; which being couered with earth, suffer no water to enter, and are very warme; the doore in the most part of them performes the office also of a chimney to let out the smoake: its made in bignesse and fashion like to an ordinary scuttle in a ship, and standing slopewise: their beds are the hard ground, onely with rushes strewed vpon it, and lying round about the house, haue their fire in the middest, which by reason that the house is but low vaulted, round, and close, giueth a maruelous reflexion to their bodies to heate the same.

Their men for the most part goe naked; the women take a kinde of bulrushes, and kembing it after the manner of hemp, make themselues thereof a loose garment, which being knitte about their middles, hanges downe about their hippes, and so affords to them a couering of that which nature teaches should be hidden; about their shoulders they weare also the skin of a deere, with the haire vpon it. They are very obedient to their husbands, and exceeding ready in all seruices; yet of themselues offring to do nothing, without the consents or being called of the men.

As soone as they were returned to their houses, they began amongst themselues a kind of most lamentable weeping and crying out; which they continued also a great while together, in such sort that in the place where they left vs (being neere about 3 quarters of an English mile distant from them) we very plainely, with wonder and admiration, did heare the same, the women especially extending their voices in a most miserable and dolefull manner of shreeking.

Notwithstanding this humble manner of presenting themselues, and awfull demeanour vsed towards vs, we thought it no wisedome too farre to trust them (our experience of former Infidels dealing with vs before, made vs carefull to prouide against an alteration of their affections or breach of peace if it should happen), and therefore with all expedition we set vp our tents, and intrenched ourselues with walls of stone; that so being fortified within ourselues, we might be able to keepe off the enemie (if they should so proue) from comming amongst us without our good wills: this being quickly finished, we went the more cheerefully and securely afterward about our other businesse.

Against the end of two daies (during which time they had not againe beene with vs), there was gathered together a great assembly of men, women, and children (inuited by the report of them which first saw vs, who, as it seems, had in that time of purpose dispersed themselues into the country, to make knowne the newes), who came now the second time vnto vs, bringing with them, as before had beene done, feathers and bagges of *Tobáh* for presents, or rather indeed for sacrifices, vpon this perswasion that we were gods.

When they came to the top of the hill, at the bottom whereof wee had built our fort, they made a stand; where one (appointed as their chiefe speaker) wearied both vs his hearers, and himselfe too, with a long and tedious oration; deliuered with strange and violent gestures, his voice being extended to the vttermost strength of nature, and his wordes falling so thicke one in the necke of another, that he could hardly fetch his breath againe: as soone as he had concluded, all the rest, with a reuerend bowing of their bodies (in a dreaming manner, and long producing of the same) cryed *Oh*: thereby giuing their consents that all was very true which he had spoken, and that they had vttered their minde by his mouth vnto vs; which done, the men laying downe their bowes vpon the hill, and leauing their women and children behinde them, came downe with their presents; in such sort as if they had appeared before a God indeed, thinking themselues happy that they might haue accesse vnto our Generall, but much more happy when they sawe that he would receiue at their hands those things which they so willingly had presented: and no doubt they thought themselues neerest vnto God when they sate or stood next to him. In the meane time the women, as if they had beene desperate, vsed vnnatural violence against themselues, crying and shrieking piteously, tearing their flesh with their nailes from their cheekes in a monstrous manner, the blood streaming downe along their brests, besides despoiling the vpper parts of their bodies of those single coeuerings they formerly had, and holding their hands aboue their heads that they might not rescue their brests from harme, they would with furie cast themselues vpon the ground, neuer respecting whether it were cleane or soft, but dashed themselues in this manner on hard stones, knobby hillocks, stocks of wood, and pricking bushes, or whateuer else lay in their way, itterating the same course againe and againe; yea women great with child, some nine or ten times each, and others holding out till 15 or 16 times (till their strengths failed them) exercised this cruelty against themselues: a thing more grieuous for vs to see or suffer, could we haue holpe it, then trouble to them (as it seemed) to do it. This bloudie sacrifice (against our wils) beeing thus performed, our Generall, with his companie, in the presence of those strangers, fell to prayers; and by signes in lifting vp our eyes and hands to heauen, signified vnto them that that God whom we did serue, and whom they ought to worship, was aboue: beseeching God, if it were his good pleasure, to open by some meanes their blinded eyes, that they might in due time be called to the knowledge of him, the true and euerliuing God, and of Jesus Christ whom he hath sent, the saluation of the Gentiles. In the time of which prayers, singing of Psalmes, and reading of certaine Chapters in the Bible, they sate very attentiuely: and obseruing the end at euery pause, with one voice still cried, Oh, greatly reioycing in our exercises. Yea they tooke such pleasure in our singing of Psalmes, that whensoeuer they resorted to vs, their first request was commonly this, *Gnaáh*, by which they intreated that we would sing.

Our Generall hauing now bestowed vpon them diuers things, at their departure they restored them all againe, none carrying with him anything of whatsoeuer hee had receiued, thinking themselues sufficiently enriched and happie that they had found so free accesse to see vs.

Against the end of three daies more (the newes hauing the while spread itselfe farther, and as it seemed a great way vp into the countrie), were assembled the greatest number of people which wee could reasonably imagine to dwell within any conuenient distance round about. Amongst the rest the king himselfe, a man of a goodly stature and comely personage, attended with his guard of about 100 tall and warlike men, this day, viz., *June* 26, came downe to see vs.

Before his comming, were sent two embassadors or messengers to our Generall, to signifie that their *Hióh*, that is, their king, was comming and at hand. They in the deliuery of their message, the one spake with a soft and low voice, prompting his fellow; the other pronounced the same, word by word, after him with a voice more audible, continuing their proclamation (for such it was) about halfe an houre. Which being ended, they by signes made request to our Generall, to send something by their hands to their *Hióh* or king, as a token that his comming might be in peace. Our Generall willingly satisfied their desire; and they, glad men, made speedy returne to their *Hióh*. Neither was it long before their king (making as princely a shew as possibly he could) with all his traine came forward.

In their comming forwards they cryed continually after a singing manner, with a lustie courage. And as they drew neerer and neerer towards vs, so did they more and more striue to behaue themselues with a certaine comelinesse and grauity in all their actions.

In the forefront came a man of a large body and goodly aspect, bearing the Septer or royall mace, made of a certaine kind of blacke wood, and in length about a yard and a halfe) before the king. Whereupon hanged two crownes, a bigger and a lesse, with three chaines of a maruellous length, and often doubled, besides a bagge of the herbe *Tabáh*. The crownes were made of knitworke, wrought vpon most curiously with feathers of diuers colours, very artificially placed, and of a formall fashion. The chaines seemed of a bony substance, euery linke or part thereof being very little, thinne, most finely burnished, with a hole pierced through the middest. The number of linkes going to make one chaine, is in a manner infinite; but of such estimation it is amongst them, that few be the persons that are admitted to weare the same; and euen they to whom its lawfull to use them, yet are stinted what number they shall vse, as some ten, some twelue, some twentie, and as they exceed in number of chaines, so thereby are they knowne to be the more honorable person-ages.

Next vnto him that bare this Scepter, was the king himselfe with his guard about him; his attire vpon his head was a cawle of knitworke, wrought vpon somewhat like the crownes, but differing much both in fashion and perfectnesse of worke; vpon his shoulders he had on a coate of the skins of conies, reaching to his wast; his guard also had each coats of the same shape, but of other skins; some hauing cawles likewise stucke with feathers, or couered ouer with a certaine downe, which groweth vp in the countrey vpon an herbe much like our lectuce, which exceeds any other downe in the world for finenesse, and beeing layed vpon their cawles, by no winds can be remoued. Of such estimation is this herbe amongst them, that the downe thereof is not lawfull to be worne, but of such persons as are about the king (to whom also it is permitted to weare a plume of feathers on their heads, in signe of honour), and the seeds are not vsed but onely in sacrifice to their gods. After these, in their order, did follow the naked sort of common people, whose haire being long, was gathered into a bunch behind, in which stucke plumes of feathers; but in the forepart onely single feathers like hornes, euery one pleasing himselfe in his owne deuice.

This one thing was obserued to bee generall amongst them all, that euery one had his face painted, some with white, some blacke, and some with other colours, euery man also bringing in his hand one thing or other for a gift or present. Their traine or last part of their company con-sisted of women and children, each woman bearing against her breast a round basket or two, hauing within them diuers things, as bagges of *Tobáh*, a roote which they call *Petáh*, whereof they make a kind of meale, and either bake it into bread, or eate it raw; broyled fishes, like a pilchard; the seede and downe aforenamed, with such like.

Their baskets were made in fashion like a deep boale, and though the matter were rushes, or such other kind of stuffe, yet was it so cunningly handled, that the most part of them would hold water: about the brimmes they were hanged with peeces of the shels of pearles, and in some places with two or three linkes at a place, of the chaines forenamed: thereby signifying that they were vessels wholly dedicated to the onely vse of the gods they worshipped; and besides this, they were wrought vpon with the matted downe of red feathers, distinguished into diuers workes and formes.

In the meane time, our Generall hauing assembled his men together (as forecasting the danger and worst that might fall out) prepared himselfe to stand vpon sure ground, that wee might at all times be ready in our owne defence, if any thing should chance otherwise than was looked for or expected.

Wherefore euery man being in a warlike readinesse, he marched within his fenced place, making against their approach a most warlike shew (as he did also at all other times of their resort), whereby if they had beene desperate enemies, they could not haue chosen but haue conceiued terrour and fear, with discouragement to attempt anything against vs, in beholding of the same.

When they were come somewhat neere vnto vs, trooping together, they gaue vs a common or generall salutation, obseruing in the meane time a generall silence. Whereupon, he who bare the Scepter before the king, being prompted by another whom the king assigned to that office, pronounced with an audible and manly voice what the other spake to him in secret, continuing, whether it were his oration or proclamation, at the leaste halfe an houre. At the close whereof there was a common *Amen*, in signe of approbation, giuen by euery person: and the king himselfe, with the whole number of men and women (the little children onely remaining behind) came further downe the hill, and as they came set themselues againe in their former order.

And being now come to the foot of the hill and neere our fort, the Scepter bearer, with a composed countenance and stately carriage began a song, and answerable thereunto obserued a kind of measures in a dance: whom the king with his guard and euery other sort of person following, did in like manner sing and daunce, sauing onely the women, who danced but kept silence. As they danced they still came on: and our Generall perceiuing their plaine and simple meaning, gaue order that they might freely enter without interruption within our bulwarke. Where, after they had entred, they yet continued their song and dance a reasonable time, their women also following them with their wassaile boales in their hands, their bodies bruised, their faces torne, their dugges, breasts, and other parts bespotted with bloud, trickling downe from the wounds, which with their nailes they had made before their comming.

After that they had satisfied, or rather tired themselues in this manner, they made signes to our Generall to haue him sit down; unto whom both the king and diuers others made seuerall orations, or rather, indeed, if wee had vnderstood them, supplications, that hee would take the Prouince and kingdome into his hand, and become their king and patron: making signes that they would resigne vnto him their right and title in the whole land, and become his vassals in themselues and their posterities: which that they might make vs indeed beleeue that it was their true meaning and intent, the king himselfe, with all the rest, with one consent and with great reuerence, ioyfully singing a song, set the crowne vpon his head, inriched his necke with all their chaines, and offering vnto him many other things, honoured him by the name of *Hyóh*. Adding thereunto (as it might seeme) a song and dance of triumph; because they were not onely visited of the gods (for so they still iudged vs to be), but the great and chiefe God was now become their God, their king and patron, and themselues were become the onely happie and blessed people in the world.

These things being so freely offered, our Generall thought not meet to reiect or refuse the same, both for that he would not giue them any cause of mistrust or disliking of him (that being the onely place, wherein at this present, we were of necessitie inforced to seeke reliefe of many things), and chiefely for that he knew not to what good end God had brought this to passe, or what honour and profit it might bring to our countrie in time to come.

Wherefore, in the name and to the vse of her most excellent maiesty, he tooke the scepter, crowne, and dignity of the sayd countrie into his hand; wishing nothing more than that it had layen so fitly for her maiesty to enioy, as it was now her proper owne, and that the riches and treasures thereof (wherewith in the vpland countries it abounds) might with as great conueniency be transported, to the enriching of her kingdome here at home, as it is in plenty to be attained there; and especially that so tractable and louing a people as they shewed themselues to be, might haue meanes to haue manifested their most willing obedience the more vnto her, and by her meanes, as a mother and nurse of the Church of *Christ*, might by the preaching of the Gospell, be brought to the right knowledge and obedience of the true and euerliuing God.

The ceremonies of this resigning and receiuing of the kingdome being thus performed, the common sort, both of men and women, leauing the king and his guard about him, with our Generall, dispersed themselues among our people, taking a diligent view or suruey of euery man; and finding such as pleased their fancies (which commonly were the youngest of vs), they presently enclosing them about offred their sacrifices vnto them, crying out with lamentable shreekes and moanes, weeping and scratching and tearing their very flesh off their faces with their nailes; neither were it the women alone which did this, but euen old men, roaring and crying out, were as violent as the women were.

We groaned in spirit to see the power of Sathan so farre preuaile in seducing these so harmelesse soules, and laboured by all meanes, both by shewing our great dislike, and when that serued not, by violent withholding of their hands from that madnesse, directing them (by our eyes and hands lift vp towards heauen) to the liuing God whom they ought to serue; but so mad were they vpon their Idolatry, that forcible withholding them would not preuaile (for as soone as they could get liberty to their hands againe, they would be as violent as they were before) till such time, as they whom they worshipped were conueyed from them into the tents, whom yet as men besides themselues, they would with fury and outrage seeke to haue againe.

After that time had a little qualified their madnes, they then began to shew and make knowne vnto vs their griefes and diseases which they carried about them; some of them hauing old aches, some shruncke sinewes, some old soares and canchred vlcers, some wounds more lately receiued, and the like; in most lamentable manner crauing helpe and cure thereof from vs; making signes, that if we did but blowe vpon their griefes, or but touched the diseased places, they would be whole.

Their griefes we could not but take pitty on them, and to our power desire to helpe them: but that (if it pleased God to open their eyes) they might vnderstand we were but men and no gods, we vsed ordinary meanes, as lotions, emplaisters, and vnguents, most fitly (as farre as our skills could guesse) agreeing to the natures of their griefes, beseeching God, if it made for his glory, to giue cure to their diseases by these meanes. The like we did from time to time as they resorted to vs.

Few were the dayes, wherein they were absent from vs, during the whole time of our abode in that place; and ordinarily euery third day they brought their sacrifices, till such time as they certainely vnderstood our meaning, that we tooke no pleasure, but were displeased with them; whereupon their zeale abated, and their sacrificing, for a season, to our good liking ceased; notwithstanding they continued still to make their resort vnto vs in great abundance, and in such sort, that they oft-times forgate to prouide meate for their owne sustenance; so that our Generall (of whom they made account as of a father) was faine to performe the office of a father to them, relieuing them with such victualls as we had prouided for our selues, as Muscles, Seales, and such like, wherein they tooke exceeding much content; and seeing that their sacrifices were displeasing to vs, yet (hating ingratitude) they sought to recompence vs with such things as they had, which they willingly inforced vpon vs, though it were neuer so necessarie or needfull for themselues to keepe.

They are a people of a tractable, free, and louing nature, without guile or treachery; their bowes and arrowes (their only weapons, and almost all their wealth) they vse very skillfully, but yet not to do any great harme with them, being by reason of their weakenesse more fit for children then for men, sending the arrowes neither farre off nor with any great force: and yet are the men commonly so strong of body, that that which 2 or 3 of our men could hardly beare, one of them would take vpon his backe, and without grudging carrie it easily away, vp hill and downe hill an English mile together: they are also exceeding swift in running, and of long continuance, the vse whereof is so familar with them, that they seldome goe, but for the most part runne. One thing we obserued in them with admiration, that if at any time they chanced to see a fish so neere the shoare that they might reach the place without swimming, they would neuer, or very seldome, misse to take it.

After that our necessary businesses were well dispatched, our Generall, with his gentlemen and many of his company, made a iourny vp into the land, to see the manner of their dwelling, and to be the better acquainted with the nature and commodities of the country. Their houses were all such as we haue formerly described, and being many of them in one place, made seuerall villages here and there. The inland we found to be farre different from the shoare, a goodly country, and fruitfull soyle, stored with many blessings fit for the vse of man: infinite was the company of very large and fat Deere which there we sawe by thousands, as we supposed, in a heard; besides a multitude of a strange kinde of Conies, by farre exceeding them in number: their heads and bodies, in which they resemble other Conies, are but small; his tayle, like the tayle of a Rat, exceeding long; and his feet like the pawes of a Want or moale; vnder his chinne, on either side, he hath a bagge, into which he gathereth his meate, when he hath filled his belly abroade, that he may with it, either feed his young, or feed himselfe when he lists not to trauaile from his burrough; the people eate their bodies, and make great account of their skinnes, for their kings holidaies coate was made of them.

This country our Generall named *Albion*, and that for two causes; the one in respect of the white bancks and cliffes, which lie toward the sea; the other, that it might haue some affinity, euen in name also, with our own country, which was sometime so called.

Before we went from thence, our Generall caused to be set vp a monument of our being there, as also of her maiesties and successors right and title to that kingdome; namely, a plate of brasse, fast nailed to a great and firme post; whereon is engrauen her graces name, and the day and yeare of our arriuall there, and of the free giuing vp of the prouince and kingdome, both by the king and people, into her maiesties hands: together with her highnesse picture and armes, in a piece of sixpence currant English monie, shewing itselfe by a hole made of purpose through the plate; vnderneath was likewise engrauen the name of our Generall, etc.

The Spaniards neuer had any dealing, or so much as set a foote in this country, the vtmost of their discoueries reaching onely to many degrees Southward of this place.

And now, as the time of our departure was perceiued by them to draw nigh, so did the sorrowes and miseries of this people seeme to themselues to increase vpon them, and the more certaine they were of our going away, the more doubtfull they shewed themselues what they might doe; so that we might easily iudge that that ioy (being exceeding great) wherewith they receiued vs at our first arriuall, was cleane drowned in their excessiue sorrow for our departing. For they did not onely loose on a sudden all mirth, ioy, glad countenance, pleasant speeches, agility of body, familiar reioycing one with another, and all pleasure what euer flesh and blood might bee delighted in, but with sighes and sorrowings, with heauy hearts and grieued minds, they powred out wofull complaints and moanes, with bitter teares and wringing of their hands, tormenting themselues. And as men refusing all comfort, they onely accounted themselues as cast-awayes, and those whom the gods were about to forsake: so that nothing we could say or do, was able to ease them of their so heauy a burthen, or to deliuer them from so desperate a straite, as our leauing of them did seeme to them that it would cast them into.

Howbeit, seeing they could not still enioy our presence, they (supposing vs to be gods indeed) thought it their duties to intreate vs that, being absent, we would yet be mindfull of them, and making signes of their desires that in time to come wee would see them againe, they stole vpon vs a sacrifice, and set it on fire erre we were aware, burning therein a chaine and a bunch of feathers. We laboured by all meanes possible to withhold or withdraw them, but could not preuaile, till at last we fell to prayers and singing of Psalmes, whereby they were allured immediatly to forget their folly, and leaue their sacrifice vnconsumed, suffering the fire

# CHAPTER 8

# Settling into the Dream:
# The Pioneer Epic of Gaspar
# Castaño de Sosa (1590)

*In theory New Spain and its frontiers were far from lawless landscapes. Less than twenty years after Columbus's first landfall, the Laws of Burgos (1512) were drafted to protect the rights and property of Indians—as well as to compel them to wear clothes (Olson 1992, 118). Earlier and later laws, both religious and civil, controlled such things as what people read, how they worshipped, where they could explore, and what equipment they were required to take along when they went exploring.*

*History shows that the Spanish laws protecting Indians were frequently broken, often with impunity. Still New Spain was not such a lawless place that any sane person would dare to disobey the viceroy, the king's own representative in the New World.*

*Enter Gaspar Castaño de Sosa. Twice refused viceregal permission to head an expedition into the north, Castaño gathered together a group of fewer then two hundred settlers and, in July of 1590, set off northward from the played-out mines of Almadén (near present-day Monclova, Coahuila) (Thrapp 1988, 242). On horseback and in clumsy carts, fighting hunger, thirst, and Indians, Castaño and company pushed through Texas and into New Mexico in search of new territories to mine and farm. The expedition's advance guard, including Castaño, traveled at least as far north as the site of present-day San Ildefonso, New Mexico (Schroeder and Matson 1965, 120).*

*In 1591 Castaño's luck ran out. In early March of that year, he was tracked down and arrested by Captain Juan Morlete, an old rival operating under the authority of the viceroy. Castaño was returned to Mexico City in chains and there convicted on a variety of charges, including illegal entry into the lands of peaceful Indians (Thrapp 1988, 243). This conviction would later be overturned, but by then Castaño, exiled to the Philippines, was dead.*

*The following account of Castaño's expedition reveals a full appreciation of the precariousness of its protagonist's legal situation. With the one-sided vision of a good defense attorney, the narrative presents Castaño in the best possible light. Courageous, kind, humble, just, Christian, and above all loyal to his king and viceroy, Castaño is presented as a paragon of pioneer virtue. By the end of the narrative, it is impossible not to feel sorry for such a hero, especially as he humbly submits to the indignity of shackles, his quixotic run through the West having reached its tragic end.*

*Shackles are not the only quixotic element in Castaño's story. If Castaño's flagrant disobedience of the viceroy was not the New World equivalent of tilting at windmills, his attacking a good-sized pueblo with a tiny force of soldiers certainly was.*

*At times it is almost possible to believe that the author of the narrative (which dates from 1592) had read Cervantes's* Don Quixote *(the first part of which dates from 1608). This is as impossible, though, as the author having been exposed to North American pioneer diaries or Hollywood westerns— two genres whose wagon-train clichés are prefigured in this narrative. Castaño himself fits the stereotype of the strong, decisive, but ultimately democratic pioneer leader. Also featured are a main body of fearful-but-plucky settlers; a necessary handful of cowardly quitters who want to turn their backs on the dream; and, of course, the pioneer's familiar host of enemies: heat, thirst, hunger, cold, madness, rough country, wild animals, and hostile Indians.*

*Although the effects of the Castaño narrative on later works of western literature can only be guessed at, it cannot be denied that this tale includes many examples of what would become the archetypes of the pioneer saga.*

*The original narrative of Castaño's expedition was possibly written by Andrés Pérez de Verlanga, Castaño's secretary (Hammond and Rey 1966, 245). The translation reprinted here was based on a version of the narrative entitled "Memorial del descubrimiento que Gaspar Castaño de Sosa hizo en el Nuevo México, siendo teniente de gobernador y capitán general del Nuevo Reino de León," which was printed in Joaquín Francisco Pacheco and Francisco de Cárdenas y Espejo's 42-volume* Colección de Documentos Inéditos *(Madrid 1864–84) (Hammond and Rey 1966, 245). The notes in square brackets were added by Hammond and Rey. The notes in braces were added by the editors of this volume.*

## Selected Bibliography

Hammond, George P., and Agapito Rey, eds. and trans. "Castaño de Sosa's 'Memoria.' " *The Rediscovery of New Mexico, 1580–1594.* Albuquerque: University of New Mexico Press, 1966.

Olson, James S. *Historical Dictionary of the Spanish Empire, 1402–1975.* New York: Greenwood, 1992.

Schroeder, Albert H., and Dan S. Matson, eds. and trans. *A Colony on the Move: Gaspar Castaño de Sosa's Journal 1590–1591.* Salt Lake City: School of American Research, 1965.

Thrapp, Dan L. *Encyclopedia of Frontier Biography.* 3 vols. Glendale, Cal.: Arthur H. Clark, 1988.

GASPAR CASTAÑO DE SOSA

# Settling into the Dream: The Pioneer Epic of Gaspar Castaño de Sosa (1590)

**Report on the exploratory expedition to New Mexico undertaken on July 27, 1590, by Gaspar Castaño de Sosa while he was Lieutenant Governor and Captain General of New León. . . .**

ON JULY 27, 1590, Gaspar Castaño de Sosa started out with his entire force, including wagons, and spent the night at a marsh two leagues from the town, leaving behind many friendly natives who were deeply grieved by his departure because of their association with the Spaniards and their friendship for them. Two days earlier an Indian named Miguel came to the town. He was a native of Caqualco who had lived among the Cacuares for fourteen years, having been left with that tribe by a group of soldiers. Miguel had learned the native language of the region, which pleased Gaspar Castaño and the army very much, since he could serve as an interpreter. After Castaño had clothed him like the other members of the expedition, he gladly gave up his association of fourteen years with the Cacuares.

On the twenty-eighth of the month we reached the Río de los

Nadadores, where we remained for several days. During this time many Indian chiefs, including some who had previously been friendly, came to us with protestations of amity; and Gaspar Castaño ordered that they be given written guarantees of protection, which they had not had before. While the camp was relying on the sense of security thus established, reports reached us that the natives were stealing horses, whereupon the lieutenant governor {Castaño} set out in pursuit with twelve soldiers and overtook the culprits at the foot of a mountain to which they were taking the animals. He seized three of the Indians; and these captives, besides being caught with the loot, confessed when they were brought back to camp. As a warning to the rest of the Indians in the camp, as well as to admonish the natives of the region through which the army would later pass, Castaño ordered two of the thieves to be hanged; the other, who was very young, he entrusted to a soldier in the company.... The eleventh we went to Boca del Potrero, where we saw many Indians on a mountain. The lieutenant governor sent for them, but they refused to come down. He sent a second summons on the following day, but despite all our exhortations and kind words, we could not induce them to descend from the mountain....

On the eighteenth we went on and spent the night at a place where we were drenched by a heavy downpour, making it impossible to travel, for the wagons mired down.

We left this place on the twenty-first and went as far as the marshes of the river thought to be the Salinas, where we were visited by a friendly cacique named Jácome, whom the lieutenant governor treated kindly. Jácome was asked to pledge obedience to the king our lord, which he did, and thereupon received a security warrant. We remained here for several days to await the return of Francisco Salgado, Manuel de Mederos, and two other men whom our leader had sent to Mexico city with letters for the viceroy. During this period of waiting, the lieutenant governor set out in person with a number of soldiers and natives to explore the sierras in that region, hoping to discover some mines, and saying that if he located any, he would colonize the valley, as it was the best and most suitable to be found anywhere in the world. He made every possible effort to trace the mines, since there were old reports of their existence; but he was unable to locate any, nor could the natives who accompanied him give any information about them. So, finding none in that area, he decided to go on; and, while still searching for the mines, he and his companions came to two rancherías, where the people—men, women, and children—received them gladly. The lieutenant governor and his men treated the

Indians well, and they in return gave many of the small articles they had in their rancherías. . . . On the twenty-seventh we camped at Barranca, where Viruega's horse got mired down in some deep pools. The twenty-ninth we left Barranca and spent the night in some hills where we found a large water hole. On the thirtieth we left this place and camped in a gully or ravine where some showers fell, supplying us with water. Otherwise we should have had none; and thus the Lord cared for us.

On September 1 we started out again and passed through a ravine where our big cart broke down and the oxen were sent back. The second we went on to spend the night in another ravine, without water. On September 3 we continued our journey and camped in a walnut grove where we found many nuts. . . .

On the ninth we traveled on to spend the night at the Río Bravo {Río Grande}, where we tarried many days waiting for Francisco Salgado, Manuel de Mederos, and a number of other men who were expected with the viceroy's answer. The lieutenant governor had told them that he would wait for them at the Bravo to receive the Viceroy's orders, for which purpose he had sent them to Mexico city. Seeing that they were so long in coming back, the lieutenant governor commanded that all corn and wheat be measured in order to find out what provisions were left, and we found that there were only one hundred fanegas. This grieved him, for he thought we had more provisions than that. The cause for the scarcity was the fact that the supplies had not been distributed carefully, since the grain was carried in large baskets and no record had been kept, as the food was in the care of Juan Pérez de los Ríos. The lieutenant governor had not failed to tell him days earlier that he should distribute measured rations to everyone; but Pérez countered on several occasions by saying that his people were not going to be put on short rations, and in order to please him our leader did not compel him to ration the grain. Now, when the corn and wheat finally were measured, the lieutenant governor ordered that the grain should be distributed among the wagons in definite amounts and that the various groups should account for the quantities entrusted to them. He also ordered that from then on each person be given one almud per week; and this command was obeyed.

Meanwhile, in view of the delay in the return of Salgado, Mederos, and their men, and mindful of the scanty provisions, the lieutenant governor decided to go ahead with the expedition. In the process of establishing the route that the army would have to follow, many points of view were expressed by the men, who all differed from the leader with the exception of Captain Cristóbal de Heredia, Francisco López de Ricalde,

Martín de Salazar, and Juan de Carvajal. The opinion of this group was that they should look for the Río Salado. In the end the lieutenant governor instructed Captain Cristóbal de Heredia to start the search. In compliance with this command, Juan Pérez de los Ríos and several companions set out in search of the said river, but could not find it because of the difficult nature of the terrain. Pérez came back with news of a different river, saying that it could be followed, though with difficulty because of the ruggedness of the land bordering it. He added that the trail lay at some distance from the river, and that it would be laborious and costly to send the oxen and horses to the stream itself on account of the many rocks. . . .

The seventh we continued in search of the Río Salado, the object of our journey; and Captain Cristóbal de Heredia sent out Juan de Carvajal, Martín de Salazar, Domingo de Santiesteban, and Blas Martínez de Mederos for this purpose. They succeeded in finding the river, which pleased them very much. Domingo de Santiesteban came back to convey the good news that he and his companions had at last discovered the Salado, although it was impossible to reach it because of the many high rocks and gullies. We spent the night in a ravine where there was a pool that supplied water for our people; but the oxen and horses were sent back. We tried every means of reaching the stream, but to no avail; and so we turned back to look for the other river, which we had noted before. Captain Cristóbal de Heredia went ahead to see if it was far away and soon found it, about three leagues from the spot where we had halted. . . .

The twelfth we left this place and reached some hills where we found a small pool of water; since we looked in vain for the Río de las Laxas {Devil's River}, which was no longer visible, we sent the oxen and horses back to that river and continued vigorously to search for the Río Salado. Salazar, Diego Díaz de Berlanga, and Cristóbal Martín went on this mission. In three or four leagues they again caught sight of it and returned to camp saying that we could not get down to it. Nevertheless, we decided to proceed on our way; and, as we started out, God sent a heavy shower for our relief. We trusted that He would provide, for we knew He was merciful to us.

The fourteenth we left this place and moved on, camping for the night at the place were Cristóbal de Heredia was given his commission as maese de campo {camp master}. Then the lieutenant governor, realizing that the journey was being drawn out too long, ordered that only one half an almud of wheat or corn should be given to each person per week; as the ration was small, he tried to buy some oxen from Juan Pérez de los Ríos, to be slaughtered and the meat to be distributed among the people in the camp. In the course of the negotiations with Juan Pérez de los Ríos, who could see that the need was great, he replied that he would not sell a single animal, but that if the lieutenant governor needed oxen in this emergency, they were all available and he would make a gift of them in the name of the king our lord. The lieutenant governor accepted the offer and immediately held a roll call of all his people. Finding that there were upward of one hundred and seventy persons, he ordered the distribution of one and a half pounds of meat per day for each person. With this ration and the grain portion above-mentioned, we were able to get along; but we began at that point to roast maguey in order to supplement the shortage. . . .

When we set out again on the eighteenth, Cristóbal de Heredia and some soldiers went ahead to see if there was an approach to the Río Salado. In the course of his search we found that it could not be reached because of the bad terrain and complete lack of water; so he sent Francisco López de Ricalde and Jusepe Rodríguez back to camp while he himself rode on with the rest of his men. The two who came back told the lieutenant governor that there was no possible way of going forward, since they could not find the river, which must have turned abruptly to the west, and since the wagons could not travel by that route. This information displeased everyone, particularly Juan López [Pérez] de los Ríos, who feared that his capital would be lost, though he was even more concerned about his wife and children than his possessions. He complained bitterly, blaming the lieutenant governor for leading him astray. This was what grieved him most. As far as he was concerned, if things turned out badly, he could withdraw to a ranchería and end his days there, since the lieutenant governor had chosen a different route from the one he wanted to follow.

The lieutenant governor listened to all the hysterical complaints of Pérez and others. Then, during a lull, he called the people together and asked them what they thought should be done. There were some who expressed the opinion that they ought to go back and pick up the route that a number of the men had wanted to follow in opposition to the choice of the lieutenant governor. The latter, since the other route was the one he favored, encouraged us as kindly as he could, urging us all—men, women, and children, including the Indians—to commend ourselves to God and to have faith that He and His holy Mother would guide and enlighten us, giving wisdom to our leader so that he would not be wanting in anything, for it was his desire to serve God our Lord and his Majesty. Accordingly, he gave orders to leave this place and to go on, which we did.

Immediately afterward, the lieutenant governor sent some men to look for water along the route we were to follow. When we had gone about a quarter of a league, Francisco López de Ricalde came to the governor (who was bringing up the rear, as was his custom) to tell how Juan Pérez de los Ríos, downhearted and weeping, had asked him to intercede with Castaño to turn back, for the love of God. As soon as Ricalde broached the subject, our leader told him angrily that he did not want to have anyone talk to him about the matter; that, if the Spaniards showed fright, it would be taken as a sign of weakness on their part and they would lose their rights; and that Ricalde should tell Juan Pérez to hold his peace and go on with the trip, instead of discouraging the people. For he, the lieutenant governor (as he had already said) trusted in God, who would not let them lack water, but would provide it for them.

The lieutenant governor now withdrew from the army and marched to one side, accompanied only by a servant named Juan López. After going about half a league he came to a very large pool of water, which delighted him, for in that area such a big pond had never before been found. It seemed that the Lord had indeed provided it, as He always makes provision. Our leader hastened to the wagons and halted them so that the oxen and horses could be driven to water, as was done. Here we decided to wait for Cristóbal de Heredia. He arrived the following day, reporting that he had been unable to reach the river. Some thought that it had disappeared from our route, as had the Laxas. . . .

On the twenty-third, as we were yoking our oxen and getting ready to leave, Pedro Flores arrived with the report that water had been found. We went back with him to spend the night in the place described, where we rejoiced to find that the water was plentiful. The next day the men who had discovered the river returned to report that the hills and sierras came to an end at this point, and that the river was about four leagues from our location. They were welcomed for their good news, in view of the hardships we had endured thus far, the poverty of the land, the scanty water, and the exhaustion of the horses, which was what we most regretted. For we were all in the depths of despair because of the rocky terrain on the journey in search of the long-sought Río Salado.

Twenty-five dozen horseshoes were worn out on the mountains here, since there was no way to travel save on horseback. Many horses wore out their shoes in two or three days, incredible as it may seem, and a large number of the animals became lame. So great was the hardship endured before we reached water that only those of our people who witnessed the ordeal will believe how much we suffered. If the discovery of this route were to be paid for in money, it would take an enormous sum.

The lieutenant governor expressed thanks to his companions and the fervent hope that God our Lord and his Majesty would reward them. He also assured them that in so far as might be in his power, he would grant, in the name of the king, any favor they might ask. They should not hesitate to speak, because he could never repay with money their many labors or the enthusiasm with which they had helped him; for if they were to be rewarded with cash it would require a great sum. As if with one voice, his followers replied that they would always be ready to withstand such hardships as they might have to endure, since their main interest lay precisely in doing what the lieutenant governor ordered, in the name of his Majesty. For this he thanked them and said that, by God's will and with His favor, he trusted that they would accomplish their purpose, since it was a very worthy one, and that the king would reward them as he does all who serve him. The lieutenant governor was pleased at the sturdy spirit displayed by his men, and they were no less gratified by what he told them. I cannot exaggerate nor even describe here the aforementioned hardships. In short, after finding the river we were seeking, we thought we had been through the worst of the struggle, and so we remained there in great contentment for two days. . . .

On the twenty-sixth we set out for the river we had sought so eagerly, but could not find a way down to it except by some steep slopes which we descended with great difficulty. These hardships seemed very light to all of us in our eager desire to serve God and the king. In the descent some wagons broke down, among them one containing the coffer for the royal fifths. We all dismounted and the lieutenant governor told us to go down to the river for a rest with the [undamaged] wagons and the people, while he would remain there with some men to watch the royal coffer, which he did. The next day the wagon [holding the coffer] was made ready and taken to the river.

The following day, while we were at the river, Alonso Jaimez arrived with the men he had taken along, saying [at first] that he had followed the trail specified by the lieutenant governor, and that after three days of travel he had come upon a large number of people of the Depesguan {Jumano Apaches} nation, who received him cordially. When he explained to them through the interpreter the purpose of the trip, the natives were highly pleased and gave him many buffalo and chamois skins, fine shoes of the type they themselves wore, and a quantity of meat. They also indicated that we might travel through their region and that they would lead us to places where there were settlements and an abundance of corn. So Alonso Jaimez turned back, very satisfied with the friendship shown him by the Indians.

After his return to the camp, Jaimez [finally] explained to the lieutenant governor that he had not followed the route suggested by the latter, and the governor laughed at him upon learning how widely Jaimez's route deviated from the one specified, at the same time displaying all the gratification that could be desired. . . .

On November 2 we traveled on and camped for the night at a place where the Indians attacked Juan de Vega with arrows. This happened when Diego de Viruega, Alonso Lucas, Andrés Pérez, and others who were leading the way, crossed the river upon reaching an impassable spot, at which moment they saw a group of Indian men and went toward them. We all began to talk to the group by signs, some from one side of the river and some from the other. Our men drew away from the Indians, but Juan de Vega, himself a native, lagged behind. Some of the Indians, seeing that he was alone, seized him, took some ropes away from him, threw him into the river, and shot him with three arrows. The next morning a large number of natives appeared, and the lieutenant governor tried in every way to get them to come to the camp, but to no avail.

While we were at this place, where we rested for a day, the men in the camp noticed the Indians driving away some oxen. The lieutenant governor, seeing their shameless behavior, ordered Cristóbal de Heredia and five soldiers to go after the thieves. During the pursuit, Heredia and his men encountered a group of Indians, who, they said, attacked them with arrows. Our men in self-defense killed some of the assailants, apprehended four, and brought them to camp. In view of the theft of the oxen and other offenses, the lieutenant governor ordered that one of the prisoners be hanged as punishment and that the other three, since they were mere youths, be kept as interpreters for the expedition. In order that they might be taught our language quickly, he entrusted one each to Juan Pérez de los Ríos, Pedro Flores, and Cristóbal de Heredia. Despite our extreme care, they escaped with an ox as the other Indians fled. At this same place we watered our animals by hand. We found quantities of mesquite, which the humbler members of the party ate, thus saving us some provisions; this was much appreciated, as the supplies were getting low. . . .

The tenth we continued our trip, sleeping at various places. We passed some mesquite groves and camped for the night at a bend of the river, after driving the cattle to a little island. A child, daughter of Francisco López de Ricalde, died at this place. We caught a lot of fish; and there was so much mesquite that occasionally it spared us the need of slaughtering. . . .

We resumed our journey on the thirteenth, traversing a very pleasant plain and halting for the night by the river in a canebrake. Viruega caught many more fish during the day. That night an Indian couple failed to return to camp, which grieved us, as we feared they had been killed by other Indians.

The fifteenth we continued to a bend in the river where there were many tracks of cattle. On the sixteenth we traveled over a fine road away from the river to a place where it made a big bend. There, a tame deer belonging to Catalina de Charles broke a leg.

The seventeenth, while we were traversing some hills, the axle of the large cart broke in descending a slope, so that we spent the night away from the river. By now our provisions of corn and wheat were well-nigh depleted. Since we had plenty of fish and mesquite, the lieutenant governor ordered that each person be given only one small tortilla for each meal, but that two pounds of meat be distributed also to every individual per day. All of this caused great dissatisfaction and privation, and our hardships increased. . . .

The nineteenth we slept on a sandy beach where Juan de Carvajal and Juan Pérez had some sort of dispute.

On the twentieth, after leaving the sandy area, we followed a fine plain lying at a distance from the river, which made a big turn at that point. We spent the night here and rested for a day, as some of the oxen had been left behind at the previous camping place. We went in search of them, found a number, and assumed that none was missing. We also saw a column of smoke on a mountain four leagues away, which some of the men wanted to investigate; but the lieutenant governor would not allow it, apparently fearing that some harm might be done to the Indians. Although he did not expressly say so, this was the interpretation given to his refusal. The men argued that he should go on to find out the cause of the fire and bring back an Indian, but he replied that the attempt would be pointless since we had no interpreter for these natives. He added that those people would not be able to furnish us with any information; that he himself was satisfied we were on the right route; and that farther on he would try to obtain an Indian, since by then we should be closer to the place we were looking for. Some of the soldiers were displeased because he did not allow them to go out immediately and get Indians to serve as guides. . . .

On December 1 we left this place. After going through beds of rushes for about half a league, we came to a river {the Hondo} which seemed to flow from a sierra rising toward the west, but we could not cross it as the water was too deep. We therefore turned east to cross the river we had previously followed, into which the other stream flowed. While we were doing so, the main wagon broke down, and Alonso Jaimez and Juan de Estrada went down with it. Not being divers, they and their horses splashed about, causing considerable merriment; and they were irked about being called divers. . . .

On the third we started out again and traveled upstream through swamps and reeds, camping for the night in a brushy hollow on the river bank. Here we blundered, permitting the lieutenant governor to go up the river alone with no one following him, because we believed he would soon come back. Instead, he traveled so far that two hours after dark he had not yet returned. We were all greatly worried and somewhat ashamed at having let him go alone, though we had erred only through negligence, assuming that he would come back in a short while. We lighted many fires, hoping that he could find his way by their light. In view of his failure to return, and our growing concern for his safety, Juan de Carvajal, Pedro Iñigo, and Pedro Flores decided to go in search of him, carrying lighted torches so that he could see them. Thus equipped, they set out and found him a quarter of a league from the camp, making his way back. All complained because the leader had gone out alone. He replied that he had not intended to go so far, and that he had done so only to explore the route, because the present trail was sandy and very difficult. Moreover, he said, the river turned there, and he wanted to get off the bad road. This was the reason for his delay. When the people saw him, their deep distress over his delay turned into joy. . . .

On the sixth we left this place, closely following the river, which turned northeast. We camped for the night on the bank in a field of tall grass. Here the grassy plain caught fire, and we were fearful of losing one of the wagons—a catastrophe which would have happened if we had not made strenuous efforts to put out the flames. . . .

On the ninth we continued up the river, which turned north again. We traveled over good trails and through many groves, stopping for the night among the trees on the bank of the stream. In this area there was abundant mesquite, without which we should have suffered severely. The

Lord always provides in time of greatest need; and not only the Indians, but all of us, men and women alike, ate mesquite. . . .

We left this place on the twenty-third and traveled east over a fine plain, since the river made a big bend. That day the lieutenant governor and Andrés Pérez, the government secretary, went ahead to explore; and from a hill they saw that some of the men who had gone with the maese de campo were on their way back, driving their pack animals. As the lieutenant governor looked at them for a long time and they did not respond with any sign of recognition, he felt very grieved, inferring that they had not found anything or had met with some disaster. Going forward, he met Juan Rodríguez Nieto, on foot, with his harquebus on his shoulder and following his exhausted, saddleless horse. When Castaño inquired why he traveled that way, the soldier was reluctant to tell what had happened. Finally, however, he said that as they marched up the river they found a footpath they followed until, from the top of a sierra, they saw a pueblo {Pecos}. They then camped for the night and the next morning they went toward the pueblo and were forced to enter it because the weather was so bitterly cold and the land was covered with snow. The Indians of this pueblo received them in a friendly manner, giving them food for that day and some eight or ten fanegas of corn.

Early the next day, wishing to turn back, the maese de campo sent some soldiers to the pueblo to ask for more corn. They went to carry out their orders; and, with a view to reassuring the Indians and further dispelling their fears, the men carried no arms. All except Alonso Lucas and Domingo de Santiesteban, who were shelling some corn the Indians had given them, walked securely about the pueblo, relying on the goodwill of the inhabitants. All of a sudden the natives began to shout and, at the same time, to hurl stones and shoot arrows. Faced with this attack, the men fell back as best they could to the place where they had left their arms. In the meantime, some Indians had come down from the flat roofs of their three- or four-story houses and had taken some of the arms, all except about five harquebuses; whereupon the soldiers seized these weapons and withdrew from the plaza where they had camped, leaving in the hands of the Indians five harquebuses, eleven swords, nineteen saddles, nine sets of horse armor, and a quantity of wearing apparel and bedding.

When the maese de campo realized the damage the Indians had caused, he decided to go back to meet the people and the wagons coming up the river. Three of his men were wounded—Domingo de Santiesteban, Francisco de Mancha, and Jusepe Rodríguez. They started the return journey that very day, all riding bareback, using halters for reins, deprived of cloaks and coverings, and traveling for three days without a morsel to eat. Then God willed that they should meet an Indian woman on the plain who gave them some corn flour and beans, so little that it hardly amounted to a handful for each person; but had it not been for this aid they would have perished from hunger, cold, snow, and fierce winds, for the weather was very severe. Let us all give some thought to the sufferings of these men! When they reached the lieutenant governor, he received them with great joy, in spite of what had happened, though God knows how sad we all felt on seeing those men return in such distress.

In view of these circumstances, we {the main expedition} decided not to follow any farther the route along the river by which those men had returned, for they told us it was scarcely passable, on account of the numerous gullies. We turned back about a league to a spot where the lieutenant governor ordered us to rest for a few days, which we did. Then, one day, mindful of what had happened to the maese de campo and his men and of the great damage they had suffered at the hands of the Indians, our leader called us together and spoke encouragingly to us, exhorting us not to worry over past misfortunes, although he was very sorry for the hardships suffered by the men. As for the property taken by the Indians, he would go personally to the pueblo where the event had occurred and make every possible effort to recover the arms and other goods. Everyone agreed to this, much pleased with his plans.

In order to exact submission from the Indians to our king, and disregarding the scarcity of provisions, the lieutenant governor decided to take along twenty soldiers and an equal number of servants, and to set out after only two or three days' rest so that the Indians would have less time to ruin the arms. . . .

On the twenty-sixth [of December], . . . [we] all departed on horseback and camped for the night a league away by the river.

We resumed our journey on the twenty-seventh, traveling over a fine plain, and spent the night at Urraca. A freak accident befell Juan Rodríguez Nieto at this place. While he was trying to start a fire, a spark flew out from somewhere, and the large and small powder flasks hanging from his belt exploded, but without doing any damage.

On the twenty-eighth we left this camp and traveled all day. One of our men, Pedro Flores, had suffered an attack of melancholia the day before, which left him exhausted and somewhat incoherent. Before starting out, the lieutenant governor asked him to go back to the others, who were following us, with instructions from our leader to camp at Urraca and await further orders. He was sure the sick man would be able to return safely and would find the wagons, at a spot four leagues away. Pedro Flores replied that he would never go back; but some insisted that he should be ordered to do so, for they felt he was really sick and so dangerously melancholic that he appeared in a measure to have lost his mind. The lieutenant governor felt sorry for him in his suffering and again asked him to return, saying that a soldier or servant would be sent to accompany him; but he would not consent. At this point the lieutenant governor talked of turning back on account of Pedro Flores, who felt very badly about it and said that there was no reason for such action.

Since he seemed to feel better, we continued our trip and stopped for the night at a place called Caballo, near a small water hole. This place is so named because here, after the experiences above related, the maese de campo had ordered a horse slaughtered for food when there was nothing else to eat. Shortly afterward Pedro Flores, very cheerful, came to the quarters of the lieutenant governor and said he was quite well and free from pain, but very hungry because, from the time he had left the wagons, he had not eaten a thing; nor had he slept for three nights— something unheard of, it seemed to me. The lieutenant governor rejoiced at what Pedro Flores said, as well he might, because he was very fond of the man. He therefore ordered that Flores be given some meat and three tortillas; these tortillas were a real luxury, since we had almost none. The next morning Pedro Flores was missing and the lieutenant governor ordered the maese de campo to search for him, which he did, accompanied by two other men; but they could not find him and returned to camp. Then, as they were rounding up the horses, they discovered that Pedro Flores's horse was missing, as were his saddle, harquebus, and armor, all of which he had taken with him. Believing he had gone back to the wagons that day, the lieutenant governor ordered the party to proceed, and we obeyed. . . .

On the thirty-first, before daybreak, the lieutenant governor ordered breakfast prepared, telling us all to eat and to feel confident that we should be well received by the Indians of the entire pueblo, because it was his firm intention to cause them no harm at all. Accordingly, he asked us not to make any move save by his orders or those of the maese de campo. Then we headed straight for the pueblo.

In order that the Indians should be aware of our approach before we came in sight, the governor asked the maese de campo to dispatch some men by a hidden route to see if they could find an Indian who might be sent ahead to the pueblo, so that he could explain to the natives that we were coming not to molest them but to place them under the protection and authority of his Majesty. Martín de Salazar undertook this mission, together with Cristóbal [Martín] and Diego de Viruega, while the lieutenant governor and his party continued on their way toward the pueblo, straight over the path which the other men would have to take after finding the Indian spokesman.

Going forward in this manner, his men in formation and with flag unfurled, the governor, as we came in view of the pueblo, ordered the buglers to blow their trumpets. When he reached the town, he noticed that the natives were in battle array, men as well as women standing fully prepared on the terraces and down below. Surveying the situation, he ordered the maese de campo to pitch camp at the distance of an harquebus shot from the pueblo, on the side where it seemed strongest, and this was done. Then he ordered the two bronze pieces set up, asking Juan Rodríguez Nieto to take charge of them and to keep the fuse lighted in order that everything might be in readiness in case the guns should be needed for defense against the Indians and their pueblo; or rather, in case the natives should try some shameless trick like the one played previously. He urged us to be very alert and to conduct ourselves like brave soldiers, as we were accustomed to do.

After making all these arrangements, the lieutenant governor called to the Indians in sign language, but none would leave his dwelling or come out from behind the barricades, trenches, or ramparts which the pueblo maintained for its defense at the most vital points. Although these had all been constructed earlier, we could not understand the present activities of the Indians; but later they explained to us that they were at war with other groups, and that this was the reason for the fortifications, except that the many earthen bulwarks on the terraces of their houses had been newly added to protect the pueblo against us.

All this took place at about eight o'clock in the morning. The lieutenant governor then left his quarters, accompanied by the maese de campo, Martín de Salazar, Juan de Carvajal, and Blas Martínez de Mederos. On nearing the houses of the pueblo, he called to the Indians and told them he would not do them any harm or injury, but this failed to calm them. On the contrary, they hastened to pile up stones on the terraces. The stones were brought by the women, for the men were all armed, at their posts, and shouting lustily at us.

The lieutenant governor and his soldiers circled the entire pueblo in an effort to soothe the natives with kind words and by signs, offering gifts to placate them, but to no avail. Instead of softening, the Indians shot arrows and hurled quantities of stones by means of slings, growing more and more clamorous. These maneuvers lasted about five hours, while the governor's group marched around the pueblo several times and the main body of soldiers remained in camp, as ordered. Then the group returned to camp, where the lieutenant governor ordered us all to remain armed and to round up the horses. Taking a few more articles of the kind he had given the natives before, such as knives and other small items, they went back to the pueblo, circled it once more, and tried again to give the inhabitants some presents in an attempt to find out who was the captain of the pueblo. As a result of this attempt, our men saw and talked with the chieftain. One of the soldiers in the group on this occasion was Diego de Viruega, who dismounted and tried to climb over a crumbling corner of the fortifications in order to give presents to some Indians near there who showed signs of wanting to be friendly; yet they would not allow him to ascend.

At that moment the captain of the pueblo came up and was given a knife and some other trifles; but even this failed to pacify the natives. So the Spaniards returned to their quarters, and the lieutenant governor said to them: "These Indians do not want to be our friends. What do you gentlemen think?" Several responded by asking what he himself wanted to do with the Indians, and he replied that it was his wish to subdue them by peaceful means without injury to either side. The soldiers countered by saying that he should not waste much time in this effort, as it was useless. The lieutenant governor then summoned Andrés Pérez, the secretary, to accompany him, which Pérez did; and when they had gone back to the pueblo and marched around it, the secretary was asked to certify that Castaño had tried to communicate with the natives by signs and had spent considerable time in circling the pueblo in company with the maese de campo, Martín de Salazar, Juan de Carvajal, Blas Martínez de Mederos, and Diego de Viruega. Since he, the secretary, had witnessed the peaceable overtures made to the Indians by the lieutenant governor, both previously and in the company of the said Andrés Pérez, the latter should so certify, drawing up an affidavit to be witnessed by the others.

The governor then returned to camp and once more asked his men what should be done, since the Indians would not listen to reason; and they all answered with one accord that he ought not to waste any more time on those dogs. He replied by inquiring what course they wished to take, and the men repeated that the natives should be overcome by force, since they refused to accept the friendship we had offered in peace and goodwill. The lieutenant governor objected that he thought it was by then too late to undertake the task suggested, to which his men replied that if God wished to grant them victory, there was time enough and to spare.

It was then about two o'clock in the afternoon, and we all believed that the lieutenant governor was acting as he did in order to allow the Indians more time. In view of the unanimous opinion of the soldiers, he ordered the maese de campo to post two men on a commanding elevation back of the pueblo so that they could see if any of the inhabitants were leaving. The maese sent Juan de Carvajal and Blas Martínez de Mederos to the observation post and they departed on this mission. The governor returned to the pueblo, where he made another appeal to the Indians and attempted to soothe them; but they would not relent. Moreover, an Indian woman came out on a terrace connecting the houses (which are four or five stories) and threw some ashes at him; and as she did so the natives began to shout. He turned back, commanding all of us who bore arms to make ready for battle and mount our horses. Then he ordered Juan Rodríguez Nieto to fire one of the guns over the pueblo, which Nieto did; at the same time the harquebuses were fired in the hope that this would frighten the natives. As we drew close to the pueblo, the Indians hurled showers of stones, by hand or with slings, and shot many arrows. Still the lieutenant governor went on appealing to them, while they derided him. In the meantime the Indian women showed fierce courage and kept on bringing more stones to the terraces.

Thereupon the lieutenant governor ordered the maese de campo to attack the pueblo in earnest. For our greater protection, Castaño and the maese de campo went to an unoccupied section of the pueblo, where they ordered Diego de Viruega, Francisco de Mancha, Diego Díaz de Berlanga, and Juan Rodríguez Nieto to climb to the top with one of the artillery pieces. The men did so, although with much difficulty, because the Indians were harrying them fiercely from behind a parapet and some trenches. To facilitate the ascent, the lieutenant governor attacked the Indians at this point and forced them to withdraw. When the soldiers reached the top, he told them to fire their harquebuses from there, aiming wherever the attack would be most effective. Then he returned to the maese de campo and the other men, who were facing the main forces of the pueblo. This being the strongest point, we attacked it with a large number of guns; and the Indians, realizing the strength of our onslaught, replied in kind. None of them abandoned his section or trench; on the contrary, each one defended the post entrusted to him, without faltering in the least. Such intelligence among barbarians seemed incredible.

At the time when the Spaniards were fighting near that section, Thomas, one of the lieutenant governor's Indian servants armed with bow and arrow, began to shoot at the inhabitants; and another Indian, named Miguel, did likewise. When the natives noticed that we were shooting arrows, they became alarmed and showed more fear of those weapons than of our harquebuses. The lieutenant governor then ordered us to shoot in every direction, which we did. Thomas, the above-mentioned Indian, together with Domingo Fernández, a Portuguese, entered one of the houses, while the other men remained at their posts, firing their harquebuses. The Indians, finding themselves hard pressed, abandoned some of the dwellings; and the lieutenant governor, sensing that the place could be entered safely on that side, ordered some of the men to climb to the top of the fortified point and take it. After this was accomplished, he went to the section where Viruega, Mancha, Diego Díaz, and Juan Rodríguez were posted and asked them how things were going. They replied that two of their party were wounded, but that most of the natives were abandoning the stronghold we were trying to seize. One Indian displayed great bravery, going about among his people and bringing reinforcements to the stronghold, but Diego Díaz de Berlanga felled him with an harquebus shot—incredible though it may seem, since he was so far away. When the Indians in that section of the pueblo saw that he had fallen, the majority of them abandoned the position, which was the key point we were trying to take.

The lieutenant governor now left this section, since the men were holding their posts like brave soldiers, as they had done on all other occasions; but before leaving he told them not to fire their harquebuses any more, nor to cause any further damage there. Then he took Diego de Viruega to the point where the battle was still in progress; and here he told Captain Alonso Jaimez to climb to the top with some soldiers, while others from below protected their ascent. This was done. There did not seem to be as large a number of Indians at that spot as there were before; but the few who held their posts behind the barricades defended the terraces very bravely, so that no one could climb to the top except by the slender wooden hand ladders, which only one person at a time could ascend. There were no doors leading from one room to another, but only hatchways just large enough for a single person; and therefore our men, in order to get through them and climb to the terraces, had to ascend without sword or shield, after which they passed the weapons to one another as they climbed. The lieutenant governor, perceiving the danger to our soldiers, ordered the maese de campo and many others to train their harquebuses on the enemy, though he had previously given the order that we should not shoot to kill, because he hoped that God would en able us to defeat our foes without killing them.

In obedience to these orders, the maese de campo brought down an Indian with one harquebus shot, as did both Juan de Contreras and Juan López, a servant of the governor, with the result that the natives were forced to abandon the barricade and our men took it. . . . When the pueblo realized that we had occupied this block of buildings, not a soul was venturesome enough to come out on the terraces.

Thereupon the lieutenant governor and captain general entered and walked through the plazas and streets of the pueblo with a few companions, while the inhabitants all appeared on the wooden corridors extending along the streets and plazas between the houses. The natives pass from one house to the other through these corridors, and also by means of wooden bridges spanning the street from terrace to terrace. In this manner they were able to move about securely from place to place, although in any case we threatened them with no harm beyond that already described; for the lieutenant governor wanted to win by friendship rather than by war. In fact, he was very sorry that the harm done, which was necessary for the protection of our men, could not have been avoided. So strong was this sentiment that, shortly before, when we had set fire to a small wooden corridor and he saw the flames, he ordered that they be put out immediately. Diego de Viruega, with his customary zeal, rushed to do so, which pleased the lieutenant governor immensely, for he said that, as Christians, we should practice Christian conduct in all that pertained to the service of God and the king. Now, as the governor walked through the pueblo with several soldiers, not an Indian threw a stone or shot an arrow. On the contrary all tried to indicate by means of signs that they wanted our friendship. Making a cross with their hands, they cried "Friends, friends, friends," which is the method they use to express their desire for friendship.

In the course of this stroll the lieutenant governor came to a plaza where the chief of the pueblo appeared in a corridor and talked to him for awhile. One of the governor's companions on this occasion was Diego de Viruega, who climbed up to the corridor in order to talk with and cajole the chief; but when he got to the top, the Indians ran away from him. Nevertheless, one old Indian who came out remained behind where the Spaniard had entered and embraced him. Viruega then descended again.

By means of signs the governor told the chieftain and many others who stood in the corridor that he had not come to harm them in the least, and that they should not be afraid. The natives understood him clearly, and they soon brought out some food which they threw down to us from the corridors, since none of them dared to descend. In fact, when one Indian tried to climb down, the others restrained him and he abandoned the attempt. The lieutenant governor asked the Indian captain for the arms, saddles, harquebuses, and other articles taken from the maese de campo and his companions. The chieftain replied that they had burned all the saddles, harquebuses, and guards for the swords, and that the clothes and bedding had been distributed among the people or taken to another pueblo. Thus he gave us to understand very clearly that there was nothing left except some blades without guards.

The lieutenant governor then instructed a number of his men to try to seize some Indians in that section of the pueblo which we had not taken and where there were so many people, in order that we might learn from them what had become of the arms and other articles. Under strict orders not to harm the natives in any way, they proceeded to carry out the task. Then the governor went back to the place where he had left the native captain and assured him that his people need not be afraid, because they would suffer no harm. The Indians understood all he said, and gave signs of wanting our friendship. The chieftain climbed up to a terrace and from there addressed his people in a loud voice. Then we saw many natives coming out into the passageways everywhere, with signs of joy and friendship, although no one would come down into the plazas or streets. The lieutenant governor again asked the captain to order his people to hand over the articles they had taken from our men; and the Indian captain repeated that there was practically nothing left, but that he would ask his people to return what there was. They then brought out two sword blades without guards, a cuish, several pieces of sack-cloth, and some trifles of little value. Since it was getting late, the governor requested the captain to have a search made in order to gather up everything left and to hand it over the next day. . . .

Early the next day the lieutenant governor got his horse and rode out in full military array to tour the town and inspect the plazas and streets before the sentries were removed. He found the people calm, which pleased him greatly, since this was what he wished. He therefore ordered his men to return to their quarters, and there he addressed them, thanking them for the zeal they had displayed in discharging the duties we all owe to God our Lord and to his Majesty. He entreated them all, for the love of God, not to cause any harm to the Indians, their pueblo, or its houses. This exhortation was indeed unnecessary, for everyone, without being so instructed, was trying to show friendship for the Indians, inspired by the zeal of the lieutenant governor in treating them well. Then the governor told the Indian servants in his army that under no circumstances were they to leave the camp, enter any house, or trouble the Indians of the pueblo in any manner.

At this time, while all of us were together and happy to see the pueblo at peace, the lieutenant governor nevertheless sent some men back to the blockhouse where the watch had been posted, in another attempt to coax the people out, for which purpose they were to take lights with them. They entered the underground passages where the natives had hidden the day before, and they found many tunnels leading to other blockhouses and to underground estufas {kivas}. After examining these places, they turned back and reported that there were no people at all in the area searched. The lieutenant ordered that everything should be left as it was, and all was calm. He then went to the pueblo, accompanied by some soldiers on horseback and on foot, in order to reassure the entire population as best he could and to see what there was in the pueblo. Many people came out and made signs of friendship, while the party looked the pueblo over carefully. The most interesting things seen were sixteen underground estufas, very large and very well whitewashed, built for protection against the bitter cold. The natives light no fires inside them; instead, they bring in from the outside many braziers banked with ashes, in a manner so ingenious that I find no words to describe it.

These estufas are entered through small trap doors, large enough for only one person at a time, and the natives go down into them by means of ladders set up for that purpose.

The houses in this pueblo are built like military barracks, back to back, with doors opening out all around; and they are four or five stories high. There are no doors opening into the streets on the ground floors; the houses are entered from above by means of portable hand ladders and trap doors. Each floor of every house has three or four rooms, so that each house, as a whole, counting from top to bottom, has fifteen or sixteen rooms, very neat and well whitewashed. Every house is equipped with facilities for grinding corn, including three or four grinding stones mounted in small troughs and provided with pestles; all is whitewashed. The method of grinding is novel, the flour being passed from one grinder to another, as these Indians do not make tortilla dough, although from this flour they do make many kinds of bread, corn-flour gruel, and tamales.

This pueblo had five plazas. It was also provided with such an abundant supply of corn that everyone marveled. There were those who maintained that the total must amount to more than thirty thousand fanegas, since each house had two or three rooms full of it, all of excellent quality. Moreover, there was a good supply of beans. Both corn and beans were of many colors; it seemed that some of the corn was two or three years old. In the houses, the natives also store quantities of herbs, chili, and calabashes, and many implements for working their cornfields.

As for their clothing, we noticed that most of the men, if not all, wore cotton blankets and over these a buffalo skin, since this was the cold season; some covered their privy parts with small pieces of cloth, very elegant and elaborately decorated. The women wore a blanket tied over the shoulder and left open on one side, with a sash the width of a span wrapped around the waist. Over this blanket they wear another, nicely decorated and very fancy, or a kind of robe made of turkey feathers, as well as many other novel adornments, all of which is quite remarkable for barbarians.

These Indians have a great deal of pottery, red, figured, and black, such as plates, bowls (*cajetes*), salt containers, basins, and very beautiful cups (*jicaras*). Some of the pottery is glazed. They also have plentiful supplies of firewood, and of lumber for building houses. Indeed, we were given to understand that whenever anyone wanted to build a house, he had the lumber for that purpose ready at hand; and, furthermore, clay for adobes was available in quantities. . . . We spent the entire day looking at the various things in the pueblo; but not an Indian ventured outside the houses. The natives returned to us some small articles of little value that had belonged to our people. Reassured by this act, the lieutenant governor ordered the sentries removed, except at our guard quarters, which adjoined the pueblo, as has been stated. He thought that by doing so he would make the Indians feel more at ease, because they themselves had asked for the removal of the guards.

At dawn the next day, not a single inhabitant was to be found in the town, a development which distressed us all greatly when we learned of it. Nevertheless, the lieutenant governor ordered that no harm be done to the Indians, even if they had abandoned the pueblo, although he commanded that the houses be searched to see if any of our goods could be found. We did this without causing any damage, and we found some of our belongings, but they were of no use to us because they had been smashed to pieces. The lieutenant governor then ordered that we take a little corn, beans, and flour from each house, which we did, twenty-two fanegas in all, sending this to the wagons at Urraca. This load was dispatched in care of eight soldiers and eight or ten helpers, while the lieutenant governor and the rest of his men remained in the pueblo to see if the natives would come back. We stayed there for several days with that object in view; but none of the Indians came. The governor therefore decided to move his army from the pueblo so that the inhabitants might return to it. He felt sorry for them because they had abandoned their homes in the bitter cold of winter, with its strong winds and heavy snows, conduct which seemed incredible to us. . . .

On January 6, 1591, we left his place in search of these mines. The lieutenant governor asked the maese de campo to conceal four men with very good horses in the pueblo so that, if the Indians came back to that vicinity, some might be captured and persuaded to return to their homes. . . . We had not yet left our quarters when two Indians approached from one side of the settlement. We seized them and brought them to the lieutenant governor, who was with his men at a distance of two harquebus shots from the pueblo. When he saw the Indians, he treated them kindly, gave them some small presents, and told them to go back to their homes. In their presence he ordered a large cross erected on that spot, explained its meaning to them, and told the secretary to draw up a security guaranty in the name of his Majesty and on behalf of the royal service. This document he gave to one of the Indians for delivery to his chief, and then sent him away, taking the other one along as a guide on our journey. Thus we went on, the Indian contentedly leading us. . . .

On the ninth . . . we journeyed to another pueblo a league away. In addition to the people who already accompanied us, many more came to meet us along the trail. When we arrived at the settlement, the Indians proved so stubborn that we had to climb up to their houses and terraces; then they overcame their fear and approached us. We inquired for their chief, and when he appeared, the lieutenant governor treated him well, giving him some small articles such as had been presented to the other Indians previously. With friendship established, he ordered us to erect a large cross to the sound of trumpets and the firing of harquebuses, after which he explained its meaning to the natives. They pledged obedience to the king our lord, and in his name we appointed a governor, an alcalde, and an alguacil.

We spent the night in this pueblo and the inhabitants supplied an abundance of corn, flour, beans, calabashes, tortillas, and turkeys for all who were present. Here we saw an Indian carrying a bow and arrows, and the lieutenant governor called to him, asking him to hand over his arms, which he did. The governor explained to the man that no one was allowed to carry a bow or an arrow in his presence, or in that of any Spaniard; and he then broke the bow while a multitude looked on. The spectators all assured him that he would not find such weapons again; and we later learned this to be so, for we never saw the mistake repeated among them. . . .

All. . . of these settlements had canals for irrigation, which would be incredible to anyone who had not seen them with his own eyes. The inhabitants harvest large quantities of corn, beans, and other vegetables. . . .

The next day, the eleventh of the month, we left this place during a snowfall, because of which few people accompanied us. We traveled to another valley, two leagues away, and came to a large pueblo; before reaching it we were met by many people and thus we all entered it together. The pueblo consisted of four quarters and a very large square, with entrances at every corner. This town contained many inhabitants, by whom we were well received. The houses were built of adobes, very well planned and well constructed, two or three stories high, and neatly whitewashed; each house had its estufa. In the center of the plaza there was a large round building, half underground and half above ground, spanned by beams on which the Indians had built a terrace. We marveled at the thickness of the timbers, which seemed to us to be of mesquite wood. The natives gather in this building on certain days of the year to perform their idolatrous ceremonies; for they have numerous idols, a fact which I forgot to mention before. In the first pueblo where the maese de campo encountered these conditions, there were many of these idols, as there are in all the settlements. . . .

We saw in this pueblo many turquoises, and also an Indian wearing an armband which seemed to be made of rich stones. It was suggested to the lieutenant governor that he try to seize the ornament, but he replied that it was not wise to do so at present, as the Indians might get the notion that we coveted their goods and had come to their land to steal their possessions. He had faith that God would put them in such a compliant state of mind that they would accept Him and the king; other objectives could wait for the appropriate time, which had not yet come. All the lieutenant governor tried to do was to examine the armband, and he approached the Indian in order to look at it. This Indian was also wearing a beautiful buffalo skin. When the lieutenant governor came up to him to examine the ornament (as I have said), the Indian refused to show it, and the matter rested there.

We returned to the pueblos through which we had come, crossing a river frozen so solidly that the ice must have been two spans thick and we had to use pickaxes to break it. . . .

On the twenty-seventh we went to Urraca, where the wagons were and the expedition had its headquarters. We were very well received, because it was more than thirty days since we had bade farewell to our people. There was little food left in the camp—none, to be accurate—and with the scanty amount we brought, we decided to leave that place and make our way toward the populated areas. . . .

On February 1 we resumed our journey and spent the night at Estero, three leagues distant. February 3 we traveled on, crossed the river, and camped for the night on its bank. On the fourth we set forth again, but it took us four days to travel a league, because many of the wagons broke down and the weather was cold and it snowed. . . .

We resumed our journey on the eighth {of March 1591}, going toward a pueblo named Santo Domingo, situated on the bank of a large river; we planned to use this settlement as a center of operations while searching for the new mines. On the way, we stopped for the night at an abandoned pueblo, a league from Santo Domingo. The lieutenant governor and many of the men from the expedition went on to Santo Domingo, where he ascertained that it was possible to bring the wagons all the way to this settlement. He therefore returned to the wagons, which were with the main force of the expedition, and found some of his men already there. When he discovered this, he sent Maese de Campo Cristóbal de Heredia to the pueblo of Santo Domingo, where the governor had left many of this people, with orders to arrest a certain soldier.

The maese de campo, who was also fiscal, went on this errand and cleared up the case. The fact was that five or six soldiers from the governor's company, who had remained at the pueblo of San Mateo, had discussed a plot to kill him and return to Mexico because he would not let them do what they pleased. He restrained them from annoying or plundering the natives; and this was the basis of their complaints and the reason for their plotting. When the maese de campo arrived at the pueblo to arrest the soldier, by order of the lieutenant governor, Alonso Jaimez came out from his quarters, gun in hand, and asked, "Who is calling me?" No one had done so, and accordingly he was told that no one wanted him. Then Jaimez responded, "Let each man look out for himself." In view of this threat, the maese de campo lunged at him, but he fled. The maese de campo then returned with the arrested soldier to the wagons and the camp where the lieutenant governor was waiting. As soon as the soldier was brought there, our leader commanded that he should be garroted, because the finger of suspicion pointed to this man more than to any of the others. When the execution was about to be carried out, according to orders, the whole expedition, men and women, begged the governor to pardon the prisoner, for the love of God; and so, moved by pity and the pleading of the entire force, the governor ordered the execution stopped, although he had let his people think he would carry it out so that they would be disciplined by fear. We do not give the names of the soldiers here, because this affair was handled with great charity.

On the eighth [ninth?] of the month we left the abandoned pueblo and went on to Santo Domingo, where we were accorded a very friendly reception. Here the lieutenant governor learned that Alonso Jaimez had run away. The next day, the eighth [tenth?]—after the entire expedition with its wagons had settled in this pueblo for a few days in order that we might conduct from here our search for the mines we had heard about—all of the soldiers and other people in the expedition assembled and asked the lieutenant governor, for the love of God, to overlook certain incidents that had occurred in his camp, since he had forgiven many offenses with great clemency. They pointed out that Alonso Jaimez had absented himself from the camp because he was afraid that the lieutenant governor would certainly punish him, which was the reason why he had run away; and he was very repentant for having offended his leader in any manner. Now all the soldiers and the maese de campo in unison entreated the governor to favor them by pardoning Jaimez; and he answered that, in the name of his Majesty, moved by charity and the suffering they had all endured, he would grant a pardon to Jaimez and to all others who had transgressed the law in any way. Nevertheless, Alonso Jaimez was to be relieved of his commission as captain of the party that was to go to the city of Zacatecas, the Río Grande, and other places, on a recruiting mission. In fact, this commission was revoked publicly and without delay at the time when the governor pardoned all the culprits in the name of his Majesty. We do not record here the names of the others who erred on this occasion, since they have now been pardoned.

On the eleventh a man appeared before the lieutenant governor, asking him to grant some of the company permission to leave for Mexico. He ventured to present this request because they had heard the governor say that anyone who wanted to leave could do so. Our leader told them that the statement was true, and that he reaffirmed it. All those who wanted to leave were free to depart; and he gave them permission because he would rather remain there alone to die than give occasion for unworthy acts. In view of this concession, the group did not actually leave, because there were no longer any soldiers who wanted to go. So, even though there were several disgruntled individuals, nevertheless, when it became apparent that the lieutenant governor was right and that those who wanted to leave were wrong, all the men—the former malcontents as well as the others—remained quietly and in agreement with him. They performed such duties as arose, never alluding to the recent incidents.

While we were in this pueblo of Santo Domingo, the lieutenant governor and a party of twenty men went out to look for mines and a certain pueblo which he had not visited before. As they went along, taking possession of various settlements, they crossed some mountains where they found two pueblos that had been deserted only a few days earlier on account of wars with other pueblos which forced the inhabitants to leave their homes. This was the explanation given by the Indians who accompanied us, and we ourselves could see plainly that it was true, because there were signs of many having been killed. In these towns we found an abundance of corn and beans.

From these two abandoned settlements we went back to the Río Grande where we had established a camp for our army and the wagons. From what we had seen there and were told everywhere in the land, we deduced that these were the pueblos whose people had killed the friars reported to have come this way. When we reached the first of the two pueblos, there were no natives left in it. While we were there, we noticed that the one across the river was being evacuated in part, and in order to prevent its complete abandonment, the lieutenant governor sent the maese de campo with some soldiers to stop the evacuation. Then the governor and all the rest of us crossed the river, although it was in full flood, and forced some of the people who were fleeing to turn back. Many, however, had remained in the pueblo. Our leader reassured the natives, giving them to understand that they were not to desert their homes, and they were very pleased. When we asked why the people of the other pueblo had fled, we were told they had done so from fear, because they had killed the friars. We explained that they need not run away, and the governor sent some Indians from this [second] pueblo to call the others back. We took possession of the pueblo in the name of his Majesty and named a governor, an alcalde, and an alguacil; then we raised a large cross with the same kind of ceremonies already described. . . .

Traveling on, we met Juan de Carvajal, Joseph Rodríguez, and Francisco de Mancha, who were coming to notify the lieutenant governor of the arrival of Captain Juan Morlete with fifty men. The governor asked who they were, and the three soldiers named most of them; but there were none in the group from among the many men whom he had sent to Mexico and whom he was awaiting. He was puzzled by the fact that the party included none of the most important people he was expecting, although he did not show his perplexity. In the afternoon he ordered that we travel at a gallop, because he wanted to enter by day the pueblo where Captain Morlete had his entire camp. Those of us who accompanied the lieutenant governor never heard him say a word beyond what has been stated. As he advanced, he was warned not to enter the pueblo, nor even to approach it, because Captain Morlete and his men were coming to arrest him. When our leader realized the situation, he asked that not a word be said, adding that if they wanted to arrest him, they were welcome to do so, although he was serving his Majesty and had ample authorization for what he was doing. If it was the king's will to have him arrested, he would gladly submit.

Accordingly, the governor accelerated his pace in order to reach his destination before dark. When he arrived at the pueblo, he went to one side of the plaza while Captain Juan Morlete was passing through the center, on his way to his quarters; and as they met they greeted each other. After dismounting, the lieutenant governor walked toward Captain Juan Morlete and his men; the captain, seeing him approach, drew near with his men closely grouped about him. They greeted each other again and embraced; and then many of the others who were friends of the governor embraced him also.

When these demonstrations were over, Captain Morlete drew from his pocket a royal decree, saying that he came by order of Viceroy Don Luis de Velasco in the name of his Majesty to carry out a royal command, which he read to him word for word. The lieutenant governor listened to the reading of the decree, and when it was finished, the captain asked him to submit to arrest. Our leader replied that he was quite willing, if that was the wish of his Majesty, for he was entirely subject to his authority. Then all of them walked to the tents, and Captain Juan Morlete gave orders that the lieutenant governor should be shackled, to which he submitted meekly. Other orders were read to him, containing provisions that concerned him, and he replied that he would obey them all since they came from his king and lord. Whereupon he took the papers, placed them on his head, and then kissed them in the presence of Juan Morlete and the men of Morlete's force and his own. All members of both contingents were greatly pleased at the humility and submissiveness shown by the lieutenant governor; and Captain Juan Morlete, observing Gaspar Castaño's meekness, honored him and treated him in the manner due his rank and merits, which gratified the soldiers of both armies.

# CHAPTER 9

# Rey of the Wild Frontier: Hernán Gallegos's Narrative of the Chamuscado-Rodríguez Expedition (1591)

*In the first chapter of his narrative of the 1591 Chamuscado-Rodríguez expedition, Hernán Gallegos presents himself as a humble soldier, possessed of "an earnest desire to serve my king and lord in some important cause worthy of my ambition" (Hammond and Rey 1966, 67). Anyone reading Gallegos's narrative from the perspective of the twentieth century will recognize the author for something else—a dyed-in-the-buckskin frontiersman.*

*Gallegos and his handful of companions—the group totals nine soldiers and three Franciscan friars—lack the numbers to act with the arrogant military force of the larger expeditions of de Soto and Coronado. Instead this small party relies on the combination of blustery courage and shrewd cunning that would become the hallmark of the trapper, ranger, scout, and other frontier heroes. The cruel-but-clever bluff Gallegos and his companions pull on a group of horse-killing Indians is worthy of no less than a Davy Crockett or Natty Bumppo at his finest.*

*Along with the typical frontiersman's cunning, Gallegos also carries the frontiersman's baggage of violence and prejudice. An experienced Indian fighter even before his trip into New Mexico, the author is convinced that all Indians are barbarous and deceitful, that force is the only kind of reasoning such beings understand. He also expresses a frontiersman's rough contempt for men of the cloth, though this stance is softened by his conviction that the hand of God is visible in everything.*

*Besides going into the wilderness with fewer men than previous expeditions, the expedition on which Gallegos reports goes with fewer expectations.*

*Not expecting to find treasure cities to rival Tenochtitlán, the narrator is ecstatic over encountering adobe pueblos inhabited by a few hundred simple farmers in need of salvation (and in possession of food). Not expecting to simply pick up a fortune in refined gold, the explorers seek out potential sites for mines of all types, and the narrator frequently comments on the potential value of the farm-, grazing, and timberlands he crosses. On such matters Gallegos is a pragmatic commentator, a realist who has shed some of the wilder dream delusions about the West that so blinded his predecessors.*

*Still this at-times pragmatic author comes off as no less superstitious than the "barbarous" peoples he describes, and his understanding of Indians is far from complete, even if the tactics he and his companions practice against the natives apparently succeed. In his blindness toward Indians, Gallegos prefigures an entire literature that would portray the Indian as childishly superstitious and easily fooled by a clever white man of action who relies as much on his wits as his Winchester.*

*Gallegos's narrative, written upon his return to New Spain from the wilds of New Mexico, was intended as a report to the viceroy. The translation reprinted below was made by George P. Hammond and Agapito Rey, from a manuscript in the Archives of the Indies in Seville. The notes in brackets are those of Hammond and Rey. The notes in braces were added by the editors of this volume.*

## Selected Bibliography

Bolton, Herbert Eugene, ed. "Exploration and Settlement in New Mexico and in Adjacent Regions, 1581–1605." In *Spanish Exploration in the Southwest 1542–1706.* New York: Scribners, 1930.

Gallegos Lamero, Hernán. *The Gallegos Relations of the Rodríguez Expedition to New Mexico.* George P. Hammond and Agapito Rey, trans. and eds. Santa Fe, N.M.: El Palacio Press, 1927.

Hammond, George P., and Agapito Rey. *The Rediscovery of New Mexico, 1580–1594.* Albuquerque: University of New Mexico Press, 1966.

HERNÁN GALLEGOS

# Rey of the Wild Frontier: Hernán Gallegos's Narrative of the Chamuscado-Rodríguez Expedition (1591)

**Telling how, upon our arrival at the settlement, we gave orders that the inhabitants should provide us with food supplies.**

WHEN WE ARRIVED at the settlement, a pueblo which we named Piedra Aita, we decided that we would start there to explain how we had run short of provisions, in order that the natives of this and other towns should give us the food necessary for our sustenance. Moreover, if this pueblo gave us provisions, they would be given to us everywhere in the province. Up to that time, the natives had not been asked to supply anything for our maintenance.

We all assembled to consult with our leader and to determine the method which should be used in obtaining the provisions. It was decided first of all to tell the natives by means of signs that we had used up the supplies brought with us, and that since they had plenty they should give us some because we wanted to go on. When they realized this and saw that the supplies we had brought were exhausted, they thought of starving us to death and acted as if deaf. We told our leader that the natives had paid no attention to us and pretended not to understand.

To this he replied that it was not advisable to use force, for we could see plainly that the people in these pueblos were very numerous and that within an hour after their call to arms three thousand men would gather and kill us. When the leader expressed this opinion, the soldiers argued that, inasmuch as he had authority to seize the provisions we needed for men and horses, he should make use of it, because we preferred to die fighting rather than from starvation, especially since we were in a land with ample food. Since our leader was ill, he replied that we could do what we thought best, provided that we did not incite the natives to re-volt and that they gave us the provisions willingly.

When our men found that the Indians rebelled at our request for food, our leader, rising from his sick bed, and seven companions armed themselves and went to the pueblo with their horses in readiness for war. When the Indians saw we were armed, they withdrew into their houses and fortified themselves in the pueblo, which was composed of three hundred houses of three and four stories, all of stone. Seeing that the In-dians had retired to their houses, we entered the town, and, carrying a cross in our hands, asked them for some corn flour because we had noth-ing to eat. The natives understood, but held back, not wishing to give it. Confronted with the hostile attitude of the Indians, some of our men fired a few harquebuses, pretending to aim at them in order to intimidate them into giving us the food we needed. We wanted them to understand that they had to give it, either willingly or by force.

In order that no one should complain of having provided much while another gave less, the soldiers decided that each house should contribute a little and that for this purpose a measure should be made which held about half an almud {peck} of ground corn flour. Then the natives brought us quantities of ground corn from every house in the pueblo, fearing us and the harquebuses—which roared a great deal and spat fire like lightning—and thinking we were immortal, since we had told them that we were children of the sun and that the sun had given us these weapons for defense. Seeing that we did not ask for anything except food for ourselves, all gave something and told us they were our friends, though the friendship they feigned was due more to fear than to anything else. We remained on our guard lest, being Indians, they should treacher-ously plan some trick and attack us unawares.

Since this pueblo had contributed nine loads of flour as a present and the news had spread throughout the province, we were given exactly the same amount, no more and no less, at the other pueblos, so that we did not lack food during the entire trip. For all this, and the many favors He had granted us, insuring that we should never be without provisions, we offered thanks to God. All the pueblos thus gave us supplies as tribute; and as they are now accustomed to it, they will not resent giving such tribute when someone goes to start settlements. Together with the supply of corn and flour, they presented us with large numbers of turkeys, of which they have many flocks and do not value highly. Of the provisions that they offered us we took only what was necessary, and what was left over we returned to them. This pleased them very much, and they told us they were our friends and would give us food and whatever else we might need. They did this due to fear rather than from any desire to befriend us. It was presumably because of that attitude and the fact that we had asked for and taken provisions from them that they attempted to unite the province in order to seize us by force and kill us.

## Concerning the attempt of the Indians to kill us, the gathering that they held, and how they overcame their fear of us.

After the events related above, and after the natives had given us what we needed for our support, in characteristic Indian fashion, they determined to seize us treacherously by night and kill us if they could. The cause for this was the fact that, after we had seen the settlement, with which we were very much pleased, Father Fray Juan de Santa María, one of the friars in our party, decided to return to the land of the Christians in order to give an account and report of what had been discovered to his prelate and to his Excellency, the viceroy.

Everyone condemned the decision as inadvisable, for he would not only endanger his own life, but imperil the soldiers, and in addition would jeopardize further exploration of the land. We urged him to wait until we had inspected everything about which the natives had informed us, and had gone to see the buffalo, in order that a complete report of all this might be taken to the friar's prelate and to his Excellency, as any account that he could give now would be incomplete, since we had not seen the most important things. To this advice Fray Juan de Santa María replied that he was determined to return to Christian territory and report on what he had seen. His departure caused much unrest in the land and trouble for us. Without the permission of his superior, he left the party at vespers on the feast of Our Lady of September.

When the natives saw that the friar was leaving, they became alarmed, believing he was going to bring more Christians in order to put them out of their homes; so they asked us by signs where he was going, all alone. We tried to dissuade them from their wicked thoughts, but, as they were Indians, this did not prevent them from doing evil. They followed the friar and killed him after two or three days of travel. We knew nothing of this until we returned from our trip to the buffalo; and even though the natives told us they had slain the father in the sierra, which we named the Sierra Morena, we pretended not to understand. Seeing that we paid no attention to the death of the friar and that they had killed him so easily, they thought they would kill us just as readily. From then on they knew we were mortal; up to that time they had thought us immortal.

When we learned that the natives had killed the friar and that they intended to slay us also, we decided to withdraw gradually. We stopped at a pueblo which we named Malpartida, and at a distance of one league from that spot we discovered some mineral deposits. While we were at this pueblo, some Indians from another settlement, which we named Malagón, killed three of our horses. We soon missed the animals and learned how the Indians of this district of Malagón had killed them. When the leader and the soldiers realized what had happened, they determined that such a crime should not go unpunished. The leader ordered five of the party—Pedro de Bustamante, Hernán Gallegos, Pedro Sánchez de Chaves, Felipe de Escalante, and Pedro Sánchez de Fuensalida—to go to the pueblo of Malagón, where it was reported the three horses had been killed; to find and bring before him the culprits, either peaceably or by force; and to make some arrests at the pueblo in order to intimidate the natives.

When the five soldiers learned of their leader's orders, they armed themselves, made ready their horses, and proceeded to Malagón, which they found to consist of eighty houses of three and four stories with plazas and streets. Entering the pueblo in fighting order, as men who were angry, they found the Indians keeping watch on the housetops and asked who had killed the three missing horses. In order to protect themselves from the harm that might befall them, the natives replied they had committed no such deed. As soon as we heard this answer, we discharged the harquebuses to make the Indians think we were going to kill them, although we incurred great risk in doing so, for we were only five men facing the task of attacking eighty houses with more than a thousand inhabitants. When we had fired our harquebuses, the natives became frightened, went into their houses, and stayed there. To placate us they threw many dead turkeys down the passageways to us, but we decided not to accept the offering so that they would know we were angry. Then we asked twenty or thirty Indians who appeared on the roofs and who seemed to be the chief men of the pueblo—the cacique among them—to give us either the horses or the culprits who had killed them. To this they replied that their people had not slain the animals; and they asked us not to be angry, declaring that they were our friends.

Since the natives did not surrender those who had killed the horses, Hernán Gallegos, Pedro Sánchez de Fuensalida, and Pedro de Bustamante dismounted and went up to the houses to see if they could find any trace of horseflesh. The other soldiers guarded the pueblo to protect their companions from danger. Hernán Gallegos and Pedro de Bustamante soon found pieces of horseflesh in two houses of the pueblo and came out to notify their comrades of the discovery. We then fired the harquebuses once more, and the Indians, observing our conduct, were more frightened than defiant, since we had expressed our will with such determination. Gallegos and Bustamante then mounted; and all five of us, holding horseflesh in our hands, again asked the Indians who were keeping watch to tell us which men were guilty of killing the horses. We warned them to deliver those men to us, because we wanted to kill them or take them to our leader so that he might have them put to death; and we added that if the natives would not give up the culprits, we would have to kill them all. We challenged them to come out of their pueblo into the open so that we might see how brave they were; but they were very sad and answered that they did not want to fight us, for we were brave men, and that it was the Indians in the next pueblo who had killed our horses, thinking they were animals like the native buffalo.

Then we soldiers attacked the pueblo again in order to capture some Indians. They took refuge in the pueblo, but some hurled themselves from the corridors into the open in an attempt to escape, whereupon Hernán Gallegos and Pedro de Bustamante rushed after them and each seized an Indian by the hair. The natives were very swift, but the horses overtook them. After apprehending them, the soldiers took them to the camp of the leader to be punished, in view of their crime and as an example to the others.

Before this happened and before returning to camp, we decided to set fire to the pueblo so that the inhabitants would not perpetrate such a crime again. Pedro de Bustamante then picked up a bit of hay, started a fire by means of an harquebus, and prepared to burn the pueblo; but his companions would not allow the town to be burned and so many people to perish, lest all should suffer for the guilt of perhaps eight individuals.

Thus we returned to the camp with the prisoners and delivered them to our leader, who ordered that they should be beheaded on the following morning. To this the soldiers replied that he should consider what it meant to imprison these Indians for a day; that it was not good policy; that if they were to be executed it should be done at once, for there were more than a thousand Indians in the camp who might attempt some wickedness on account of the imprisonment of the two Indians. When the leader realized that the soldiers were right, he ordered Pedro de Bustamante, the notary [Gallegos], and the other soldiers to place a block in the middle of the camp's plaza, where the rest of the Indians were watching, and to cut off the heads of the prisoners with an iron machete as punishment for them and as an example to the others. The preparations were carried out as ordered; although, as the friars had decided to remain in that settlement, it was agreed that at the time when the Indians were to be beheaded the friars should rush out to free them—tussle with us, and snatch the victims away from us in order that the Indians might love their rescuers, who were resolved to remain in the land.

All was so done. At the moment when the soldiers were about to cut off the heads of the Indians, the friars came out in flowing robes and saved the captives from their perilous plight. As we pretended that we were going to seize them, the Indians who were watching immediately took hold of the friars and the prisoners and carried all of them off to their houses, mindful of the great support they had found in the priests. Because of what we had done and proposed to do, the natives became so terrified of us that it was surprising how they trembled. This was willed by God on high, for we ourselves were but a small force.

The following morning, many Indians from the pueblo of Malagón came, heavily laden with turkeys and other food for our use, entreating us not to be angry with them, since they would not commit such deeds again. In the future they would watch and round up the horses, so that none would be lost. They assured us that they were our friends. We were very much pleased at this, although we did not show it, in order that they and the other natives might hold us in even greater fear.

A few days later the Indians assembled for the purpose of killing us, but that did not deter us from going to explore the land in order to verify the information that we had been given. When we left, and again after we returned to camp, we realized clearly and definitely that they wanted to kill us, and that the people of the entire region were gathering for this purpose; so we decided to take precautions and to continue keeping careful watch, as we had done up to that time. Since we watched with more zeal than in the past, the natives became aware of it. If they had shown great friendship for us before, they showed even more now.

In spite of their fear, we came to the conclusion from their conduct that they wanted to kill us; wherefore we determined to attack and kill them, and to burn some of their small pueblos even though we should perish in the attempt, in order that they might fear the Spaniards. We challenged them many times so that they might know there was no cowardice in us. But as the friars had decided to remain in the said settlement, we sometimes—in fact, most of the time—relinquished our rights in order that the fathers might remain in the province and be content. Nevertheless, their decision to stay was against the judgment of all, because the natives had killed the other friar and because they were to remain among such great numbers of idolatrous people.

## Evil practices of these people.

We learned nothing of the rituals performed by the people of this settlement, except that when someone dies they dance and rejoice, for they say that he goes to the one whom they worship. They bury the dead in cavelike cellars, and every year on designated days they place many things as an offering at the foot of the cellars where the bodies lie.

The *mitotes*, or ceremonial dances, which they perform to bring rain when there is a lack of rainwater for their cornfields, are of the following nature. During the month of December the natives begin their dances, which continue more than four months, at intervals of a certain number of days—every fortnight, I believe. Attendance at the mitotes is general, so the people gather in large numbers, though only the men take part, the women never. The ceremonies, which begin in the morning and last until evening, are held around an altar maintained for this purpose and continue throughout the night. An Indian chosen for the occasion sits elevated in their midst, and the participants dance before him. Close to this Indian are six others holding fifteen or twenty sticks. They walk about and dance. During each movement of the dance, one of them steps out and puts into his mouth seven sticks, three spans in length and two fingers in width. When he finishes putting them in his mouth and taking them out, he pauses, seemingly fatigued. Then he dances with two or three of the said sticks in his mouth. Next, the man who is seated as "lord" receives seven lashes from whips made of light flexible willow for that purpose. These lashes are administered by the Indians standing close to him, for he has six Indians on each side who lash him thirty-six times in the course of each movement, in such a manner as to draw blood, making him look like a flagellant. After inflicting the original seven lashes, they continue to dance and to give him an equal number of lashes until they make the blood flow as if he were being bled. Although they do this until it seems that he will collapse, he shows no sign of pain. On the contrary, he talks to a large snake as thick as an arm, which coils up when it is about to talk. The whipped "lord" calls to it, and the reptile answers in such a manner that it can be understood. We thought this snake might be the devil, who has them enslaved. For this reason God our Lord willed that the settlement and its idolatrous people should be discovered, in order that they might come to the true faith.

At these dances, furthermore, two Indians carrying two rattlesnakes in their hands walk around in the midst of the people. The snakes are real; one can hear their rattles. They coil around the necks and creep all over the bodies of the two Indians who come, dancing and executing their figures, toward the lashed man, whom they acknowledge and obey as "lord" on this occasion. They hold the reptiles in their hands and, falling on their knees before the flayed one, give him the two snakes. He takes them, and they creep up his arms and over this body, making a great deal of noise with their rattles, until they reach his throat. Then the flayed one rises and swings around quickly. The snakes fall to the ground, where they coil and are picked up by those who brought them. Kneeling, the two Indians put the reptiles in their mouths, and disappear through a little doorway.

When this is over two Indian coyotes appear and go around among the dancers, howling in a startling and pitiful manner. As soon as the mitote has concluded, the flayed lord makes an offering of a certain number of sticks, adorned with many plumes, so that the people may place them in the cornfields and waterholes; for they worship and offer sacrifices at these holes. The natives do this, they say, because then they will never lack water. The men flayed are so badly lacerated that their wounds do not heal in two months. The participants are so neat and well adorned in these mitotes and dances that the spectacle is well worth seeing.

The local marriage customs will be described here to show how much wisdom God our Lord has bestowed upon the people of this settlement. Whenever anyone wishes to marry according to their custom, all his relatives and some of the other inhabitants assemble and perform their dances. The wedding and attendant festivities last more than three days. The first thing given the couple is a house in which to live. This is presented to them as a dowry by the father- and mother-in-law, parents of the bride. The house is two, three, or four stories high, with eight or ten rooms. The couple to be married are seated on a bench. At the side of the bride stands an Indian woman as bridesmaid and at the side of the groom an Indian who acts as groomsman. Apart from them stands a very old man, well dressed in colored and nicely woven blankets. He acts as the priest, telling the couple from time to time to kiss and embrace, and they do what the old man commands.

Their colored and ornamented blankets are set before the couple. The groom covers his bride with her blankets and she places his on him, in such a way that they clothe one another. Then the old man talks. As we did not know the language we did not understand what he was saying, but from his gestures we supposed he was telling them that they should love each other very much, since that was the purpose for which they had been united. When this is over the people place before the bride a grindstone, an olla, a flat earthenware pan *(comal)*, drinking vessels, and *chicubites*. They also put a grinding stone *(metate)* in her hand. The old man tells the bride that the gifts set before her, which are all entirely new, signify that with them she is to grind and cook food for her husband; that she is to prepare two meals every day for him, one in the morning and the other in the afternoon; that they are to dine and retire early, and rise before daybreak. She answers that she will do so.

Then the priest speaks to the groom, before whom are placed a Turkish bow, spear, war club, and shield, which signify that with them he is to defend his home and protect his wife and children. They give him his crate *(cacoxte-cacaxtle)* and leather band *(mecapal)* for carrying burdens. Then they place a hoe in his hand to signify that he is to till and cultivate the soil and gather corn to support his wife and children. He answers that he will do everything indicated. In addition to this, he is given lands in which to plant corn. Then the dances continue. Afterward the couple are taken to their house. All that day there is food in abundance, which consists of turkeys, buffalo meat, tamales, tortillas, and other things. The orderliness with which these Indians perform the ceremony described above is amazing. For a barbarous people the neatness they observe in everything is very remarkable.

CHAPTER 10

# Sunken Ships and Winged Corrals: The Juan de Oñate Expedition to New Mexico (1598)

Herbert Eugene Bolton (1930, 199) writes that in the aftermath of the Chamuscado-Rodríguez and Antonio de Espejo expeditions: "There were now dreams, not only of conquering and settling New Mexico, but of going beyond the Llanos del Cíbola and Quivira to plant settlements on the Strait of Anian, and so there was a crowd of competitors for the position of adelantado of New Mexico."

Some dreamers, such as Gaspar Castaño and the leaders of the ill-fated Humaña-Leyva expedition, tried to beat the crowd by joining the competition without official permission. Others played by the rules, and of this group the winner was the wealthy, aristocratic, Mexican-born Juan de Oñate, the son of a prominent conquistador and a relative by marriage to both Montezuma and Cortez.

In February of 1598, following years of delay in obtaining royal approval, Oñate led a large party of soldiers, families, wagons, and livestock north from the Conchos River toward the Rio Grande. On July 11 he established his headquarters at Caypa Pueblo, which he called San Juan, and there the work of establishing the colony of New Mexico began in earnest.

By fall of 1598, however, Oñate himself was on the move. He traveled west in hopes of reaching the South Sea and a fortune in pearls. He traveled north and east, going as far as Kansas. In 1604–5 he followed the Colorado River to the Gulf of California. During his ramblings Oñate fought Indians on the plains and at the pueblo of Acoma, which his troops destroyed at *the cost of an estimated eight hundred Indian lives (Thrapp 1988, 1083).*

*Though he claimed, "For my part, I have sunk my ships" (Bolton 1930, 221), Juan de Oñate saw more of the West than both Coronado and Espejo. He was in fact a better explorer than a governor. When he returned from his trip to the north in 1601, the colony of New Mexico was in such disarray that he had to use force to compel weary settlers and friars to stick with the venture (Simmons 1991, 164–71). Oñate maintained his rule until 1608, but after returning to Mexico he was convicted (in 1614) on charges of misconduct stemming from his time as governor of New Mexico. He was later pardoned.*

*As might be expected, the literary documents issuing from Oñate's controversial tenure as governor tend to whitewash the governor's actions and to overstate the value of the colony. In his letter to the viceroy, for example, Oñate defends his attack on Acoma by legalistically pointing out that he did not destroy the pueblo in simple revenge or to further his own power, but "as punishment for its crime and its treason against his Majesty" (Bolton 1930, 218). In the account of the Oñate expedition to the east, the land is promoted as a veritable Garden of Eden, full of ripe fruit and docile buffalo that "do not become angry like our cattle, and are never dangerous" (Bolton 1930, 255).*

*This description is in contrast to another Oñate-expedition document, Vicente de Saldívar Mendoza's "The Discovery of the Buffalo." The Mendoza party's attempt to corral and domesticate the buffalo ends in utter failure, leaving the narrator with nothing more than the hope that crossing the buffalo with Spanish cattle will make them tamer. (This hope persists in reverse in the twentieth-century West, where the crossbred "beefalo" has been developed to supply domestic cattle with the wild buffalo's hardiness.)*

*The Spaniards' inability to comprehend the buffalo—as well as their failure to make it conform to their notions of the proper relationship between man and animal—provides a striking example of what happens when the fragile balloon of dream meets the hard horns of reality. It also provides a metaphor for the many cultural and environmental misunderstandings that have marked the last four hundred years of human experience in the American West, misunderstandings that have shaped the literature of the region from its earliest days to the present.*

*"Letter Written by don Juan de Oñate from New Mexico, 1599" was published in Pacheco and Cardenas,* Colección de Documentos Ineditos, *16:302–15. The English translation was made by Herbert Eugene Bolton. Both "The Discovery of the Buffalo, 1599" and "The Account of the Expedition of Oñate toward the East, 1601," were translated by Bolton from*

*manuscripts in the Lowery Collection, Library of Congress. The author of "The Account of the Expedition of Oñate toward the East, 1601," is unknown. The notes in brackets were added by the editors of this volume.*

### Selected Bibliography

Bolton, Herbert Eugene, ed. *Spanish Exploration in the Southwest, 1542–1706.* New York: Scribners, 1930.

Thrapp, Dan L. *Encyclopedia of Frontier Biography.* 3 vols. Glendale, Cal.: Arthur H. Clark, 1988.

Simmons, Marc. *The Last Conquistador: Juan de Oñate and the Settling of the Far Southwest.* Norman and London: University of Oklahoma Press, 1991.

JUAN DE OÑATE

# Sunken Ships and Winged Corrals: The Juan de Oñate Expedition to New Mexico (1598)

**Copy of a letter written by Don Juan de Oñate from New Mexico to the Viceroy, the Count of Monterey, on the second day of March, 1599.**

From Rio de Nombre de Dios I last wrote to you, Illustrious Sir, giving you an account of my departure, and of the discovery of a wagon road to the Rio del Norte [Rio Grande], and of my certain hopes of the successful outcome of my journey, which hopes God has been pleased to grant, may He be forever praised; for greatly to His advantage and that of his royal Majesty, they have acquired a possession so good that none other of his Majesty in these Indies excels it, judging it solely by what I have seen, by things told of in reliable reports, and by things almost a matter of experience, from having been seen by people in my camp and known by me at present. . . .

I departed, Illustrious Sir, from Rio de Nombre de Dios on the sixteenth of March, with the great multitude of wagons, women, and children, which your Lordship very well knows, freed from all my opponents, but with a multitude of evil predictions conforming to their desires and not to the goodness of God. His Majesty was pleased to accede to my desires, and to take pity on my great hardships, afflictions, and expenses, bringing me to these provinces of New Mexico with all his Majesty's army enjoying perfect health. . . .

At the end of August I began to prepare the people of my camp for the severe winter with which both the Indians and the nature of the land threatened me; and the devil, who has ever tried to make good his great loss occasioned by our coming, plotted, as is his wont, exciting a rebellion among more than forty-five soldiers and captains, who under pretext of not finding immediately whole plates of silver lying on the ground, and offended because I would not permit them to maltreat these natives, either in their persons or in their goods, became disgusted with the country, or to be more exact, with me, and endeavored to form a gang in order to flee to that New Spain, as they proclaimed, although judging from what has since come to light their intention was directed more to stealing slaves and clothing and to other acts of effrontery not permitted. I arrested two captains and a soldier, who they said were guilty, in order to garrote them on this charge, but ascertaining that their guilt was not so great, and on account of my situation and of the importunate pleadings of the religious and of the entire army, I was forced to forego the punishment and let bygones be bygones.

Although by the middle of September I succeeded in completely calming and pacifying my camp, from this great conflagration a spark was bound to remain hidden underneath the ashes of the dissembling countenances of four of the soldiers of the said coterie. These fled from me at that time, stealing from me part of the horses, thereby violating not only one but many proclamations which, regarding this matter and others, I had posted for the good of the land in the name of his Majesty.

Since they had violated his royal orders, it appeared to me that they should not go unpunished; therefore I immediately sent post-haste the captain and procurator-general Gaspar Perez de Villagran and the captain of artillery Geronimo Marques, with an express order to follow and overtake and give them due punishment. They left in the middle of September, as I have said, thinking that they would overtake them at once, but their journey was prolonged more than they or I had anticipated, with the result [death] to two of the offenders which your Lordship already knows from the letter which they tell me they wrote from Sancta

Barbara. The other two who fled from them will have received the same at your Lordship's hands, as is just. . . .

There must be in this province [Teguas] and in the others above-mentioned, to make a conservative estimate, seventy thousand Indians, settled after our custom, house adjoining house, with square plazas. They have no streets, and in the pueblos, which contain many plazas or wards, one goes from one plaza to the other through alleys. They are of two and three stories, of an *estado* and a half or an *estado* and a third each, which latter is not so common, and some houses are of four, five, six, and seven stories. Even whole pueblos dress in very highly colored cotton *mantas,* white or black, and some of thread—very good clothes. Others wear buffalo hides, of which there is a great abundance. They have most excellent wool, of whose value I am sending a small example.

It is a land abounding in flesh of buffalo, goats with hideous horns, and turkeys; and in Mohoce there is game of all kinds. There are many wild and ferocious beasts, lions, bears, wolves, tigers, *penicas*, ferrets, porcupines, and other animals, whose hides they tan and use. Towards the west there are bees and very white honey, of which I am sending a sample. Besides, there are vegetables, a great abundance of the best and greatest salines in the world, and a very great many kinds of very rich ores, as I stated above. Some discovered near here do not appear so, although we have hardly begun to see anything of the much there is to be seen. There are very fine grape vines, rivers, forests of many oaks, and some cork trees, fruits, melons, grapes, watermelons, Castilian plums, *capuli*, pine-nuts, acorns, ground-nuts, and *coralejo*, which is a delicious fruit, and other wild fruits. There are many and very good fish in this Rio del Norte, and in others. From the ores here are made all the colors which we use, and they are very fine.

The people are in general very comely; their color is like those of that land, and they are much like them in manner and dress, in their grinding, in their food, dancing, singing, and many other things, except in their languages, which are many, and different from those there. Their religion consists in worshipping idols, of which they have many; and in their temples, after their own manner, they worship them with fire, painted reeds, feathers, and universal offering of almost everything they get, such as small animals, birds, vegetables, etc. In their government they are free, for although they have some petty captains, they obey them badly and in very few things.

We have seen other nations such as the Querechos, or herdsmen, who live in tents of tanned hides, among the buffalo. The Apaches, of whom we have also seen some, are innumerable, and although I heard that they lived in rancherías, a few days ago I ascertained that they live like these in pueblos, one of which, eighteen leagues from here, contains fifteen plazas. They are a people whom I have compelled to render obedience to His Majesty, although not by means of legal instruments like the rest of the provinces. This has caused me much labor, diligence, and care, long journeys, with arms on the shoulders, and not a little watching and circumspection; indeed, because my *maese de campo* was not as cautious as he should have been, they killed him with twelve companions in a great pueblo and fortress called Acóma, which must contain about three thousand Indians. As punishment for its crime and its treason against his Majesty, to whom it had already rendered submission by a public instrument, and as a warning to the rest, I razed and burned it completely, in the way in which your Lordship will see by the process of this cause. All these provinces, pueblos, and peoples, I have seen with my own eyes.

There is another nation, that of the Cocóyes, an innumerable people with huts and agriculture. Of this nation and of the large settlements at the source of the Rio del Norte and of those to the northwest and west and towards the South Sea, I have numberless reports, and pearls of remarkable size from the said sea, and assurance that there is an infinite number of them on the coast of this country. And as to the east, a person in my camp, an Indian who speaks Spanish and is one of those who came with Humaña, has been in the pueblo of the said herdsmen. It is nine continuous leagues in length and two in width, with streets and houses consisting of huts. It is situated in the midst of the multitude of buffalo, which are so numerous that my *sargento major*, who hunted them and brought back their hides, meat, tallow, and suet, asserts that in one herd alone he saw more than there are of our cattle in the combined three ranches of Rodrigo del Rio, Salvago, and Jeronimo Lopez, which are famed in those regions.

I should never cease were I to recount individually all of the many things which occur to me. . . . I shall only note these four, omitting the rest as being well known and common:

First, the great wealth which the mines have begun to reveal and the great number of them in this land, whence proceed the royal fifths and profits. Second, the certainty of the proximity of the South Sea, whose trade with Pirú, New Spain, and China is not to be depreciated, for it will give birth in time to advantageous and continuous duties, because of its close proximity, particularly to China and to that land. And what I emphasize in this matter as worthy of esteem is the traffic in pearls, reports of which are so certain, as I have stated, and of which we have had ocular experience from the shells. Third, the increase of vassals and tributes, which will increase not only the rents, but his renown and dominion as well, if it be possible that for our king these can increase. Fourth, the wealth of the abundant salines, and of the mountains of brimstone, of which there is a greater quantity than in any other province. Salt is the universal article of traffic of all these barbarians and their regular food, for they even eat or suck it alone as we do sugar. These four things appear as if dedicated solely to his Majesty. I will not mention the founding of so many republics, the many offices, their quittances, vacancies, provisions, etc., the wealth of the wool and hides of buffalo, and many other things, clearly and well known, or, judging from the general nature of the land, the certainty of wines and oils... there is such a surplus there. Particularly do I beg your Lordship to give a license to my daughter Mariquita, for whom I am sending, and to those of my relatives who may wish so honorably to end their lives.

For my part, I have sunk my ships and have furnished an example to all as to how they ought to spend their wealth and their lives and those of their children and relatives in the service of their king and lord, on whose account and in whose name I beg your Lordship to order sent to me six small cannon and some powder, all of which will always be at the service of his Majesty, as is this and everything else. Although on such occasions the necessities increase, and although under such circumstances as those in which I now find myself others are wont to exaggerate, I prefer to suffer from lack of necessities rather than be a burden to his Majesty or to your Lordship, feeling assured that I shall provide them for many poor people who may look to me if your Lordship will grant the favor, which I ask, of sending them to me. . . .

## Account of the Discovery of the Buffalo, 1599. . . .

Bidding them [Indians] goodby, he [Saldivar Mendoza and his companions] left that place and travelled ten more leagues in three days, at the end of which time he saw the first buffalo bull, which, being rather old, wandered alone and ran but little. This produced much merriment and was regarded as a great joke, for the least one in the company would not be satisfied with less than ten thousand head of cattle in his own corral. . . .

He camped for the night at that river, and on the following day, on his way back to the camp, he found a ranchería in which there were fifty tents made of tanned hides, very bright red and white in color and bell-shaped, with flaps and openings, and built as skilfully as those of Italy and so large that in the most ordinary ones four different mattresses and beds were easily accommodated. The tanning is so fine that although it should rain bucketfuls it will not pass through nor stiffen the hide, but rather upon drying it remains as soft and pliable as before. This being so wonderful, he wanted to experiment, and, cutting off a piece of hide from one of the tents, it was soaked and placed to dry in the sun, but it remained as before, and as pliable as if it had never been wet. The *sargento mayor* bartered for a tent and brought it to this camp, and although it was so very large, as has been stated, it did not weigh over two *arrobas* [about fifty pounds].

To carry this load, the poles that they use to set it up, and a knapsack of meat and their *pinole*, or maize, the Indians use a medium-sized shaggy dog, which is their substitute for mules. They drive great trains of them. Each, girt round its breast and haunches, and carrying a load of flour of at least one hundred pounds, travels as fast as his master. It is a sight worth seeing and very laughable to see them travelling, the ends of the poles dragging on the ground, nearly all of them snarling in their encounters, travelling one after another on their journey. In order to load them the Indian women seize their heads between their knees and thus load them, or adjust the load, which is seldom required, because they travel along at a steady gait as if they had been trained by means of reins.

Having returned to camp they had a holiday that day and the next, as it was the feast of Señor San Francisco, and on the 5th of October they continued their march so as to reach the main herd of the cattle. In three days they travelled fourteen leagues, at the end of which they found and killed many cattle. Next day they went three more leagues farther in search of a convenient and suitable site for a corral, and upon finding a place they began to construct it out of large pieces of cottonwood. It took them three days to complete it. It was so large and the wings so long that they thought they could corral ten thousand head of cattle, because they had seen so many, during those days, wandering so near to the tents and houses. In view of this and of the further fact that when they [buffalo] run they act as though fettered, they took their capture for granted. It was declared by those who had seen them that in that place alone there were more buffalo than there are cattle in three of the largest ranches in new Spain.

The corral constructed, they went next day to a plain where on the previous afternoon about a hundred thousand cattle had been seen. Giving them the right of way, the cattle started very nicely towards the corral, but soon they turned back in a stampede towards the men, and, rushing through them in a mass, it was impossible to stop them, because they are cattle terribly obstinate, courageous beyond exaggeration, and so cunning that if pursued they run, and that if their pursuers stop or slacken their speed they stop and roll, just like mules, and with this respite renew their run. For several days they tried a thousand ways of shutting them in or of surrounding them, but in no manner was it possible to do so. This was not due to fear, for they are remarkably savage and ferocious, so much so that they killed three of our horses and badly wounded forty, for their horns are very sharp and fairly long, about a span and a half, and bent upward together. They attack from the side, putting the head far down, so that whatever they seize they tear very badly. Nevertheless, some were killed and over eighty *arrobas* of tallow were secured, which without doubt is greatly superior to that from pork; the meat of the bull is superior to that of our cow, and that of the cow equals our most tender veal or mutton.

Seeing therefore that the full grown cattle could not be brought alive, the *sargento mayor* ordered that calves be captured, but they became so enraged that out of the many which were being brought, some dragged by ropes and others upon the horses, not one got a league toward the camp, for they all died within about an hour. Therefore it is believed that unless taken shortly after birth and put under the care of our cows or goats, they cannot be brought until the cattle become tamer than they now are.

Its shape and form are so marvellous and laughable, or frightful, that the more one sees it the more one desires to see it, and no one could be so melancholy that if he were to see it a hundred times a day he could keep from laughing heartily as many times, or could fail to marvel at the sight of so ferocious an animal. Its horns are black, and a third of a *vara* long, as already stated, and resemble those of the [Asian] *búfalo;* its eyes are small, its face, snout, feet, and hoofs of the same form as of our cows, with the exception that both the male and female are very much bearded, similar to he-goats. They are so thickly covered with wool that it covers their eyes and face, and the forelock nearly envelops their horns. This wool, which is long and very soft, extends almost to the middle of the body, but from there on the hair is shorter. Over the ribs they have so much wool and the chine is so high that they appear humpbacked, although in reality and in truth they are not greatly so, for the hump easily disappears when the hides are stretched.

In general, they are larger than our cattle. Their tail is like that of a hog, being very short, and having few bristles at the tip, and they twist it upward when they run. At the knee they have natural garters of very long hair. In their haunches, which resemble those of mules, they are hipped and crippled, and they therefore run, as already stated, in leaps, especially down hill. They are all of the same dark color, somewhat tawny, in parts their hair being almost black. Such is their appearance, which at sight is far more ferocious than the pen can depict. As many of these cattle as are desired can be killed and brought to these settlements, which are distant from them thirty or forty leagues, but if they are to be brought alive it will be most difficult unless time and crossing them with those from Spain make them tamer. . . .

### True Account of the Expedition of Oñate Toward the East, 1601. . . .

Each day the land through which we were travelling became better, and the luxury of an abundance of fish from the river greatly alleviated the hardships of the journey. And the fruits gave no less pleasure, particularly the plums, of a hundred thousand different kinds, as mellow and good as those which grow in the choicest orchards of our land. They are so good that although eaten by thousands they never injured anybody. The trees were small, but their fruit was more plentiful than their leaves, and they were so abundant that in more than one hundred and fifty leagues, hardly a day passed without seeing groves of them, and also of grapevines such that although they hid the view in many places they produced sweet and delicious grapes. Because of this the people were very quiet and [not] inclined to injure us in any way, a favor granted by our Lord, for which we did not cease to praise Him and to render a thousand thanks, and in acknowledgment of which the majority of the people endeavored to unburden their consciences and their souls; and God being pleased that on the feast of the Porciuncula, which is the 2d of August, we should reach a place which from times past had been called Rio de San Francisco, with very special devotion to the Most Blessed Confessor the greater part of the army confessed and received communion.

Proceeding on the day of the Glorious Levite and Martyr, San Lorenzo, God was pleased that we should begin to see those most monstrous cattle called *cibola*. Although they were very fleet of foot, on this day four or five of the bulls were killed, which caused great rejoicing. On the following day, continuing our journey, we now saw great droves of bulls and cows, and from there on the multitude which we saw was so great that it might be considered a falsehood by one who had not seen them, for, according to the judgment of all of us who were in any army, nearly every day and wherever we went as many cattle came out as are to be found in the largest ranches of New Spain; and they were so tame that nearly always, unless they were chased or frightened, they remained quiet and did not flee. The flesh of these cattle is very good, and very much better than that of our cows. In general they are very fat, especially the cows, and almost all have a great deal of tallow. By experience we noted that they do not become angry like our cattle, and are never dangerous.

All these cattle are of one color, namely brown, and it was a great marvel to see a white bull in such a multitude. Their form is so frightful that one can only infer that they are a mixture of different animals. The bulls and the cows alike are humped, the curvature extending the whole length of the back and even over the shoulders. And although the entire body is covered with wool, on the hump, from the middle of the body to the head, the breast, and the forelegs, to just above the knee, the wool is much thicker, and so fine and soft that it could be spun and woven like that of the Castilian sheep. It is a very savage animal, and is incomparably larger than our cattle, although it looks small because of its short legs. Its hide is of the thickness of that of our cattle, and the native Indians are so expert in dressing the hides that they convert them into clothing. This river is thickly covered on all sides with these cattle and with another not less wonderful, consisting of deer [elk?] which are as large as large horses. They travel in droves of two and three hundred and their deformity causes one to wonder whether they are deer or some other animal.

CHAPTER 11

# The Dream in Verse: Gaspar Pérez de Villagra's New World Epic (1610)

*When the natives of Acoma Pueblo killed a troop of Spaniards under the command of Juan de Zaldívar, the* maese de campo *of Juan de Oñate's army, Oñate dispatched soldiers to punish the Indians responsible. Led by Zaldívar's brother Vicente, these troops destroyed Acoma, slaughtering much of the population. Among those who attacked the rock of Acoma was Gaspar Pérez de Villagra, Oñate's quartermaster. At Acoma Villagra distinguished himself as a brave and competent soldier; later, he served Oñate in a less violent way by returning to Mexico City to recruit reinforcements for the struggling colony (Thrapp 1988, 1486).*

*After his adventures in New Mexico, Villagra returned to his native Spain where, in 1610, he published his* Historia de Nueva México *(History of New Mexico), an epic poem on the colonization and settlement of New Mexico. The publication of the poem did not serve as a conclusion to Villagra's New Mexico adventures, however, for in 1614 the slow wheels of Spanish justice finally rolled around to try Villagra for killing some Acoman Indians and enslaving others (Leal 1989, 49–50). Like his leader Oñate, Villagra was convicted and then pardoned. He died in 1620 while en route to take a post in Guatemala.*

*Though his life was undoubtedly colorful, Villagra would not be remembered today were it not for his* Historia de Nueva México. *Long valued by historians as a primary account of the Oñate expedition, Villagra's poem also has long been dismissed as a work of literature. Reflecting the popular opinion is New Mexico historian Ralph Emerson Twitchell's remark that Villagra was "a better chronicler than poet" (1924, 1). While it may be conceded that Villagra's poetry is too conventional to be considered inspired,* Historia de

Nueva México *is so much a work of the imagination that it doesn't need the benefit of great poetics to qualify as literature.*

*One example of the poem's literary character is Villagrá's highly imaginative attempt to convey the thoughts and motivations of the Indians of Acoma. In scenes that could only have come from the poet's imagination, Villagrá portrays oratorical Acomans making speeches that neatly serve to divide the members of the tribe into good Indians (led by the noble Gicombo) and bad Indians (led by the sneaky Zutacapan). Villagrá similarly tries to imagine Indian sexuality, which in his hands takes the form of either the bad Indian's lust for white women or the good Indian's incredibly romanticized monogamous love. It hardly needs to be said that the good Indian/bad Indian and the lusting Indian/romantic Indian would all reappear as stock figures in the popular literature of the American West.*

*Further qualifying* Historia de Nueva México *as literature is the way the university-educated Villagrá calls on Old World literary ideas to relate a New World experience. Villagrá's epic poem is shot through with references to European literary sources: chivalric romances, the Bible, the Greek and Latin classics. Clearly the mighty fortress of Acoma bears a more-than-passing resemblance to Homer's Troy, and the reluctant warrior Gicombo is something of a New World Achilles.*

*Of course the Acomans were no more Trojans than they were, in the most literal sense,* Indians. *Nor was Acoma another Troy. Nor Oñate a new Ulysses. Villagrá the poet casts them as such because such casting makes the experience of New Mexico easier for the European mind to comprehend. In* Historia de Nueva México, *the reality of the New World has once again been fitted to the dream of the old. That Villagrá chose to fit the reality to the dream form of the epic poem only makes the forced nature of the fit more apparent.*

*The first printing of* Historia de la Nueva México *was made in Acala de Henares in 1610. The first published English version, a prose translation by Gilbert Espinosa, was produced by the Quivira Society in 1933. An authoritative, and much needed, English-Spanish edition was published by the University of New Mexico Press in 1992. Translated and edited by Miguel Encinias, Alfred Rodríguez, and Joseph P. Sánchez, the 1992 edition was used for this anthology. The portion of the poem reprinted here begins with Canto XXVI, in which Gicombo receives word of the killing of the Spaniards, then follows with selections describing the destruction of Acoma by the vengeful Spanish. The notes in brackets have been added by the editors of this volume; the footnotes are those of Encinias, Rodríguez, and Sánchez.*

## Selected Bibliography

Leal, Luis. "The First American Epic." *Pasó por Aquí: Critical Essays on the New Mexican Literary Tradition, 1542–1988.* Ed. by Erlinda Gonzales-Berry. Albuquerque: University of New Mexico Press, 1989.

Thrapp, Dan L. *Encyclopedia of Frontier Biography,* 3 vols. Glendale, Cal.: Arthur H. Clark, 1988.

Twitchell, Ralph Emerson. *Captain Don Gaspar de Villagra, Author of the First History of the Conquest of New Mexico by the Adelantado Don Juan de Oñate.* (Santa Fe: Historical Society of New Mexico), 1924.

Villagra, Gaspar Pérez de. *Historia de la Nueva México, 1610: A Critical and Annotated Spanish/English Edition.* Ed. and trans. by Miguel Encinias, Alfred Rodriguez, and Joseph P. Sanchez. Albuquerque: University of New Mexico Press, 1992.

GASPAR PÉREZ DE VILLAGRA

# The Dream in Verse: Gaspar Pérez de Villagra's New World Epic (1610)

How the news about the [death of the] Army Master came to the ears of Gicombo, one of the Acoman captains, who had been absent, and of the activity he showed gathering the Indians in council, and of the discord they had. . . .

When Gicombo, a valiant barbarian,
A gentleman, affable, sagacious,
Who then was thirty leagues from the fortress [Acoma],
Through the arts of the devil, who sleeps not,
Learned what had happened, and without delay,
Fearing such crime would be ascribed to him
As being a man of influence, esteemed
As captain in that same fortress,
Where he was married to Luzcoija,

A famous, beauteous barbarian,
Who for her great beauty and noble air
Was reverenced and respected
In all that fortress and its neighborhood,
For this just cause and many more
That were all joined in his noble person,
Affronted at the deed and infamous affair,
He ordered Buzcoico to depart at once
For the Apaches, who were foreigners,
Remote and set apart from his nation,
And call to him Bempol, his greatest friend,
A native born in that land there,
Extremely valiant and a great soldier,
And he should say as his message
That within six suns 'twas convenient
They should both meet at Acoma, nor should there be
Any failure or delay in this,
Because he had serious things
To tell him and discuss with him, of importance.
And hardly was the powerful lamp of heaven
Closing the sixth of his revolutions
When the two spirited warriors
Did meet in Acoma, where, together,
They were well served and well supplied
By noble Luzcoija, and, together there,
After having considered and conferred
Through all the night upon the ugly case,
They determined that at the break of day
All the captains should be called in,
Who were but six valiant barbarians,
Popempol, Chumpo, Calpo, Buzcoico,
Ezmicaio, and Gicombo, that brave man
By whose command all were gathered.
And seeming like the sower who scatters
The grain and spreads it well about,
Lost in the soil, so, seeming quite carefree,
Addressing the assembly, he thus spoke:
"Ye powerful men, right well you know
'Tis necessary an offender always wear

His chin upon his shoulder,[1] suspicious
Of all misfortune and all sad outcome.
You see well that he who has made
Eleven Spaniards leave without a cause
This sad and miserable life
May well expect them, 'spite of him, to force,
When he is most careless and most secure,
Him to depart and follow after them
Upon the sorry route which they pursued.
And since there is no remedy to recall them,
Those who depart from out this life,
It seems to me that with all due prudence,
If you would make yourselves safe in fact,
All our children and our wives, too,
Should leave this citadel, and we remain,
No more than we men, in the meantime, till
The Spaniards indicate or show
The courage which they have and the forces
They will set to avenge their friends.
It was for this cause that I wished
Bempol should come and join himself with us
And give his opinion and vote
As one who always had, in arms,
Place most prominent, and more in things
That are of so great weight and import
As these are, upon which we see
The honor of so many hang, not to speak of
The many lives that will be risked and lost
Of stern necessity unless quick remedy be used
To ill so dangerous as time will tell
Right speedily unless it be cut short,
Its miserable sickness known."
Now, like the madman who does turn
His rage against his doctor and, enraged,
Tries to destroy and make an end of him,
Not seeing that he watches, seeks, attempts,

[1]The popular Spanish expression graphically suggests one constantly looking back in apprehension.

A method to cure him and give him health,
Thus, raging, wild and without sense,
Hearing these words from the outside,
Zutacapán was approaching
With a feigned and disdainful laugh
And spoke in this wise, with disdain:
"Surely I am ashamed and it galls me
That for so cowardly and base a thing
Such brave and lofty captains should
Have joined in council, for of seven
Who are in this noble, famous body,
Any of the five honorable men
Whom I shall soon point out with my finger
Is shelter enough and sufficient
To be, within this post and fort, able
To break to pieces all the universe
And quite destroy it, leaving naught
Not subject and vassal to him.
And if Gicombo has so great a fear,
Let him shelter beneath the shadow of this mace,
For here his life will be preserved all safe
And also will prevent a foreigner
From coming to defend us and to vote
Where forces and advice more than suffice,
Especially among soldiers as brave
As all those fears are cowardly
With which they now come skulking in."
The two warriors, alike wounded
By the rude stroke of but one stone,
Immediately left their seats
And, like swift sakers, they attacked,
Their palms open widely,[2] and if
Popempol, Chumpo, and Calpo had not
Swiftly smoothed o'er their roused and kindled wrath,
There would Zutacapán entirely
Have lost forever his honor.
And, turning to him, Bempol said:
"Tell me, infamous wretch, since when you dare

---

[2] The image corresponds well to the bird of prey, with its talons spread, and with the Mediterranean offensive norm of slapping instead of punching.

To speak where you have never had
The hands to do by force of arms
What you wish now to do by tongue alone?"
At this, Cotumbo said, enraged:
"There is reason for no one to excel,
For, in this fort, this arm alone
Suffices to conquer the entire world.
And to think otherwise is cowardice,
Infamy, and vile affront that stains
The valor and the grandeur which we have,
As though we were the gods, on top
Of these valiant and mighty walls."
Then, after this, Tempal, insidious,
Like cruel, poisonous scorpion
Grazing amid the poisoned grass,
Whirring its three impudent tongues
And with its sting elevated,
Said it would be great baseness should
Their arms be governed by all those who had
Fears for a place so notoriously safe.
As bits of flint do strike out sparks
With blows from steel, and glowing flakes,
Others beyond these few approved,
Joining their party, and they said
That those were poor in valor and in shame
Who ever feared or even thought
That, placed in that position, there could come to them
Any more evil than to the stars, whose great height
Does not permit that anything should come
Which might obscure them or stain them.
Hearing this, the noble Zutancalpo [son of Zutacapán],
Like skillful musician who doth lower
The high first string and loosen it,
Did throw his powerful war club
In the midst of the council, and he said:
"If this poor fatherland could be
Defended by a single valiant arm
I know that it would be set free by this.
But tell me, you unconquered men,
How many, throned upon a lofty peak,
Ourselves have seen in miserable wreck

Fall from their elevated seats?
How many, valiant, strong, and courageous,
We see consumed by weak forces?
How many lofty stars, unfixed,
From out the huge and mighty heavens
We see extinguished in a little time?
What boots it, gentlemen, that my father
With but the shadow of his mace doth make
Our lives secure, and that, beside,
Others, too, wish with but a single arm
To overthrow and conquer a whole world,
If, coming to the truth, they, together,
Like sorry kites,[3] without respect,
Must be despised and so demeaned,
As you see that club on the ground,
Mute, cowardly, and without management
Of the bellicose hand that governs it?"
Not letting him finish, at that instant,
Discharging living fire from his eyes,
Bempol stood forth, saying defiantly:
"Let no one think that his own strength
Extends or in itself is raised as far
As is the lowest, most despised, dust,
For I shall make him place his worthless eyes,
Spite of himself, where I do place my foot."
Gicombo then was ired, with many more,
And this party all did desire
To plead through arms, and, that the fire
Might not be kindled more and so burst out,
After they had exchanged with much anger
Many great demands and replies,
There did remain three against three opposed,
Gicombo, Zutancalpo, and the great Bempol
Against Zutacapán, Cotumbo, and Tempal,
Whose fierce combat was suspended
Until they gained a victory from Spain. . . .
Here Zutacapán made reply at once:
"I wish that these Castilians whom you fear

---

[3]Among birds of prey, the kite is considered cowardly by Spaniards.

Might, like gods in a passion,
Hurl their most ardent lightnings upon us,
But it would be proper for you to tell
Of each one hundred thousand bolts how many you
Have seen that have struck on our walls?
And if you have seen one that did
More damage ever than to tear away
A few pounds, counting it at most,
From our valiant and lofty cliffs?
Now if the power of Heaven does not extend
Further than you have heard, why speak
Of infamous wretches, all more mortal
Than those we have seen left without their souls,
Their miserable bodies being dead?"
"I know that they are mortal," then declared
The valiant, temperate Gicombo, "For,
Because of you alone, being such,
Eleven in this stronghold died.
And you know also that there is no rock
Nor strength so haughty in this life
That it cannot be leveled and destroyed
If with deceit and treacherous dealing
We wish to fight and destroy it."
"I know this very well," said Amulco [a wizard],
"But when good comes it is but just
That all acknowledge its greatness.
The sun is not so sure to give us light
As it is sure we shall have victory.
Break down the bridges, then, and block
All passageways so that nothing
May be left for the Spaniards,
For from henceforward we must settle on
The moon's most elevated horn.
To you, strong Gicombo, I give,
Though Luzcoija is most beautiful,
Twelve beautiful Castilian maids,
And six to brave Bempol, that he may go
Back honored with such booty to his friends,
His kinsmen, fatherland, and his near relatives."
At this point, both at once replied,

Not to give more suspicion of weakness,
"Arms shall you give to us and not women
If we are to have prize of battle.
And lest it be thought that we wish,
From fear of death, to be exempted here
From seeing the Castilians, we promise
On our part, and for those who wished
To leave this place and not to wait for them,
To remain here more firmly than
The lofty mountains do when they await
Those who would break and penetrate and destroy them."
And since the Spanish folk do now
Prepare themselves in haste, I wish at once
To prepare me, lord, for I must
Come with them all unto this fortalice.

### How the battle was carried forward until gaining victory and how fire was set to all the pueblo, and of other things that happened. . . .

Because of their [the Acomans'] great fury the astute
Sergeant [Vicente de Zaldívar] did order that there be brought up
Two fieldpieces, and, in the interim,
Addressing his men, he thus spoke to them:
"Ye founders of manorial houses,
Ye columns of the Church invincible,
Ye mirrors for brave men, whose breasts
Deserve with reason to be honored
With crosses red and white and green,
Today your deeds attain the highest point
And to the highest homage that Spaniards
Have ever yet raised them on high.
Let them not fall, sustain the scale
That thus sustains and weighs the true greatness
Of the most honorable, gallant deed
That noble arms were ever seen to do."
Just then the two pieces came up
And were set at the place and spot
Where an attack, by chance, was being made
By three hundred brave, furious barbarians,

All delivering terrible shouts.
And as they made their charge, at last,
The two pieces did suddenly belch forth
Two hundred spikes from each, at which,
Just as we see the magpies, terrorized,
Suspend their chirping and their cackling
At the charge of powder which scatters
Great store of small shot, and we see
A few escaping and others
Remain with shattered limbs, and others dead,
And others beating their wings on the ground,
Their black beaks gaping and their bowels
Pouring from out their torn bellies,
We then beheld, not otherwise than this,
A sudden great heap of the dead,
Mangled, without hands, legs, shattered,
Deep wounds opened into their breasts,
Their heads laid open and their arms,
Pierced a thousand times, their flesh
Pouring out blood in mortal agony,
Took leave of their immortal souls,
Leaving the bodies quivering there. . . .
The Sergeant, then, seeing the bravery,
Endurance and persistence with which all
Of the barbarians yet fought furiously,
That he might see no more of butchery,
Just as the clever, cautious pruner does
Who judges well the vine and looks and runs
His careful glance over each spreading bough,
And when he has surveyed, doth act and prune
The ill-shaped branches and the withered ones,
With all superfluous and useless ones,
And leaves with skill and good judgment
The stems with runners and new shoots
Which are considered fruitful ones,
That great soldier, surveying all the field,
Withdrawing all the soldiery
From their appointed stations,
He ordered that from him the foe be told
They should observe the slaughter, the destruction

Of all the miserable wretches that there were
Stretched out upon the ground and they should grieve
At such corpses and blood, and he gave them
The word and faith of noble gentleman
To do them justice and with clemency
To hear their case as if he were
Their own true father. And immediately
Loosing a great flight of arrows,
Like to mad dogs, they made reply
They would not speak of this, but they would take
Their arms and teeth and fists, as well,
Because they, their wives and children
Perforce would die and would give up
Their lives and souls and their honor
In this struggle. And, upon this,
They, fighting furiously, did charge
To die or conquer with such force
That they caused fear and terror to us all.
Now at this time, turned cowardly
And thinking to find safety here,
Zutacapán did come and beg for peace
Before the gallant Sergeant; he, content,
Not knowing who that traitor was,
Told him that he should give and hand over
Only the chief ones who had caused
The recent mutiny and that with this
He would do all that he well could.
The tender cinquefoil was never seen
To tremble so at single gentle touch
Of a soft hand as he then shook,
That brutal savage, at the word.
And so, hesitant, sad, suspicious,
Hardly had there driven to his settling,
In mighty and precipitous course,
The sun his beauteous chariot and hid
The light with which he lighted us,
When in the sorry town all was
Divided and set off in two parties,
Both one and the other being timorous
About the Spaniards' strength and their courage.

And when the light did grow once more
The barbarians, having discussed
All the grave matters of this peace,
Seeing Zutacapán had been the chief
Who had brought on the recent mutiny,
With all his friends and all his followers,
Like leafed forests that are rustled
By powerful Boreas, shaken,
So in a confused mass they move
Hither and thither, shaking off
Their dust, raising and altering
Their lofty tops, and all about
Are all moved to and fro and everywhere,
These poor barbarians, ruined,
Took refuge in their arms to such effect
That for three whole days the soldiers
Nor ate nor slept nor drank a drop,
Nor sat down nor laid aside
Their strong weapons from out their hands,
Shedding such store of blood they now
Were flooded, tired out with shedding it.
And now the fire kept sending up
A ruddy vapor, bit by bit,
Attacking all the sad houses,
And then in a short time it mustered up
Sufficient vigor and in the dry pine
Of the resinous houses and dwellings
It crackled in the roofs and in a thousand spots,
A very thick and dense and sluggish smoke,
Like great fleeces, was puffing out thickly
From windows here, there, and everywhere,
And like the most ardent of volcanoes
They poured out, whirling toward the sky
Great store of embers and of sparks.[4]
And thus, those wild and mad barbarians,
Seeing themselves now conquered, 'gan to kill
Each other, and did so in such fashion

[4]This described burning of Acoma is, not surprisingly, somewhat similar to the burning of Troy as narrated in Virgil. See the *Aeneid* II.

That sons from fathers, fathers from their loved children,
Took life away, and further, more than this,
Others in groups did give aid to the fire
So that it might leap up with more vigor,
Consume the pueblo and destroy it all.
Only Zutacapán and they his friends,
Fleeing as cowards lest they see themselves
Within Gicombo's hands, did hide themselves
Within the caves and hollows which there were
Upon the fortress rock, whose great extent
Did show itself a second Labyrinth
Because of many caves and hiding holes,
Their entrances and exits and chambers.
The General [Gicombo] and brave Bempol, seeing
That all did kill themselves and seal
Truly the pact which all had sworn
To suicide if they as conquered should
Come from the struggle with the Castilians,
Determined jointly they would kill themselves.
And so, fearful, because of this,
Of such incurable evil, not to see all
In death's own arms, some of their friends,
Sad, much dismayed, did speak to them,
Begging sincerely they would surrender
And so, together, they might save their lives.
At this appeal they instantly replied,
Those furious, obstinate barbarians:
"Tell us, ye Acomans unfortunate,
What state is this of Acoma today
To undertake so infamous a thing
As this you ask us? Tell us now
What refuge you do think that fate doth leave
As soon as peace might be secured
All firmly with these Castilians?
Do you not see that we have now arrived
At that last sorrow and that final point
Where we all must, without our liberty,
Live out our sorry life as infamous wretches?
Acoma was once, and upon the peak
We saw her name, heroic, lifted high,

And now the very gods who gave
Their hands to her, to raise and honor her,
We see only did so that her ruin
Might be more miserably felt
By those poor wretches who did hope
For such firmness in such feeble weakness.
For this reason, we, all of us, agreed,
If you are, as we two do feel you are,
Firm in the promise which we swore
That we would give our throats to happy death
And submit them since there remaineth not
Another greater remedy for this our health
Than to give up the hope that yet remains
For us to gain it and to secure it." . . .

## . . . of the end and death of Gicombo and Luzcoija. . . .

I think, lord, that we should return
To the unhappy spot where yet remain
The poor General and the brave Bempol,
Who, as I say and said before,
Were like illustrious Brutus and Cassius,
Who wished to take away their lives
Because they saw themselves conquered.
Thus, never to live as subjects,
The one departed to leap off the cliff,
The other to give undeserved death
To his dear Luzcoija, lest he might see her
In hands of Spaniards who could
Enjoy her beauty, now wasted.
Now, coming from the mighty labyrinth,
Desperate, reckless, furious,
They then spoke to each other in this wise:
"Oh how the harsh fates do now destroy us
And violent tempest doth batter us
And troubles us with living fire and blood,
Oppresses, subdues, conquers, ruins us!
And you, infamous men of Acoma,
Shall be most horribly punished,
With such penalty as 'tis well should come

Upon such coward spirits as yours are.
And you, vile Zutacapán, who have been
The instrument of such calamity,
Know that for you there are waiting, prepared,
Most cruel beatings, cruel punishments,
For this evil and this shameful disgrace,
And are entrusted to most fearsome gods,
Who for your monstrous crimes will give to you
A very late and profitless reward."
Having said this, the two did separate.
Gicombo made his way to his own house,
Which was enveloped in smoke and live flames,
And, forcing passage through the hostile coals
And embers, and through leaping flames,
He came into the very room where was
His most beloved wife, she lamenting
With a great store of matrons and maidens
Who, openmouthed, were all gasping
Most heated breath out of their lungs
And implanting sad kisses on the wall.
As he entered, it was impossible
Amid the confused cries and lamentings
And the thick smoke that hovered over all,
For him to find her, and because of this
He held the doorway so that all of them
Might there consume and be burnt up.
As the fire, gaining strength, approached
The miserable palace, unconsoled,
The Sergeant came in search of the barbarian
With a good squadron of our warriors,
And when the brute Arabian saw him
He fixed his eyes on him, inflamed with rage
And violent with insane anger.
Like a ferocious boar hemmed in
By speedy greyhounds and foxhounds,
Grinding foam freely from his mouth
And threatening with his curving tusks,
Thus did the General display his rage,
Obstructing the exit for those who were
Within that perilous dwelling.

And Luzcoija's beauteous face showing,
Like those who go by a shortcut
To shorten the course of the road,
So the poor, afflicted savage
Offered her broad, spacious forehead
To the force of the powerful mace
That caused her two most beautiful eyes
To spring from out her solid skull.
Never was seen in the eager hunter
Greater content when he possessed
His longed-for game, already caught,
Than this barbarian had having
Now quite destroyed his dearest pledge
And deprived her of all feeling.
The Sergeant, then, seeing the hardihood
Of that valiant, stern General,
Attempted to make a true friend of him
By dint of promises and reasoning,
Giving to him his word as a soldier
And faith as cavalier of noble birth
To settle his affairs in such fashion
That he alone should govern that fortress
For your Majesty, and no other one
Except Don Juan should give commands in it,
As he himself had been a living coal,
Which at its time of dying, going out,
Doth kindle its light higher and show it,
The furious, bloody idolater,
Smiling disdainfully, thus replied to him:
"You now can give me no greater sorrow
Than life, this woman being now dead.
But if you wish to do me a favor,
Then allow me to fight with six or seven
Of the best soldiers found within your camp,
And then kill me yourself, for 'tis unjust
To refuse such a trifling favor
To me whom you see now so bound for death.
I shall do more for you, as you must see
That all these women must be burnt,
Let them all be freed from this fire

And not one of them stay on my account."
Seeing that his cause was hopeless,
By this and other things which had happened,
He ordered Simón Pérez to shoot him
Right quickly and with certain aim,
And, without being seen nor understood,
He struck the unhappy General to the earth,
His face all tainted in ugly yellow.
When he had ended and was quite lifeless,
Those savage women, amazed, whom he kept
In killing heat, almost unconscious,
Pouring out streams of sweat, boiling,
All their closed pores now open wide
And their hot mouths and their nostrils
Being satisfied by air alone,
Did then escape in greatest haste. . . .

# CHAPTER 12

# The Basic Stuff of the West: Pierre Esprit Radisson (1651)

*"Roll the stone!" The great boulder rocks, teeters, then goes bouncing hugely down the narrow canyon, sweeping along in its landslide Tull and his pursuing henchmen, while sealing the escaping threesome forever in their idyllic mountain valley. From henceforth, one supposes, Lassiter, Jane, and little Fay will live out their lives sweetly, secure in the bosom of nature while the mad world rushes by (Grey 1912, 280).*

*It's easy enough to throw brickbats at the Ohio dentist turned avid western novelist—for his mawkish plots, stereotypical characters, and convenient division of the West into good and evil camps. Whatever the several charges, however, Zane Grey's stone-rolling incident marks one of the most dramatic moments in western American literature, a thrilling last page to a story of survival among lawless men played out against the backdrop of a vast landscape. But it would be to tumble into the pitfall of some glib critics to suggest that these two elements—violence and a mysteriously wild nature—are in any way unique to western American literature. As a glance at tales ranging from the* Ramayana *to* Beowulf *readily reminds us, the literatures of most cultures deal with these major features of the human experience. Perhaps if one is to suggest a distinction beyond the formulaic treatment that eventually subsumes such forces, it would lie not only in the degree but also in the manner of reporting. Almost by definition, the frontier offers dual pivots on which most of its literature saws back and forth: on a nature alternately a source of threat and a source of abundance, and on good men according to their own lights representing the concept of civilization contending with the forces of lawlessness and darkness. And such on the western frontier were not the artificial high points of a St. George finally meeting his dragon but arose, at least in the popular imagination, from the immediate reality of daily struggles facing every settler.*

As to sources for this particular literary phenomenon, it would be about as silly to ascribe the existence of California to Las Sergas de Esplandián *as to identify any one book as the singular fountainhead of a western novel owing its shape to many combined factors coming together through the years. Yet we can point to early strands contributing to its later development. One surely is the life and writings of the seventeenth-century* coureur de bois, *Pierre Esprit Radisson.*

*Born in France about 1636, Radisson arrived in pioneer Canada in 1651, then inhabited by less than three thousand white people. The next year while he was out hunting, marauding Iroquois pounced on the teenager and dragged their captive off into the depths of the wilderness. There he was tortured and among the screams of other prisoners witnessed horrific acts: "They burned a French woman. They pulled out her breasts and took a child out of her belly, which they broiled, and made the mother eat of it; so in short [she] died" (Radisson 1961, 22). Three years later he escaped, but the long nightmare hadn't dulled his edge for adventure. Over the next decades he made trip after trip into the unknown west and north, and though his geography isn't always identifiable, he may deserve credit for several feats significant to the frontier's expansion. Some students claim that Radisson was the first Frenchman to reach the Mississippi River as well as the first to explore the country between Lake Superior and Hudson's Bay. Switching his loyalties back and forth between France and rival England with an aplomb that suited his convenience, the swashbuckling Radisson helped found the famous Hudson's Bay Company, important to the development of the far north and western Canada. More than that, as we'll see in the first selection, his influence was psychological. Radisson's explorations heightened Frenchmen's awareness of the West as a vast promised land awaiting their settlement.*

*Radisson's role as first pathfinder showed that the process would be one of conflict, of prolonged brutality. As also reflected in Grey's later* Riders of the Purple Sage, *the violence would be of two sorts, both played out against nature's magnificent backdrop. There would be the immediacy of men spilling blood for possession of the land and its fruits. And, as the final excerpt from Radisson's* Explorations *shows, it also would involve quick-witted tests to compensate for one's weaknesses, bluffing and conniving to gain the upper hand over powerful competitors, a tactic Lassiter and untold numbers of later western heroes also well understood.*

*The explorer's fearful and wonderful English can be nearly as horrific as some of the tortures he witnessed and on occasion perpetrated. Burpee (1936, 213) calls it ". . . the execrable English of one possessing scarcely even an elementary knowledge of the language." The persnickety focus on this shortcom-*

*ing slights the robustness of Radisson's writing. Boatfield and Dobson (1935) praise the Frenchman as "vigorous" and "picturesque." They hold him valuable for his "vivid portrayal" of the frontier (1935, 320). Radisson's riotous spelling and grammatical transgressions aside, his prose foreshadows western tales that pull readers through largely on the strength of exuberant derringdo, with the garish colors of suspense promised on the covers of many a nineteenth-century dime novel about the West. The text here is a modernization by Loren Kallsen, done for Arthur T. Adams' edition. Kallsen's technique is to strike a balance between rendering ". . . Radisson's chaotic narrative palatable. . . " and preserving ". . . the essential flavor of the original" (Radisson 1961, xxix).*

*Nevertheless some explanation may prove helpful. When Radisson talks about large bodies of water, such as "the great sea," it can't be certain whether he has in mind Lake Michigan or the Gulf of Mexico; such was the mistiness of geography at the time. As to vocabulary, read "carriage" as "portage." "Castors" are beaver or beaver pelts. A fort refers to any structure made for protection, whether a building or logs and boulders hastily thrown together. "Gabions" are wicker baskets filled with earth and used in fortifications. Radisson and his Indian allies mourn the death of their parents, that is, their close companions, thought of in familial terms. The notes in brackets are those of Adams.*

### Selected Bibliography

Boatfield, Helen C., and Dobson, Eleanor Robinette. "Radisson, Pierre Esprit." *Dictionary of American Biography* 8 (1): 320–21. Ed. by Dumas Malone. New York: Scribner's, 1935.

Burpee, Lawrence J. *The Search for the Western Sea: The Story of the Exploration of North-Western America.* [1907]. 1:64–84, 212–23. New York: Macmillan, 1936.

Grey, Zane. *Riders of the Purple Sage.* New York: Harper and Row, 1912.

Radisson, Pierre Esprit. *The Explorations of Pierre Esprit Radisson.* [1885]. Ed. by Arthur T. Adams. Minneapolis: Ross and Haines, 1961.

Vestal, Stanley. *King of the Fur Traders: The Deeds and Deviltry of Pierre Esprit Radisson.* Boston: Houghton Mifflin, 1940.

PIERRE ESPRIT RADISSON

# The Basic Stuff of the West:
# Pierre Esprit Radisson (1651)

WE EMBARKED ourselves on the delightsomest lake of the world. I took notice of their cottages and of the journeys of our navigation because the country was so pleasant, so beautiful, and fruitful that it grieved me to see that the world could not discover such enticing countries to live in. This I say because the Europeans fight for a rock in the sea against one another, or for a sterile land and horrid country that the people sent here or there by the changement of the air engenders sickness and dies thereof. Contrariwise, these kingdoms are so delicious and under so temperate a climate, plentiful of all things, the earth bringing forth its fruit twice a year, the people live long and lusty and wise in their way.

What conquest would that be at little or no cost, what labyrinth of pleasure should millions of people have, instead that millions complain of misery and poverty? What should not men reap out of the love [of] God in converting the souls? Here is more to be gained to heaven than what is by differences of nothing; there should not be so many dangers committed under the pretense of religion. Why [are] so many thresors [rewards?] hid from us by our own faults, by our negligence, covetousness, and unbelief? It's true, I confess, that the access is difficult, but must say that we are like the coxscombs of Paris when first they begin to have wings, imagining that the larks will fall in their mouths roasted; but we ought [remember] that virtue is not acquired without labor and taking great pains.

We meet with several nations, all sedentary, amazed to see us, and were very civil. The further we journeyed the delightfuller the land was to us. I can say that [in] my lifetime I never saw a more incomparable country, for all I been in Italy; yet Italy comes short of it, as I think [of] when it was inhabited and now forsaken of the wildmen.

Being about the great sea, we conversed with people that dwelleth about the salt water, who told us that they saw some great white thing sometimes upon the water, and [which] came towards the shore, and men in the top of it, and made a noise like a company of swans, which made me believe that they were mistaken. I could not imagine what it should be, except the Spaniard; and the reason is that we found a barrel broken as they use in Spain. . . .

We runned to the height of the carriage. As we were agoing, they took their arms with all speed. In the way we found the bundle of castors that the enemy had left. By this means we found out that they were in a fright as we and that they came from the wars of the upper country, which we told the wildmen, [and] so encouraged them to gain the water-side to discover their forces, where we no sooner came but two [Iroquois] boats were landed, and charged their guns either to defend themselves or to set upon us. We prevented this affair by our diligence and shot at them with our bows and arrows, as with our guns. They, finding such an assault, immediately forsook the place. They would have gone into their boats, but we gave them not so much time. They throwed themselves into the river to gain the other side. This river was very narrow, so that it was very violent. We had killed and taken them all if two boats of theirs had not come to their succor, which made us gave over to follow them, and look to ourselves, for we knewed not the number of their men. Three of their men nevertheless were killed. The rest is on the other side of the river, where there was a fort which was made long before. There they retired themselves with all speed.

We pass our boats to augment our victory. Seeing that they were many in number, they did what they could to hinder our passage, but all in vain, for we made use of the bundle of castors that they left, which were to us instead of gabions, for we put them at the heads of our boats and by that means got around in spite of their noses. They killed one of our men as we landed. Their number was not [enough] to resist ours. They retired themselves into the fort and brought [in] the rest of their [equipage] in hopes to save it. In this they were far mistaken, for we furiously gave an assault, not sparing time to make us bucklers, and made use of nothing else but of castors tied together. So without any more ado we gathered together. The Iroquois spared not their powder, but made more noise than hurt. The darkness covered the earth, which was somewhat favorable for us, but to overcome them the sooner we filled a barrel full of gunpowder and, having stopped the hole of it well, tied it to the end of a long pole, being at the foot of the fort. Here we lost three of our men. Our machine did play with executions. I may well say that the enemy

never had seen the like. Moreover, I took three or four pounds of powder; this I put into a rind of a tree, then a fuse to have the time to throw
the rind, warning the wildmen as soon as the rind made his execution
that they should enter in and break the fort upside down, with the
hatchet and the sword in their hands. In the meantime the Iroquois did
sing, expecting death, or to their heels. At the noise of such a smoke and
noise that our machines made with the slaughter of many of them, seeing
themselves so betrayed, they let us go free into their fort that thereby they
might save themselves. But having environed the fort, we are mingled
pell-mell so that we could not know one another in that skirmish of
blows. There was such an noise that should terrify the stoutest men.

Now there falls a shower of rain and a terrible storm that to my
thinking there was something extraordinary: that the devil himself made
that storm to give those men leave to escape from our hands to destroy
another time more of these innocents. In that darkness everyone looked
about for shelter, not thinking of those braves that laid down half dead to
pursue them. It was a thing impossible; yet do believe that the enemy was
not far. As the storm was over, we came together making a noise, and I
am persuaded that many thought themselves prisoners that were at liberty. Some sang their fatal sang, albeit without any wounds, so that those
that had the confidence to come near the others were comforted by assuring them the victory and that the enemy was routed.

We presently make a great fire and with all haste make up the fort
again, for fear of any surprise. We searched for those that were missing.
Those that were dead and wounded were visited. We found eleven of our
enemy slained, and two only of ours, besides seven were wounded, who
in a short time passed all danger of life. While some were busy in tying
five of the enemy that could not escape, the others visited the wounds of
their companions, who for to show their courage sunged louder than
those that were well. The sleep that we took that night did not make our
heads giddy, although we had need of reposing. Many liked the occupation, for they filled their bellies with the flesh of their enemies. We
broiled some of it and [filled a] kettle full of the rest. We burned our
comrades, being their custom to reduce such into ashes [those] being
slained in battle. It is an honor to give them such a burial.

At the break of day we cooked what could accommodate us, and fling
the rest away. The greatest mark of our victory was that we had ten heads
and four prisoners, whom we embarked in hopes to bring them into our
country, and there to burn them at our own leisures for the more satisfaction of our wives. We left that place of massacre with horrid cries, for-

getting the death of our parents. We plagued those unfortunate. We plucked out their nails one after another. . . .

I arrived before him, the 26th of August, on the western coast of Hudson's Bay, and we met the 2nd of 7ber, at the entrance of the river called Kavivvakiona by the Indians, which signifies "let him that comes, go." Being entered into this river, our first care was to find a convenient place where to secure our vessels and to build us a house. We sailed up the river about 15 miles, and we stopped at a little canal, wherein we lay our vessels, finding the place convenient to reside at.

I left my brother-in-law busy about building a house, and the next day after our arrival I went up into the country to seek for Indians. To this purpose I went to a canoe with my nephew and another of my crew, being all 3 armed with firelocks and pistols, and in 8 days we went about 40 leagues up the river, and through woods, without meeting one Indian or seeing any sign where any had lately been. Finding several trees gnawed by beavers, we judged there was but few inhabitants in those parts. In our traveling we killed some deer.

But the 8th day after our departure, our canoe being drawn ashore and overturned near the waterside, reposing ourselves in a small island about evening, an Indian pursuing a deer espied our canoe. Thinking there were some of his own nation, he whistled to give notice of the beast, that passed by to the little island not far off from us. My nephew, having first spied the Indian, told me of it, not minding the deer. I presently went to the waterside and called the Indian, who was a good while before he spoke, and then said he understood me not, and presently run away into the woods. I was glad of meeting this Indian, and it gave me some hopes of seeing more ere long. We stood upon our guard all night.

Next morning I caused our canoe to be carried [to] the other side of the island, to have it in readiness to use in case of danger. I caused a fire to be made a 100 paces off.

In the morning we discovered nine canoes, at the point of the island, coming towards us, and being within hearing, I demanded who they were. They returned a friendly answer. I told them the cause of my coming into their country and who I was. One of the eldest of them, armed with his lance, bow and arrows, etc., rose up and took an arrow from his quiver, making a sign from east to west and from north to south, broke it in 2 pieces and flung it into the river, addressing himself to his companions, saying to this purpose: "Young men, be not afraid. The sun is favorable unto us. Our enemies shall fear us, for this is the man that we have wished for ever since the days of our fathers."

After which they all swimmed ashore unto me, and coming out of their canoes, I invited them unto my fire. My nephew and the other man that was with him came also within 10 paces of us without any fear, although they see the Indian well armed. I asked them who was their chief commander, speaking unto him unknownst to me. He bowed the head, and another told me it was he that I talked unto. Then I took him by the hand and, making him sit down, I spoke unto him according to the genius of the Indians, unto whom, if one will be esteemed, it is necessary to brag of one's valor, of one's strength and ableness to succor and protect them from their enemies. They must also be made believe that one is wholly for their interest and have a great complaisance for them, especially in making them presents; this amongst them is the greatest band of friendship.

I would at this first interview make myself known. The chief of these savages sitting by me, I said to him in his language: "I know all the earth. Your friends shall be my friends, and I am come hither to bring you arms to destroy your enemies. You nor your wife nor children shall not die of hunger, for I have brought merchandise. Be of good cheer. I will be thy son, and I have brought thee a father. He is yonder below, building a fort where I have 2 great ships. You must give me 2 or 3 of your canoes, that your people may go visit your father."

He made a long speech to thank me and to assure me that both himself and all his nation would venture their lives in my service. I gave them some tobacco and pipes, and seeing one of them used a piece of flat iron to cut his tobacco, I desired to see that piece of iron and flung it into the fire, whereat they all wondered, for at the same time I seemed to weep and, drying up my tears, I told them I was very much grieved to see my brethren so ill-provided of all things and told them they should want for nothing whilst I was with them, and I took my sword I had by my side and gave it unto him from whom I took the piece of iron; also I caused some bundles of little knives to be brought from my canoe, which I distributed amongst them. I made them smoke and gave them to eat, and whilst they were eating I set forth the presents I brought them, amongst the rest a fowling piece with some powder and shot for their chief commander. I told him, in presenting him with it, I took him for my father. He in like manner took me to be his son in covering me with his gown. I gave him my blanket, which I desired him to carry unto his wife as a token from me, intending she should be my mother. He thanked me, as also did the rest, to the number of 26, who in testimony of their gratitude cast their garments at my feet and went to their canoes and brought all the fur skins they had. After which ceremonies we parted. They promised before noon they would sent me 3 of their canoes, wherein they failed not. They put beavers in them.

We went towards the place where I left my brother-in-law. I arrived the 12th of 7ber, to the great satisfaction of all our people, having informed them [of] the happy success of my journey by meeting with the natives.

The very day I returned from this little journey, we were alarmed by the noise of some great guns. The Indians that came along with us heard them, and I told them that these guns were from some of our ships that were in the great river called Kawirinagaw 3 or 4 leagues' distance from that where we were settled. But being desirous to be satisfied what it should mean, I went in a canoe unto the mouth of our river, and seeing nothing, I supposed we were all mistaken, and I sent my nephew with another Frenchman of my crew back with the savages unto the Indians. But the same evening, they heard the guns so plain that there was no farther cause of doubt but that there was a ship. Upon which, they returned back to tell me of it.

Whereupon I presently went myself with 3 men to make the discovery. Having crossed over this great River Kawirinagaw, which signifies "the dangerous," on the 16th, in the morning, we discovered a tent upon an island. I sent one of my men privately to see what it was. He came back soon after and told me they were building a house and that there was a ship. Whereupon I approached as near as I could without being discovered, and set myself with my men as it were in ambush, to surprise some of those that were there and to make them prisoners to know what or who they might be. I was as wary as might be and spent the whole night very near the place where the house stood without seeing anybody stir or speak until about noon next day, and then I see they were English, and drawing nearer them the better to observe them, I returned to my canoe with my men.

We showed ourselves a cannon-shot off and stayed as if we had been savages that wondered to see anybody there building a house. It was not long before we were discovered, and they hallowed unto us, inviting us to go unto them, pronouncing some words in the Indian tongue, which they read in a book. But seeing we did not come unto them, they came unto us along the shore, and standing right opposite unto us, I spoke unto them in the Indian tongue and in French, but they understood me not. But at last, asking them in English who they were and what they intended to do there, they answered they were Englishmen come hither to trade for beaver. Afterwards I asked them who gave them permission and what commission they had for it. They told me they had no commission and that they were of New England. I told them I was settled in the country before them for the French company and that I had strength sufficient to hinder them from trading to my prejudice; that I had a fort 7 leagues off, but that the noise of their guns made me come to see them, thinking that it might be a French ship that I expected, which was to come to a river farther north than this where they were, that had put in there by some accident contrary to my direction; that I had 2 other ships lately arrived from Canada, commanded by myself and my brother, and therefore I advised them not to make any longer stay there and that they were best begone and take along with them on board what they had landed.

In speaking I caused my canoe to draw as near the shore as could be, that I might the better discern those I talked with. Finding it was young Guillam that commanded the ship, I was very glad of it, for I was intimately acquainted with him. As soon as he knew me, he invited me ashore. I came accordingly, and we embraced each other. He invited me on board his ship to treat me. I would not seem to have any distrust but, having precautioned myself, went along with him. I caused my 3 men to come out of my canoe and to stay ashore with 2 Englishmen whilst I went on board with the captain. I see on board a New England man that I knew very well. Before I entered the ship the captain caused English colors to be set up and, as soon as I came on board, some great guns to be fired. I told him it was not needful to shoot any more, fearing lest our men might be alarmed and might do him some mischief. He proposed that we might traffic together. I told him I would acquaint our other officers of it and that I would use my endeavor to get their consent that he should pass the winter where he was without receiving any prejudice, the season being too far past to be gone away. I told him he might continue to build his house without any need of fortifications, telling him I would secure him from any danger on the part of the Indians, over whom I had an absolute sway, and secure him from any surprise on my part. I would before our parting let him know with what number of men I would be attended when I came to visit him, giving him to understand that, if I came with more than what was agreed betwixt us, it would be a sure sign our officers would not consent unto the proposal of our trading together. I also advised him he should not fire any guns and that he should not suffer his men to go out of the island, fearing they might be met by the Frenchmen that I had in the woods, [so] that he might not blame me for any accident that might ensue if he did not follow my advice. I told him also the savages advised me my ship was arrived to the northwards, and promised that I would come visit him again in 15 days and would tell him farther, whereof he was very thankful and desired me to be mindful of him. After which, we separated very well satisfied with each other, he verily believing I had the strength I spoke of, and I resolving always to hold him in this opinion, desiring to have him be gone or, if he persisted to interrupt me in my trade, to wait some opportunity of seizing his ship, which was a lawful prize, having no commission from England nor France to trade. But I would not attempt anything rashly, for fear of missing my aim. Especially I would avoid spilling blood.

Being returned with my men on board my canoe, we fell down the river with what haste we could, but we were scarce gone three leagues from the island where the New England ship lay but that we discovered another ship under sail coming into the river. We got ashore to the southwards, and being gone out of the canoe to stay for ship that was sailing towards us, I caused a fire to be made. The ship being over against us, she came to anchor and sent not her boat ashore that night until next morning. We watched all night to observe what was done, and in the morning, seeing the long boat rowing towards us, I caused my 3 men, well armed, to stand at the entrance into the wood 20 paces from me, and I came alone to the waterside.

Mr. Bridgar, whom the [Hudson's Bay] Company sent [as] governor into that country, was in the boat, with 6 of the crew belonging unto the ship whereof Capt. Guillam was commander, who was father, as I understood afterwards, unto him that commanded the New England ship that I had discovered the day before. Seeing the shallop come towards me, I spoke a kind of jargon like that of the savages, which signified nothing, only to amuse those in the boat or to make them speak, the better to observe them and to see if there might be any that had frequented the Indians and that spoke their language. All were silent, and the boat coming around 10 or 12 paces from me, seeing one of the seamen leap in the water to come to shore, I showed him my weapons, forbidding him to stir, telling him that none in the boat should come ashore until I knew who they were. Observing by the make of the ship and the habit of the sailors that they were English, I spoke in their language, and I understood that the seamen that leaped in the water, which I hindered to proceed any farther, said aloud, "Governor, it is English they spoke unto you." Upon my continuing to ask who they were, who commanded the ship, and what they sought there, somebody answered, "What has anybody to do to inquire? We are English." Upon which I replied, "And I am French, and require you to be gone," and at the same instant making sign unto my men to appear, they showed themselves at the entrance of the wood. Those of the shallop, thinking in all likelihood we were more in number, were about to have answered me in mild terms and to tell me they were of London, that the ship belonged unto the Hudson Bay Company and was commanded by Capt. Guillam. I informed them also who I was, that they came too late, and that I had taken possession of those parts in the name and behalf of the King of France. There was several other things said, which is not needful here to relate, the English asserting they had right to come into those parts, and I saying the contrary.

But at last, Mr. Bridgar saying he desired to come ashore with 3 of his crew to embrace me, I told him that I should be very well satisfied. He came ashore and, after mutual salutations, he asked of me if this was not the River Kakiwakionay. I answered it was not and that it was farther to the southward; that this was called Kawirinagaw, or "the dangerous." He asked of me if it was not the river where Sir Thomas Button, that commanded an English ship, had formerly wintered. I told him it was and showed him the place, to the northwards.

Then he invited me to go aboard. My crew, being come up, dissuaded me, especially my nephew. Yet, taking 2 hostages, which I left ashore with my men, for I suspected Capt. Guillam, having declared himself my enemy at London, being of the faction of those which were the cause that I deserted the English interest, I went aboard, and I did well to use this precaution; otherwise Capt. Guillam would have stopped me, as I was since informed, but all things passed very well. We dined together. I discoursed of my establishment in the country; that I had good numbers of Frenchmen in the woods with the Indians; that I had 2 ships and expected another; that I was building a fort; to conclude, all that I said unto young Guillam, master of the New England ship, I said the same unto Mr. Bridgar, and more too. He took all for current, and it was well for me he was so credulous, for would he have been at the trouble I was of traveling 40 leagues through woods and brakes, and lie on the cold ground to make my discoveries, he would soon have perceived my weakness. I had reason to hide it and to do what I did. Moreover, not having men sufficient to resist with open force, it was necessary to use policy. It's true I had a great advantage in having the natives on my side, which was a great strength, and that indeed whereupon I most of all depended.

# CHAPTER 13

# The Self as Myth: Father Louis Hennepin (1675)

*Imaginations flourish on frontiers. Frontier regions, after all, present us with the unknown, and the unknown offers unlimited possibilities, the mother's milk of the creative mind.*

*Tall tales, bizarre humor, and marvelous stories are the result, and over the years these can work their way into literature. We chuckle over Mark Twain's "The Celebrated Jumping Frog of Calaveras County," a product of California's mining camps, and muse on the Duke and the Dauphin in Twain's* Huckleberry Finn. *The two itinerant con artists manage to keep just a few steps ahead of the law, with continual recreations of outlandish personalities. The two stories represent two poles. The frog story manipulates outer reality into an entertaining tale. In contrast, with the scheming Duke and Dauphin, the frontier is a stage on which two sociopathic liars create their own inner realities, their own identities.*

*Among the historical precursors of such types on the northwestern frontier, Father Louis Hennepin appears as one of the earliest. Appropriately the hard facts of his life blur at the edges—not even his birth and death dates are certain—while the manufactured image of himself appearing in Hennepin's writings is sharp and colorful, heroic and patently untrue. Further whetting the irony of Hennepin's story, he was a Catholic missionary, a frontier priest so dazzled by himself as he soared into his imagined life that he earned the spite of his fellow clerics and evokes the continuing amusement of modern scholars.*

*Louis Hennepin was born in Belgium and while still a youth entered the Recollect Order. Once a priest, he developed an itch to travel and spent 1675–81 in French Canada and the upper Mississippi region of the United States, most notably accompanying La Salle on some of his expeditions. Back in Europe Hennepin began turning his travels into books. Though they were widely translated and wildly popular, titillating Europeans' cravings for adventure tales, the problem was that in large part Hennepin wove his entertaining stories out of the stuff of bright lies and stolen material. These tales celebrated Hennepin and incautiously bad-mouthed such powerful men as La Salle.*

*As Bernard DeVoto (1952, 142) puts it: "Hennepin was a fascinating man: a devout Franciscan with Jansenist leanings who became a heretic, jovial, adventurous, intrepid, tireless, a sound geographer, a good observer, a braggart, a liar, and an indefatigable admirer of Louis Hennepin." The historian (1952, 143) continues: "So Hennepin took up the literary life, creating staggering and entirely fictitious achievements for himself and trying to pass off La Salle's explorations as his own."*

*Even in his own time, however, the happily wayward priest began paying for his literary frolics. His fantastic claims caused his credibility to sag among men who knew better. Shunned in France, a Hennepin desperate to continue his forays in America was forced to make the rounds of European courts in hopes of begging support for his plans. It's not clear how successful he was in this, but the upshot is that he probably never made it back to America. In any case the French king put out an order for the priest's arrest, should Hennepin again appear in Canada (Hennepin 1903, xli).*

*Some of the reasons for such ire can be seen in the selections below, which show Hennepin manufacturing his own bright self. An alternately vainglorious and fawning Hennepin pretends to have beaten La Salle in his discovery of the mouth of the Mississippi River. Claiming to destroy the myth of the Straits of Anian, an imagined sea connection between the Atlantic and Pacific, the hoodwinker is in turn hoodwinked as he swallows substitute Indian mythologies. He grossly paints himself as the woods-wise hero who saves the trembling explorer Duluth from threatening Indians, whereas the reverse was the truth. The passage ends with a typical flare of Hennepinian proportions, a remark on the correlation of his name with the Indian word for the sun. Throughout, the present editors have somewhat modernized the text of the 1698 English version of Hennepin's* A New Discovery of a Vast Country. *The notes in brackets have been added by the editors of this volume.*

## Selected Bibliography

DeVoto, Bernard. *The Course of Empire.* Boston: Houghton Mifflin, 1952.

Hennepin, Louis. *A New Discovery of a Vast Country in America.* [1698]. Ed. by Reuben Gold Thwaites. Vol. l. Chicago: A. C. McClurg, 1903.

FATHER LOUIS HENNEPIN

# The Self as Myth: Father Louis Hennepin
## (1675)

**The course of the Mississippi River from the mouth of the river of the Illinois to the sea; which the author did not think fit to publish in his *Louisiana*; with an account of the reasons he had to undertake that discovery.**

THERE IS NO MAN but remembers with pleasure the great dangers he had escaped; and I must confess that, when I call to mind the great difficulties I was under at the mouth of the river of the Illinois and the perils I was exposed to in the discovery of the course of the Mississippi, my joy and satisfaction cannot be expressed. I was as good as sure that M. la Salle would slander me and represent me to my superiors as a willful and obstinate man if I presumed to go down the Mississippi instead of going up to the north as I was desired and as we had agreed together; and therefore I was very loath to undertake it. But on the other hand, I was exposed to starvation and threatened by my two men that if I opposed their resolution of going down the river, they would leave me ashore during the night and carry away the canoe wherever they pleased; so that I thought it was reasonable to prefer my own preservation to the ambition of M. la Salle; and so I agreed to follow my men, who seeing me in that good disposition, promised that they would be faithful to me.

We shook hands to seal these promises; and after prayers embarked in our canoe the 8th of March 1680. The ice which came down from the north gave us a great deal of trouble; but we were so careful that our canoe received no hurt; and after six hours rowing, we came to a river [Missouri] of a tribe called Osages, who live toward the Messorites. That river comes from the westward and seems as big as the Mississippi; but the water is so muddy that it's almost impossible to drink of it.

The Issati, who inhabit toward the source of the Mississippi, make sometimes excursions as far as the place where I was then; and I understood afterwards from them, having learned their language, that this river of the Osages and Messorites is formed from several other rivers which spring from a mountain about twelve days' journey from its mouth. They told me further that from that mountain one might see the sea and now and then some great ships; that the banks of that river are inhabited by several tribes; and that they have abundance of wild bulls and beaver.

Though this river is very big, the Mississippi does not visibly swell by the accession of it; but its waters continue muddy to its mouth, albeit seven other rivers fall into it, which are near as big as the Mississippi and whose waters are extraordinary clear.

We lay every night on islands, at least if it were possible, for our greater security; and as soon as we had roasted or boiled our Indian corn, we were very careful to put out our fire; for in these countries they smell fire at two or three leagues distance, according to the wind. The savages take a particular notice of it, to discover where their enemies are and endeavor to surprise them.

The 9th we continued our voyage and, six leagues from the river of the Osages, discovered on the south side of the Mississippi a village, which we thought to be inhabited by the Tamaroa, who had pursued us, as I have related. Seeing nobody appear, we landed and went into their huts, wherein we found Indian corn, of which we took some bushels, leaving in lieu of it six knives and a small quantity of little glass beads. This was good luck for us; for we dared not leave the river and go hunting for fear of falling into the hands of the savages. . . .

Two days after, we saw a great number of savages near the riverside; and heard immediately after a certain noise, as of a drum; and as we came near the shore, the savages cried aloud "Sasacouest?"; that is to say, "Who goes there?", as I have been informed. We were unwilling to land; but they sent us a pirogue, or heavy wooden canoe, made of the trunk of a tree, which they make hollow with fire; and we discovered amongst them the three savages we had met two days before. We presented our calumet of peace, which they received; but gave us to understand by signs that we must go to the Akansa; for they repeated so often that word, pointing at the savages ashore, that I believe this is the right name of their tribe. We could not avoid it; and as soon as we were landed, the three Chikacha took our canoe upon their shoulders and carried it to the village. The savages received us very kindly and gave us a shelter for ourselves alone; and presented us with beans, Indian corn, and meat to eat.

We made them also some presents of our European commodities, which they admired. They put their fingers upon their mouths, especially when they saw our guns; and I think this way of expressing their surprise is common to all the savages of North America.

These savages are very different from those of the north, who are commonly sad, pensive, and severe; whereas these appeared jovial, civil, and free. Their youth are so modest that they dare not speak before old men, unless they are asked any question. I observed they have tame poultry, as hens, turkey cocks, and bustards, which are as tame as our geese. Their trees began to show their fruit, as peaches and the like, which must be a great deal bigger than ours. Our men liked very well the manner of these people; and if they had found any furs and skins to barter for their commodities, they would have left me amongst them; but I told them that our discovery was more important to them than their trade; and advised them to hide their commodities underground, which they might take again upon our return and exchange them with the savages of the north. They approved my advice and were sensible that they should prevent many dangers; for men are covetous in all countries.

The 18th we embarked again, after having been entertained with dancing and feasting; and carried away our commodities, though the savages were very loath to part with them; but having accepted our calumet of peace, they did not presume to stop us by force.

## A continuation of our voyage on the Mississippi River.

. . . The Mississippi divides itself into two channels and thereby forms a large island, which to our thinking was very long and might be about sixty leagues broad. The Koroa obliged us to follow the channel to the westward, though the Chikacha, who were in their pirogues, endeavored to persuade me to take the other. But as we had some suspicion of them, we refused to follow their advice, though I was afterwards convinced that they designed only to have the honor to bring us to several tribes on the other side of the river, whom we visited on our return.

We lost quickly the company of our savages; for the stream being very rapid in this place, they could not follow us in their pirogues, which are very heavy. We made that day near forty leagues and landed in the evening upon the island, where we pitched our shelter.

The 24th we continued our voyage; and about five and thirty leagues below the place we had lain we discovered two fishermen, who immediately ran away. We heard some time after a great cry and the noise of a drum; but as we suspected the Chikacha, we kept in the middle of the river, rowing as fast as we could. This was the tribe of the Quinipissa, as we understood since. We landed that night in a village belonging to the tribe of Tangibao, as we have been informed; but the inhabitants had been surprised by their enemies, for we found ten of them murdered in their huts; which obliged us to embark again and cross the river, where we landed and, having made a fire, roasted our Indian corn.

The 25th we left the place early in the morning; and after having rowed the better part of the day, came to a point where the Mississippi divides itself into three channels. We took the middle one, which is very broad and deep. The water began there to taste brackish, but four leagues lower it was as salt as the sea. We rowed about four leagues farther and discovered the sea, which obliged us to go ashore to the eastward of the river.

### An embassy sent to the Issati by the savages that inhabit to the west of them. Whence it appears that there is no such thing as the Straits of Anian; and that Japan is on the same continent as Louisiana.

Under the reign of the Emperor Charles V, the fathers Recluse of our order were the first that were sent by his command into New Mexico; since which time there have been of them [sic] beyond the Vermillion Sea. The most remarkable mention of the Straits of Anian commences from the time of that most excellent religious of our order, Martin de Valencia, who was the first bishop of the great city of Mexico. We have spoken of him elsewhere.

In process of time it was believed that the said straits were only imaginary. Many persons noted for great learning are of this opinion; and to evince the truth of it, I will here subjoin one evident proof to those which are already produced by them: and it is this. During my stay amongst the Issati and Nadoussians there arrived four savages to embassie to these people. They had come above five hundred leagues from the west and told us by the interpreters of the Issati that they were four moons upon the way, for so it is they call their months. They added that their country was to the west and that we lay to the east in respect of them; that they had marched the whole time without resting, except to sleep or kill game for their subsistence. They assured us there was no such thing as the Straits of Anian and that in their whole journey they had neither met with nor passed over any great lake, by which phrase they always mean the sea, nor any arm of it.

They further informed us that the tribe of the Assenipoulacs whose lake is down in the map and who lie northeast of the Issati was not above six or seven days journey from us; that none of the tribes within their knowledge who lie to the west and northwest of them had any great lake about their countries, which were very large but only rivers, which coming from the north, run across the countries of their neighboring tribes, which border on their confines on the side of the Great Lake, which in the language of the savages is the same as sea; that spirits and pygmies, or men of little stature, did inhabit there, as they had been informed by the people who lived farther up than themselves; and that all the tribes which lie beyond their country and those which are next to them do dwell in meadows and large fields, where are many wild bulls and beaver, which are grayer than those of the north and have their coats more inclining to black; with many other wild beasts, which yield very fine furs.

The four savages of the said embassy assured us further that there were very few forests in the countries through which they passed on their way hither; insomuch that now and then they were so put to it for fuel that they were forced to make fires of bulls' dung to boil their victuals with in earthen pots, which they make use of, as neither having nor knowing of any better.

All these circumstances which I have here inserted make it appear that there is no such thing as the Straits of Anian as we usually see them set down on maps. To assert the truth of what I say, I here frankly offer myself to return to these parts with such ships as His Britannick Majesty or their High and Mightinesses, the States General, shall think fit to send thither, in order to a full discovery; in which I have no other aim but the glory of God, the propagation of the Gospel, instruction of those blind and ignorant people who have been neglected for so many ages, improvement of trade, which, the better it is understood, the more will it daily increase between the subjects of the King of Spain, my Master, and those of His Britannick Majesty and States General. And lastly that correspondence and union so necessary to be maintained amongst them, that they may live and labor together for the common good. I declare I have no other design; that my intentions are sincere and upright, and that my desire is to be serviceable to all Europe; respect being first had, as I am in duty bound, to my natural Prince, the King of England, and the States; to whom I am singularly engaged for the good reception they were pleased to honor me with. Others perhaps would have used me ill, in return of all my services and the many dangerous voyages I have made, with no other design but to contribute what in me lay to the Glory of God, the salvation of souls, and the good of all Christendom. I know well what I say. But to return. Whatever efforts have been made for many years past by the English and Dutch, the two nations of the world, who are the greatest navigators, to find out a passage to China and Japan through the frozen sea, they have not as yet been able to effect it. But by the help of my discovery, and the assistance of God, I doubt not to let all Europe see that a passage may still be found thither, and that an easy one, too. For example, one may be transported into the Pacific Sea by rivers, which are large, and capable of carrying great vessels, and from thence it is easy to go to China and Japan, without crossing the Equinoctial Line. Those that read my relation and will never so little examine the maps which are annexed to it will soon acknowledge the truth of what I say.

### The Sieur du Luth is in a great consternation at the appearance of a fleet of the savages, who surprised us before we were got into the River Ouisconsin.

The Sieur du Luth had reason to believe that the three savages but now mentioned were really spies sent to observe our actions; for indeed they knew that we had taken away the beaver robes from before the Fall of St. Anthony. He could not forego his fears but told me we should serve the fellow that did it but right if we should force him to carry them back and leave them in the place where he found them. I foresaw discord would be our destruction and so made myself mediator of the peace once more. I appeased the friar by remonstrating that God who had preserved us hitherto in the greatest dangers would have a more peculiar care of us on the occasion because the man's action was good in itself.

Two days after, all our provisions being dressed and fit to keep, we prepared to depart. But the Sieur du Luth was mightily surprised when he perceived a fleet of a hundred and forty canoes carrying about a hundred and fifty men bearing down directly upon us. Our men's consternation was no less than the Sieur's. But when they saw me take out from amongst our equipment a calumet of peace, which the Issati had given us as a pledge of their friendship and protection, they took heart and told me they would act as I should direct.

I ordered two of them to embark with me in a canoe to meet the savages, but the Sieur desired me to take a third to row, that by standing in the middle of the canoe I might the better show the pipe of peace, which I carried in my hand, to appease the barbarians, whose language I understood indifferently well. The other four of our men I left with the Sieur du Luth and told them, in case any of the young warriors should land and come up to them, they should by no means discourse or be familiar with them; but that they should keep their posts with their arms ready fixed. Having given these orders, I went into my canoe, to the barbarians who were coming down the river in theirs.

Seeing no chief amongst them, I called out as loud as I could, "Ouasicoude! Ouasicoude!", repeating his name several times. At last I perceived him rowing up towards me. All this while none of his people had affronted us, which I looked upon as a good omen. I concealed my reed of peace, the better to let them see how much I relied upon their word. Soon after, we landed and entered the shelter where the Sieur du Luth was, who would have embraced their captain. Here we must observe that it is not the custom of the savages to embrace after the manner of the French. I told the Sieur du Luth that he need only present him with a piece of the best boiled meat that he had and that in case he ate it we were safe.

It happened according to our wish. All the rest of the captains of this little army came to visit us. It cost our folks nothing but a few pipes of Martinico tobacco, which these people are passionately fond of, though their own be stronger, more agreeable, and of a much better scent. Thus the barbarians were very civil to us, without ever mentioning the beaver robes. The chief Ouasicoude advised me to present some pieces of Martinico tobacco to the chief Aquipaguetin, who had adopted me for his son. This civility had strange effects upon the barbarians, who went off shouting and repeating the word "Louis," which, as we said, signifies the sun. So that I must say without vanity my name will be as it were immortal amongst these people, by reason of its matching so accidentally with that of the sun.

CHAPTER 14

# Retaking the Dream: Diego Vargas Zapata y Luján Ponce de León and the Reconquest of New Mexico (1695)

*Before the invention of the atomic bomb, the one American nightmare that could match terrifying thoughts of the Day of Doom or fears of a slave rebellion was the idea of an Indian uprising. If seismographs could have measured the force and intensity of nightmares become real, any seismographs in the New Mexico of August 1680 would have been knocked off their bases by the Pueblo Revolt that began on the tenth day of that month. Increasingly angered by seven decades of Spanish domination, and led by Popé (a Tewa religious leader from San Juan Pueblo), the Pueblos united and rose against the Spanish throughout New Mexico. In the rebellion's early stages, the Indians killed twenty-one missionaries and four hundred colonists, and by August 21 all of New Mexico's Spaniards were either dead or fleeing for their lives to El Paso. Over the next several years, authorities made a few halfhearted attempts at the reconquest of New Mexico, but the Indians successfully drove off their former masters.*

*Enter Vargas. Or more precisely, Diego Vargas Zapata y Luján Ponce de León, scion of a noble family famed in the annals of Spain. Vargas had arrived in Mexico in 1672 and successively received appointments as mayor in Teutila and Talpujagua. In 1688 the king gave him a five-year appointment as governor and captain general of New Mexico—a not-very-promising assignment, since the province was still under Indian control. And it might have stayed that way—in spite of Vargas's desire to reconquer it—if the viceroy had not received a report that an incredibly rich quicksilver mine was there for the taking in New Mexico. Desperate for more quicksilver for the other mines of New Spain (quicksilver, or mercury, was used to extract silver and gold from ore), the viceroy ordered Vargas to retake New Mexico.*

*And Vargas did just that; he did it, in fact, without firing a shot or killing anyone. How did he manage such a feat? As Vargas recounts the adventure, his superior intelligence, his nerves of steel, his understanding of his foes, his command of the troops—in short, his almost superhero nature—made it possible for him to maneuver almost all the pueblos into surrendering. Like any skilled novelist, he doesn't tell us all this; rather, he shows it by placing himself at the center of tales worthy of European literary paragons from Ulysses to El Cid. Similar paragons would be, in the American West, embodied in characters from Natty Bumppo to John Wayne and would play a central role in our metanarrative of the conquest of the West. Most of the West's best authors have, in one way or another, attacked the superhero myth; but it still lives in countless novels, movies, and TV shows.*

*What Vargas doesn't emphasize is that he brought to the Pueblos a full pardon for their earlier misdeeds. In his desperate desire for quicksilver, the viceroy willingly overlooked murder, rape, and robbery (just as he had earlier overlooked similar crimes when perpetrated against the Pueblos), if only his generous pardon would persuade the Indians to resubmit to Spanish rule, thereby making possible a search for the fabulous quicksilver mine. Add to the viceroy's leniency not only dissension among the Pueblos but also the effects of a drought that had been hitting hard at the agricultural base of their economy. Faced with hunger, squabbling among themselves, and attacked by Utes and Apaches, the Pueblos were ripe for an offer of help and protection from the Spaniards. Nevertheless we should credit Vargas with the courage it took to face down a foe that outnumbered his forces and had proven its ability to rout the Spaniards.*

*After the reconquest Vargas returned to El Paso and sent word of his success to the viceroy. Then, without waiting for settlers sent by the viceroy, Vargas raised his own band of recolonizers and led them to Santa Fe in 1693. Seeing several hundred hungry mouths to feed, the Pueblos weren't as receptive to Vargas as they had been only a year before and denied him and his party entrance into the villa of Santa Fe. The Spaniards won the ensuing conflict, killing many of the Tano defenders in battle, executing seventy men after the town was taken, and seizing the women and children to serve as slaves to the settlers. That victory sparked resistance among other Pueblos, however, and Vargas and his soldiers and Indian allies spent much of 1694 putting down uprisings throughout the province. Crop failures in 1695–96 forced the hungry Indians to attempt another rebellion, but Vargas crushed it, too. In his triumph, though, he returned Indian captives to their pueblos, angering his own colonists by denying them slave labor.*

*When Governor Cubero (Vargas's replacement) arrived in 1697, some of the resentful colonists filed charges against Vargas, accusing him of embezzlement, mismanagement, and bad judgment that had caused the Indian uprisings. Cubero put his predecessor behind bars, fined him 4,000 pesos, and confiscated his property. It took months for news of all this to reach Mexico City, but when it did, Vargas's release was ordered, and he left for Mexico in July 1700. Reappointed governor of New Mexico in 1703, Vargas returned in July of that year (Cubero had fled before his arrival). Back in charge Vargas soon had to lead a campaign against the Apaches, but he became ill and died near Bernalillo on 8 April 1704.*

*Numerous editions of Vargas's account have appeared over the years, and many others have told the story, too, including one of Vargas's famous contemporaries, Carlos de Sigüenza y Góngora, who added melodrama by inventing an emotionally charged dialogue. Here, for example, is Sigüenza y Góngora's version of Vargas's address to the Moqui:*

> The General made a halt and forced the Indians, who were most conspicuous in their impudence and insults, to come up to where he was, and he said to them: "Ah Indians, ah you dogs of the worst breed that the sun warms! Do you think that my tolerance is owing to fear of your numbers and arms? Pity is what I have had for you in not killing you, for by a single threat on my part, you would all perish!"

*Sigüenza y Góngora's twentieth-century editor, Irving Albert Leonard, rightly says in a footnote that "Vargas is much less rhetorical in describing this incident."*

*Vargas's exploits have been handed down in folk legend, too, for each year since the reconquest, New Mexicans have celebrated on the day of its anniversary. The notes in brackets have been added by the editors of this volume.*

## Selected Bibliography

Brandon, William. *Quivira: Europeans in the Vicinity of the Santa Fe Trail, 1540–1820.* Athens: Ohio University Press, 1990.

Espinosa, J. Manuel, ed. and trans. *First Expedition of Vargas into New Mexico, 1692.* Albuquerque: University of New Mexico Press, 1940.

Sigüenza y Góngora, Don Carlos de. *The Mercurio Volante of Don Carlos de Sigüenza y Góngora: An Account of the First Expedition of Don Diego de Vargas into New Mexico in 1692.* Trans. and ed. by Irving Albert Leónard. Los Angeles: The Quivira Society, 1932. Reprint. New York: Arno, 1967.

Thrapp, Dan L. *Encyclopedia of Frontier Biography.* 3 vols. Glendale, Cal.: Clark, 1988.

DIEGO VARGAS

# Retaking the Dream: Diego Vargas Zapata y Luján Ponce de León and the Reconquest of New Mexico (1695)

## Vargas Wins Back Santa Fe with Words

AFTER THE MILITARY INSTRUMENTS had been played, they [Indians holding the villa of Santa Fe] answered that they were ready to fight for five days and that they would kill us all, and that we would not escape as we did the first time, for all of us would be killed.

At that moment they commenced to shout furiously. This lasted well over an hour. At the same time I kept a close watch, with the interpreters, and it was seen that many warriors were covering up the openings in the intrenchments and fortifying them anew with many rocks, and large metate stones, and other objects with which to harm and kill our men whenever they should dare advance, should the height of the walls not be sufficient to resist them, for, in fact, this alone entailed great risk and danger to our lives because the walls were well intrenched and connected. They were confident that they would kill us. During the shouting and yelling some of their chiefs were conspicuous, uttering many impudent statements in their language which were translated and told to me by the interpreters, among them the sergeant of the company, and so I ordered him to tell them to calm themselves and to rest assured that I did not come to harm them in any way. They answered that I should not permit the horses to graze in their planted fields. I said that they were safe and would in no way be harmed; that I had already given orders to that effect which my people and soldiers were observing.

When the sun came out I advanced about twenty paces with the above-mentioned interpreter, my secretary of government and war, and the captain of the presidio, and I told them that I had been sent from Spain by his Majesty, the king, our master, to pardon them, and that they should become Christians as they had been, and not remain under the power of the devil, who had them deceived. To assure them that I spoke the truth, since they knew well the Virgin, our Lady, who was represented there on the banner, I ordered the royal alférez to show them the image of the Virgin, as testimony of the truth of that which I spoke to them and in order to convince and assure them of my good intentions. I myself took it in my hand, pointing it out to them and asking them if they did not see and recognize it as the Queen of Queens, our Lady, the Blessed Virgin. I showed them the coat of arms of our lord, the king, which was represented on the other side of the banner, so that they would know that he had sent me and that the soldiers had come under my command by his orders; that I was his governor and captain general and was also theirs; that they should not doubt my word, but instead realize that I was speaking the truth and felt sorry for them in their worship of the devil, who had them deceived, instead of God, our Lord; that they should realize that they were Christians like us.

They answered that if it were true that I was their new governor then I should take off my morion so that they could better see my visage. I asked my arms bearer to give me my hat, whereupon I took off my morion and advanced closer toward them so that they could see and easily recognize me, even removing the kerchief from my head. They told me that when the Spaniards formerly lived in this kingdom they offered peace to the Apaches and then hunted them down and killed them, and that I would treat them in like manner. To this I answered that the Apaches were not Christians, rather they were traitors who entered under the guise of peace in order the easier to rob and kill them, as they had done when the Spaniards lived in this land; that in fact the latter had come out from their houses to defend them and protect the lives of their women and children, and their clothing and horses, in order to prevent them from being carried off; and that, despite the vigilance of the Spaniards, in those pueblos where no military guard resided or was stationed the Apaches succeeded in killing them, robbing them, carrying off their produce, and taking their women and children as slaves.

In order to convince them of a certainty that I would grant them peace and pardon in the name of his Majesty, the king, our lord, I placed before them as witness the image of the Blessed Virgin, which I again pointed to on the royal banner. Again I held it in my hand, and, resting on my stirrups, I made the demonstrations necessary to win them from their incredulity. I took my rosary from my pocket and showed them a holy cross of Jerusalem which I have attached to it, and I said to them that I held up that holy cross and the Blessed Virgin, our Lady, who could be seen on the royal banner, as witnesses; that I would pardon them in the name of his Majesty, and that they should believe me and come down with extended hands; that likewise I had brought the three priests to absolve them from the grave sin which they had committed by abandoning our holy faith. They answered that they believed that what the governor and the fathers said was true, but that they also knew that they would be ordered to rebuild the churches and the houses of the Spaniards, that they would have to work hard, and that they would be whipped if they did not do as they were told, as had been done by the Spaniards formerly. They proceeded to name and designate certain set-tlers—Xavier, Quintana, Diego López—asking if they were among us. I answered in the negative, saying that I did not know whether or not they were still alive, but that they could rest assured and be certain that they would never again return to these parts. An Indian among them, very clever, whose name I later learned to be Antonio, and who has been given the nickname of Bolsa ["The Pouch"], standing over the great intrench-ment over the doorway, was speaking in the name of all his comrades. These, holding their weapons, which consisted of sturdy lances, bows and arrows, and large darts, also occupied different embrasures. They were very much on their guard, and at every movement made by the soldiers they became disturbed as though believing that they were about to be at-tacked.

At this time the squads which were stationed at the sides and corners saw that a large host was approaching, some on horseback and others afoot, from the surrounding pueblos. Without doubt they had planned to hurl themselves upon us from the rear upon my arrival. Some Indian, or perhaps some of those who may have been in the corn fields and fortified towers they have there, must have gone to notify the said pueblos, whose warriors, as I say, were advancing rapidly, afoot and on horseback, and with their weapons. Most of them carried lances with long shafts. From what I later asked them, it seems that they have an Indian blacksmith who makes them for them. I ordered the captain of the presidio to go out with a squad from the said place and, without venturing any great distance from it, meet the said troop and prevent it from passing. The other squad was ordered to advance in like manner from the other side. I remained, holding the said position, which was the location of the said force, with the soldiers of the third squad and the others who were distributed at different places. The captain carried out my order, as did the leader of the second squad. The said rebels, who were aware of all that was taking place, although resenting very much that the aid to them might be intercepted, were gladdened, and repeated from the intrenchments that the troops were now coming to their aid, and that we would soon see; to which I answered them that they would not join forces, and that it was indeed a pity that they did not believe in the goodness of my heart, and what I had told them to the effect that they had been deceived by the devil; that if I had wished to kill them I would not have said the alabado, but rather, upon my arrival, without making a sound or having aroused them with the alabado, I would have made certain of their death and would not have given them time to permit the warriors who are coming to their aid to find them alive and help them, as they may think; and that I have not ordered that they be killed because my only wish is that they become Christians, for I come to pardon them, as I have told them.

Rebellious, and paying no attention to my benign words, but on the contrary obstinate, they persisted in making themselves more secure in their fortifications, bringing anew many stones, painting themselves with vermilion, and making gestures and demonstrations anticipating the outbreak of war. Having observed that they had in front of the stronghold, near their doorway, many small reservoirs, and noticing that, being without water, they had conduits which led into the said stronghold, I, said governor and captain general, with regard to the above-mentioned, ordered four companions in my squad to go and cut off the water from the ditch which served the stronghold. They did accordingly, taking with them, in compliance with my order, native allies and tools to perform the task, which was accomplished successfully.

As a result, the besieged rebels were saddened and very much disturbed, saying that if we had come as messengers of peace, why was it that we took their water from them. To this I answered that as for me peace was assured them, and that in order that they acknowledge it, they should climb down from the intrenchments and come out and make peace, to which they persisted in repeating that the fathers should enter, and that they would then proceed to come out. The fathers all repeated their desire to enter. Father Fray Miguel Muñiz asked my permission to do so, for which I thanked him, and told him, "Father, it is not time for your Reverence and the other fathers to enter, for the rebels are treacherous and may perpetrate some cruel act upon your Reverences, at the same time taking your lives, and it is not licit for me to place you in such danger, nor to permit you to enter." Seeing that it was about eleven o'clock in the morning, and that they continued with their renewed demonstrations, some coming out, and others going in, I decided not to take any further risk nor to waste any more time, for in all justice I had on my part endeavored, as a Catholic and a loyal vassal of his Majesty, to persuade them, his vassals, humbly to render obedience and vassalage to him, as well as to our holy faith and his divine Majesty.

Finding myself with forty men in the plaza and at positions surrounding it, and others guarding the entrances, and, of the native allies, some fifty or sixty Indians being with me at the said place, for the rest were at the encampment guarding their horses and supplies, I told them, through the interpreters, that again it was my plea to them, in the name of his Majesty, that they accept the peace which I had offered them. I repeated that I was awaiting a favorable answer, and that I would carry out my promise without doing them any harm, pardoning all of them. Again I assured them of this by displaying as witness the said Blessed Virgin, our Lady, and the holy cross. In this manner I gave them a time limit of one hour in which to resolve and decide to render obedience and make peace, otherwise I would consume and destroy them in fire and blood without quarter; that thus did I make known to them my request and give them the said time limit of one hour; afterward let them not complain of their misfortune. They answered that I might do whatever I pleased, and they spoke in desperation, which is of record to the entire camp. Then I ordered the reverend fathers to come with me to the said encampment to take breakfast, and I commanded that during that hour the soldiers do likewise. Thus was it carried out, chocolate and biscuit being given to every one. I also ordered that a supply of powder and ball be distributed and taken, and likewise that the captain of artillery take down to the edge of the plaza the large stone mortar and the bronze piece, loaded properly.

At this time, the Indian Domingo came to me, said governor and captain general, and told me, very sadly, that he had already told his people that it was to their advantage to make peace; and, reminding them of the plight of the pueblo, he had told them not to be foolish but rather to believe me, for if they did not, I was tired of talking to them, and answering finally that, if they wished to be destroyed, neither he nor the people of his pueblo would be ruined; that I could see that they would not obey him, and that he had come out and taken leave of them to tell me that he could do nothing with them, as well as that which he has told me, and that there is nothing more that he can do.

To this, the rebels having returned to their intrenchments, occupying them by virtue of the security of seeing me in the said place and plaza speaking with their captain, I, said governor and captain general, with the interpreters, and calling up also the royal alférez and my secretary of government and war, and being near by and facing the said intrenchment and the doorway, again exhorted, persuaded, and pleaded with them in a loud voice, telling them that it was necessary that they answer me with a decision as to whether or not they wished to be Christians and to render the obedience and submission which they owed to our holy faith and the king, our lord, after which I ordered them to come down and render it to the divine and human Majesties; that I again guaranteed them pardon, and set up as witness, as I had already told them on numerous occasions, the Blessed Virgin, our Lady, whose image I displayed to them on the royal banner which I carried, and also the holy cross, which I displayed to them again; that, therefore, they now should give me an answer, one speaking for all of them, and not all together, so that I might decide at once whether or not to make peace or war.

To this they answered me that they would make peace, provided that I withdraw to my encampment with all the soldiers, removing also the said large harquebuses, and that I should return unarmed with the said soldiers; that under these conditions, disarmed, they would come out into the plaza to sue for peace. To which I answered that I was no longer afraid of them, nor was I fatigued as they were, enclosed and besieged, without water, and subject to the danger of my setting fire to the place and killing them all; that I could have done all this ever since I had arrived. At this time Domingo, the interpreters, and the reverend fathers again spoke to them from the plaza, below the intrenchments, and two Indians came out unarmed to make peace. I received them, extending my hands to them, and dismounting from my horse I embraced them. Meanwhile, the reverend father, Fray Francisco Corvera, entered the patio of the stronghold, the captain of the presidio behind him, followed by the reverend father, Fray Miguel Muñiz. They were peeping from their intrenchment; and the said Indians, although afraid, continued to come out to make peace, which I extended to all of them with great love, as I stood there dismounted, embracing them, shaking hands with them, and speaking to them with tender and loving words, in order to assure them of my good will and of the said peace. I told them to make this known to the rest, who had not come down, although some women, old and young, had done so.

After the plaza had been cleared, and after they had reentered their stronghold, the captain of the presidio came to ask me if the squads should permit the said people who had been halted, the ones recently seen on the said mesa, as recorded, to enter, to which I told the said captain to come with me, with the squad which had assisted me, also ordering my secretary of government and war to do likewise. Passing over to the said mesa, I found there a very large squad of warriors, some on foot and others mounted, residents of the villa, of those who had gone to the dance at the pueblo of Santa Clara; and the captain of the said pueblo was also there, with the greater part of his people, to all of whom I said as I approached close to them, "Praise be to the blessed sacrament!" Through the interpreters I told them of my coming, and of the peace as related above, and I embraced them and shook hands with them, for they had alighted from their horses and had set down their arms. I told them to order the people of their pueblo not to leave it, that they were safe in their houses, that as they were living in their pueblo they would remain, with their same governor and captains, if it was to their liking, and that all that was demanded by his Majesty, the king, our lord, who was theirs as well and the lord of all the land, was that they be Christians and not idolaters.

With this, they being satisfied, I took leave of them and returned to the said plaza, where I ordered the captain of the said rebels and stronghold to command that everybody hang crosses from their necks, and also set up a large cross in the middle of the patio of the said dwelling. Since it was already past four or five o'clock in the afternoon, I withdrew with the fathers to eat, leaving the soldiers distributed in the plaza and at the sides of the stronghold, and leaving orders to the effect that without fresh orders from me, they should not permit anyone to enter the place, because, reorganizing with their aid, which they might secure from the outside, they might make themselves strong by means of an ambush on the encampment, or on the horses, which we could fear might result in a misfortune; and, therefore, they should not be without suspicion because of the said peace, but rather with the watchfulness and vigilance which they should have as good soldiers and loyal vassals of his Majesty.

# CHAPTER 15

# Defending the Dream: The Diary of Juan Mateo Manje (1697)

*The Spanish Jesuit Father Eusebio Kino gained a secure niche in history by exploring much of northern Sonora and southern Arizona and by naming the Colorado River. Captain Juan Mateo Manje (or Mange) accompanied Kino and kept a diary on each of their journeys of exploration. In 1907 Herbert Eugene Bolton, twentieth-century historian of the Spanish borderlands, discovered some of Manje's manuscripts in the Archivo General de México; and in 1926 the Mexican Archives published Francisco Fernández del Castillo's edition in the original Spanish of the Manje manuscripts. An English translation by Harry J. Karns "and associates" appeared in 1954; and its publisher, Arizona Silhouettes, tried to convey the magnitude of Kino and Manje's explorations with these statistics (Manje 1954, vii–viii):*

> Between 1694 and 1701 Captain Manje accompanied Father Kino on nine major trips of discovery, which included 7,500 miles of unexplored trails—three times the distance from Los Angeles to New York. On the seven expeditions included in this account, they covered 4,675 miles in 200 days—an average of 23 miles per day—including time out for illnesses, baptisms, conversions and study of the resources of the country. It was not unusual to cover 45 miles in a single day.

*Of Kino's and Manje's lives before and after their great treks of discovery, we have what Bolton tells us in several works on Kino and what personal background Manje supplies in his first diary. His uncle, Manje (1954, 3) tells us, had left Spain in 1680, with letters requesting that he be given a royal appointment in the New World as a reward "for his services during the war against Portugal." In New Spain the viceroy first appointed the uncle governor of Mextitlán and then in 1683 "promoted" him to the position of "governor and captain general of the kingdom of New Mexico."* The Pueblo Indians of that kingdom had rebelled in 1680, killing or driving the Spaniards from all but the province of El Paso; and three years later they still threatened to destroy that last bastion of Spanish power in the region. Manje's uncle, General Domingo Jironza Petris de Crouzat, successfully defended El Paso and reasserted Spanish control over some of the nearby territory. Retired and reappointed, then again retired and reappointed, General Jironza eventually left New Mexico and became governor of Sonora in March of 1693.

Ten months earlier, his nephew, Juan Mateo Manje, had sailed from the port of Cádiz for the West Indies of New Spain. Making his way to Sonora, Manje asked his uncle for an appointment and received one as a soldier in the Compañía Volante *(Flying Column)*, a troop of fifty soldiers formed to fight the Apaches and other hostile Indians. When Father Kino and his missionary associate, Father Agustín de Campos, asked for a military escort to accompany them on explorations into Pimeria Alta (northern Sonora and southern Arizona), Governor Jironza assigned his nephew Manje to the expedition. Manje tells us almost nothing else about himself. We know only that he waited until 1716 to compile (and possibly transcribe and expand) his diaries.

In the selections that follow, Manje mentions a possible source of quicksilver (needed to separate the elements in refining gold and silver ores). Given his strong antipathy toward the Apaches, it's surprising that he expresses considerable admiration for other native peoples, such as the Yumas. He even repeats some native legends and myths. In defending Father Kino from harsh criticism that his efforts have been foolish and fruitless, Manje says such attacks distort the good priest's work much as a reflected image can be distorted by tricks with mirrors. Manje doesn't seem to realize that his own perceptions have been filtered through the lenses of his dreams, the same sort of dreams that had fueled Spanish conquest for over a century and a half and that still fuel much "progress" in the American West.

The notes in brackets have been added by the editors of this volume.

### Selected Bibliography

Bolton, Herbert Eugene. *Rim of Christendom: A Biography of Eusebio Francisco Kino.* New York: Macmillan, 1936. Reprint. New York: Russell, 1960.

———. *The Padre on Horseback.* San Francisco: Sonora, 1932. Reprint. Chicago: Loyola University Press, 1963.

Kino, Eusebio Francisco. *Kino's Historical Memoir of Pimeria Alta.* Ed. by
    Herbert Eugene Bolton. 2 vols. Cleveland: Clark, 1919.

Manje, Juan Mateo. *Unknown Arizona and Sonora, 1693–1721: From the
    Francisco Fernández del Castillo Version of* Luz de Tierra Incognita *by
    Captain Juan Mateo Manje.* Ed. and trans. by Harry J. Karns and associ-
    ates. Tucson: Arizona Silhouettes, 1954.

Powell, Lawrence Clark. *Southwest Classics: The Creative Literature of the Arid
    Lands; Essays on the Books and Their Writers.* Los Angeles: Ward Ritchie,
    1974.

FATHER EUSEBIO KINO

# Defending the Dream: The Diary of Juan Mateo Manje (1697)

## [Nov. 18, 1697]

WE CONTINUED to the west. After four leagues, we arrived at mid-day at
*Casas Grandes,* inside of which Father Kino said mass even though he had
traveled without eating until then. One of the houses was a large building
four stories high with the main room in the center, with walls two *varas*
of width made of strong *argamasa y barro* and so smooth inside that they
looked like brushed wood and so polished that they shone like Puebla
earthenware. The corners of the windows are square and very straight,
without sills or wooden frames. They must have been made in a mould.
The same may be said of the doors, although these are narrow, and by
this they are known to be the work of Indians. The walls are 36 paces in
length and 21 in width. Good architecture is apparent from the founda-
tions up, as shown by the design on the edge and surface.

At a distance of an *arcabuz* shot are seen 12 more houses partly caved
in. They have thick walls, and the roofs are burnt with the exception of
one lower room which is built with smooth round beams—apparently
cedar or juniper. On top of these are *otates* and over these a heavy coating
of *argamasa* and hard clay has been placed. The room has a high ceiling

of very interesting construction. All around there is evidence of many other ruins and high mounds for a stretch of two leagues.

There are many pieces of broken pottery, plates and *ollas* made of fine clay, painted in various colors similar to the pottery made at Guadalajara, a city of this New Spain. It is believed that this was a large city or town of political people with an established government. There is a main canal that flows from the river over the plain, encircling and leaving the town in the center. It is three leagues in circumference, 10 *varas* wide and four *varas* deep, where, perhaps, half of the water of the river was diverted to serve as a defensive moat as well as a reservoir to provide water to the suburbs and to irrigate its neighboring fields. The guides said that at a distance of a day's journey towards the north there are other buildings of the same character of construction, and also on the other side of the river there is another *arroyo* which unites with the one they call Verde.

All those buildings were built by people whose chief was called *el Siba*, which in their language means "The cruel and bitter man". Because of the bloody wars waged against them by the Apaches and 20 allied nations many were killed on both sides. Some of the Indians left, divided themselves and returned to the north, from whence they had come in previous years; but the majority went to the east and south. From all this information we judge it is likely they are the ancestors of the Mexican nation. This belief is corroborated by like constructions and ruins located at 34 degrees, and those in the vicinity of the Presidio of Janos at 29 degrees—also called Casas Grandes—and by many others, we were told about, which are seen towards 37 and 10 degrees to the north.

On the banks of the river at a league's distance from *Casas Grandes* we found a settlement *(al margen Tucsan)* where we counted 130 souls to whom we preached eternal salvation. The priest baptized nine children. They had fear of the soldiers and horses since they had not seen them until this time.

On the 19th, after mass, we continued to the west over arid plains. On all lands where these buildings are located there is no pasture. It seems that the land has a saline character. After having traveled four leagues, we arrived at a settlement called Tucsoni Moo, named thus on account of a great mound of wild sheep horns piled up, looking like a mountain. These animals are so plentiful that they are the people's common source of sustenance. This pile of horns is so high that it is higher than some of their houses. It appears as if there are more than 100,000 horns. The heathen Indians welcomed us profusely, sharing with the soldiers some of their supplies. We counted 200 courteous and peaceful people. We camped here for the night. Father Kino and I, through the interpreters, instructed them in the knowledge of God and the mysteries of the Holy Faith. They asked us to baptize 15 children and seven sick adults. . . .

While we were there [San Andres], a young Indian appeared all painted up with some red material that had the appearance of vermilion, or very fine red earth. Upon asking him where he had obtained this paint, he said that at five days journey to the northwest and the Colorado River there was a place where it could be found. He brought a ball of this color covered with chamois. It was very red, heavy and oily, and it oozed out of the chamois. It seemed to me, from what I have read in the Philosophy of Barúa on Metals, to be mercury or quicksilver.

*Alférez* Francisco de Acuña asked him many questions; and the young Indian said that upon breaking the red metal, which they bring to paint themselves with, it drops like thick white water. The color is like a lead bullet, when divided with a knife. On putting it in your hands it runs through your fingers, falling to the ground where it makes small holes. Upon taking enough of it to fill a hat it could not be lifted, it was so heavy. These are indications of quicksilver; and, if this be so, it would be of great service to His Majesty and useful to the mines of New Spain to discover such a treasure. There are in the world quicksilver mines only at Almadén in Spain, at Cuancabelica in Perú and at Carintia in Germany. When our mines stopped producing, it cost our Majesty a great deal of money to bring the metal from Carintia so that the gold and silver mines of the Indies would not have to shut down. The reason we did not go to look at these mines was that our horses were worn out, and there was not enough soldiers to resist the Apache enemies who live on the way. In order to discover it, we decided to return later with more provisions and soldiers.

However, in a short time several wars broke out against the Apache enemy, and Don Jacinto de Fuensaldaña succeeded to the command as Captain of the *Compañía Volante*. Many changes, battles and casualties occurred so everybody concerned maintained silence with regard to this discovery.

They also told us about some white people who, at certain times of the year, came from the Colorado River on horseback with saddles, *arcabuces* and swords. They never shoot their firearms. These we surmised were the *Moquinos*, who, in state of apostasy, had gone on the war path in 1680; but because they had no powder they could not shoot their firearms. We must add that this statement is somewhat contradictory as these men are white. It might be that they are Englishmen who lived towards the coast of the Gulf of California, or it might be that they are Spaniards who, long ago, may have been shipwrecked and who, by swimming or on rafts, succeeded in coming out to the mainland and now lived there. They too, having no powder for their firearms, could not shoot them. Also, they may have been able to break the wild horses which are said to be toward the north.

We talked to the Indians about our Holy Faith; and we baptized 12 children, I myself, acting as godfather for some of them. They were given staffs of justice as insignia of authority to establish their own government. . . .

## [Feb. 12, 1699]

On the 12th, after mass, we continued west over hills covered with pasture; and after five leagues, we came to a spring of crystal water which we named Santa Eulalia. Nearby we found a small settlement where we counted 60 persons, who took us to a big square *corral* with stone walls. Near this there was a smoked cave on a rocky hill.

We were told that a giant monster with the features of a woman, mouth of a pig and claws of an eagle had come from the north and made his home in this cave. (I do not know whether or not they are telling a fable.) This monster would fly around catching as many Indians as he could to eat. The Pima Indians began very carefully to gather large quantities of wood. One day the Indians invited the monster to this place and sacrificed for him two Indian prisoners they had caught from the enemies, with whom they were at war. When the monster was satiated, the Indians started a dance which lasted three days in the *corral*—built so that the monster would come in.

When the Indians who were dancing got tired and sleepy, others would take their place. When the monster became sleepy and went to his cave, the Indians followed him. When he was sound asleep, they closed the door of the cave with the wood they had gathered and set it on fire. The flames and smoke asphyxiated the monster, which died growling. Thus the Indians got rid of this terrible beast.

It is not new that in both North and South America are to be found bones and traces of giants. In the *pueblo* of Oposura, in this Province of Sonora, the Indians have a tradition that they killed another giant using the same strategy. Its bones have been found just recently. During the pacification of Mexico, General Don Fernando Cortés found bones of giants which he sent to Spain. At the promontory of Santa Elena, in the kingdom of Perú, there was once a large town of giants who were destroyed by the fire of Heaven which fell on them like that of the Sodomites, and many bones can be seen even now.

We continued to the west and after another five leagues, we slept near a well of water so deep that we had to water the horses by hand, or with gourds. . . .

I was carrying on this trip an ancient report of a previous trip of discovery made by Governor Don Juan de Oñate, in 1606. He went from New Mexico—after he had pacified that nation—to the sea of California; the Colorado River; and others; and several other nations which he enumerates, and which we have now found (I have already written about this in the first book).

We asked some of the oldest Indians whether they had heard anything from their ancestors about their having seen a Spanish captain with horses and soldiers. They answered that they had, and that this captain had talked with the old Indians, who were already dead, and that he had passed toward the sea with armed white men and that he had returned to the east of Asia from whence he had come.

The Indians added (without our suggesting such a thing) that when they were young a beautiful white woman dressed in white, gray and blue, covered with a veil from head to foot, had come to these lands. She spoke to them and shouted and chided them in an unknown language. She carried a cross. They said the nations of the Colorado River had shot her twice, leaving her for dead, and that returning to life she would fly away without their knowing where her home was. After a few days she would return and chide them again.

This same story had been told to us when we arrived five days previously at the settlement of San Marcelo. We did not believe it, but now that these Indians who live so far away from each other confirm this tale, we wonder whether she could have been the venerable María de Jesus Agreda. In the diary of her life, written about 1630, she had preached to the heathen Indians of North America and around New Mexico. Now, after 68 years, we received this information from very old men who were at least 80 years of age.

The only thing we do not understand is the fact that she could not make herself understood. God having performed the miracle of bringing her from Spain to these regions, he also could have endowed her with the gift to learn the dialect of the Indians so that she could make herself understood. Thus we are of the belief that she is the one and the same woman of the tradition above referred to, but so much time has elapsed it is very probable that the Indians, who were young, did not pay a great deal of attention to what they were being taught; or, on the other hand, the demon of confusion confounded them, obliterating from their minds what they had learned.

It could also be what we have noted among these tribes that when anyone talks to them in a different language they may understand they will use the phrase "we do not understand" to explain that it is not their dialect. My only purpose in making this observation is that, perhaps, at some later day further inquiries and investigations might be made in regard to the nations of the north.

We were also told that toward the north and along the coast there are to be seen white men—dressed—who come at times with arms as far as the Colorado River to trade and to barter cloth for *gamuzas* with the Indians. We were told the same thing some two years ago by the Indians of *Casas Grandes*. This has also been noted in ancient narratives and is a matter of tradition with others who sailed and discovered the Gulf of California.

We do not know whether these were Spaniards from the ships which, at the time of the first viceroys of Mexico, were sent to discover lands and tribes. The expedition never returned and is supposed to have been shipwrecked near the coast. The survivors, by swimming or on rafts, may have been able to reach the mainland.

Again, perhaps these could be Chinese or Japanese people (if there be any whites among them) or heretical foreigners married to Indian women; and who, by reason of such relationships, are allowed to trade without being molested. . . .

The science of reflected light consists of a curious art, which by the use of different kinds of mirrors—plain, convex, concave, cylindrical and of various other forms and degrees of gradation—depending upon the place and distance at which they are placed, gives a reflexion which seems supernatural to those ignorant of the art. It changes the faces of handsome people into ugly and deformed ones and changes human beings into four-footed animals and birds. On the other hand, it can give the appearance of women of rare beauty and angelical features the look of ferocious animals. With these lenses and with a small calf skin invisible to the naked eye, and by the aid of a candle and lenses, graduated in a lantern, it is possible to reflect large images and adorn a bare-walled room with rich paintings. Other lenses are made which are called magnifying-glasses, use of which makes very small seeds, like beans, mustard and other seeds take on the appearance of a variety of candies which are good to look at and which are inviting to the taste. In reality, they are nothing more or less than a quantity of useless seeds. I will not mention the armies that can be marshalled by the use of only one soldier which can be seen through a window of the lens.

Divergent reports were made, by those opposed to the saving of souls, against Father Eusebio Francisco Kino, the author who wrote of these trips, and the discoveries of new lands, rivers, valleys and tribes of docile and courteous Indians. He had given a detailed and accurate account of everything in order to stimulate interest among missionary priests to come and convert such a great flock, such a delight to our Lord, who shed His precious blood to redeem mankind. But those adverse to the proposition of the conversion of the Indians claimed that the land is unproductive, unhealthy, and that the Indians are incapable, differing very little from animals, and that it would be wasted time and money to do anything for them.

They claimed that Father Kino's devotion to the souls, with very little counsel and judgment, caused him to speak in hyperboles and superlatives in favor of the Pima and other nations, which have been discovered. From this small ant they say he has created an elephant and given great significance to little and useless things of no value, exaggerating and augmenting, like the mirrors, great things which could not be found in the Pimería where there was no use for missions.

There are also some other antagonists (I do not know if with good reason) like the above, who frustrated the arrival of the priests who were on their way but who would rather stay in some old mission, than come to the Pimería since they had heard so many false reports. Those spreading such false testimony will be called to account by the Supreme Judge, as they are the reason that the Pimería is not today a thriving, large and flourishing Christianity. To refute such pernicious opinions, rumors and reports, the Reverend Father Visitor Antonio Leal, of the missions and priests in the Province of Sonora, set out on the present trip, that I am describing, in company with Father Eusebio Francisco Kino and Francisco Gonzálvo, priests of the Pimería missions. I acted as Lieutenant Governor and Military Governor. There also were two soldiers, Antonio Ortíz and Diego Rodríguez, who were sent by orders of General Don Domingo Jirónza de Cruzat, Captain Governor of the *Compañía Volante* of Sonora, to make the trip and write a diary about it. After we traveled 40 leagues from the Real de San Juan Bautista, capital of Sonora, to the mission of Nuestra Señora de los Dolores, the first mission of the Pima nation, I joined with the priests on October 22, 1699. Having loaded 60 horses with viaticum and the ornaments and vestments necessary to celebrate the Holy Sacrifice of the Mass, we departed on October 24, after mass. We left the mission of Nuestra Señora de los Dolores, traveling north over plains and hills covered with pasture. After going eight leagues, we camped at the mission of Nuestra Señora de los Remedios which is under the jurisdiction of Father Eusebio Kino. The Indians engaged in the construction of the church, which when completed will be the best in all the Province of Sonora.

On the 29th, after having heard mass, we left this place and traveled north through a fertile land; and after going 10 leagues, we arrived at noon at the great settlement of San Javier del Bac, where the natives came out quite a distance on the road to meet us. There were 50 Indians, each one carrying a cross and chanting a song of the Christian doctrine that the fiscal Indian of the mission of Dolores had taught them before. With this show and demonstration of pleasure, they went ahead of us and gave us lodgings in the *adobe* and flat roofed houses with beams, which on another occasion they had built for us. Near this house the rest of the Indians and women of the town were formed in two rows as in the Christian towns. There were 400 men.

In a short time after we had arrived, the governor of a settlement located west, called Otcan, arrived with 270 heathen men together with their corresponding families to greet the Father Visitor. We exchanged compliments with them. Since it was early and a quiet and pleasant evening, the soldiers and I, accompanied by the Reverend Father Visitor, started afoot to a nearby hill where we could see in all directions a good portion of the extensive plains. There was no other hill besides this one. We went to the top and found all around a wall of stone with a plaque in the middle. In the center of this there was a white stone, like a sugar loaf of half a *vara* in height, imbedded in the ground. We guessed it might be some idol that the heathen Indians worshipped, so with great effort we pulled out the stone which was stuck in about one-third of the way, thereby exposing a large hole. At the time, we did not know what it could be. While we were coming down the hill, and before we arrived at the settlement, a great and furious hurricane developed. We could scarcely walk because of the terrific windstorm. None of the Indians had gone with us to the top of the hill; but when the furious wind arose they started to yell, saying in sort of rebellion, *"Vbiriqui cupioca,"* which meant that the House of the Wind (god) had been opened. All evening and all night the

# CHAPTER 16

# Embroidering the Dream: The Fabulous Tale of Mathieu Sagean (1701)

*What lay in the interior of the West? Was it possible to make an overland crossing through that vast terra incognita? And how vast was the West? Such questions intrigued eighteenth-century scientists almost as much as scientists of our day are fascinated by questions about the size of the universe and the composition of the atom. Then as now, whenever evidence was in short supply, theories abounded. And then as now, the competition between competing theories helped fuel further exploration—dreams compelling the search for reality.*

*Failing to find enough of reality, searchers sometimes succumb to the temptation to expand and embroider the few facts they have, until their tales are exposed through the close scrutiny of the skeptical. Often forgotten, however, are the modest nuggets of fact salted in such mountains of fabrication. Are any such nuggets to be found in the tales of Louis-Armand de Lom d'Arce Baron de La Hontan and Le Page du Pratz?*

*La Hontan arrived in the New World in 1683. Although his service as a French officer in the fight against the Iroquois in 1684 supplied him with enough material for dozens of fascinating stories, he most influenced the course of American history with what historians generally consider a fable. After La Hontan had returned to Europe, he published in 1703 a book said to be the best seventeenth-century work on New France:* Nouveaux Voyages de M. le Baron de Lahontan dans l'Amérique Septentrionale (New Voyages to North America). *In* Discovery of the Great West (1869; *later entitled* La Salle and the Great West, 1052), *the historian Francis Parkman delivered what remains the consensus about La Hontan and his book:*

La Hontan had seen much, and portions of his story have a substantial value; but his account of his pretended voyage up the
"Long River" is a sheer fabrication. His "Long River" corresponds in position with the St. Peter, but it corresponds in nothing else; and the populous nations whom he found on it—the
Eokoros, the Esanapes, and the Gnacsitares, no less than their
neighbors the Mozeemlek and the Tahuglauk—are as real as the
nations visited by Captain Gulliver.

*Bernard DeVoto agrees, and his treatment of another Frenchman's
tale—that of Le Page du Pratz—matches in its scornful and derisive dis-
missal the tenor of Parkman's assessment of La Hontan's account. Le Page
du Pratz claimed to have met, near Natchez, an old Yazoo Indian who said
that around the year 1700 he had first traveled to the Atlantic Coast and
then had reversed his direction, traversed the continent, and reached the
shores of the Pacific. The old man, named Moncacht-Apé, gave few details of
the journey, but he described the people he met near the Pacific, and some of
their characteristics seem similar to those of several Northwest Coast peoples.
Du Pratz included Moncacht-Apé's story in his Histoire de la Louisiane
(1758), and as DeVoto (1952, 66–68, 566–68) notes, "It got rid of the Western Sea, which would seem to have been the end in view, offering exploration
instead an equally convenient route to the Pacific, by way of the Great River
of the West." After carefully scrutinizing the geography of the tale, DeVoto
concludes, "The journey of Moncacht-Apé appears to have been invented in
the interest of a particular geographical theory and with maps of a particular
school on the inventor's desk."*

*DeVoto also informs us that an acquaintance of du Pratz, one Monsieur
Dumont, had scooped du Pratz by five years. Before writing his book, du
Pratz had told Moncacht-Apé's story to Dumont, who included an abbre-
viated version of it in his own Mémoires Historiques sur la Louisiane
(1753). What DeVoto doesn't mention is that Dumont's version seems more
credible and suggests that the tale-stretcher was du Pratz, not Moncacht-Apé.*

*In any case only eighteenth-century cartographers and imperialists hunt-
ing for a Northwest Passage would become excited by these tales, for although
they may be as fictional as Jonathan Swift's Gulliver's Travels, they lack
narrative and dramatic flair and seem almost untouched by fantasy. Fantasy
fairly reeks, however, in the account of Mathieu Sagean, an illiterate French
soldier who tantalized authorities in Brest in 1701 by telling them about his
"true adventures" in America. His long narrative was written down, and the
written copy convinced Minister Ponchartrain that an expedition should be*

sent to explore the wonderful kingdom that Sagean describes, the Kingdom of Acaaniba. Less credulous officials recognized just how tall Sagean's tale was, and no exploring party was sent to try to find his imaginary pathway. Sagean's description of Acaaniba was translated into English and published in London in 1755. It was later reprinted in New York in 1863 and again in 1866 in The Historical Magazine, the source of the following selection.

In La Salle and the Great West, Parkman summarizes Sagean's account of Acaaniba; but although the historian renders faithfully all the details, he has squeezed the imaginative juice out of the Frenchman's fantasy and gives us only the dry pulp. Readers of this anthology will notice an Elysian aura in the account of Acaaniba similar to that in Garci Rodríguez Ordóñez de Montalvo's sixteenth-century fantasy of an imaginary California (from which this volume's second selection was taken). The wonder is not that the myth was so powerful that it could seduce a high government official (after all, Spanish ships had returned to Europe loaded to the decks with Aztec and Incan gold). What's amazing is that for the past two centuries we have scorned the lie so much that our contempt has blinded us to the entertainment provided by Sagean's dream fabrication.

As for Sagean, he was sent to Louisiana, where, as Parkman (1983, 1054) puts it, "Sauvolle and Bienville, chiefs of the colony, were obstinate in their unbelief; and Sagean and his King Hagaren [of Acaaniba] lapsed alike into oblivion."

## Selected Bibliography

Davis, Andrew McFarland, ed. *The Journey of Moncacht-Apé.* Fairfield, Wa.: Ye Galleon Press, 1966.

DeVoto, Bernard. *The Course of Empire.* Boston: Houghton Mifflin, 1952.

"Matthew Sagean and His Adventures." *The Historical Magazine* 10(2) (March 1866): 65–71.

Parkman, Francis. *La Salle and the Great West.* 1869. In *France and England in North America.* Vol. 1. New York: Library of America, 1983.

MATHIEU SAGEAN

# Embroidering the Dream: The Fabulous Tale of Mathieu Sagean (1701)

## Extract of the Relation of the Adventures and Voyages of Matthew Sagean

THE SAID SAGEAN is the son of John Sagean, in the Regiment of Ohrignan Salieres, and Mary Carsaute; the father, a native of Bordeaux; and mother, of Rochelle: both Roman Catholics. They were married on the island of Montreal, about sixty leagues south-west of Quebec. Said Sagean was born in the village of Lachine; he is thirty-eight or forty years of age; can read a little, but not write.

About twenty years ago, he set out from Montreal in a bark canoe to follow the late Monsieur de la Sale in his discoveries. After some excursions of the Sieur de la Sale, he halted with his party in the country of the Illinois, an Indian nation on the banks of the Mississippi, which the Spaniards call El Rio de la Magdalena, where he built Fort St. Louis, on an island near the mainland, with which it communicates by a bridge, which is drawn into the fort. This fort was built by the aid of the Indians, and the Sieur de la Salle, leaving the command to the Sieur de Tonty, returned to Canada with nineteen men and the Recollect Father Francis, he left the rest of his people, to the number of 100 men, among whom was said Sagean.

Some time after said Sagean took a fancy to go on an exploration, and having obtained leave of said Sieur de Tonty, he took with him eleven other Frenchmen and two Mahegan Indians (also called Loups); they took three bark canoes to ascend the said river Mississippi, on which, having made about 150 leagues, they came to a fall which obliged them to make a portage of about six leagues, after which they embarked on the same river, which they ascended for forty leagues without meeting any nation, and having stopped about a month and a half to hunt and try some new discoveries, they found a river fourteen leagues off which ran south southwest, which made them think it emptied in the South Sea, its course being entirely different from those that go and discharge in the North Sea. They resolved to navigate it, and accordingly made the portage of that road, during which they met many lions, leopards and tigers, which did them no harm. They entered said river with their canoe, and after making about 150 leagues on it, they found the Acaaniba, a great nation, occupying at least 200 leagues of country where they have several towns defended by earthworks, and many villages with houses built of wood and bark. They have a king who calls himself a descendant of Montezuma, and who is generally dressed in human skins, which are common in that country—the people are also dressed in them. They are polished in their manners; they are idolaters, and have idols of frightful shape and enormous size which are in the king's palace: there are two, among others, one of which is the figure of a man armed with lances, arrows and quivers, holding one foot on the ground and the other in the air, with his hand on the figure of a horse, as if wishing to mount him. They say that this human statue is the representation of one of their kings, who was one of the greatest conquerors of that country; and this statue holds in its mouth, and as it were between its teeth, a precious stone of square form, and as large as a goose's egg, which shines and lights up at night like a fire: he believes it to be a carbuncle. The other of these idols is the statue of a woman who he believes was an empress or queen, mounted in a saddle on a figure of a horse or unicorn, having one horn in the centre of the forehead more than a fathom long, and around this horse or unicorn there are figures of four large dogs, and that of another unicorn, with also that of a man, who holds said unicorn chained. All the figures are of fine gold and massive, but very badly made and misshapen. They have no pedestal; they are placed on a kind of platform, which is also of gold, thirty feet square, for each of said statues, between which is a path leading to the King's apartment by a magnificent vestibule more than a hundred feet long, where there are lattices of caracoly. Here the King's guard is kept, consisting generally of two hundred men. At the four corners of this vestibule are four small open cabinets, with lattices of caracoly, where the King's music is kept, which is very poor compared to that of Europe. All the people of this State come once a month to render the same worship to these idols, having none at home.

The King's palace is of very great extent, and his private apartment is twenty-eight to thirty feet square, and three stories high, the walls, eighteen feet high, are of massive gold, in squares, laid one on another, and, like very large bricks, fastened together with clamps and bars of the same material; the floor of this apartment is also of very large massive gold bricks, made square. The rest of this magnificent apartment is of beams covered with wood. The King dwells here alone, and no one enters except his wives, whom he changes every night, and the one who has the honor of sleeping with him prepares his food in her apartment, brings it into his, and eats with him, without their having any to wait on them.

He promised (permitted) the French alone to enter the interior of his room, and was pleased to see them. These people carry on a great trade in gold. Sagean cannot say positively with what nation, unless it is the Japanese, as he believes, for they carry it very far in caravans, and he has often heard them say, in their way of counting, that there was six moons' journey from their country to that nation. He saw one of these caravans set out while he was among them, composed of more than 3,000 oxen, all loaded with gold on their backs. This caravan was escorted by a like number of horsemen, armed with lances and arrows, with a kind of dirk. They make their trade at the point of the lance, and the nation they deal with gives them in exchange iron, steel, and edged arms.

They have no writing like ours. The said Sagean says that they gave each of the leaders of the caravan a piece of bark dressed like paper, on which is set down the quantity of gold confided to him, for which he gives an account on their return, in the same manner that they engrave their extraordinary events and epochs on stones and metals. The King of the Anniba is called Hagaaren, which means in their language Great King. He is at war with no nation, yet he has nearly one hundred thousand men, cavalry and infantry, on foot; but three fourths of the cavalry are around the city where he resides. His troops have straight gold trumpets, which they blow very badly, and a kind of drums, or, rather, cymbals, also of gold, and like great gold kettles, covered with deer skin, on which they beat with sticks, and these cymbals are carried by oxen, on which a man mounts to beat them. Their tents are made of leather or ox skins, dressed like chamois, which they cover with bark of trees, flexible as cloth, to keep off the rain.

He does not know whether they observe any military discipline—he only knows that one day in the week they practice shooting at a target with their arrows. The King presides at this exercise, and rewards those who hit the mark either with some office or one of his wives. These men are of dark complexion, and their faces seem hideous, and much narrower than natural, because, when children, their mothers compress the head tightly, on both sides, between flat pieces of wood.

The women are as handsome and white as in Europe, and are mod-est. Their deformity, shared by the men, is the extraordinary size of the ears, which is a mark of beauty among them, and to enlarge and lengthen them they pierce the ears and load them with gold and bones of animals; they also wear their nails very long, and it is not only one of their points of beauty, but also a mark of distinction, and the higher a person is in dignity, the longer the nails are, and so on to the King, who in this sur-passes all others. They also let the hair grow on the face, stomach, and chest, and the most hairy are esteemed the most handsome. Polygamy prevails among them, and every man takes as many wives as he wishes.

They do not trouble them as to the conduct of the young men and women, provided they are not engaged in childhood by their father and mother by a promise for the future, which is quite common; but for girls thus promised, and married women, it is a matter of life and death, as well as for their paramours, if they go astray to the knowledge of their husband or betrothed.

These people like enjoyment, are great dancers, great eaters, and have no rule or order in their meals, but are sober in drinking. They make wine from roots and herbs. They are great smokers, and their tobacco is good and very common, growing without cultivation.

They received the French very well, and they were the first Europeans that they had seen; during the five months that they remained among them, they were always feasted, so that they lacked nothing useful or agreeable. Girls were even forbidden to refuse them anything under pain of death, and six were stabbed on the complaint of one named Francis, when drunk with palm wine, that they had refused him. The country is fruitful in Europe [the translator notes that this sentence is not intelli-gible in the French, either].

The King made every effort to retain them in his service. He even wished said Sagean one of his daughters, aged fourteen, in marriage, and on his departure told him that he would keep her for him, having made him promise to return; and as each Frenchman had a gun and ammuni-tion, fearing that the King or others of the nation might take a fancy to one, they made a great mystery of them, saying that they were familiar spirits who killed all who approached, except themselves, just as they killed birds and beasts at the command of the French. To make it more mysterious, they took care never to load before them, and they were left in wondrous amazement at the sight of the effect of said arms, and so great was their fear of them that they durst not approach, and showed no desire to do so.

This country is very temperate, being neither too warm nor too cold, and the natives live to extreme old age. During the stay of the French in that country they saw no one sick or die, except with decrepitude and old age.

The country abounds in all sorts of fruit, both European and Indian; apples, pears, peaches, figs, almonds, walnuts, chestnuts, mulberries, hazelnuts, gooseberries, strawberries, raspberries, melons of all kinds, courges, giraumons, potatoes, oranges, citrons, sweet and sour, very large olives, bananas, grapes, much larger and better than in Europe. They have also Indian corn, and wild rice as good and white as rice. They make bread of both, cultivating only the maize. Verdure reigns the whole year, and fruit is found all the year, and the woods and plains are the most beautiful that can be seen, and where affording the best pasturage, are full of all kinds of beasts and birds, particularly wild oxen, larger than those in Europe. They tame them, and use them to carry burdens and for caravans. There is an animal called pitiou, in fact, smaller than ordinary cattle; it is large and round, with short legs, and cloven hoof like an ox. It has no horns, and long pendant ears; the tail is like a sheep's, covered, not with hair, but with a very fine black wool, curly like a negro's hair. The women spin it very neatly, and make it into pagnes and blankets. Its flesh is delicious, and resembles mutton. The rivers are very well stocked with fish, and the woods full of India fowl, wild pigeons, turtledoves, partridge, common and painted hens, ducks, swans, all of extraordinary size, which they take in a kind of net. There are also many parrots, strangely formed animals, and monkeys.

These nations live in wonderful concord and harmony, although they have no form of justice but what they make for themselves. Yet there is a kind of pillory where the luckless maltraitteurs are exposed.

The capital of the Acaanibas, where the king resides, is about six leagues from the river, which is called Milly, in the language of the country; it signifies gold river, or river from the north-west.

The French obtained the King's leave to depart only on the promise, which he exacted of them by the heavens, which is their ordinary oath, that they would return at the end of thirty-six months and bring coral, wampum, beads, and others from Canada, trifles exchanged with that nation for gold, which they have so abundantly, and esteem so lightly, that the King gave them liberty to take what they pleased; they accordingly loaded themselves with it, and each took sixty bars, about a palm long, and weighing four pounds. The two Indians who were with them would not take any, and wondered to see our Frenchmen burden themselves with it. They told them that it was to make kettles, which they believed, the kettles of the Acaaniba, as well as all their dishes and cooking utensils, being of that precious metal.

The said Sagean says that he did not see the mines which gave this prodigious quantity of gold, but he says that they could not be far from the town, as two of his comrades, with one of that nation, took only three days to go and return; that his comrades, who died subsequently, told him that this gold was in crevices of several mountains and hills; that in the inundations, which are frequent in those parts, the waters separate the gold and carry it down, and when the dry season comes great heaps are found in the former bed of the rivers, which remain dry four months of the year, and here the people gather it.

Sagean assures, on his life, that if they will send him to the Mississippi, no matter at what point on the river, he will easily find the road, and conduct any one to the Acaanibas, with canoes which he will build himself, provided there are tools, and men with arms and ammunition to hunt, and that they will be well received by these people on giving them presents of the things already mentioned, being what they most esteem. The King, having taken leave of them, gave them also more than two hundred horsemen, more to honor than to protect them, there being no risk among a people who loved them to adoration. The horsemen, besides a quantity of all kinds of provisions, carried their gold even to their canoes, which followed, coasting the shore of the river, for five days, after which they bade them farewell with frightful howls.

And the sequel of this relation contains the extraordinary adventures of said Sagean, and the massacre of almost all who accompanied him on the river St. Lawrence, near its mouth, where they were taken by an English pirate, his imprisonment, and of some of his comrades who remained, and of the last voyages in which he found himself engaged, to the West and East Indies, and to China, and his return to Brest, where necessity drove him to enlist as a marine. He has here given this relation, having been unwilling to disclose his secret either to the Dutch or English, among whom he was employed during the long stay he was obliged to make with them. This is confirmed by his replies to the interrogatories made by Monsieur Dechoureux.

He adds that on this river of the Acaaniba, which they call Milly, which means River, he saw much gold dust on the banks, and gives positive assurance of the fact.

# CHAPTER 17

# How Miracles Prove Dreams: Fray Francisco de Céliz's Account of the Alarcón Expedition to Texas (1718)

*By the mideighteenth century, Spanish archives contained enough reports from New World cities and missions that entire diaries could be misplaced. One such "lost" diary resurfaced in 1933, was translated into English by Fritz Leo Hoffmann, and was published in Los Angeles by the Quivira Society in 1935. Written by Fray Francisco de Céliz, it tells the story of Don Martín de Alarcón's Texas expedition of 1718. Spain sent the Alarcón expedition, as Hoffmann (Céliz 1935, 3) explains in his introduction, for the same three reasons that impelled the Spanish to explore other parts of North America: "(1) the search for gold and [other sources of wealth]; (2) the conversion of the natives. . .; and (3) the fear of foreign encroachment on lands already claimed but not yet occupied by Spain."*

*The more immediate cause of the Alarcón expedition occurred on 18 July 1714: the arrival of a Frenchman, Louis Juchereau de St. Denis, at the Spanish presidio of San Juan Bautista on the Rio Grande. Earlier reports of La Salle's ill-fated Texas colony (1689) and of the French settlement at Mobile (1710) had prompted Spanish activity in Texas, but not enough to satisfy Francisco Hidalgo, a zealous missionary who (according to Hoffmann) decided to trick his Spanish superiors into sending more support to Texas. Hidalgo asked the French governor of Louisiana, La Mothe Cadillac, for help in converting the natives of Texas; and Cadillac responded by sending St. Denis to the Rio Grande. When authorities in Mexico heard about St. Denis, they ordered more Spanish settlement in Texas, leading by the end of 1717 to a total of six missions and a presidio. To strengthen these Texas outposts, the viceroy ordered Alarcón to establish a new mission at what is now San Anto-nio and to explore the territory to determine the extent and strength of the French presence.*

*Although Alarcón's expedition took place during much of the period from April until January of 1718 and covered hundreds of miles from near Eagle Pass, Texas, to near Natchitoches, Louisiana, Céliz's diary is relatively brief. The good father obviously enjoyed the beauty of the countryside, and much of his diary describes groves of oak, pecan, plum, and other trees. Some of these groves must have been impressive, indeed, for at one point the expedition halted before a flooded river and set about building a dugout canoe from a log that measured three brazas (eighteen feet) in circumference. Apart from such references to the local flora, most of the remainder of the diary consists of pedestrian bureaucratic reporting: how many leagues traveled, how many natives baptized, what goods distributed to the new converts, etc.*

*In the brief selections that follow, however, Céliz tells more entertaining tales. A few days after experiencing the frightening explosions of a Texas thunderstorm, the expedition had to cross a river swollen by the previous days' downpour. The intrepid Alarcón spurred his horse into the flood—and almost drowned when the horse was swept downriver. To understand why Céliz regarded as a near "miracle" the rescue of Governor Alarcón from the rushing river, modern readers must know that the governor's pants came un-buttoned, but since his pant legs were tied at the knees, the raging water could pull the pants only as far down as his ankles, "thus forming a sort of ball and chain on his feet" (and all of that on someone who didn't know how to swim). After Céliz describes another near miracle (the governor's long nap on a snake that doesn't budge), we can see that New England Puritans weren't the only New World settlers who persisted in seeing miracles all around them. What better validation of one's dreams than such miracles?*

*Nothing miraculous happened when the party later recrossed the river (although Céliz says that the governor's silver table service was lost when a raft sank—apparently Don Martín traveled in fine style). Nor did any mir-acles occur when the natives welcomed Alarcón. But Céliz's account of one reception reveals what a good time was had by all, even Europeans inclined to look down their noses at "savage" doings. Note, too, that the Indians, sup-plied by the French, had more firearms than their Spanish visitors. Given such odds, it seems a miracle that Céliz and Alarcón survived an expedition among savages—unless the natives weren't always so savage as one-half of the European stereotype of them had it. (Survive they did, although Hoff-mann gives no information about Céliz and says that Alarcón's subsequent career remains largely a "mystery.") Had the natives not been so friendly and had European diseases not decimated so many of them, the survival of European colonists might seem even more miraculous. Such as it was, the "miracle" of their survival still serves as validation for the New World dreams of those who think they own the land.*

*The notes in brackets are Hoffmann's; the notes in braces have been added by the editors of this volume.*

### Selected Bibliography

Céliz, Francisco. *Diary of the Alarcón Expedition into Texas, 1718–1719.* Trans. by Fritz Leo Hoffmann. Los Angeles: Quivira Society, 1935.

FRANCISCO DE CÉLIZ

# How Miracles Prove Dreams: Fray Francisco de Céliz's Account of the Alarcón Expedition to Texas (1718)

### The Miracle of the Savin Branches

ON THE 13TH {of May}, after having left this place, at about noon we reached the ford of the San Marcos river, and until now we could not believe that it was the San Marcos, because everyone says that the San Marcos river enters the sea several leagues distant from the Guadalupe. The crossing is about eight to nine leagues from the above-named place. The ford is wide and good, and at the entrance there is a thick wood of the same kind of trees that are downstream. This day we traveled in search of the Guadalupe river over the same road that leads to Texas and went about four leagues, so that in all this day we covered thirteen. We stopped because a cloudburst caught us, which lasted unceasingly all night; and here as well as in San Antonio the thunderstorms are so frightful that all those who have experienced them in Spain, as well as in these parts, say that they have not seen any like them, for the shortest last six hours, with thunder pealing like harquebus-shots in battle. . . .

On the 16th {of May}, we crossed the river with great difficulty; but first it is necessary for us to consider the things which occurred the day before. It so happened that after we had seen the swollen river and had investigated to see if it could be crossed or gone around, and had found no recourse whatsoever, the melancholy and sadness that fell upon the governor was so great that in his heart he felt no less than that the last days of his life had arrived; and thus, observing the obligations of a Catholic in such danger, he wanted to prepare himself, calling his secretary and dictating to him some things that had to be done if God should take him upon crossing this river. It so happened that, twenty-four buzzards having come to tarry close to where we were stopping, the governor asked the father chaplain, "Father, what are those birds looking for?" To which the father replied, "They may have come to make happy over the funeral rites of somebody present," at which the anguish was even greater, even before entering the water. He began, therefore, to cross with great difficulty, and the greatest fatality would have befallen us that can be imagined had not God and the most holy Virgin extended the arms of their omnipotence and mercy to protect and favor the governor against the extremely dangerous situation in which he found himself. He, having started to cross on the strongest horse that could be found, carried on the haunches the sergeant of the company. Upon arriving at the opposite bank, after having crossed most of the river, he reined the horse back, and, the current catching its haunches, it was swept downstream with both riders submerged and grasping the horse, for about half the distance of a musket-shot. At this place they came up still holding on to the horse, and, going down again, they lost their grasp on the horse, and the water carried them submerged for more than another half the distance of a musket-shot where they again arose. The anxiety they experienced may well be imagined, especially since the governor, who was dressed, did not know how to swim. And, although the said sergeant knew how to swim well, this would not have enabled him to rescue himself, because of the great force of the water, if here God had not performed a miracle through the intercession of His most pure Mother who provided them with two savin branches to which they held on, and from there, because of the great depth, they were rescued by ropes. After this miraculous occurrence, I have asked the governor several times about the case, and he has always assured me that he does not know how he went [down the stream], whether under the water or over the water. The truth is that those who saw him say that he went downstream motionless, all of which proves that it was entirely a miracle, because the rescue could not have been attributed to natural causes, especially when the horse with the saddle nevermore turned up and the governor lost the buttons off his pants, thus forming a sort of ball and chain on his feet. [For all of this] we thank unceasingly only God and His most holy Mother, and, moreover, we invoke their favor in the furtherance of this expedition and [place the] conquest under their charge. Furthermore, although [the governor] carried in his pocket a small silver box with the rosary and the prayer book in which the most holy Virgin is praised, they not only did not fall into the water when his pants came down, but the prayer book did not even get wet. This same day we traveled about six leagues to a high hill where we stopped. . . .

On the 22d {of September}, we continued our journey in the direction of southeast, and at about seven leagues we stopped to rest. Soon thereafter we proceeded in the same direction until we ran into a large inlet which we were obliged to circle, because it was very wide and deep, and, it seems, navigable. We traveled four leagues to the south, the west, and in the direction of the north along a creek that contains some water, having gone this day twelve leagues. It happened that on this day, from noon until the evening prayers, the governor lay on a large snake at this place, without the reptile having moved, in spite of its known ferocity. This occurrence was taken to be almost a miracle. . . .

The Indians of the tribes which had assembled spent the 16th and 17th {of October} in building the house, which they did in accordance with their custom, of timber, in a pyramidal form, covered with grass, and this day, in the afternoon, they called together all the chiefs in order to make his reception more solemn. They celebrated it that night in the following order: the Indians having dressed in gala form with their hides, and all the people—men, women, and children—having assembled, a great bonfire was [kindled] in the patio of the house, in front of which they put a small wooden bench and skins of bison for carpets. After the principal Indians and chiefs had entered the house, they took the governor by his arms and with great care placed on his head some feathers from the breasts of white ducks and on his forehead a strip of black cloth which fell to his cheeks. Then they placed him on the skins, a leading Indian who was seated on the small bench and who was holding him by the shoulders, serving him as a thing to lean on. At this time the drum or kettledrum (which they make of a large water-jug, covered with a stretched and dampened skin) commenced to resound, accompanied by the timbrels and singing of the whole multitude. The people, arranged in order, sang while being seated in their manner, the men being uniformly separated from the women and children, who, without disagreeing one point in their voices, made a gentle, although coarse harmony. Four bonfires were made by the Indians, which make a remarkable light, and the Indian superintendents carried in their hands torches of burning reeds and walked about very carefully in order to keep all the Indians in order. From time to time a leading Indian of the proctors who are in the settlement interrupted the singing, and standing before the governor, he began his discourse, telling [him] of the great pleasure with which they received him into their lands and all the Spaniards and fathers whom they already had, and that thenceforward their friendship and relations would be closer, and that since he had permitted to let himself be received according to their custom, they no longer looked upon him as a stranger but as if born among them. [They said that] they received him as their chief, and in consequence of this they would help him and his people in anything that might present itself, and that they were asking him to do the same, defending them with the Spaniards against the enemies who were harassing them. [In answer] to this, his Lordship, by means of an interpreter, promised to perform for them all the good services that he could, and that this courtesy was showing it and had shown it in the name and person of his king and lord, to whom, he declared, they should be always grateful and submissive because of the great deal that he had spent and was spending in loving them. The discourses having ended, the singing and shouting continued very gaily and joyfully, all the Indians saying in their language that they would do as they were told and took it as very good and acceptable. The other proctors were doing the same thing in the name of all the nations, those whom each nation had in the presence of the governor exchanging places so that all would have a part in the ceremony. This function lasted until three in the morning, thus giving all those at the assembly an opportunity to catch a little rest.

Tuesday, the 18th, all the chiefs of the settlements of La Concepción de Agreda and San Joseph de Ayamonte assembled, and by means of their spokesman, renewed the agreements of their recognition with the governor, who repeated his mission in the name of his Majesty; and after they had spent a long time with their discourses, alternating their pipe of peace with the conversation, the governor gave them tobacco and a goodly portion of clothing of all colors, which they were to distribute among themselves. This the spokesman adjusted with due promptness, leaving the chiefs of both nations and other chiefs who happened to be present from the tribe of the Caudachos very contented. The latter pointed out that they desired to receive the Spaniards in their villages. This day all the Indians came in marching order, firing their muskets with such precision that it seemed that they had been well disciplined in the militia; and as was noticed by all, the governor was received with shots from more muskets than the said governor had on his side, because a great number of them had been introduced among the Indians in the neighborhood of the French, who gave them to the Indians in exchange for horses and skins.

# CHAPTER 18

# Chasing a Nightmare into the Dream: The Valverde Campaign (1719)

*With memories of New Mexico's Pueblo uprising of 1680 still strong, the Spaniards faced the dawn of the eighteenth century with fears of new menaces: the French were rumored to be encroaching on Spanish territory from the east; and Utes and Comanches were riding down from the north to attack not only the Indians under Spanish domination but also Spanish settlers. To meet the Ute-Comanche threat, provincial governors sent troops out of New Mexico to chase the enemy into hitherto unexplored territory. In 1719 Governor Antonio Valverde y Cosio received orders from the viceroy to send another punitive expedition after the Utes and Comanches.*

*Convening a council of war in Santa Fe, Valverde enlisted a force of about forty soldiers, five or six private citizens, and sixty Indian allies. The expedition started north on September fifteenth, crossed into what is now Colorado after some days of travel, and eventually reached a place near present-day Las Animas. They saw signs that their enemies had preceded them, but the Utes and Comanches always kept far enough ahead that they were never spotted. Frustrated by their failure to catch up with the enemy and fearful that winter would soon arrive—possibly stranding them over two hundred leagues from Santa Fe and then freezing and starving them— the Spanish forces headed back to New Mexico.*

*By then rumors had raised the specter of a French force of six thousand outside Taos. Rumor also insisted that the French had been busy arming hostile Indians against the Spanish. Modern historians such as Bernard DeVoto say the rumors were not true, but such false reports fueled Spanish fears that their frontiers were dangerously vulnerable.*

*Worried about the rumored French troops and about the Utes and Com-*

*anches, the viceroy sent Valverde new orders to travel north again to find and punish the enemy. The governor complied—sort of. Instead of leading the expedition himself, he stayed in Santa Fe and gave the command to Don Pedro de Villasur. One hundred strong, the Villasur force traveled north farther than any of the earlier expeditions, probably to somewhere in the vicinity of the present Kansas-Nebraska border. Wherever the location of their last camp, there most of them were massacred by Pawnees in August of 1720. Some Spanish soldiers escaped, but, ironically, it was a French force that came upon the bodies of Villasur and his slain comrades and preserved the record of his ill-fated expedition.*

*Survivors straggled back to Santa Fe, and their reports of the massacre gave one of Valverde's enemies, former governor Félix Martínez, the grounds to charge Valverde with cowardice, incompetence, and bad judgment. Formal proceedings against Valverde dragged on into 1726, when, on July fifth, General Pedro de Rivera questioned Valverde about the charges. The governor's answers survive in a report of the hearing, translated in the twentieth century by Alfred Barnaby Thomas and published in his collection* After Coronado: Spanish Exploration Northeast of New Mexico, 1696–1727. *Although the authorities absolved Valverde of some of the blame for the massacre, they fined him two hundred pesos for appointing as leader of the expedition someone as inexperienced as Villasur.*

*After Coronado gives no information about Valverde's later life, and of his early life it provides only the brief statement he made in answer to one of Rivera's questions (Barnaby 1935, 231):*

> He testified that his name was Don Antonio Balverde Cosio; that he was a native of Burgos, Kingdom of Castile; that he is Spanish, a bachelor; and that his profession has been that of a soldier, having obtained the offices in this kingdom of captain of its presidios and governor and captain-general of it; and that at the present his residence is at the presidio of El Paso del Rio del Norte; and that he is fifty-five years of age; so he answers.

*Whatever happened to Valverde after 1725, he had already made his mark on the history of the West by being one of the first Europeans to travel into eastern Colorado, arriving there almost a century before Zebulon Pike would wander into the area and gaze upon the peak that now bears his name.*

*Western American literature should also include some mention of Valverde, for his diary brings to life the expedition he led in 1719. Although not complete (some passages were torn out, and the account of the expedition's return is missing) and not as detailed as the Lewis and Clark journals, Val-*

verde's diary deserves to be read in its entirety. Since this anthology's limited space precludes reprinting even a brief diary in full, the selections that follow must be seen only as representative; taken out of context, they cannot convey the building tension and the sense of pursuit and retreat that come from reading all the entries in succession.

Still the selections do describe the dwellings of the Apaches, as well as the abundance of their crops and the success of their irrigation system (facts that refute the old stereotype of Indians as nothing but hunters and nomads). If we are disappointed that Valverde wastes so few words in describing the magnificent scenery, we must remember that he wrote when Europeans had not yet learned to appreciate the aesthetic grandeur of mountains (see Marjorie Hope Nicolson's Mountain Gloom and Mountain Glory for a history of that change in perception). At least we can chuckle at the serendipity of the Spaniards' remedy for their unfortunate encounter with poison sumac, and we can wish we had been there to sample the nectarous wine brought from El Paso and to see the teeming herds of deer and buffalo.

The edenic Colorado countryside furnished nightmare as well as dream, however. First the writer casually mentions soldiers torturing a bear. Then the diary ends with the little army's decision to retreat after learning that to the north Indians are being armed by the French.

The notes in braces have been added by the editors of this volume.

## Selected Bibliography

Brandon, William. *Quivira: Europeans in the Region of the Santa Fe Trail, 1540–1820.* Athens: Ohio University Press, 1990.

DeVoto, Bernard. *The Course of Empire.* Boston: Houghton Mifflin, 1952.

Thomas, Alfred Barnaby. *After Coronado: Spanish Exploration Northeast of New Mexico, 1696–1727; Documents from the Archives of Spain, Mexico, and New Mexico.* Norman: University of Oklahoma Press, 1935.

ANONYMOUS

# Chasing a Nightmare into the Dream: The Valverde Campaign (1719)

## Chasing the Utes and Comanches

THE TWENTY-SEVENTH of the month {September} dawned as the preceding day; with much more snow and rain. The señor governor, with the wisdom of experience, commanded that the horseherd should not be collected until the weather cleared up. He distributed this day [torn out] pinole and mutton, giving it to the ones who were sick from an attack of an herb called ivy, caused strangely by lying down upon it or being near it. Those affected swelled up. He ordered Antonio Durán Armijo, a barber by trade who had some knowledge of blood letting, to attend and assist them and that whatever might be necessary should be asked for, and his lordship with his charitable zeal would order it be done.

On this day about ten o'clock in the morning Chief Carlana, the Apache chief of the Sierra Blanca, arrived in camp with sixty-nine Apaches of his ranchería and tribe. They circled the camp on their horses, jubilantly singing and shouting. In the evening these same messengers danced according to their custom, some covered with red and others with white paint. They came to the tent of the said governor, who received them with great kindness. After they had danced for a good part of the night, he ordered them entertained and feasted.

On the twenty-eighth of the month, the weather having cleared, the camp set out from the above mentioned spot and river. After marching some six leagues, they arrived on an arroyo with little water but much timber, where the camp was supplied with wood. On this journey they caught many deer so that the Indians were sufficiently provisioned with good fat meat. While the command was camped in this spot, Chief Carlana of the Apache nation came to the tent of the governor about four o'clock in the afternoon with seven young braves of his ranchería, all armed with arrows, machetes, and oval leather shields. By means of the interpreters, he told the governor that now was the time to send out spies to reconnoiter the regions in which their enemies, the Utes and Comanches, were. To this the governor responded that it seemed very wise, and after ordering them to be given chocolate and tobacco, he sent them off, impressing upon them the care and vigilance they ought to exercise in this affair in order to bring about the success and happy outcome of this campaign. The governor blessed the spot.

According to the order he gave to Ensign Torres and Captain Luís Garzía, in whose care the Indian pueblo people had come, the horseherd that the natives were bringing was counted. When done, six hundred and eighty beasts were found. These horses were never mixed in the number or body of the horseherd of the presidio and settlers.

The twenty-ninth day of the month, on which is celebrated the festivity of the glorious archangel San Miguel. After mass was said, to which the whole camp listened, they set out from this locality. Having crossed the river, they arrived at another more pleasant, with a grove of plum trees, many willows and many wild grapes, from which vinegar was made. In the woods some deer were caught by the Indians who, surrounding them, drove them into the camp, at which there was great glee and shouting. The journey this day had been five leagues up to their arrival on the river, which the señor governor named the San Miguel. It has plenty of good water and runs through a very broad and pleasing valley. A number of deer were caught, for many abound in this valley, thus verifying what the Apaches had said on many occasions, namely, that there was good hunting here. But from fear of the Utes, they are fleeing from their hunting grounds, which those of their nation have, where they were maintaining themselves and securing many pelts.

On the thirtieth of this month of September, the governor in prosecution of their journey moved the camp from this spot on the San Miguel River a distance of two leagues. They always followed the route to the north, leaving a high sierra on the west, with much level ground stretching towards the east. On the road they hunted many deer, with which the camp was supplied. A halt was made on the river, where they arrived at ten o'clock under the guidance of the Apache chief, Carlana. In this region, for greater protection, the said señor governor ordered four squads of settlers formed as a guard, in whose custody the camp would be during the night. For this purpose, he named four leaders under the orders of Sergeant-Major Don Alonso Real de Aguilar of this kingdom. In the camp there were seven soldiers and some settlers considerably ill from the evil effects of the ivy mentioned above, for stepping on it or passing near it causes such great discomfort that their bodies swell, they appear hydropical, and the skin peels off. The most harm is done to the genital organs. From this sickness they suffered for some time when relief was found by chewing chocolate and then applying and rubbing the saliva on the parts. This remedy, accidentally discovered by Francisco Casadas whose face had swollen, relieved him to a great degree. The rest of the sick followed his example. . . .

On the second of October, the governor with all his camp set out from this river of Santo Domingo. Having marched some four leagues all over level ground, the route always to the north, and the river on the left hand, they came to where another, which comes down from the north with more copious clear water, joins it. At the union of both streams they put up the camp at about the middle of the day. The señor governor called this river the San Lorenzo. It has many plums, which though wild are of fine flavor and taste. With these and many very delicious wild grapes the people satisfied themselves. It was leafy here and the command took a nap, enjoying the coolness and shade of the many poplars and deep woods. While they were in this happy state, a bear came out of the thicket and threw the entire camp into an uproar. The people took great delight in teasing it for some time until they killed it.

On this day the señor governor took advantage of his many experiences in military affairs in this country, as he had been reared from a tender age in its service, and ordered the army to set out at sunset from this spot, and march during the night in order to avoid the great deal of dust that was made, as this could be a means by which the enemy might learn that they were being followed. After setting out they marched about two leagues to a river they call Chiopo, to which the governor gave the name of San Antonio. It is an admirable stream much resembling the Del Norte because of its large volume of water and broad, spacious meadows, filled with poplars. On its banks camp was set up at about ten o'clock at night. At about three or four o'clock in the morning three Apaches of the spies who set out from the spot of the sacrament, arrived with the news that on the road, of the many which go to and fro from Santa Fé and its settlements, which goes to the Teguas [Tiguas] they found that three Comanche and Ute enemies had with them twenty beasts and a colt, whose trail led straight to their land and ranchería. They themselves returned in order to communicate the news they had. At this very hour Chief Carlana sent out other spies whom he ordered to report immediately and without delay what they discovered.

On the third of October, the governor set out with the camp from this river San Antonio and after marching over level ground some four leagues, arrived at a very pleasant river with many large poplars and other graceful trees. To this river his lordship gave the name of San Francisco. Here they hunted and caught many deer and a lot of good fat prairie hens with which they made very delicious tamales. After recognizing that the river did not have good watering places for the horses to drink, the governor mounted his horse and with some of his military chiefs went out to find where they could do this more favorably. This having succeeded, the horseherd was divided into groups and drank until satisfied. Afterwards, the governor returned to his tent, where the Reverend Father Fray Juan del Pino was.

He wished to entertain him, as he did. They celebrated together with the military chiefs the eve of the glorious patriarch San Francisco, having ordered out a small keg of rich spirituous brandy made at the Pass of the Río del Norte of the governor's own vintage. It was of such good flavor, taste and quality and though vinted without the carefulness with which other wines are made, that that of Castile does not surpass it. The health of the reverend father chaplain was toasted in celebration of his patriarch. This they did, both the governor and the others who were present, wishing each other fortune with pleasure and concord.

The señor governor, having received news that the Apaches had found a horse which was believed to belong to their enemies, had called the Apache and Chief Carlana to learn and investigate the truth, so that through the interpreters the latter should tell what it meant. Having demanded of him why he had not given an explanation of the horse that had been found, he answered that when the enemies were attacking the Apaches of La Jicarilla, they had left there that horse which they had taken from them. Then the governor ordered the horse returned [to the Jicarilla] and gave them pinole and tobacco.

On the fourth of the month of October, the señor governor set out with all his camp from this spot and river of San Francisco. After mass was heard and after the governor and the father chaplain and officers of war had breakfasted, his lordship ordered a cask of wine which had been made at the pass to be brought out. With it they all drank to the health of the governor and of the chaplain, and celebrated the saint's day of San Francisco. To this the chaplain, who had behaved on this campaign like a real true son of such a good father, responded with propriety and urbanity. The governor himself so declared in toasting his saint's day, with appropriate actions both as to what has been referred to, as well as in the great pleasure he had in regaling them under the circumstances with the best rich bread and melon preserves he carried for such an occasion to entertain the reverend father chaplain and himself.

The expedition having set out as said above, from this locality, crossed the river, the route to the north, and went along its meadows for four leagues over level ground. While so marching they recognized two tracks of some of their enemies, which were followed a considerable distance. For this reason his lordship ordered the camp to stop on the same Río San Francisco, giving to the place the name of San Francisco. It is a very cheerful spot, with a beautiful view and excellent springs and many thick poplar groves. On the left hand, about three leagues away, there is a range of mountains and on the right, a very extensive plain in the distance.

On this road today many deer and prairie chickens which moved about in flocks were caught to such an extent that nowhere else were more caught because of their abundance in this region. The governor hunted deer and chicken. Having been given news that one of the settlers was very sick with a pain in his stomach, the governor ordered him called to his tent and a cup of tea given him to strengthen him. This made him better, and he sent him something to eat every day, for which he was very thankful. On this day a mountain lion and a wildcat were killed. At about sunset some Indians came in, running from a bear which plunged into the middle of the camp, throwing the people into confusion. With great shouting and uproar, they killed him with many spear thrusts and arrows. His strength and size were so formidable that the governor was impelled to go with the chaplain to view it.

On the fifth of the present month, the señor governor and his command left this site of San Onofre and River of San Francisco, keeping it always on the left hand and the mountain ridge also. Having traveled two short leagues, the governor commanded the expedition to stop because Chief Carlana said that in the region where they were to spend the night there was but little water. The governor, accordingly, guided by experience, ordered a halt so that the horseherd might drink. The place where we rested is very pleasing, with large groves of plum trees and cherries, so that the soldiers gathered considerable. After the siesta was over and the horseherd brought in, the governor ordered the march to proceed, still keeping the range of mountains on his left hand. Having traveled some four leagues, keeping the route always to the north and following a dry creek on his left hand, a short distance opposite the brook, they made camp, on a spring which the governor called Nuestra Señora de Dolores. It was mountainous all around. Plum trees, roses of Alexandria, and a great deal of rockrose were found. There was sufficient water for the people, and they dexterously gave the horses, that came saddled, water they poured out in containers.

On the sixth of the present month of October, the señor governor and all his camp left this spring of Nuestra Señora de Dolores and marched over level land and through many good pastures because it was grassy. On the road to the left was a summit sloping to the east heavily wooded with pines. Having traveled some six leagues, they arrived at a spring which had considerable water. There the camp was put up and the governor called it Nuestra Señora del Carmen. On this day before the halt a bear was met. It was larger than the preceding ones, for its size and height were probably greater than that of a donkey. One of the soldiers went out and put a spear into him up to the middle of the shaft. The brute, turning around, seized the lance and grasped the horse by the hocks. At the same time another soldier went to the rescue and gave the bear another spear thrust. The bear, seizing the horse by the tail, held him down and clawing viciously, tore a piece of flesh off the rump. Having tied the bear up finally, they finished killing him. The soldiers who were bringing up the rear guard of the cavalry met a female and two cubs, which they also killed. . . .

On the twelfth of October, the governor with his command set out and continued down the river, following the route to the east. After traveling some four leagues, they halted on the banks of the said river. The name of San Nicolás Obispo was given to the spot. That night about eleven o'clock, while the governor was talking around the fire with the sergeant-major and the lieutenant of the company, and Captain Miguel Thenorio de Alva, such a furious hurricane came up that it obliged them to withdraw to their tents, which it seemed would be uprooted. The hurricane lasted all night.

On the thirteenth of the month the governor with his camp set out and marched down the river, keeping the route to the east. After we had marched some six leagues, camp was set up on the banks of the river; the spot was called Nuestra Señora del Pilar de Zaragosa. Along the way on the journey, they noticed where their enemy had stopped. According to the ranchos and the fires they made, they must have exceeded two hundred. From this it ought to be understood that there were no less than five persons, and in some cases more, about each fire. There were also

many buffalo herds, walking about feeding and wandering in all directions on those plains which are so extensive that nothing is seen to ob-
struct the view.

On the fourteenth of the aforesaid month, the governor with all his
camp set out downstream, always keeping his route to the east. After they
marched some two leagues, the track of the enemy was recognized, which
left a clear trail wherever it went, both on account of the great number of
people and the multitude of horses, as well as the tent poles they carried
dragging along behind. Their road went northeast. Marching on, the governor ordered a halt. He told the Chief Carlana through the interpreters
that he was going immediately to where it appeared to him that the enemy was, according to what he judged from the trail. He was minded to
follow it until they should all be punished. To this reasoning the Chief
Carlana responded that it would not be possible to follow them because
they had changed direction and had taken another route along which
there were very few springs, and those too scanty to support the main
body of the horseherd and command.

After listening to these reasons which Carlana had given, the governor called a council of all the soldiers and settlers. Assembled, he told
them that they should give their opinions as to what ought to be done in
the light of what Chief Carlana had proposed.

His lordship told them that he had still sufficient vigor and strength
for greater campaigns and journeys, and that he was entirely unaffected
by the severity of the weather and the few conveniences which these journeys hold out. But as they were aware, he knew how to perform and bear
the hardships that had presented themselves on other occasions, so that
they should set forth, without respect to him, according to their experiences that which appears to them ought to be done. All having understood this, and in compliance with what was ordered, answered unanimously that they were of the opinion that the señor governor and all the
camp should return, for by continuing to follow the enemy there was a
manifest risk that thereby all the cavalry, which was the principal means
by which the kingdom was sustained, might be lost. This his lordship well
knew, for he was familiar with the rigor of the snow and cold weather,
which in these lands is so extreme that it benumbs and annihilates. Such
had happened in the year '96 under the governorship of the Marqués de
la Nava de Brazinas, when his lordship was captain of the presidio. At
that time the Picuríes Indians had abandoned their pueblo and, uniting
with the Apaches, become apostates from our holy Catholic faith. He set
out to punish them. In his pursuit at this very time of the year he lost the

major part of his horseherd. Valverde was a good witness of this event, as he was commanding the armed forces. These latter remained helpless for a long time until delivered by Providence.

To fulfill his obligation in the royal service—since no other person would have penetrated through so many and such unknown lands, never before seen or discovered by the Spaniards, as those his lordship has explored in the present campaign—he has demonstrated his great zeal in the service of his majesty. For these reasons, it appeared that his lordship should suspend following the enemy and retire with his army to the presidio in the center of the kingdom. . . .

On the twenty-second of the aforesaid month {October} the governor had information that one of the Apache chiefs of that ranchería had a wound which appeared to be from a gun shot. To inform himself of this, he ordered Lieutenant Frances Montes Vigil to bring him into his presence. This was done. When the Apache had come with many other Indians of his tribe, the governor examined the wound, asked him who had given it to him and with what he had been wounded. He answered that while he and his people were in his land, which is farther in from El Cuartelejo, on the most remote borderlands of the Apaches, the French, united with the Pawnees and the Jumanos, attacked them from ambush while they were planting corn. Placed on the defensive, they fought, and it was then that they gave him that oblique wound in the abdomen which was still healing. The Apache also said that had not the night settled on them, so that they could escape from their ranchería, none would have remained. They have seized their [Paloma] lands, and taken possession of them and held them from that time on.

The French have built two large pueblos, each of which is as large as that of Taos. In them they live together with the said Pawnees and Jumanos Indians, to whom they have given long guns which they have taught them to shoot. With one of these they had wounded him. They also carry some small guns suspended from their belts. At the time of the fight the Apaches had told them that they would advise their friends, the Spaniards, in order that they might defend them. To this the French responded that they were greatly pleased to have them notify them and bring them there, for they are women *criconas* (these are words, however rude, that the Indians are accustomed to use to incite ire). All the enemy were dressed in [torn out] that they have done them much damage in taking away their lands and that each day they are coming closer. This is the reason that moved the Apaches to come, establishing themselves on this lower part of the river to be able to live in safety from their enemies.

Likewise, they added that the French have three other settlements on the other side of the large river, and that from these they bring arms and the rest of the things they bring to those which they have recently constructed. They know this because they were told by some women of their tribe who were made captives among the French on the occasions when they had war, but who had fled and returned with their kinsmen.

# CHAPTER 19

# The Stuff of Dreams: Pierre Gaultier de La Vérendrye (1730)

*Though Herbert E. Bolton's claims for Sir Francis Drake's "plate of brasse" may be the eminent historian's greatest faux pas, there was a precedent for his excited credulity. One Sunday afternoon in 1913, some students found a similar tablet on a hill near their high school in Fort Pierre, South Dakota. It was, by most accounts, genuine, and it commemorated the La Vérendrye brothers' deep penetration into the northwestern mystery. In a larger sense the relic also honors the accomplishments of the brothers' father, Pierre Gaultier de La Vérendrye, the last and greatest of the French explorers in Canada and the American West. His story is a curious though telling one, for it shows how a dedicated and literal-minded, even skeptical, soldier can be taken up by the powerful stuff of dreams that buoys much literature.*

*The elder La Vérendrye was born in Three Rivers, Quebec, a frontier town where Indian threats and calls to arms were normal hazards of existence. Beginning his military career as a youth, La Vérendrye saw action in New England, Newfoundland, and Europe, receiving numerous wounds from musket balls and sabers. After that he returned to the Three Rivers area and took up farming and trading with the local Indians. In middle age, however, La Vérendrye began a more ambitious enterprise—establishing trading posts west of the Great Lakes. Here he left his mark for the history books. A statistical outlier—an honest and patriotic man among the corruption and bureaucratic bêtise that typified the fur industry under control of the French king—La Vérendrye pushed ever westward, gathering information from the Indians as he went and trying to separate fact from fantasy about the unknown lands ahead. His most immediate contributions were outflanking the British of the competing Hudson's Bay Company and, secondly, understanding the geography of the Saskatchewan and Missouri rivers. The first river was the key to western Canada, the second the key to the American*

*West. Thus, as concerns the Missouri, La Vérendrye set the stage for Lewis and Clark more than half a century before their expedition took place. At La Vérendrye's urging, his sons struck far out across the Great Plains, and though scholars dispute whether they sighted the Black Hills of South Dakota or the Big Horn Mountains farther on, with their famous trip the brothers ranged deeper into the unknown than had any previous European.*

*Our concern here, however, is not so much the elder La Vérendrye's successes where others had failed at determining the truth of geography, but the process leading up to his conclusions. Those conclusions often were flawed, for along with other men La Vérendrye wrestled and sometimes lost with the old mythologies that could overwhelm him as they had overwhelmed others. As he sat through the winters in his posts west of Lake Superior, the trader invited Indians to come in and chat, and he'd write down what they told him about the lands beyond the edge of the white men's knowledge. Bernard DeVoto (1952, 196) describes the dangers of the process:*

> Made affectionate by brandy and warmed by the big log fires, while auroras flamed beyond the stockade or the fort shook to gales out of the Arctic, they told him what they knew, what they had heard, what they guessed, and what it amused them to invent. They scratched maps on pieces of bark or hide or in the ashes of the hearth. In a year Vérendrye had heard all that his predecessors had heard and a great deal more.

*Hardly a gullible man, this trader with decades of experience dealing with the wiles and superstitions of white and Indian alike knew that all of what he was hearing couldn't possibly be true. Though it would have been to France's long-term advantage to do otherwise, the French bureaucracy overseeing the fur trade demanded ever more profits from their most capable man in the field, thus limiting his ability to take time out to explore and verify with his own eyes what he heard. It came down to this: he had no other choice but to listen to his Indian friends, dutifully report the details to his distant superiors, then try to sort out fact from fantasy. This was no easy task. Perhaps the reported tribe of dwarf Indians and the mountain range that glowed through the night were a bit much for the rational European mind. But what about rumors of silver? Many years before, French adventurers had found lead and copper in the Upper Mississippi region. Then why not silver farther on? Hadn't the Spanish, as everyone knew, grown fat by finding the gold in Mexico that was the fixation of their beliefs? One could hardly afford to eliminate possibilities.*

*And even when the Indians weren't entertaining themselves by spinning the stuff of fairy tales, they could get what they'd heard second- or third-hand wildly scrambled. One current theory has it that our nighttime dreams are meaningless, yet the stories they tell are the mind's attempt to manufacture order out of the daily harvest of chaotic detail. Something similar seems to have gone on with the Indians. They developed "stories" that took on their own authority. La Vérendrye had a vague notion of the Spanish colonies to the southwest in New Mexico, but in the flux of rumor these became blended in the daydreaming mind with the lighter-skinned Mandan Indians and with the Indians' own familiarity with Frenchmen into a credible but misty report of other white men dwelling somewhere in the wilderness, as reported in the third selection by one of La Vérendrye's sons. It had just the ring of fact to it yet was open-ended enough that the listener could bend it to any reality he willed.*

*Such an atmosphere compounded the confusions that La Vérendrye and other Europeans brought with them. Geography, reasoned eighteenth-century minds, obsessed with logic and order, should be symmetrical. If there was a range of mountains in eastern America, well, then, there must be another in the West to balance things out. And there really should be a great river flowing out of it, the dreamed-of easy waterway to the Pacific Ocean. When Indian after Indian supplied bits of evidence that might be construed to shore up the concept, again the dream became a reality in the listener's mind. And at times, as seen in the second passage, all this became ever more twisted and blurred, as information filtered down through two and sometimes three intermediary languages to an explorer cautiously trying to winnow out fact from fiction.*

### Selected Bibliography

DeVoto, Bernard. *The Course of Empire*. Boston: Houghton Mifflin, 1952. 195–217.

Kavanagh, Martin. *La Vérendrye: His Life and Times*. 2d ed. Brandon, Manitoba: published by the author, 1967.

La Vérendrye, Pierre Gaultier de Varennes de, et al. *Journals and Letters of Pierre Gaultier de Varennes de La Vérendrye and His Sons*. Ed. by Lawrence J. Burpee. Toronto: Champlain Society, 1927.

Smith, G. Hubert. *The Explorations of the La Vérendryes in the Northern Plains, 1738–1743*. Ed. by W. Raymond Wood. Lincoln: University of Nebraska Press, 1980.

PIERRE LA VÉRENDRYE

# The Stuff of Dreams: Pierre Gaultier de La Vérendrye (1730)

**Continuation of the Report of the Sieur de la Vérendrye touching upon the discovery of the Western Sea. (Annexed to the Letter of M. de Beauharnois, of October 10, 1730.)**

A SAVAGE named Pako, Chief of Lake Nipigon, Lefoye, and Petit Jour his brother, Cree chiefs, reported to me that they had been beyond the height of land and reached a great river which flows straight towards the setting sun, and which widens continually as it descends; that in this great river there are only two rapids about three days' journey from its source, and that wood is only found along about two hundred leagues of its course, according to the estimate they made in their travel.

They give a great account of that country, saying that it is all very level, without mountains, all fine hard wood with here and there groves of oak; that everywhere there are quantities of fruit trees, and all sorts of wild animals; that the savage tribes are there very numerous, and always wandering, never staying in any fixed place, but carrying their cabins with them continually from one place to another and always camping together to form a village. They call these nations Assiniboin and Sioux because they speak all the Sioux languages. The nations about three hundred leagues lower down are sedentary, raise crops, and for lack of wood make themselves mud huts. The wood comes to an end on the shore of a great lake formed by the river about two hundred leagues from its source; on the left as you follow down, at the outlet of the lake, you come to a little river the water of which looks red like vermilion, and is held in great esteem by the savages. On the same side of the river, but much lower down, there is a small mountain, the stones of which sparkle night and day. The savages call it the Dwelling of the Spirit; no one ventures to go near it. This kind of mountain and the Red river, where in places a very fine

gold-coloured sand is found, seem to all the nations of the region something very precious.

As I am going to report such new facts as I have learnt this year, 1729,
respecting the country I have just been speaking about, I conclude by
mentioning the other particulars which I learnt last year so as to give a
more exact account of them on the testimony of other savages who have
explored the same river.

Having neglected nothing, Monsieur, since I arrived last autumn as
commander of the Northern post, that could help to give me the fullest
possible knowledge of the fine and mighty river which flows straight to
the west and the route to be taken to get to it, I have taken care also to secure a savage able to conduct a party thither in case, with the consent of
His Majesty, you should be so good as to honour me with your commands to discover it, and, on the strength of the new information I have
received, I can now positively state as follows:

The savages of the interior have knowledge for the most part of this
river; some speak as having been there, others have heard of it, and all
agree in what they say about it. Last autumn some Cree came to fort
Camanistigouia with some people of the region.

Tacchigis, a chief of the Cree, told me then that he had been as far as
the lake of the great river of the West, and several times afterwards he
told me the same story that the others had already done. I asked him if he
did not know of other great rivers; he replied that he knew of several, but
that the one running west exceeded all the others in width. He then gave
me a statement in regard to several other larger rivers that he had seen
from a height of land sloping to the south-west.

He told me that four great rivers take their rise there, one of which,
flowing north as far as the lake of the great river of the West, turns west
at the outlet of the lake; another flowing north-east falls into a river
which, flowing west-north-west, empties into the same lake. The third,
flowing at first south-east and afterwards running south, goes to the
country of the Spaniards. The fourth, taking its course between the last
two, forms the Mississippi. With a piece of charcoal he made me a map of
those regions, and placed these rivers on them according to his marks.

I am expecting this spring some savages who, I am assured, have been
very far down the river of the West, and who will be able to supply a map
of the road to the places at which they have been.

A slave adopted by the people of the territory, and given to Vieux
Crapaud, chief of the flat country, by the Cree, after having been made
prisoner by the Assiniboin on the stretch of country to the left of the river

of the West, reports that the villages there are very numerous, many of them being nearly two leagues in extent, and that the back country is inhabited like that fronting on the river. All the savages there, according to his report, raise quantities of grain, fruits abound, game is in great plenty and is only hunted with bows and arrows; the people there do not know what a canoe is; as there is no wood in all that vast extent of country, for fuel they dry the dung of animals.

He adds that he passed several times within sight of the mountain the stone of which shines night and day, and that from that point you begin to notice a rise and fall of tide; also that from the lake near which is the Red river to far below the mountain there are no settlements of savages; that he had never heard tell whether it was far from the sea, and that he did not think there was any man bold enough to pass by the different tribes that are to be found in great number lower down in order to make an exploration.

He makes mention of all the special points contained in the Memoir which I had the honour to send you last year by the Reverend Father Gonner and affirms that on the right bank of the river there is a tribe of dwarfs not over three feet or so in height, but numerous and very brave. At the place where the ebb and flow begins the river is more than three leagues in width.

With reference to the guide, the man I have chosen is one named Auchagah, a savage of my post, greatly attached to the French nation, the man most capable of guiding a party, and with whom there would be no fear of our being abandoned on the way. When I proposed to him to guide me to the great river of the West he replied that he was at my service and would start whenever I wished. I gave him a collar by which, after their manner of speaking, I took possession of his will, telling him that he was to hold himself in readiness for such time as I might have need of him, and indicating to him the season of the year when I might be in the flat country for the purpose of proceeding to the discovery of the Western Sea; if, Monsieur, I should have the honour of receiving your orders to do so. I then made him some presents to increase his affection for us, and make sure that he would fulfil his promises.

Apart from that I acquainted myself with the route through different savages, who all made the same statement, that there are three routes or rivers which lead to the great river of the West. Consequently I had a map made of these three rivers, in order that I might be able to choose the shortest and easiest road. I had the honour, Monsieur, of sending you that map as it was traced for me by Auchagah, showing the three rivers which flow into Lake Superior, namely the one called Fond du Lac river, the Nantouagan and the Kaministikwia. The two latter are those on which everything is marked with exactness on the map, lakes, rapids, portages, the side on which the portage must be made, and the heights of land; all this is represented or indicated. Comparing these two routes, the river Nantouagan, which is two days' journey from the river Kaministikwia going towards the extremity of the lake, is, it seems to me, the one to be preferred. It has, it is true, forty-two portages, while the Kaministikwia has only twenty-two; but, on the other hand, it has no rapids, while the other has twelve, two of which are long and very shallow. Besides, the road is straight and one third shorter. The height of land for this route is not over fifty leagues distant, and after seventy leagues at most there is a steady descent. Finally, in spite of all the portages, the savage assures me that, with easy travelling, we shall get from Lake Superior to Lake Tecamamiouen in twenty days at the most, and from there in four days to the Lake of the Woods, and in ten to Lake Winnipeg. Some Cree or Christinaux, who live towards the outlet of the Lake of the Woods, where the great River of the West has its beginning, came this spring. These savages are La Marteblanche and two other chiefs of the same tribe. They made me a map of their own country and of that of which they have knowledge, and it agrees with the first; it is in the lands that are to the left of the great river as you follow it down that minerals and metals are found in quantity. Amongst the metals, they are acquainted with lead and copper; but there is a third kind which does not flatten out, but breaks, when hammered. They do not know what it is, but its white colour makes them think it is silver. According to their map, which agrees with the one made by Auchagah, the lower portion of the Western river runs west-north-west. They state that there are whites at the mouth of the river, but that they do not know to what nation they belong, the length of the journey being such that none of them venture to go there; one would have to start from the Lake of the Woods in the month of March in order to make the journey and could not hope to get back before November. What they report is founded on hearsay. What chiefly deters them from making the journey to the sea is that on a former occasion, according to their story, two of their canoes were lost in the ice ten days' journey from Lake Winnipeg. Fear holds them back, and besides, as they can get all their wants supplied by the English of the near north, who are distant only twenty days' travel, what more would they go to seek at the Western Sea? Looking at the map as they have traced it there is no appearance of the river communicating with the Northern Sea. As there are several rivers, in the latitude shown by the map, to the south-west towards Lake Winnipeg, it is probable that from the same latitude there are also some flowing to the Western Sea. To be able to settle this point, we should have to establish a post at Lake Winnipeg. La Marteblanche has promised to take me there, or, as he is old, to have me taken by his son. This lake is about five hundred leagues from the river Kaministikwia. Leaving Montreal in May, you can get to Lake Winnipeg in September. From the head of Lake Superior to the Lake of the Woods the distance is the same as from the outlet of the latter to Lake Winnipeg, with this difference that there are only two rapids requiring portages in the whole great river of the West, whereas from Lake Superior to the Lake of the Woods, a distance of a hundred leagues, you have portage after portage all the way. The two rapids I have just mentioned are in a rocky formation consisting of gun flint. The great river which goes to the sea is the discharge of the lake and of the large river which empties into it flowing west. This great river (the first mentioned) also flows west a distance of ten days' journey, after which it turns for a little west-north-west; and it is from that point that the rise and fall of the tide becomes perceptible. Such is the information given me by the Cree chiefs. Their map shows all the countries they have traversed from north to south and from the Lake of the Woods to the river of the West. The whole right bank of the great river as you go down from the Lake of the Woods as far as Lake Winnipeg is held by the Cree, and it is the country of the moose and marten, while beaver is so plentiful that the savages place little value on it and only collect the large skins which they send to the English. These people dress themselves in winter in beaver skins and in spring they throw them away, not being able to sell them. The left bank of the same river is inhabited by the Assiniboin and the Sioux; the country is rich in metals, and buffalo are abundant. If they speak of places beyond it is nearly always on hearsay and without any great certainty.

After these details, Monsieur, it only remains for me to represent to you the importance, as it seems to me, of proceeding promptly with this exploration. The Cree are trading with the English, finding interpreters in the Indians of the neighbourhood, and it is natural that they should speak there of the prospect of having French among them, and that they should give the same information they have given to us here. The English have every interest in getting ahead of us, and if we allow them time they will not lose the chance of doing it. Besides, the colony will receive a new benefit independently of the discovery of the Western Sea through the quantity of furs that will be produced and which now go to waste among the Sioux and Assiniboin, or by means of the Cree go to the English. I hoped this spring to see many Cree and Assiniboin, according to the promise they made me last spring, 1729, to come to my post at Kaminis-tikwia. The death of one of their principal chiefs, a man of high consider-ation, has caused them to change their plan and decided them to go to war in the direction of the Spaniards to avenge his death according to their custom. I have only succeeded in getting information from two sav-ages of the country, one of whom is a Monsoni chief, who relates that he went as far as the height of land to the north-west of the river in 1728: they state positively that there are whites, and that they have seen wood sawn into boards; these people, too, use boats, according to the descrip-tion they give of their canoes. This appeared to astonish them a good deal, because in all that great extent of country such a thing as an axe or a gun is never seen. There are a great many different kinds of wood there, and the animals are strange to them. Others have told me that they had seen people who said that they had gone down to the foot of the great river, and only savage tribes were met with; at the mouth of it they had seen a great island in the sea which seemed to be inhabited.

That is all, Monsieur, in the way of new information that I have been able to obtain this year. If, subject to His Majesty's good pleasure, you should see fit to honour me with your instructions to go and establish a fort at Lake Winnipeg, I shall have the honour in the second year there-after to give you positive information respecting the Sea in question.

### Journal in the form of a letter covering the period from the 20th of July 1738, when I left Michilimackinac, to May, 1739, sent to the Marquis de Beauharnois. . . .

Shortly afterwards I was informed that my interpreter, whom I had paid well to make sure of him, had decamped, in spite of all the offers my son the Chevalier could make him, in order to follow an Assiniboin woman of whom he was enamoured, but who had refused to remain with him. He was a young man, a Cree by nationality, who spoke good Assiniboin, and as there are several Mandan who speak it pretty well I made myself perfectly understood. My son spoke in Cree, and the Cree interpreted it into Assiniboin; but now, to crown our misfortunes, we were reduced to trying to make ourselves understood by signs and gestures. If I had dis-trusted my interpreter, who every day assured me that he would always stay with me and never abandon me, I would have taken advantage of the time he was with me to ask the questions that I wished to ask the

Mandan; but, flattering myself that I had a man whom I could depend on, I had put off doing so till after the departure of the Assiniboin.

All day long I was greatly perplexed. All that I succeeded in learning in the evening, after all the people had gone, in reply to any questions that I asked, such as whether there was much population along the river banks farther down, and of what nations it consisted, and whether they had any knowledge of a country far beyond, was that there were five forts of their own people on the two sides of the river much larger than the one we were in; that at a day's journey from the last of their forts were the Panaux, who had several forts, and beyond them the Pananis; that these two tribes occupied a large territory, and that at present they were at war with the Mandan and had been for the last four years. Formerly they had always been their close allies, and I should hear later what had caused the falling out.

The Panana and the Pananis built their forts and lodges in the same way in which they themselves did. In the summer corn and tobacco grew lower down the river, which was very wide so that you could not see the land on the other side. The water was not drinkable; all the land there was inhabited by people white like ourselves who worked in iron. Among all the tribes of this region the word iron seems to be applied indiscriminately to all metals. Those people, I was told, never went on foot, but always on horseback, both when they hunted and when they went to war. You could not kill any of these men with arrow or gun as they had iron armour, but that by killing a horse you could capture the man easily enough as he could not run. They had iron bucklers, very bright, and fought with lances and sabres, which they handled with great skill. You never saw a woman in their fields; their fort and houses were of stone.

I asked if the country was well wooded, and if the prairies continued to be marked by risings and depressions. They said that wood was found along the river in places, and also in clumps through the prairies; the further you went down, the higher the hills became, and that there were many that were bare rocks of fine stone, especially along the river. I asked if it took a long time to go to the country where the whites, the men who rode horses, were. They replied that the Panana and Pananis had horses like the whites; it took them a whole summer to make the journey with men alone; but since they had been at war with the Panana they did not venture to go very far. The roads were blocked so far as they were concerned. Buffaloes abounded in the prairies, much larger and heavier beasts than those we see in the prairies here, their hides white and of several colours. They showed us some horns cut across the middle which hold nearly three pints, their colour being greenish. There are some in all the lodges which are used as ladles, a proof that they killed a great many of them when the road was open.

That was all I was able to learn, and even so there was a good deal of chance about it . . . .

## Journal of the Expedition of the Chevalier de la Vérendrye and one of his brothers to reach the Western Sea, addressed to M. the Marquis de Beauharnois. 1742–43.

Up to that point we had been very well received in all the villages we had passed through, but nothing in comparison with the gracious manners of the head chief of the Gens de l'Arc, a man entirely disinterested unlike the rest, and who always took the very greatest care of everything belonging to us.

I attached myself to that chief, who merited all our friendly feelings. In a short time, through the pains he took to teach me, I learnt the language sufficiently to make myself understood and also to understand what he said to me.

I asked him if they knew the whites of the coast and if they could take us thither. He replied: "We know them through what has been told us by prisoners of the Gens du Serpent, amongst whom we shall shortly arrive. Don't be surprised if you see so many villages assembled with us. Word has been sent in all directions for them to join us. You are hearing war shouts every day; it is not without intention; we are going to march in the direction of the high mountains which are near the sea to find the Gens du Serpent. Do not be afraid to come with us, you have nothing to fear, and you will be able to see the sea that you are in search of."

He pursued his discourse thus: "The French who are on the coast are numerous; they have a large number of slaves whom they settle on their lands in each tribe; they have separate apartments: they marry them to one another and do not oppress them, so that they like being with them and do not seek to run away. They breed a great many horses and other animals which they use in tilling the land. They have many chiefs for the soldiers and have some also for prayer."

# CHAPTER 20

# Sailing into the Northern Mists: Georg Wilhelm Steller (1741)

*While from their settlements to the east and south the English, French, and Spanish probed the unknown continent, Russian explorers began testing the terra incognita by sea from outposts on the Siberian peninsula of Kamchatka. Excited by rumors and dreams of colonial expansion and scientific discoveries, the Russian crown charged Vitus Bering with finding out where northwestern America really was. In 1741 after weeks of touch-and-go sailing through misty northern waters, Bering finally sighted his goal. The fog that had dogged his voyage at last parted, and there before his ship appeared the dramatic, snow-covered peak of Alaska's Mt. St. Elias.*

*It should have been a thrilling moment, of the order that inspires bands to play, bards to scribble, and that launches a passionate scramble inland. Instead the captain gazed at the peak, shrugged, and as the clouds closed back around the 18,000-foot apparition, turned the St. Peter around and headed back toward Russia (Steller 1988, 61–64). The captain's lack of enthusiasm and his perfunctory reaction seem strange. Explorers, we like to think, are made of stronger stuff. When a vast, unknown land appears at their feet, they don't shrug and then retreat toward home, but plunge boldly forward.*

*Necessity, however, forced the captain to land in the New World. Realizing that the St. Peter needed a fresh supply of water for the return trip, he sent sailors to Kayak Island to fill the ship's water barrels. But he almost refused naturalist/doctor Georg Wilhelm Steller, champing at the bit to discover new plants and animals, permission to go ashore. As it was, after weeks of sailing, Steller spent only a few hours in the New World, and the irony led him to quip (1988, 64) that the expedition had come all that distance "only to take American water to Asia."*

*On the other hand, Bering apologists can cite reasons for the captain's hesitancy. From its inception the expedition had been tangled in hair-tearing* bureaucratic snarls. Then, early into the voyage, the St. Peter's sister ship, the St. Paul, became lost in the drizzle. She was never sighted again, hardly a confidence-building development for the frazzled captain (Golder 1922, 1:65). Conditions became steadily worse. The fogs were terrible, storms threatened, winter was approaching, and the sailors joined their captain in fearing that as they sailed blind, victims of the unpredictable winds, they'd smash into the rocky coast of America. With such considerations wearing on his mind, Bering decided to turn around, thus choosing safety over the dubious benefits of exploring a savage land (Fisher 1977, 149–50).

The fogs, the mists, the alternately appearing and disappearing features of the ghostly shore, combined with the dangers of a fragile ship scudding along a threatening coast, rightly stand as a metaphor for the uncertainties surrounding the early explorations. The metaphor also applies in another, more nitty-gritty sense. In Cabeza de Vaca's Relación, we can read of the tensions between the narrator and the commander of his expedition, the haughty Narváez. We can also see how the querulousness of Padre Font was sparked by his disapproval of Anza's leadership. Whatever bright colors their reputations achieve in the history books, in daily life explorers are no more cardboard figures than the rest of us. They have eccentricities, edges that rub each other raw, energy-draining conflicts. Their personalities and backgrounds sometimes clash and pique tempers, and their attempts to deal with the conflicts in their writings can lead to the creation of literature.

In many ways the German-born Georg Steller was a man out of place aboard the St. Peter. A product of the German Enlightenment, young Steller graduated from the University of Halle, one of the most intellectually generous institutions in Europe. He combined his passions for nature and healing by studying herbal medicine, an art that brought him into contact with Europe's inquisitive minds and influential personages. Still in his twenties yet a member of the international fraternity of scientists, he became the personal physician of the archbishop of Novgorod, Russia's preeminent churchman. But despite his high position, Steller was a young man "ever outward bound" for new frontiers to explore in natural history (Steller 1988, 15). His appointment to Bering's expedition, promising to take him to unknown America, made the youth's heart leap at the possibilities of discovery.

Independent, capable, expansive, Steller found himself subject to a timid captain whose indecision soon undermined the confidence and discipline of his crew. Perhaps worse, both officers and seamen scoffed at Steller's zeal for science—so much so that they refused to take the remedy for debilitating scurvy that the young doctor had discovered. Yet Steller did not repay in kind. In Bering's headlong rush to reach the safety of his home port, the St.

Peter *wrecked on an island, and in the midst of the ensuing chaos among the men, Steller calls to mind Cabeza de Vaca, who also assumed a leadership role when lesser spirits flagged. The doctor nursed the sick, buried the dead, and sent out parties to search for food. He organized work crews to help get the survivors through the winter, so they could build a new ship from the wreckage of the old and sail for home.*

*Intellectually isolated, all the while Steller was writing in his journal, creating an interior monologue studded with sarcasm, irony, complaints, and vivid imagery. In the first of the three excerpts below, Steller vents his ire at his captain, then reveals high excitement as he spends his precious few hours exploring America.*

*The second brief selection is an out-and-out puzzle, the description of a sea creature so fantastic it contradicts the naturalist's reliability in his other accounts of animals. But the passage dovetails with the third selection, Steller's first encounter with Native Americans. Readers will have no trouble picking up on the parallels and confusions of these two, related passages. Together they illustrate the difficulties of even one of Europe's fine minds in comprehending the strange, new world.*

## Selected Bibliography

Fisher, Raymond H. *Bering's Voyages: Whither and Why.* Seattle: University of Washington Press, 1977.

Golder, F. A., ed. *Bering's Voyages: An Account of the Efforts of the Russians to Determine the Relation of Asia and America.* 2 vols. New York: American Geographical Society, 1922, 1925.

Steller, Georg Wilhelm. *Journal of a Voyage with Bering: 1741–1742.* [1781, 1793]. Ed. by O. W. Frost. Stanford: Stanford University Press, 1988.

GEORG WILHELM STELLER

# Sailing into the Northern Mists: Georg Wilhelm Steller (1741)

## Cape St. Elias...

ALTHOUGH THE ORDERLY conduct as well as the importance of the matter would have called for single-minded consideration of what to do and how to use the time and opportunity to best advantage, what to explore on shore and in what manner; also, if, considering time and provisions and distance, we should continue to follow the coast or if it was too late and we should here pass the winter—all of this was not considered worthy of calling a council, but everybody kept silent and did what he himself pleased. They were of one mind in only this, that we should take on fresh water. That's why I said, "We have come only to take American water to Asia."

Besides, it was agreed to use the small yawl for transporting water and to turn over the larger one to Master Khitrov, together with sufficient crew and ammunition, to explore the country, an assignment for which he possessed the greatest aptitude. When I asked to be sent off at the same time as Master Khitrov since he did not, after all, know everything (Khitrov himself, knowing his strengths, also asked for my company), our request was denied, and at first the attempt was made to scare me with some gruesome murder stories.

But I answered that I had never acted like a woman, nor did I know any reason why I should not be permitted to go ashore. To get there was, after all, to follow my chief work, profession, and duty. Up to now I had served Her Majesty faithfully according to my ability and was willing to maintain the honor of my service for a long time yet. And I said that if for reasons contrary to the purpose of the voyage I was not to go, I would report such conduct in terms it deserved.

I was then called a wild man who would not be kept from work even by a treat to chocolate, which was just then being prepared.

When I realized that I was to be forced against my will to inexcusable neglect of duty, I put aside all respect and uttered a particular prayer by which the Captain-Commander was immediately mollified and let me go with the water carriers but without giving me the least help or a single person other than the cossack Thoma Lepekhin, whom I myself had brought along.

On my departure from the ship, the Captain-Commander attempted to find out if I could take a joke by having trumpets sounded after me. Without thanking him, I took the matter the way it had been ordered. But I have never been one to blow my own horn and would not have appreciated it if trumpets had been sounded in my honor. . . .

I had gone scarcely one verst along the coast before I found in one spot signs of people and what they were like. Under a tree I found an old piece of log hewn as a trough in which a few hours earlier the savages, lacking kettles and dishes, had cooked meat with glowing stones according to Kamchatkan ways described elsewhere. Where they had been sitting, bones lay scattered, some with meat remaining, that had the appearance of having been roasted at the fire. From the characteristics of the bones, I recognized that they were not from any sea animals but from land animals, and it seemed to me that these, according to their form and size, should most likely be considered reindeer bones, even though I never afterwards managed to see such an animal, perhaps because this one had been brought here from the mainland. In addition to these bones there was leftover *iukola,* or dried fish, which in Kamchatka is consumed at all meals in place of our bread. Next to these leftover fish, very large Jacob's mussels eight inches in diameter were lying about in large quantities, as well as blue mussels or *musculi* as found in Kamchatka and undoubtedly eaten raw as is the custom here. I likewise found lying in various shells, as in bowls, sweet grass over which water had previously been poured in order to extract the sweetness, which struck me as quite remarkable and led me to the following conclusions.

This rare grass was up to now thought to be unique to the Kamchadals, is called *slatkaia trava* by the Russians and *kattik* by the Kamchadals, and is a true species of *Sphondylium.* The way of preparing it by cleaning the outer part with clamshells, as well as the way in which it is eaten, corresponds exactly with American practice. On the other hand, this custom is unknown to the neighboring Tungus and Olenni Koriaks living in Kamchatka. Nor was its discovery and use an absolute necessity; just as, lacking steel, they make fire without it. All this is almost certain proof that this invention comes from Kamchatka, and it follows that both nations have previously had traffic with each other, or that possibly this nation is one and the same with the Kamchadals and emigrated from them.

Considering the distance of 500 miles between the two, it can be assumed that America continues farther to the west and, opposite Kamchatka, is much closer in the north than others, without any reason, have supposed. Otherwise, the possibility of a crossing could not very well be imagined since neither nation is equipped with capable seafaring craft now nor are there indications that better craft were previously available on Kamchatka. Be that as it may, most American objects and inventions are identical to Kamchatkan or Asian ones or little different.

Besides the tree, not far from the site of the fire, where there were still fresh embers, I also found a wooden fire starter. Lacking steel, just as on Kamchatka and elsewhere in America, the people customarily make fire by friction. But the tinder made on Kamchatka is different from the Americans', a species of algae, *fontinalis*, which was bleached by the sun. I took along a sample to send back.

The felled trees lying about here and there were so cut up with many blunt blows that one can only surmise that they fell trees with stone or bone axes just as on Kamchatka and just like the old Germans in ancient times before the invention of iron—axes that now that their use has died out are considered thunderclubs.

After I had looked at these things briefly and made some notes, I continued on my way. Having traveled about three versts, I found a path leading into the very thick, dark forest right by the shore.

I held a brief consultation with the cossack, who had a loaded gun besides a knife and ax, to decide what action we should take if we should meet one or more persons, and I ordered him to do nothing at all without my command. I was furnished with only a Iakut *palma*, which was to serve for digging out rocks and plants.

I noticed right away that somebody had wanted to cover the path but had been hindered by our speedy arrival and had therefore made it all the more noticeable. We saw many trees recently stripped of their bark and surmised that it had been used for dwellings or *ambars*, which must be nearby, since wherever we looked there was no lack of beautiful woods. But since the path divided into several smaller ones leading into the woods, we explored some not too far into the forest and came, after half an hour, to a place strewn with cut grass.

I immediately cleared the grass away and underneath found a covering of rocks. When these were likewise put aside, we came to tree bark placed over poles in an oblong rectangle three fathoms long and two fathoms wide and found under it a dug-out cellar two fathoms deep in which the following items were present.

1. *Lukoshki,* or receptacles made of bark, one and a half arshins high, which were all filled with smoked fish of a Kamchatkan species of salmon, at Okhotsk called *nerka* in Tungus and in Kamchatka by the common name *krasnaia ryba,* that were so cleanly and well prepared that I have never seen any so good on Kamchatka; they also greatly excel the Kamchatkan in taste.

2. *Slatkaia trava,* from which liquor is distilled on Kamchatka.

3. Several kinds of grass, skinned like hemp; I took these for nettles, which grow here in abundance and perhaps are used as in Kamchatka to make fishnets.

4. The innermost bark of larch or spruce, rolled up and dried, which is eaten in times of emergency and hunger not only in Kamchatka but also throughout Siberia and even in Russia as far as Khlynov or Vyatka.

5. Large bundles of straps made from seaweed, which by testing I found to be extraordinarily strong and firm. Among these I also found some arrows, which in size far surpassed the Kamchatkan ones and approached the arrows of the Tungus and Tatars; they were scraped very smooth and painted black so that it might indeed be supposed that these people had iron instruments and knives.

Despite my fear of being surprised in the cellar, I searched everything thoroughly, but finding nothing further, I took, for proof of having been there, two bundles of fish, the arrows, a wooden fire starter, tinder, a bundle of straps from seaweed, bark, and grass, and sent them with my cossack to the place where the water was being loaded, with the command to take them to the Captain-Commander and ask for two or three persons to assist me further in exploring the region. I also had him warn the persons on shore not to feel too safe but to be well on their guard. I then covered the cellar as it had been and, now quite alone, pursued my purpose to further investigate plants, animals, and minerals until my cossack should return.

But after I had covered about six versts, I came to a steep cliff that extended into the sea beyond the beach so far that it was impossible to go further. I resolved to climb the cliff, and after much exertion, got on it, but saw that the east side was steep as a wall and it was impossible to go on. I therefore walked south in the hope of getting to the other side of the island, there along the shore to get to the channel to investigate my theory of the presence here of a river and harbor. But when I was climbing down the hill, which was very densely overgrown everywhere with a thick, dark woods, without finding a trace of a path so that I could not get through, I considered that it would be impossible for my cossack to find me, also that I was too far from the others in case something should happen, and that I could not get back before night, to say nothing of other dangers, which I would not have feared if I had had the slightest help from my companions.

I therefore climbed the hill and looked mournfully at the depressing limits set for my explorations, wistful about the behavior of those who held in their hands these important matters; for which actions, all have allowed themselves to be regaled with visions of money as well as honor. When I had come again to the top of the hill and turned my eyes to the mainland, at least to take a good look at the region on which I was not allowed to extend my efforts productively, I saw at a verst from me smoke rising from a breezy knoll covered with conifers, and I now had the certain hope of meeting people and learning from them what I needed for a complete report.

I therefore climbed down the hill with great haste and, loaded with my collections, headed back to the place where I had been put ashore. Here, through the men who were just then hurrying from shore to ship in the boat, I sent news to the Captain-Commander and asked him to let me have the small yawl and several men for a few hours. Meanwhile on the beach, utterly exhausted, I described the rarest plants, which I was afraid would wilt, and revived myself by being able to check out the excellent water for tea.

After approximately an hour, I got the patriotic and gracious answer: I was to get my butt on board pronto, or, without waiting, they would leave me stranded.

On August 10, we saw a very unusual and new animal, about which I shall write a short description since I watched it for two whole hours.

The animal was about two ells long. The head was like a dog's head, the ears pointed and erect, and on the upper and lower lips on both sides whiskers hung down which made him look almost like a Chinaman. The eyes were large. The body was longish, round, and fat, but gradually became thinner toward the tail; the skin was covered thickly with hair, gray on the back, reddish white on the belly, but in the water it seemed to be entirely red and cow-colored. The tail, which was equipped with fins, was divided into two parts, the upper fin being two times as long as the lower one, just like on the sharks.

However, I was not a little surprised that I could perceive neither forefeet as in marine amphibians nor fins in their place.

As for its body shape, for which there is no drawing, it corresponds in all respects to the picture that Gesner received from one of his correspondents and in his *Historia animalium* calls *Simia marina Danica*. At least our sea animal can by all rights be given this name because of both its resemblance to Gesner's *Simia* and its strange habits, quick movements, and playfulness.

For more than two hours it stayed with our ship, looking at us, one after the other, as if with admiration. It now and then came closer and often so close that it could have been touched with a pole. Then, as soon as we moved, it retired farther away.

It raised itself out of the water up to one-third of its length, like a human being, and often remained in this position for several minutes.

After it had observed us for almost half an hour, it shot like an arrow under our ship and came up again on the other side, but passed under the ship again to reappear in its first position. It repeated this maneuver back and forth about thirty times.

Now, when this animal spotted a large American seaweed, three to four fathoms long, which at the bottom was hollowed out like a bottle and from there to the outermost end became gradually more pointed like a phial, it shot toward it like an arrow, grabbed it with its mouth, and swam with it toward our vessel, and did such juggling tricks that one could not have asked for anything more comical from a monkey. Now and then it bit off a piece and ate it.

When I had observed it for a long time, I had a gun loaded and fired at this animal, intending to get possession of it to make an accurate description. But the shot missed. Although it was somewhat frightened, it reappeared right away and approached our ship gradually.

But when another shot at it was in vain, or perhaps only slightly wounded it, it retreated into the sea and did not come back. However, it was seen at various times in different parts of the sea.

## Meeting Americans...

When they were still half a verst away, the two men in the boats, while paddling steadily, began to deliver a long, uninterrupted oration to us in a high-pitched voice, not a word of which any of our interpreters could understand. We took it for either a prayer or a conjuration, the incantation of shamans or a ceremony welcoming us as friends, since both customs are in use on Kamchatka and in the Kurile Islands, as may be seen in more detail in my *Historical Description of the Kuriles*. As they paddled closer and closer, shouting continually, they began to speak to us with pauses between statements. But since no one could understand their language, we beckoned them with our hands to come closer without fear. But they pointed their hands toward the shore to signify that we should come to them there. They also pointed to their mouths and scooped up seawater to signify that we could have food and water with them. But we beckoned to them rather to come to us. When we called *nitschi* back to them, which in Baron Lahontan's description of America means "water," they repeated it many times and pointed again to the shore to indicate undoubtedly that water was available there.

Nonetheless, one of them came quite close to us. However, before he approached us altogether, he stuck his hand into his bosom, took some iron- or lead-colored shiny earth and painted himself with it from the wings of his nose across the cheeks in the shape of two pears, and stuffed his nostrils full of grass; the wings of his nose on both sides were pierced by fine pieces of bone. Then he took a stick of spruce wood lying behind him on top of the skinboat, painted red like a billiard cue and three arshins long. On this he stuck two falcon wings and bound them fast with baleen, showed it to us, and then, laughing, threw it toward our ship into the water. I cannot tell if it was meant as a sacrifice or a sign of friendship. Then, for our part, we bound two Chinese tobacco pipes and Chinese glass beads to a small piece of board, and threw it in exchange to them. He picked it up, looked at it a bit, and handed it over to his companion, who put it on top of his boat. Then he became somewhat braver, came still closer to us, yet with the greatest caution, bound a whole falcon to another stick, and presented it to our Koriak interpreter, to receive from us a piece of Chinese silk and a mirror. But it was not his intention at all that we should take the bird for ourselves; rather, he wanted us to put the piece of silk between the bird's claws so that it wouldn't get wet. But when the interpreter held on to the stick and pulled the American, who held the other end in his hands, together with his boat to our vessel, he let go of the stick, and it remained in our hands. Then he got frightened and paddled a little to the side; nor did he want to come so close again. So we threw the mirror and silk to him; with that they paddled toward the shore, signaling us that we should follow so that they might give us food and drink.

# CHAPTER 21

# Rescued from the Dream: Miguel Costanso and the 1769 Expedition by Sea to San Diego

*In 1542, the same year that Alvar Núñez Cabeza de Vaca's* Relación *was published in Spain, another Spaniard, Juan Rodríguez Cabrillo, ventured along the unknown coast of the Far West, sailing into San Diego Bay. Another sixty years and the expedition of Sir Francis Drake would pass before another Spaniard, Sebastian Vizcaino, sailed along the California coast in 1602. Then more than a century and a half would go by before the Spanish government sent more expeditions to explore the discoveries of Cabrillo and Vizcaino. Such a long delay occurred not because the Spanish authorities weren't anxious about Drake's voyage and the Russian exploration of Alaska, but because Spain had emptied its treasury, and its government saw no need to spend money exploring and colonizing remote lands that had already been claimed for the Spanish crown.*

*Anxiety finally assumed the upper hand over lethargy, however, for in 1768 the Spaniards in Mexico convened a meeting at San Blas to plan the occupation of Alta California. Present at that meeting was Miguel Costanso, author of the brief selection that follows. Although his early life lies shrouded in obscurity, we do know that Costanso had arrived in New Spain in 1764 and that he had distinguished himself by his service in the Corps of Engineers, drawing plans of the Port of San Blas. At the 1768 meeting, he was chosen for the ocean-going group of a two-pronged California expedition that was also sending a party by land. Sailing on the* San José, *he and his shipmates encountered such strong winds that they didn't reach San Diego until their supplies had been exhausted and they had all come down with scurvy.*

*Our selection from Costanso's narrative tells about this harrowing trial and about the last-minute rescue by the party that had come by land. If the reader sees in this story similarities to the endings of countless westerns, that may be because, in this case at least, popular western American art actually imitated life: travel in an unknown and harsh land sometimes brought explorers and settlers to the brink of disaster. And sometimes, of course, no cavalry arrived to save those who were about to perish. We're haunted by the fate of the Donner Party and others for whom help came too late, and we celebrate rescues because they give us hope of survival and satisfy our hunger for a happy ending.*

*Costanso's subsequent career also sounds a happy note. Picked to join the expedition that Gaspar de Portola led to Monterey in 1769, Costanso kept a diary during the journey. When Portola was replaced as governor by Pedro Fages in 1770, Costanso accompanied the former governor on the return sea voyage to San Blas. For the last quarter of the eighteenth century, Costanso distinguished himself in government service in Mexico, doing survey work, giving advice on solving problems in the northern outposts of New Spain, and designing buildings and drawing plans for government projects such as the sewer system in Mexico City. As with his early life, however, little is known about Costanso's last years.*

*His* Narrative *was published in 1770, although the historian Ray Brandes thinks that Spanish authorities probably suppressed a first printing to keep the information out of the hands of Spain's imperial rivals. At least half a dozen subsequent editions and translations have appeared, including one by the nineteenth-century western editor Charles F. Lummis, who published it in 1901 in his journal* The Land of Sunshine.

### Selected Bibliography

Costanso, Miguel. *The Costanso Narrative of the Portola Expedition: First Chronicle of the Spanish Conquest of Alta California.* Trans. and ed. by Ray Brandes. Newhall, Cal.: Hogarth, 1970.

Johnson, Allen, and Dumas Malone, eds. *Dictionary of American Biography.* New York: Scribner's, 1943.

MIGUEL COSTANSO

# Rescued from the Dream: Miguel Costanso and the 1769 Expedition by Sea to San Diego

### Suffering from Scurvy in a New Land

THE NAVIGATION of the California coast has an inseparable difficulty in the constancy of the north and northwest winds, which last through all the year with little interruption, and are directly opposed to the voyage. The coastline angles from northwest to southeast, which obligates every vessel to withdraw from the coast and run out to sea until it encounters winds more favorable and variable with which, running as far north as they need, they can stand in to windward of the port to which they are bound.

On this presumption, and with orders to follow the method indicated, the two packets made their voyage to the Port of San Diego, but with different fortunes. The *San Carlos* experienced such contrary winds and calms, that finding itself driven to sea more than 200 leagues from the coast, and short of water, it had to stand in to the coast to seek water. It did so on the Island of Cerros (Cedros) with great difficulty and hard work, the ship keeping under sail, tacking between land and the Island, with no shelter nor anchorage whatever where an anchor could be dropped without risk of losing it on account of the bad nature of the bottom.

Having concluded taking on water, the ship put to sea on March 26, and on April 29, entered the Port of San Diego, one hundred and ten days out of La Paz. But its crew, and the troops it transported—whose hardships could not fail to be excessive in so long and painful a voyage, and in the rawest of the winter, arrived in a deplorable state. Scurvy had infected all without exception, in such a way that on entering San Diego, two men had already died of the sickness; most of the seamen, and half of the troops found themselves prostrate in their beds. Only four sailors remained on their feet, and attended, aided by the troops, to trimming and furling the sails and other work on board ship.

The packet *San Antonio,* although it had put forth one month after the *San Carlos,* had the fortune to finish the voyage in 59 days, and had been lying in the Port of San Diego since April 11. But it had half of its crew equally affected by scurvy, of which illness two men had also died. Amid so much sickness, all showed happiness in being reunited, and with common accord, after the *San Carlos* had tied up in a convenient spot, the officers resolved to attend to the prompt alleviation of the sick.

The first business was to seek a place to get water from which to supply and fill the barrels with good water for the use of the men. For that purpose on May first, the Officers Don Pedro Fages, Don Miguel Costanso, and the second Captain of the *San Carlos,* Don Gorge Estorace, with the troops and mariners who found themselves in better shape for fatigue-duty, numbered twenty-one men. Following the west shore of the Port, they discovered a short distance away a group of Indians armed with bows and arrows, to whom they made signs with white cloths calling them to a parley. But, keeping at a distance, moving away as our men moved toward them, prevented a meeting. Nor was it possible, either, for our men to make greater speed, for they were weak, and after such a long voyage had, as it were, lost the use of their legs. These Indians stopped every little while upon some height, watching our men, and showing the fear which the strangers caused them by the very thing they did to hide it. They thrust one point of their bows down in the soil, and grasping it by the other end they danced and whirled about with indescribable velocity. But, as soon as they saw our men draw near, they again withdrew themselves with the same swiftness. At last it was contrived to attract them by sending toward them one soldier, who, depositing his arms on the earth, and using gestures and signs of peace, they consented to let him near. He distributed some gifts to them while the others were coming up, who finished assuring these Gentiles with some more considerable presents of ribbons, glass, beads, and baubles. They asked them by signs where the watering-place was, and the natives, pointing toward a grove which was made out in the distance to the northeast, gave to understand that within it ran some river or arroyo, and to follow, that they would take them to it.

They walked some three leagues, until they arrived on the banks of a river hemmed in on either bank by a low ridge of very leafy willows and cottonwoods. Its channel must have been twenty varas wide, and it discharges into an estuary which at high tide could admit the launch, and make it convenient for accomplishing the taking on of water. Within the grove was a variety of shrubs and odoriferous plants, as the Rosemary, the Sage, Roses of Castile, and above all a quantity of wild grapevines, which at the time were in blossom. The country was of joyous appearance, and the lands contiguous to the river appeared of excellent friableness, and capable of producing every species of fruits. The river came down from some very high mountains through a spacious ravine which was penetrated by a bend from the east and northeast. At a gunshot aside from it, and outside the trees was discovered a pueblo or rancheria of the same Gentiles who were guiding our people. It was composed of various brush and bough shelters and of huts of a pyramidal shape covered with earth. On sighting their companions with the followers they were escorting, all came out to receive them: men, women, and children proffering their houses to the guests. The women came in modest garb, covered from waist to knee with close-woven and doubled nets. The Spaniards arrived at the rancheria, which must have consisted of thirty or forty families, and at one side of it a protective enclosure, made of branches and trunks of trees. Inside this, they gave us to understand, they took refuge to defend themselves from their enemies when they saw themselves attacked: a fortification inexpugnable to the arms in use among them.

These Indians are of good figure, well-built and agile. They go naked without more clothing than a girdle of *ixtle*, or very fine maguey fiber, woven in the form of a net. They take out this thread from a plant called *Lechugilla*. Their quivers, which they bind in between the girdle and the body, are of skins of wild cat, coyote, wolf or male deer, and their bows are two varas long. Besides these arms, they use a kind of war club of very hard wood, whose shape is like that of a short and curved cutlass, which they fling edgewise and it cleaves the air with much violence. They hurl it a greater distance than a stone. Without it they never go forth to the field, and if they see a rattlesnake or other noxious animal, they throw the *macana* at it and commonly sever it in half. According to the experience afterward in the continual discussions which our Spaniards had with them, they are of haughty temper, daring, covetous, great jesters, and braggarts, although of little valor; they make great boast of their powers, and hold the most respect for the most valiant. They greatly crave whatsoever rag, but when we have clothed different ones of them on repeated occasions, they would present themselves the following day stark naked.

There are in the land, deer, antelope, many hares, rabbits, squirrels, wild cats, and rats. The ring-necked turtle-doves abound, and so do the quail, calendar-lark, mockingbird, thrush, cardinal, and hummingbird, jackdaw, crow and hawk, pelican, gull, divers and other maritime birds of prey. There is no lack of ducks nor of geese, of different shapes and sizes. There is a variety of fish. The best are the flounder and the sole which besides being of delicate taste, are of extraordinary size and weigh from fifteen to twenty pounds. In the months of July and August one can catch as much bonito as one wishes. During all the year there are halibut, burgaos, horse-mackeral, dogfish, rays, mussels and cockles of all species. In the winter months the sardine runs in as great abundance as on the coasts of Galicia and Ayamonte. The principal sustenance of the Indians that inhabit the shore of this Port is fish. They eat much cockles, for the greater facility they have in catching them. They use balsas (rafts) of rushes, which they manage dexterously with a paddle or oar of two blades. Their harpoons are of some varas in length. The point is of bone, very much sharpened, inserted in the shaft of wood. They are so dexterous in hurling this that rarely do they miss their target.

Having reconnoitered the watering place, the Spaniards returned back on board the vessels. As these were found to be very far away from the estuary in which the river discharges, their Captains Don Vicente Vila and Don Juan Pérez resolved to approach it as closely as they could, in order to give less work to the men in the handling of the launches. These labors were too much hardship, for from one day to the next this aggravated and increased the fatigue of the few who remained on their feet.

Near the beach, on the side toward the east, a scanty enclosure was constructed, formed of a parapet of earth and brushwood. Two cannons were placed onto the parapet. They disembarked some sails and awnings from the packets, with which they made two tents, large enough for a hospital. At one side the two officers, the Missionary Fathers and the surgeon put their own tents. And everything being found in shape to receive the sick, they were brought from on shipboard in the launches and arranged in the tents as comfortably as possible.

But these caves were not enough to procure them health. They already lacked the medicines and diet, nearly all of which had been consumed during the sea voyage. The surgeon, Don Pedro Prat supplied in what manner was possible this lack with some herbs which he sought in the fields, with a thousand anxieties. Of the virtues of the herbs of which he had knowledge, and he himself was in as sore need of them as were the sick, since he found himself little less than prostrated with the same affliction as they. The cold made itself felt with rigor at night in the tents, and the sun likewise by day, alternations which made the sick suffer cruelly, two or three of them dying every day. This whole expedition which had been composed of more than ninety men was reduced to only eight soldiers and as many sailors able to attend to the protection of the boats, the working of the launches, guarding the camp, and caring for the sick.

There was no news of the expedition by land. The neighborhood of the Port had been searched, looking for tracks of a horseherd, but none were discovered and it was not known what to think of this delay. But on May 14, the Indians told some soldiers who were on the beach that from the direction of south of the Port some men were coming, armed as they; and explained very well by signs that they were coming mounted on horses. All were joyous at this news, which was verified from there in a short time, sighting the people and the packtrain of the first division of the expedition by land. They exchanged salutes with festive salvos from their weapons; later explaining with arms and voices their gladness, which was equal on both sides, since all hoped to find from the others relief in their needs. The men who had traveled overland had done so without having lost one man, and without bringing one sick one, after a march of two months, but on half rations, and with no more provisions than three sacks of flour, of which they were issuing as the entire daily ration two tortillas to each individual.

# CHAPTER 22

# Mixing Fact and Fiction: Jonathan Carver (1769)

*Most schoolchildren know that the amateur soldiers of the American colonies drew on their frontier experience fighting Indians to make life nettlesome for the polished British troops during the Revolutionary War. That does not mean that the colonials necessarily were an uncouth lot. Plucky, practical, largely self-taught, they also shared the airy rationality of eighteenth-century Europeans. Thus balanced, Jonathan Carver, a veteran of the French and Indian Wars who taught himself mapmaking, was well-equipped for his travels in the wilds of the upper Mississippi River.*

*Hardly a gullible bumpkin, he commented, "This story I acknowledge appears to carry with it marks of great credulity in the relator." While exploring the depths of the wilderness, he had just beheld a fantastic event. An Indian Houdini came out of a trance, impossibly burst the ropes around his body, then delivered a prophecy that soon came true. Admitting the "extraordinary nature" of the performance, the observer nonetheless maintained a gently skeptical attitude toward the "magic" he'd just seen (Carver 1781, 129).*

*The caution, however, didn't dull the poetic nicety of the traveler's descriptions or blunt his passions. Paddling across Lake Superior on a placid day, Carver feels suspended in the air and pauses in his journalistic fact giving to appreciate a sensuous moment (1781, 132–33). Armed with his own extraordinary vision, he peers into the unknown West and sees riches greater than those of "Indostan and Malabar" awaiting future generations (1781, 122)—an estimate that proved true, though whether from perspicacity or a chance hit no one can say. And neither can it be said precisely which parts of Carver's* Travels *accurately record the writer's experiences and which, if any, he spun out of his own imagination; which were by his hand and which by unknown London editors characteristically fluffing up a text in hopes of increasing book sales.*

*We do know that Carver came from a respectable but not well-off New England family. Having risen to the rank of captain during his military service, he struck west to find the Great River of the West, the Straits of Anian, the Northwest Passage—to find the easy access to the Pacific Ocean, whatever its several names. Pursuing his hopes in a different manner, in 1769 Carver sailed to England, where he spent the rest of his life failing to turn his book into a profitable venture. Though he'd left a wife in America, he married a second time. He likely tried to raise funds by selling off parts of a large American wilderness tract he did, or did not, own. He accused the French of falsifying their maps in order to keep the riches of the West secret, then published his own map that incorporated ". . . nearly every erroneous idea that had so far been formulated. . . " by others about the region (Burpee 1936, 298). Yet much of this is cloudy, the province of continued scholarly wrangling. Perhaps the surest that can be said about shadowy Carver is that on both sides of the Atlantic his* Travels *inspired public enthusiasm for the West by mixing between two covers much of the fact and fiction then current about the lands beyond the Mississippi River.*

### Selected Bibliography

Burpee, Lawrence J. *The Search for the Western Sea: The Story of the Exploration of North-Western America*. [1907]. 2 Vols. New York: Macmillan, 1936.

Carver, Jonathan. *The Journals of Jonathan Carver and Related Documents, 1766–1770*. Ed. by John Parker. St. Paul: Minnesota Historical Society, 1976.

———. *Travels through the Interior Parts of North America in the Years 1766, 1767, and 1768*. [1778]. London: Dilly, 1781.

DeVoto, Bernard. *The Course of Empire*. Boston: Houghton Mifflin, 1952.

JONATHAN CARVER

# Mixing Fact and Fiction: Jonathan Carver (1769)

## The Shining Mountains, the Great Spirit, Pellucid Water, and Gold Dust

IN THE COUNTRY belonging to these people it is said, that Mandrakes are frequently found, a species of root resembling human beings of both sexes; and that these are more perfect than such as are discovered about the Nile in Nether-Ethiopia.

A little to the north-west of the heads of the Messorie and the St. Pierre, the Indians further told me, that there was a nation rather smaller and whiter than the neighbouring tribes, who cultivate the ground, and (as far as I could gather from their expressions) in some measure, the arts. To this account they added that some of the nations, who inhabit those parts that lie to the west of the Shining Mountains, have gold so plenty among them that they make their most common utensils of it. These mountains (which I shall describe more particularly hereafter) divide the waters that fall into the South Sea from those that run into the Atlantic.

The people dwelling near them are supposed to be some of the different tribes that were tributary to the Mexican kings, and who fled from their native country to seek an asylum in these parts, about the time of the conquest of Mexico by the Spaniards, more than two centuries ago.

As some confirmation of this supposition it is remarked, that they have chosen the most interior parts for their retreat, being still prepossessed with a notion that the sea-coasts have been infested ever since with monsters vomiting fire, and hurling about thunder and lightning; from whose bowels issued men, who, with unseen instruments, or by the power of magick, killed the harmless Indians at an astonishing distance. From such as these, their fore-fathers (according to a tradition among them that still remains unimpaired) fled to the retired abodes they now inhabit. For as they found that the floating monsters which had thus terrified them could not approach the land, and that those who had descended from their sides did not care to make excursions to any considerable distance from them, they formed a resolution to betake themselves to some country, that lay far from the seacoasts, where only they could be secure from such diabolical enemies. They accordingly set out with their families, and after a long peregrination, settled themselves near these mountains, where they concluded they had found a place of perfect security.

The Winnebagoes, dwelling on the Fox River (whom I have already treated of) are likewise supposed to be some strolling band from the Mexican countries. But they are able to give only an imperfect account of their original residence. They say they formerly came a great way from the westward, and were driven by wars to take refuge among the Naudowessies; but as they are entirely ignorant of the arts, or of the value of gold, it is rather to be supposed, that they were driven from their ancient settlements by the above-mentioned emigrants, as they passed on towards their present habitation.

These suppositions, however, may want confirmation; for the smaller tribes of Indians are subject to such various alternations in their places of abode, from the wars they are continually engaged in, that it is almost impossible to ascertain, after half a century, the original situation of any of them.

That range of mountains, of which the Shining Mountains are a part, begin at Mexico, and continuing northward on the back, or to the east of California, separate the waters of those numerous rivers that fall either into the Gulph of Mexico, or the Gulph of California. From thence continuing their course still northward, between the sources of the Mississippi and the rivers that run into the South Sea, they appear to end in about forty-seven or forty-eight degrees of north latitude; where a number of rivers arise, and empty themselves either into the South Sea, into Hudson's Bay, or into the waters that communicate between these two seas.

Among these mountains, those that lie to the west of the River St. Pierre, are called the Shining Mountains, from an infinite number of chrystal stones, of an amazing size, with which they are covered, and which, when the sun shines full upon them, sparkle so as to be seen at a very great distance.

This extraordinary range of mountains is calculated to be more than three thousand miles in length, without any very considerable intervals, which I believe surpasses any thing of the kind in the other quarters of the globe. Probably in future ages they may be found to contain more riches in their bowels, than those of Indostan and Malabar, or that are produced on the Golden Coast of Guinea; nor will I except even the Peruvian Mines. To the west of these mountains, when explored by future Columbuses or Raleighs, may be found other lakes, rivers, and countries, full fraught with all the necessaries or luxuries of life; and where future generations may find an asylum, whether driven from their country by the ravages of lawless tyrants, or by religious persecutions, or reluctantly leaving it to remedy the inconveniences arising from a superabundant increase of inhabitants; whether, I say, impelled by these, or allured by hopes of commercial advantages, there is little doubt but their expectation will be fully gratified in these rich and unexhausted climes.

But to return to the Assinipoils and Killistinoes, whom I left at the Grand Portage, and from whom I received the foregoing account of the lakes that lie to the north-west of this place.

The traders we expected being later this season than usual, and our numbers very considerable, for there were more than three hundred of us, the stock of provision we had brought with us was nearly exhausted, and we waited with impatience for their arrival.

One day, whilst we were all expressing our wishes for this desirable event, and looking from an eminence in hopes of feeling them come over the lake, the chief priest belonging to the band of the Killistinoes told us, that he would endeavour to obtain a conference with the Great Spirit, and know from him when the traders would arrive. I paid little attention to this declaration, supposing that it would be productive of some juggling trick, just sufficiently covered to deceive the ignorant Indians. But the king of that tribe telling me that this was chiefly undertaken by the priest to alleviate my anxiety, and at the same time to convince me how much interest he had with the Great Spirit, I thought it necessary to restrain my animadversions on his design.

The following evening was fixed upon for this spiritual conference. When every thing had been properly prepared, the king came to me and led me to a capacious tent, the covering of which was drawn up, so as to render what was transacting within visible to those who stood without. We found the tent surrounded by a great number of the Indians, but we readily gained admission, and seated ourselves on skins laid on the ground for that purpose.

In the centre I observed that there was a place of an oblong shape, which was composed of stakes stuck in the ground, with intervals between, so as to form a kind of chest or coffin, large enough to contain the body of a man. These were of a middle size, and placed at such a distance from each other, that whatever lay within them was readily to be discerned. The tent was perfectly illuminated by a great number of torches made of splinters cut from the pine or birch tree, which the Indians held in their hands.

In a few minutes the priest entered; when an amazing large elk's skin being spread on the ground, just at my feet, he laid himself down upon it, after having stript himself of every garment except that which he wore close about his middle. Being now prostrate on his back, he first laid hold of one side of the skin, and folded it over him, and then the other; leaving only his head uncovered. This was no sooner done, than two of the young men who stood by took about forty yards of strong cord, made also of an elk's hide, and rolled it tight round his body, so that he was completely swathed within the skin. Being thus bound up like an Egyptian Mummy, one took him by the heels, and the other by the head, and lifted him over the pales into the inclosure. I could also now discern him as plain as I had hitherto done, and I took care not to turn my eyes a moment from the object before me, that I might the more readily detect the artifice; for such I doubted not but that it would turn out to be.

The priest had not lain in this situation more than a few seconds, when he began to mutter. This he continued to do for some time, and then by degrees grew louder and louder, till at length he spoke articulately; however what he uttered was in such a mixed jargon of the Chipéway, Ottowaw, and Killistinoe languages, that I could understand but very little of it. Having continued in this tone for a considerable while, he at last exerted his voice to its utmost pitch, sometimes raving and sometimes praying, till he had worked himself into such an agitation, that he foamed at his mouth.

After having remained near three quarters of an hour in the place, and continued his vociferation with unabated vigor, he seemed to be quite exhausted, and remained speechless. But in an instant he sprung upon his feet, notwithstanding at the time he was put in, it appeared impossible for him to move either his legs or arms, and shaking off his covering, as quick as if the bands with which it had been bound were burned asunder, he began to address those who stood around in a firm and audible voice. "My Brothers," said he, "the Great Spirit has deigned to hold a Talk with his servant at my earnest request. He has not, indeed, told me when the persons we expect will be here, but to-morrow, soon

after the sun has reached his highest point in the heavens, a canoe will arrive, and the people in that will inform us when the traders will come."
Having said this, he stepped out of the inclosure, and after he had put on
his robes, dismissed the assembly. I own I was greatly astonished at what I
had seen; but as I observed that every eye in the company was fixed on
me with a view to discover my sentiments, I carefully concealed every
emotion.

The next day the sun shone bright, and long before noon all the Indians were gathered together on the eminence that overlooked the lake.
The old king came to me and asked me, whether I had so much confidence in what the priest had foretold, as to join his people on the hill,
and wait for the completion of it? I told him I was at a loss what opinion
to form of the prediction, but that I would readily attend him. On this we
walked together to the place where the others were assembled. Every eye
was again fixed by turns on me and on the lake; when just as the sun had
reached his zenith, agreeable to what the priest had foretold, a canoe
came round a point of land about a league distant. The Indians no sooner
beheld it, than they sent up an universal shout, and by their looks seemed
to triumph in the interest their priest thus evidently had with the Great
Spirit.

In less than an hour the canoe reached the shore, when I attended the
king and chiefs to receive those who were on board. As soon as the men
were landed, we walked all together to the king's tent, when according to
their invariable custom we began to smoke; and this we did, notwithstanding our impatience to know the tidings they brought, without asking any questions; for the Indians are the most deliberate people in the
world. However, after some trivial conversation, the king inquired of
them whether they had seen any thing of the traders? The men replied,
that they had parted from them a few days before, that they proposed being here the second day from the present. They accordingly arrived at
that time greatly to our satisfaction, but more particularly so to that of
the Indians, who found by this event the importance both of their priest
and of their nation, greatly augmented in the sight of a stranger.

This story I acknowledge appears to carry with it marks of great credulity in the relator. But no one is less tinctured with that weakness than
myself. The circumstances of it I own are of a very extraordinary nature;
however, as I can vouch for their being free from either exaggeration or
misrepresentation, being myself a cool and dispassionate observer of
them all, I thought it necessary to give them to the public. And this I do
without wishing to mislead the judgment of my Readers, or to make any

superstitious impressions on their minds, but leaving them to draw from it what conclusions they please. . . .

The water in general appeared to lie on a bed of rocks. When it was calm, and the sun shone bright, I could fit in my canoe, where the depth was upwards of six fathoms, and plainly see huge piles of stone at the bottom, of different shapes, some of which appeared as if they were hewn. The water at this time was as pure and transparent as air; and my canoe seemed as if it hung suspended in that element. It was impossible to look attentively through this limpid medium at the rocks below, without finding, before many minutes were elapsed, your head swim, and your eyes no longer able to behold the dazzling scene. . . .

One of the Chipéway chiefs told me, that some of their people being once driven on the island of Mauropas, which lies towards the north-east part of the Lake, found on it large quantities of a heavy shining yellow sand, that from their description must have been gold dust. Being struck with the beautiful appearance of it, in the morning, when they re-entered their canoe, they attempted to bring some away; but a spirit of an amazing size, according to their account sixty feet in height, strode into the water after them, and commanded them to deliver back what they had taken away. Terrified at his gigantic stature, and seeing that he had nearly overtaken them, they were glad to restore their shining treasure; on which they were suffered to depart without further molestation.

# CHAPTER 23

# Searching for Accounts of the Search: Father Juan Crespi and the 1774 Voyage of the Santiago

*Gold lured twenty-one-year-old Adolph Heinrich Sutro to California in 1851—but instead of digging for it, he acquired it by selling supplies to other gold-seekers. Still, dreams of gold discoveries must have continued to entice Sutro, for in 1860 he was drawn to the mines of Nevada. There he not only invented a profitable way to glean silver from mine tailings, but he also planned the formidable engineering project that earned him a secure place in the history of the Old West. Dug by a small army of workers over a nine-year period, the Sutro Tunnel cut through four miles of Mount Davidson to give better access to the fabulous Comstock Lode. But within a year of the shaft's completion in 1878, Sutro sold out for a fortune. That fortune grew when he invested it in San Francisco real estate. Then, like some other early western millionaires, Sutro used some of his wealth for cultural and philanthropic pursuits.*

*Another wealthy California merchant, Hubert Howe Bancroft, had already amassed an impressive collection of early California documents, and Sutro decided to follow his lead. He had agents search Spanish archives, and in 1883 and 1884 they sent to Sutro nineteen significant documents, which were then translated and edited by George Butler Griffin, president of the Historical Society of Southern California, and published by the society in 1891. Ironically, though—at least according to Donald C. Cutter, who re-edited the documents for republication in 1969—Sutro probably bought fool's gold when he paid his agents for their "discoveries," since most of the documents had already been published in Spain in 1882. Whatever their actual value, Sutro's collection perished in the fires caused by the San Francisco earthquake of 1906.*

*Still, even though Sutro's largess may have enriched only his sly agents rather than the world of scholarship, the tale of the scam at least spices the provenance of documents that are of considerable historical importance but that are also, with few exceptions, singularly bland. Here, for example, is a typical day's entry from one of Father Crespi's diaries:*

Thursday, the 16th [of June in 1774], dawned with much fog, although it lifted soon and we saw the Sierra of Santa Lucia, now some ten or twelve leagues distant. About seven o'clock the wind came from the north-northwest rather fresh, so that we made two miles and a half an hour. Afterwards the wind went to northwest and blew thence all day. By evening we could barely make out the land.

*The following brief selection from these largely uneventful accounts nevertheless paints a clear picture of the first encounter between Spanish navigators and the natives of Queen Charlotte Island. The encounter initiated trade that the Spanish continued, and it also gave Europeans a warning about the warlike spirit of some of the coastal peoples. Here, too, we see Spanish explorers still discovering new lands and peoples almost three centuries after Columbus's first voyage and two and a half centuries after Cabeza de Vaca trekked across the Southwest.*

*And the narrative of this discovery has about it the freshness of archetype. Before you read the following selection from Crespi's diary, imagine what the encounter between the Spanish sailors and the Northwest natives was like. Such an encounter was one of dozens, if not hundreds, that took place from the first voyage of Columbus until the era of Lewis and Clark—and those actual encounters have been reenacted hundreds of times since in historical and fictional recreations. Perhaps we go back to those first meetings between two worlds because of the possibilities they hold, possibilities of alternatives to the paths we chose to take.*

*Father Juan Crespi, author of the relatively detailed description that follows, was only one of four diarists who kept separate accounts of their 1774 voyage. According to the historian Donald Cutter, Crespi's diary is not the most accurate of the four—in part because he suffered from seasickness for most of the voyage—but Cutter (1969, xvi) adds that in Crespi's sea diaries, "one can see evidence of frequent diary writing and a dedication to certain details that escaped the less experienced but more enthusiastic Father Tomás de la Peña." Born in 1721, Crespi had more experience mainly because he was twenty-two years older than Peña. Both men had come from Europe; and like Junípero Serra, Francisco Palou, and Juan Pérez (other prominent figures in early California history), Crespi was from Mallorca. Herbert E. Bolton (1927, xv–xvi) says that "Of all the men of this half decade [1768– 74], so prolific in frontier expansion... Crespi alone participated in all the major path-breaking expeditions: from Velicata to San Diego; from San Diego to San Francisco Bay; from Monterey to the San Joaquin Valley; from Monterey by sea to Alaska. In distance he out-traveled Coronado."*

*The* vara *mentioned in the following passage was a Spanish measure roughly equivalent to 2.75 English feet. The notes in brackets have been added by the editors of this volume.*

### Selected Bibliography

Bolton, Herbert E. *Fray Juan Crespi, Missionary Explorer of the Pacific Coast, 1768–1774.* Berkeley: University of California Press, 1927.
Cutter, Donald C., ed. *The California Coast: A Bilingual Edition of Documents from the Sutro Collection.* Norman: University of Oklahoma Press, 1969.

FATHER JUAN CRESPI

# Searching for Accounts of the Search: Father Juan Crespi and the 1774 Voyage of the Santiago

## Crespi Describes the Natives of Queen Charlotte Island

AFTER THE CALM had lasted twelve hours and the ship was about a league from land, off the southwest point or hill of Santa Margarita [Cape North of Queen Charlotte Island], canoes began to put out, both from this southwest point and that running to the east-southeast; and, in a short time twenty-one canoes had come near to us. Some were very large; others of medium size; others small. Among them were two, neither of which would measure less than twelve *varas* along the keel; in one of these were twenty men and in the other nineteen. In the canoes of medium size there were ten or twelve persons, and in the smallest not less than six or seven. In a short time we saw ourselves surrounded by these twenty-one canoes, which contained more than two hundred persons, between men, women, boys and girls—for in the greater number of the canoes there were some women. Among the canoes was one containing only women, some twelve in number, and they alone paddled and managed the canoe as well as the most expert sailors could.

These canoes came alongside without their occupants manifesting the least distrust, they singing and playing instruments of wood fashioned like drums or timbrels, and some making movements like dancing. They drew close to the ship, surrounding her on all sides, and presently there began between them and our people a traffic, and we soon knew that they had come for the purpose of bartering their effects for ours. The sailors gave them knives, old clothing and beads, and they in return gave skins of the otter and other animals unknown, very well tanned and dressed; coverlets of otter skins sewn together so well that the best tailor could not sew them better; other coverlets, or blankets of fine wool, or the hair of animals that seemed like wool, finely woven and ornamented with the same hair of various colors, principally white, black and yellow, the weaving being so close that it appeared as though done on a loom.

All these coverlets have around the edge a fringe of some thread twisted, so that they are very fit for tablecloths, or covers, as if they had been made for that purpose. They gave us, also, some little mats, seemingly made of fine palm leaves, wrought in different colors; some hats made of reeds, some coarse and others of better quality, most of them painted, their shape being, as I have said, conical with a narrow brim, and having a string which passing under the chin keeps the hat from being carried away by the wind. There were obtained from them, also, some small wooden platters, well made and ornamented, the figures of men, animals and birds being executed, in relief or by incising, in the wood; also some wooden spoons, carved on the outside and smooth within the bowl, and one rather large spoon made of a horn, though we could not tell from what animal it came.

There were obtained from them two boxes made of pine, each about a *vara* square, of boards well wrought and instead of being fastened together by nails, they were sewed with thread at all the corners. They have neither hinges nor locks, but the cover comes down like that of a trunk with a fastening like that of a powder chest; and they are rather roughly fashioned within, but outside are well made and smooth, the front being carved with various figures and branches, and inlaid with marine shells in a manner so admirable that we could not discover how the inlay was made. Some of these figures are painted in various colors, chiefly red and yellow. In all the canoes we saw these boxes and some of them were nearly a yard and a half long and of a proportionate width. They use them for guarding their little possessions and as seats when paddling. They gave us, also, some belts very closely woven of threads of wool or hair, and some dried fish of the kind I mentioned yesterday. It is apparent that they have a great liking for articles made of iron for cutting, if they be not small. For beads they did not show a great liking. They accepted biscuit and ate it without the least examination of it.

As I have said, these Indians are well built; their faces are good and rather fair and rosy; their hair is long, and some of them were bearded. All appeared with the body completely covered, some with skins of otter and other animals, others with cloaks woven of wool, or hair which looked like fine wool, and a garment like a cape and covering them to the waist, the rest of the person being clothed in dressed skins or the woven woolen cloths of different colors in handsome patterns. Some of these garments have sleeves; others have not. Most of them wore hats of reeds, such as I have described. The women are clothed in the same manner. They wear pendent from the lower lip, which is pierced, a disk painted in colors, which appeared to be of wood, slight and curved, which makes them seem very ugly, and, at a little distance they appear as if the tongue were hanging out of the mouth. Easily, and with only a movement of the lip, they raise it so that it covers the mouth and part of the nose. Those of our people who saw them from a short distance said that a hole was pierced in the lower lip and the disk hung therefrom. We do not know the object of this; whether it be done to make themselves ugly, as some think, or for the purpose of ornament. I incline to the latter opinion; for, among the heathen found from San Diego to Monterey, we have noted that, when they go to visit a neighboring village, they paint themselves in such a manner as to make themselves most ugly. We saw that some of the men were painted with red ochre of a fine tint.

Although we invited these Indians to come aboard ship they did not venture to do so, except two of them, who were shown everything and who were astonished at all they saw in the vessel. They entered the cabin and we showed them the image of Our Lady. After looking at it with astonishment, they touched it with the hand and we understood that they were examining it in order to learn whether it were alive. We made presents to them, and told them by signs that we were going to their land in order to obtain water. While these two were on board the frigate two of our sailors went down into the canoes, whereat the Indians rejoiced greatly, and made a great to-do. They painted them and danced with them with such expressions of content that they could not have done more had they been well known to them, giving it to be understood by the sign of placing the hand on the breast that they loved them dearly.

From this we all inferred that this is a peaceable and very docile people. Those in the canoes invited the two sailors to their land, telling them that, if they wished, they would take them thither in their canoes; but they did not wish to go, telling them that they would go in the vessel with the rest of the people. But this was not possible, on account of the calm which lasted all the afternoon and the currents which bore us away from the land. So the canoes went away, the Indians inviting us to visit their country, and we understood them to say by signs that we should not go farther up the coast because the people there were warlike and slayers of men, this being the customary warning of almost all pagans, in order to make it understood that they are good men and the rest bad. Our attention was drawn to the pleasant faces of both men and women and their long hair well combed and braided, the women particularly keeping the head in good condition, to their using clothing almost like woven stuffs, the fabric being as good and as well made, and to the manufactured articles of wood, palm, reeds and ivory which our people got from them.

It astonished us, also, to find that the women wore rings on their fingers and bracelets, of iron and of copper. These things I saw on several women, and the sailors who saw them nearer assured me that there was a woman who had five or six rings of iron and of copper on the fingers of her hands. We saw these metals, though not to any great amount, in their possession, and we noted their appreciation of these metals, especially for large articles and those meant for cutting. The Captain, who spent a great deal of time in China and the Philippines, says that they greatly resemble the Sangleyes of the Philippines. It is certain that the weaving of the fine little mats resemble those that come from China. Although the night is very short, for the sun rises before four o'clock, yet this night was long for us, on account of the desire we had to go ashore. Some of the sailors who bought cloaks passed a bad night, for, having put them on, they found themselves obliged to take to scratching, on account of the bites they suffered from the little animals these pagans breed in their clothing.

CHAPTER 24

# Mystery Man of the Far North: Peter Pond (1775)

*Scholars, too, have their dreams. Probably not a one of them hasn't fanta-sized in idle moments about climbing creaking stairs to the attic of some old, Victorian farmhouse in, say, Cranbury, New Jersey, and discovering a man-uscript that earns a solid footnote in history. Something of the sort occurred over a century ago in a Connecticut farmhouse, when Mrs. Nathan Gillett Pond rescued a sheaf of old papers about to be burnt in the kitchen stove as trash. In those critical seconds she pulled back from oblivion the diary of one of the West's most singular adventurers. As sometimes happens, while an-swering a number of vital questions, the discovery began a controversy.*

*Peter Pond was born and died in Milford, Connecticut, yet between these events he led a life either of heroic or villainous proportions, depending on one's view. As a youth of sixteen with "a Strong Desire to be a Solge" (Gates 1965, 18), Pond joined a colonial regiment and fought in the French and In-dian Wars. Thereafter he entered the fur trade around the Detroit area. In 1775 Pond moved on to the Canadian northwest, where he spent the next thirteen years exploring and trading with the Indians. However, because Pond's diary doesn't go beyond 1775, we have scant information about him after that year. McKay says that Pond died "a poverty-stricken and forgotten old man," and there's little reason to question the statement.*

*This outline of Pond's career as a soldier and frontiersman makes him sound interesting but not outstanding. His specific accomplishments were. Far ahead of his fellow traders in the race for new lands to exploit, Pond as-cended the Churchill River and threaded a labyrinth of waterways to estab-lish a trading post on the remote Athabasca River, in present-day Alberta. He became the first white man to penetrate that far into northwestern Can-ada. Besides energetically opening new trade routes, Pond had an expansive vision of geography. This inspired Alexander Mackenzie to make the first trek through the twisted cordillera to the Pacific Ocean. And it's likely that Pond is partly responsible for the shape of the United States. Emerging from the wilderness with maps and a wealth of detail about the importance of the terra incognita, the New Englander put his information at the disposal of Benjamin Franklin. In turn, Franklin used it in the 1780s to "drive a sharp bargain" with the less knowledgeable British in drawing the northern boundary line of the United States (Gates 1965, 13).*

*Beyond Pond's few but well-deserved lines in the record books, his life contains the tempting stuff that causes mystery writers to reach for their pens. That is, shadowy intrigues and murders. Pond was a romantic but violent man, supercharged with energy but edgy and dangerous. One authority of the Canadian northwest paints him as ". . . a morose, unsociable man, suspicious, scenting offense where none was intended. He seems never to have found happiness in the company of men of his race, but preferred the wilderness and its savage inhabitants. . . " (Burpee 1936, 334). A similar estimate is seconded not only by Alexander Mackenzie but by just about every other trader who rubbed shoulders with the man. Further evidence confirms the view. The person who was implicated in at least two wilderness murders had spent years as a wartime soldier, as a trained killer. Pond's own diary somewhat casually mentions that he fatally shot a man in a duel (Gates 1965, 27–28). Despite its use to Franklin, some of Pond's map information seems deliberately calculated to mislead, though the motive for this is unclear. And the record shows that on at least one occasion, Pond worked as a spy for the United States (Gates 1965, 98–102). All this adds up to a portrait of a sleazy and violent scofflaw.*

*"Foul!" cry other scholars. In their view some historians have misunderstood both the man and his frontier context. Henry Wagner sums up the counterargument. He notes that "life was cheap" in the wilderness. Furthermore rivalries in the fur trade became so fierce that bloodletting among competitors was not uncommon. If Pond was a violent man, he was a violent man surviving among cutthroats (1955, 53). Prejudice abraded the normal jealousies over Pond's success (1955, 55). Almost all the traders in Pond's area were Scots, a shrewd and tightly knit group from the Orkney Islands. Pond was an American, an outsider scorned before the Revolutionary War as a mere colonial and after it deemed a traitor. This, and not any unusual character flaws, maintains Wagner, probably accounts for the sordid reputation surrounding Pond (1955, 33, 53). Whatever historians choose to believe, the truth is, as Wagner confesses, that mystery will continue to surround the explorer, because the evidence on either side is too slight to support a conclusion (1955, 44).*

*Pond's diary adds a literary dimension to his mystery. Most immediately the journal's extraordinary, even hilarious, spelling and its lack of punctuation and other graces seem to mark it as the confounding work of a semi-literate. Confronted by, "I Conkluded ameatly to Put a Small a Sortment of Goods Into a Canue..." (Gates 1965, 51), we might grant a certain quaint charm to the rustic writing, grant the authentic "... twang of an un-schooled colonial Yankee..." dialect (1965, xi). But one need not be an apologist to detect a native sophistication at work beneath the words' rough texture. If anything the controversial Pond was a sharp observer—and this exceptionally, when most wilderness chroniclers of the day leaned toward generalizations and overlooked many of the particulars that now interest us. As far ahead of his times in his writing as in his explorations, Pond has the later novelist's eye for detail. His realism, humor, and whimsical Yankee de-tachment equip him to pass on psychological portraits of fellow strugglers in the wilds, portraits rarely found elsewhere at the time and, in Pond, done with an incomparably keen brush.*

### Selected Bibliography

Burpee, Lawrence J. *The Search for the Western Sea: The Story of the Explora-tion of North-Western America.* [1907]. 2 vols. New York: Macmillan, 1936.

Gates, Charles M., ed. *Five Fur Traders of the Northwest.* 1933. St. Paul: Min-nesota Historical Society, 1965.

Innis, Harold Adams. *Peter Pond: Fur Trader and Adventurer.* Toronto: Irwin and Gordon, 1930.

McKay, W. A., ed. "Pond, Peter." *The Macmillan Dictionary of Canadian Biography.* Toronto: Macmillan, 1978.

Wagner, Henry R. *Peter Pond: Fur Trader and Explorer.* New Haven: Yale University Library, 1955.

PETER POND

# Mystery Man of the Far North: Peter Pond (1775)

## Descriptions of Native Scenes and Customs

A DISCRIPTION of Macenac this Plase is Kept up By a Capts Cummand of British which are Lodge in Good Baracks with in the Stockades whare thare is Sum french Bildings and a Commouds [commodious] Roman Church whare the french Inhabatans & InGasheas [*engagés*] Go to Mass Befour it was giveen up to the British thare was a french Mishenerae aStableshed hear who Resideed for a number of years hear   while I was hear thare was[?] None But traveling One who Cams sumtimes to make the a Short [stay] But all way in the Spring when the People ware ye Most numeras—then the Engasheas oftan went to Confes & Git absalution   I Had the next winter with me [one] who was aDicted to theaveing   he took from me in Silver trinkets to the amount of ten Pound But I Got them agane to a trifel   In the Spring we found one of those Preast at Mackenac who was Duing wonder among the People   My Young Man Babtest who had Cumited the theft Heard of it from his Cumrads who had Bin to Confess   his Consans [conscience] Smit Him & He Seat of to Confess   but Could not Git absalution   he went a seacant tim with out suckses But Was Informed By his Bennadict that Sumthing was wanting He Came to me Desireing me to leat him Have Two Otter Skins Promising that he would Be Bater in futer and sarve well   I Leat him Have them he went of   In a fue Minnets after or a Short time he Returnd   I askt him what Suckses   O, sade he the farther sais my Case is a Bad one But if I Bring two Otter more He will take my Case on him Self and Discharge me. . . .

We made But a Small Stay Hear and Past a Small Distans on this Lake and Entard the fox River a gane Which Leads up to the Cairing Plase of Ouiconstan [Wisconsin]   we asendead that River til we Cam to a High

Pece of Groand Whare that Nation yous to Entair thar Dead whin thay
Lived in that Part   we stopt hear a while finding Sum of that Nation on
the Spot who Came thare to Pay yare Respect to thar Departed frend
thay Had a small Cag of Rum and Seat Around the Grave   thay fild thar
Callemeat [calumet] and Began thare Saremony By Pinting the Stem of
the Pipe upward then giveing it a turn in thare and then toward ye head
of the Grave then East & West North & South after which they smoake it
out and fild it a Gane & Lade [it] By   then thay toock Sum Rum Out of
the Cag in a Small Bark Vessel and Pord it on the Head of the Grave By
Way of giveing it to thare Departed Brother   then thay all Drank them
Selves Lit the Pipe Smokd and seam to Injoie themselves Verey well   thay
Repeated this till thay the Sperit Began to Operrate and thare harts Began
to Soffon   then thay Began to Sing a Song or two But at the End of
Everey Song thay Soffend the Clay   after Sum tim Had Relapst the Cag
hat Bin Blead often   thay Began to Repete the Saisfaction thay had with
that frind while he was with them and How fond he was of his frinds
while he Could Git a Cag of Rum and how thay youst to Injoy it togather
thay amused them selves in this manner til thay all fell a Crying and a
woful Nois thay Mad for a while til thay thought wiseley that thay Could
not Bring him Back and it would not Due to Greve two much that an ap-
plication to the Cag was the Best way to Dround Sorrow & Wash away
Greafe   The Moshan was sun Put in Execution and all Began to be marey
as a Partey Could Bea   thay Contineued til Near Nite   Rite wen thay
ware More then Half Drunk the men began to approach the femals and
Chat frelay and apearantly frindley   at Length thay Begin to Lean on
Each other Cis & apeard Virey amoras   at Length two would Steapt a Sid
in y Eag [edge] of the Bushis   Prasently two more would Steap of But I
Could Obsarve Clearley this Bisnes was first Pusht on By the women who
mad thare Viseat to the Dead a Verey Pleaseing one in thare way. . . .

Thare amusements are Singing Daning Smokeing matches Gameing
and Feasting Drinking Playing the Slite of Hand Hunting & thay are
famas in Mageack   Thay are Not Verey Gellas [jealous] of thare women
In General the women find Meanes to Grattafy themSelves with out
Censent of the men   the Men often jion war parteies with Other nations
and Go against the Indans on the Miseeure and west of that   Sume time
thay Go Near St Fee [Santa Fe] in New Maxeco and Bring with them
Spanish Horseis; I have Sean Meney of them   the River aford But a fue
fish   thare woods aford Partragis a fue Rabeat Bairs & Deear are Plentey
In thare Seasons, wild foul thay have But fue   thar Religan is Like Most
of the tribes   thay a Low thare is two Sperits One Goods Who Dwelve a

Bove the Clouds Superintends over all and helps to all the Good things we have and Can Bring Sicknes on us if He pleaseis and another Bad one who dwelves in the fire and air Eaverey whare among m[en] & Sumtimes Dose Mischef to Mankind   Cortship & Mareages—[*two words illegible*] At Night when these People are Seating Round thare fiuer [fire] the Elderly one will be teling what thay Have Sean and Hard or Perhaps thay may be on Sum Intrest[ing] Subg[ec]t   the famley are lis[ten]ing   if thare be aney Young Garle in this Lodg or hut that any Man of a Differan Hut Has a Likeing for he will Seat among   the Parson of his Arrant [errand] Being Prasent hea will watch an Opertunety & through [throw] a Small Stick at Hair   if She Looks up with a Smile it is a Good Omen   he Repets a Sacond tim Perhaps ye Garle will Return the Stick   the Simtam [symptoms] ar Still Groing Stronger and when thay think Proper to Ly Down to Slepe Each Parson Raps himself up in his One Blanket   he takes Notis whar the Garl Seats for thare [she] sleep   when all the famaley are Qui[e]t and Perhaps a Sleap he Slips Soffely in to Hut and Seats himself Down By her Side PresantLey he will Begin to Lift Her Blanket in a Soft maner   Perhaps she may twish it Out of his hand with a Sort of a Sie & Snore to Gather But this is no Kiling Matter   he Seats a while and Makes a Sacond Atempt   She May Perhaps Hold the Blankead Doun Slitely   at Length She turns Over with a Sith and Quits the Hold of the Blanket   He then Creapes under and Geats as Close as he Can til allmost and than of[f] to his one Hut   this Meathard [method] is Practest a Short [time] and then ye yong Indan will Go ahanting and [if] he is Luckey to Git meat he Cums and Informs the famely of it and whare it is   he Brengs the tung and hart with him and thay Seat of after the Meat and Bring it Home   this Plesis [pleases] and he Begins to Gro Bold in the famerly the Garl after that will not refuse him under the Blanket he Will then Perhaps Stay about the famerley a Year and Hunt for the Old father But in this Intram he Gives his Consent that thay may Sleap toogther and when thay Begin to have Children thay Save what thay Can git for thare One youse and Perhaps Live In a Hut apart. . . .

In Desember the Indanes Sent Sum Young men from the Planes a Long the River to Look for traders & thay found us   after Staying a fue day to Rest them thay Departed with the Information to thare frends   In Jany thay Began to Aproach us & Brot with them Drid & Grean Meet Bever Otter Dear fox Woolves Raccone & other Skins; to trade   thay ware Welcom and we Did Our Bisnes to advantage   threw the Winter I had a frenchman for my Nighber who had winter among the Nottawaseis Saverl winters in this River well Knone By the Different Bands   I per-

seaved that he Seamd to have a Prefran & Got More trade then my Self
we ware Good frends    I told him he Got mor then his Share of trade But
Obsarvd at ye Same time it was not to be Wondread at as he had Bin
Long a Quantead    He Sade I hadnot Hit on ye Rite Eidea    he Sade that
the Indand of that Quorter was Giveen to Stealing and a Spacherley the
women in Order to Draw Custam he Left a fue Brass Rings for the finger
on the Counter Sum neadels & Alls which Cost But a trifel Leattle, Small
Knives—Hakes[?] Bell & such trifels for the Sake of Stealing these trifels
thay Came to Sea him and what thay Had for trad he Got    I Beleved
what he Sade and trid the Expereamant found it to Prove well; after
which I Kept up Sides. . . .

I Perseved that the Indans ware Uneasey In thare Minds about Sumthing    I Enquird of them what Had Befel    Thay Gave me to understand
thare was a Parson at that Plase that Had an Eevel Sperit    he Did things
Beand [beyond] thare Conseption    I wish to Sea him and Beaing In-
formd who he was I ask him Meney Questions I found him to be a french
man who Had Bin Long among the Nations on the Misurea that Came
that Spring from the Ilenoas to the Planes of the Dogs    he Had the Slite
of Hand Cumpleatly and Had Such A Swa[y] Over the tribes with whom
he was Aquanted that they Cunsendead to Moste of His Requests    thay
Gave him the Name of Minneto [Manitou] Which is a Sperite In thare
Langueg    as he was Standing Among Sum People thare Cume an Indan
up to them with A Stone Pipe or Callemeat Cureesley Rought and which
he Seat Grate Store By    Minneto ask ye Indan to Leat him Look at it and
he Did so    he wished to Purchis it from the Indan But he would not Part
with it    Minneto then Put it into his Mouth as the Indan Supposed and
Swallod it    the Poor Indan Stud A Stonished    Minneto told him Not to
trubel him Self a bout it    he Should have His Pipe agane In two or three
Days it Must firs pass threw him    at the time Seat the Pipe was Prosented
to the Indan    he Lookd apon it as if he Could not Bair to Part with it But
would not Put his Hand apon it and Minneto Kept the Pipe for Nothing

# Crossing the Desert to the Promised Land: Pedro Font's Diary of the Second Anza Expedition (1776)

*By 1773 explorers and missionaries such as Gaspar de Portolá and Father Junípero Serra had helped Spain to establish a scattering of missions and presidios in Alta California. The newly founded settlements stood virtually defenseless, however, in the face of any possible large-scale invasion by another European power. Even a possible uprising of native peoples posed a threat that might lead to the expulsion of Spanish forces from the area. Since only the Spanish had any settlements in California, and since the natives seemed relatively docile, why did mighty Spain feel so threatened by other powers and by the natives? Because the California settlements had to be re-supplied by ships sailing up the Pacific from Mexico—a voyage that could take months, the sailors battling strong head winds all the way. Moreover the Spanish still remembered the Pueblo Revolt that had driven them out of New Mexico in 1680—not to mention continuing Apache raids that had turned some Spanish presidios and missions into ghost towns. California's native peoples did seem mostly docile and pliant; but should there arise another Popé, leader of the Pueblo Revolt, every Spanish structure in Alta California could quickly be torched, every Spaniard slaughtered, and it would take months before the news would reach Mexico. (Events would soon prove that the Spanish had not overestimated the danger of native uprisings. In 1776 an Indian revolt at the San Diego mission came close to wiping out the Spanish there; and in 1781 the Yumas rebelled, killing four Franciscan friars, thirty-one soldiers, and twenty settlers, and successfully preventing any Spanish re-*

*conquest.) Spain had to find a quicker way to resupply its California outposts.*

*The viceroy, Don Antonio María Bucareli y Ursúa, decided that Spain must discover an overland route from Sonora to Alta California. To head the exploring expedition, Bucareli picked Juan Bautista de Anza, a soldier born and raised on the Sonora border. Anza's father had been captain of the presidio at Fronteras and had been killed by Apaches in 1739 when Anza was four. His father's death didn't keep Anza from volunteering for military service when he was seventeen, and the year 1759 saw him captain and commander of the presidio at Tubac in what is now Arizona. On 17 September 1773, Bucareli ordered Anza to cross the Gila and Colorado rivers and proceed overland to Alta California. Anza began the expedition on 8 January 1774.*

*During the next five months, Anza and the other thirty-three members of the expedition crossed rivers, deserts, and mountains, entered California, proceeding as far as Monterey and Carmel, and retraced their steps, arriving back at Tubac on 27 May 1774. Two years later Anza led a second Bucareli-ordered expedition over almost the same route but going on as far north as San Francisco Bay. Considering the achievements of these two expeditions, Herbert E. Bolton, distinguished twentieth-century historian of the Spanish borderlands, said (1930, viii) that "As an explorer Anza stands beside Lewis and Clark. As a colony leader it is difficult to find anyone in Anglo-American annals with whom to compare him." As a writer, unfortunately, Anza ranks not far above bureaucrats, giving only the facts and bare ones at that. His prose is clear, though not very specific, concrete, or detailed, but most of it is as arid as the desert terrain he traversed.*

*Fortunately other members of Anza's expeditions also recorded events in diaries that have survived. Herbert Bolton translated and edited these Spanish manuscripts and published them in 1930, under the title* Anza's California Expeditions. *In his modern-day narrative history of the expeditions,* An Outpost of Empire *(1930), Bolton identified the best of the diaries—that of Father Pedro Font—and praised it as "one of the great diaries of all North American history," adding that "We shall always admire him for the excellence of his observations, sympathize with him for his chills and fever, smile at him for his querulousness, and love him for his chatty gossip" (1930, 489). Among the strengths Bolton notes, Font's querulousness stands out most memorably.*

*Font complained about Anza's leadership, especially in allowing occasional fandangos and then distributing* aguardiente *that led to drunkenness.*

*Once in California, however, Font did an about-face and sided with Anza in his feud with resident military commander Fernando Rivera y Moncada. But by the time they had returned to San Miguel de Orcasitas, Font had resumed his old quarrels with Anza. All that testiness and carping keeps the reader turning the pages to find out whether Anza will manage to complete the three-thousand-mile trek without stabbing—or at least yelling at—the pesky priest.*

*Anza maintained his composure the entire journey, and afterwards he took Captain Salvador Palma, leader of the Yumas, to Mexico City, where the "heathen" was catechized, baptized, and presented to Viceroy Bucareli. The next year Anza, as he had promised, took Palma back to his people. Bucareli rewarded Anza for his services by appointing him governor of New Mexico, in which position he led campaigns against the Comanche, Apache, Ute, and Navajo. Declining health forced him to resign as governor in 1786, and he died in Sonora two years later. Fathers Garces and Diaz had already been killed in the Yuma uprising of 1781, also the year of Font's death.*

*Perhaps so little attention has been paid to Font and Anza because their great achievement coincided with an attention-monopolizing event: the American Revolution. Bolton's attempt to accord them due recognition might have had better results if he had placed Font's diary first, instead of last, in Anza's California Expeditions. Both Font and Anza point out promising locations for mining and farming, and both comment on likely sites for missions and presidios. Font agrees with a San Gabriel priest who says California looks like "the Promised Land." In the following selections, Font repeats the natives' explanation for the existence of Casa Grande (now a national monument), describes the Yumas and their customs (Bolton left some of the racier descriptions in the original Spanish), argues with Anza about allowing drunkenness at Christmas, and revealingly tells the story of a priestly soap job.*

### Selected Bibliography

Bolton, Herbert Eugene. *An Outpost of Empire*. Berkeley: University of California Press, 1930 Reprint. New York: Russell, 1966.

DeVoto, Bernard. *The Course of Empire*. Boston: Houghton Mifflin, 1952.

Font, Pedro. *Font's Complete Diary of the Second Anza Expedition*. Vol. 4 of *Anza's California Expeditions*. Ed. by Herbert E. Bolton. Berkeley: University of California Press, 1930. Reprint. New York: Russell, 1966.

PEDRO FONT

# Crossing the Desert to the Promised Land: Pedro Font's Diary of the Second Anza Expedition (1776)

## Legends and Customs of the Yumas

THE HISTORY which the governor of Uturituc recounted on the way in his Pima language, and which a servant of the commander, the only interpreter of this language, translated as we went along, is as follows: A long time ago there came to that country a man who was called The Bitter Man because of his ill nature and his harsh rule. This man was old, but he had a young daughter. And there came in his company a young man who was not a relative of his or of anybody else, and married the daughter, who was very pretty as he was handsome. And this old man brought as servants the Wind and the Clouds.

When the old man began to build that great house he ordered his son-in-law to go and look for timber with which to roof it. The young man went a long distance, but since he had no ax or anything with which to cut the trees, he was gone many days, and he finally returned without bringing any timbers. Now the old man was very angry, and he said that the son-in-law was good-for-nothing, and he would show him how he would bring the timbers. And so the old man went away to a sierra where there are many pines, and, calling on God to aid him, he cut many pines and brought many timbers for the roof of the house.

When this Bitter Man came, there were no trees in the country, nor any plants, but he brought seeds of all kinds and reaped very large harvests, with the aid of his two servants, the Wind and the Clouds, who served him. But because of his ill nature he became angry with the two servants, and discharged them, and they went a long way off. And then, for lack of servants, he was not able to reap the harvests, so he ate all that he had raised, for he was now dying of hunger. He then sent his son-in-law to call the two servants and bring them back, but he could not find them no matter how much he looked for them. Then the old man went to look for them, and having found them he took them again into his service, and with their aid he again reaped great harvests. And so they continued to live for many years in that country, but after a long time they went away, and they have heard nothing more about them.

He said also that after the old man there came to that country a man called The Drinker. He became angry with the people there and sent so much water that all the land was covered with it. Then he went to a very high sierra, which is seen from there and is called the Sierra de la Espuma, taking with him a little dog and a coyote. They call it Sierra de la Espuma because at the end of it, which is cut off with a cliff like the corner of a tower, one sees high up near the top a white ledge-like rock, which continues the same all along the sierra for a long distance. And the Indians say that this mark was made by the foam of the water which reached up to there. Well, The Drinker went up there and left the dog below so that he might tell when the water reached this ledge of the foam, and when it reached there the dog told The Drinker, for then the animals talked; and then he too went up.

After several days The Drinker sent to the Humming Birds and to the Coyote to have them bring him some mud. They brought it, and from it he made several men, some of whom turned out to be good and others bad. These men scattered out through the country, upstream and downstream, and after a while he sent some of his own people to see if the men upstream talked. They went and returned saying that although they talked they did not understand what they said. And so The Drinker became very angry because these men talked without his having given them permission. Afterward he sent other men downstream to see those who were there, and they returned saying that they had given them a friendly welcome and that they talked another language, but that they had understood them. Then The Drinker said to them that the men who lived down the stream were the good men, these being the ones as far as the Opas, with whom they are friendly. And those who lived upstream he said were the bad men, these being the Apaches, toward whom they are hostile.

He said also that once The Drinker became angry with the people, and killed many of them and changed them into saguaros, and this is why there are so many saguaros in that country. The saguaro has a green trunk, is watery, very tall and equally round, and straight from the bottom to the top, with rows of thick spines all the way up, and it usually has two or three branches of the same form, which look like arms.

Besides this he said that The Drinker at another time became very angry with the men, and made the sun come down to burn them, and so he finished them. The men begged him earnestly not to burn them, so he ordered the sun to go up, but not so high as it had been before, and told them that he was leaving it lower in order to burn them with it if they made him angry again; and this is why it is so hot in that country in the summer. . . .

These Yumas, and likewise the Cajuenches and the rest, are well formed, tall, robust, not very ugly, and have good bodies. Generally they are nearly eight spans high and even more, and many are nine and some even above nine, according to our measurements. The women are not so tall, but they also are quite corpulent and of very good stature.

Their customs, according to what I was able to learn, are the following: In religion they recognize no special idolatrous cult, although it appears that there are some wizards, or humbugs, and doctors among them, who exercise their offices by yelling, blowing, and gestures. They say that there is a god, and that they know this because the Pimas have told them so; and that these Pimas and the Pápagos, with whom they maintain peace and have some commerce, have told them that above, in the heavens, there are good people, and that under the ground there are dogs, and other animals that are very fierce. They say they do not know anything else because they are ignorant, and for this reason they will gladly learn what we may teach them, in order that they may be intelligent. And since the basis of a well-ordered monarchy, government, or republic is religion, even though it may be false, and since none is found among these Indians, they consequently live very disorderly and beastlike, without any civilization and with such slight discipline as I have previously said, each one governing himself according to his whim, like a vagabond people.

Their wars and campaigns usually last for only a few days, and they reduce themselves to this: Many of them assemble with the captain or some one who commands them; they go to a village of their enemies; they give the yell or war-cry, in order that their opponents may flee or become terrified if taken by surprise. They usually kill some woman, or someone who has been careless, and try to capture a few children in order to take them out to sell in the lands of the Spaniards. These captives are called Nixoras by us in Sonora, no matter where they come from, and this commerce in Nixoras, so unjust, is the reason why they have been so bloody in their wars. Their arms are a bow, taller than themselves, badly tempered, and a few arrows, of which generally they carry only two or three, as I saw, and these somewhat long, bad, and weak. Very few carry quivers, if indeed they carry any at all, for I did not see a single one.

Their houses are huts of rather long poles, covered with earth on the roofs and on the sides, and somewhat excavated in the ground like a rabbit burrow; and in each one twenty or thirty or more live like hogs. These houses are not close together in the form of towns, but are scattered about the bottom lands, forming rancherías of three or four, or more, or less.

The clothing of the men is nothing, although as a result of the peace treaties which they have been able to establish since the first expedition, it is noticed that they have had some commerce with the other tribes, so that now we saw some Indians wearing blankets of cotton, and black ones of wool which come from El Moqui, which they have been able to acquire through the Cocomaricopas and Jalchedunes. These they wear around their bodies from the middle up, leaving the rest of the body uncovered, y las partes mas indecentes, porque dicen que á las mugeres no les quadra que las tapen. But as a rule they go about totally naked, and they are so shameless that they are always con las manos en las partes vergonzosas, jugandose y alternadose la naturaleza. And they are so brutal that if they are reprimanded they make it worse and laugh about it, as I experienced. And if les viene gana de orinar, whether standing still or walking about they do so like beasts, and even worse, que estas se paran para mear. Asimismo quando les vienen sus flatos, los echan delante de todos con mucha frescura, and since they eat so many beans and other seeds they are very offensive with their flatulency. And if they are seated on the ground they do no more than levantar un poco la nalga por un lado, y como echan los cuescos tan largos, redondos, y recios, con el soplo levantan el polvo de la tierra. On one occasion the commander asked an Indian to bring him a brand with which to light his cigarette, and the Indian, very serious, with the lighted stick in his hand, standing in front of him echose un pedo formidable, and although the commander told him that such a thing was improper, the Indian laughed quite undisturbed. Captain Palma by now had reformed, though he used to be just like the rest, and at first when he was told that this was not proper delante de la gente, he replied that he could not do otherwise porque si no hacía assi, rebentaría. I do not know whether this freedom is to be attributed to their ignorance, innocence, and candor, or is the result of great brutality.

In the matter of incontinence they are so shameless and excessive that I do not believe that in all the world there is another tribe that is worse. The women, it might almost be said, are common, and the hospitality which they show their guests is to provide them with companions. And although among the old people there seems to be a sort of natural matrimony, recognizing as legitimate some one of the many women they have or had in their youth, yet among the young men I believe there is no such thing as matrimony, because they live with anyone they desire and leave them whenever they please—or at least polygamy is very common among them.

All the females, even though they may be small, and even infants at the breast, wear little skirts made from the inner bark of the willow and the cottonwood. This they soften a little, tear it into strips, enlace or interweave them, and make a sort of apron of them which they tie around the waist with a hair rope, one piece in front and the other behind, the one behind being somewhat longer than the one in front and reaching clear to the knees. Since they are made of so many strips or narrow ribbons the thickness of a finger, and hang loose, with the shaking which they are given on walking they make quite a noise. Among the women I saw some men dressed like women, with whom they go about regularly, never joining the men. The commander called them *amaricados*, perhaps because the Yumas call effeminate men *maricas*. I asked who these men were, and they replied that they were not men like the rest, and for this reason they went around covered this way. From this I inferred they must be hermaphrodites, but from what I learned later I understood that they were sodomites, dedicated to nefarious practices. From all the foregoing I conclude that in this matter of incontinence there will be much to do when the Holy Faith and the Christian religion are established among them. Likewise, some women, although not many, are accustomed to cover the back with a kind of cape or capotillo which they make from the skins of rabbits or of beaver, cutting the skin into strips and weaving it with threads of bark; but generally they go around with all the body uncovered except for what the skirts conceal.

On cold nights, and especially in the winter, they make a fire and crouch round it, lying down huddled together and even buried in the sand like hogs. In the daytime they are accustomed to go around with a burning brand or *tizón* in the hand, bringing it close to the part of the body where they feel the coldest, now behind, now in front, now at the breast, now at the shoulders, and now at the stomach. These are their blankets, and when the fire goes out they throw the brand away, and seek another one that is burning.

The men are much given to painting themselves red with hematite, and black with shiny black lead-colored earth, whereby they make themselves look like something infernal, especially at night. They use also white and others colors, and they daub not only the face but all the body as well, rubbing it in with marrow fat or other substances, in such a way that even though they jump into the river and bathe themselves frequently, as they are accustomed to do, they cannot remove the paint easily. And those who have nothing else, stain themselves with charcoal from the top down with various stripes and figures, making themselves look like the Devil; and this is their gala dress. The women use only red paint, which is very common among them, for I saw only one large girl who, in addition to the red hematite, had some white round spots in two rows up and down the face.

The men have their ears pierced with three or four large holes (the women not so many), in which they hang strings of wool or *chomite* and other pendants. Likewise they wear around the neck good-sized strings of the dried heads of animals that look like tumble bugs, which are found here. They are very fond of *cuentas* or glass beads, for which they bartered their few blankets, with which some members of the expedition provided themselves. They likewise traded their grain and other things which they brought, so that yesterday about five hundred watermelons and great quantities of calabashes, maize, beans, etc. were sold at the camp, and today more than twice as much. Besides this, nearly all the men have the middle cartilage of the nose pierced (I did not notice this among the women), from which the richest men, such as Captain Palma, hang a little blue-green stone, others a little white stone, half round, like ivory or bone, such as Captain Pablo wore. Others wear beads or other gewgaws in the nose, and although I saw several with nothing, on the other hand I saw some who were contented to wear a little stick thrust through the cartilage.

The coiffure of the men is unique. Most of them wear the hair banged in front at the eyes, and some have it cut at the neck, others wearing it quite long. They are accustomed to make their coiffure or dress their hair by daubing it with white mud and other paints, in order that it may be stiff. They usually do this on the banks of the water and with great care. They raise the front hair up and fix it like a crown, or like horns, and the rest they make very slick with the paints and mud, and they are accustomed also to decorate it with figures in other colors. The women do not make use of all this, their ordinary coiffure being to press the hair together and fix it with mud as in Europe the women use flour paste. Their usual custom is to wear the front hair cut off even with the eyebrows, wearing the rest somewhat long, hanging down the shoulders and back.

They are very fond of smoking, and are very lazy, and if this were not so they would reap much larger harvests; but they are content with what is sufficient to provide themselves with plenty to eat, which, since the soil is so fertile from the watering by the river, they obtain with little trouble. This consists solely in the following: before the river rises they clear a piece of land which they wish to plant, leaving the rubbish there. The river rises and carries off the rubbish, and as soon as the water goes down and recedes, with a stick they make holes in the earth, plant their seeds, and do nothing else to it. They are likewise very thievish, a quality common to all Indians. Their language is not so harsh as that of the Pimas, and to me it appeared to be less difficult to pronounce; for there is a pause like an interrogation at the end of each clause or thing which is said.

As a result of our persuasion the Yuma tribe at present is at peace with all of its neighbors, except the Indians at the mouth of the river, who are still hostile because of a war which Palma made on them a short time ago, in which he killed about twenty of their people. But this breach has now been composed by Father Garcés during his journey there, as he says in his diary. In virtue of this peace some Jalchedunes came down to the junction of the rivers, bringing their Moqui blankets and other things to barter with the people of the expedition. They did not find us there, but Father Thomás, who remained there, received them well and gave them presents.

Finally, these people as a rule are gentle, gay, and happy. Like simpletons who have never seen anything, they marveled as if everything they saw was a wonder to them, and with their impertinent curiosity they made themselves troublesome and tiresome, and even nuisances, for they wearied us by coming to the tents and examining everything. They liked to hear the mules bray, and especially some burros which came in the expedition, for before the other expedition they had never seen any of these animals. Since the burros sing and bray longer and harder than the mules, when they heard them they imitated them in their way with great noise and hullabaloo. . . .

Among the Indian women who yesterday made their voyages there was a grown-up daughter of Captain Palma, a great swimmer, and the one who went at the head of all the rest. But she was painted with red ochre according to their custom, for they stick this paint on so securely that although they may be in the water all day, as was the case yesterday, it does not come off. I had formerly told her and others that it was not good for them to paint themselves, because the Spaniards and Christians do not do it; and today when she bade me goodbye I told her the same thing, and suggested that she wash herself with water which she had there, because in this way it would be better. She replied that she did not know how to wash herself and that I should wash her, and to her great pleasure and that of those assembled I did give her a good soaping, and succeeded in removing the paint. Then I gave her a mirror in order that she might see that this way was good, and, looking at herself, she broke out laughing, "Ajot! Ajot!" which means "Good! Good!" I relate this incident as a significant circumstance, because those Indians are so enamored of their paints that it will be very difficult to succeed in taking them away from the women, and much more difficult to take them from the men, with whom I was not able to succeed so well; for they consider it gala dress to go around painted and dirty like devils.

CHAPTER 26

# Searching for a Shortcut: Fray Silvestre Vélez de Escalante's Journal of the Domínguez-Escalante Expedition (1776)

In 1774 Juan Bautista de Anza found an overland route to the California missions, but it required unpleasant and risky desert travel. In the hope of discovering a shorter—or at least easier and safer—route, a party of ten set out from Santa Fe on 29 July 1776. Heading north, in early August they entered what is now Colorado. They kept moving north, until in early September they crossed into what is now northeastern Utah. Then they turned westward, traveling until they entered Utah Valley late in September. Instead of continuing westward or going north to the Great Salt Lake, they moved south, crossing into northern Arizona in the middle of October. A few days later, early winter snowstorms forced them to change their plans, and they headed back east toward Santa Fe and spent the next month finding a way across the Grand Canyon and the Colorado River. For the following month and a half, they went homeward, visiting Hopi and Zuni pueblos on the way and arriving in Santa Fe on 2 January 1777. By then they had covered more than fifteen hundred miles and, as Bernard DeVoto points out in The Course of Empire, "most of the route lay through country as difficult as any in the United States and some of it may fairly be called the most difficult" (1952, 291).

So impressed was DeVoto by their achievement, that he called their adventure a "poem" (1952, 290), but he also called the expedition's journal—written by Fray Silvestre Vélez de Escalante as the amanuensis of his superior, Fray Francisco Atanasio Domínguez—"certainly the most serene document in the annals of American exploration" (1952, 292). That is not to *say that* The Domínguez-Escalante Journal *lacks moments of interest, but DeVoto certainly describes accurately the journalist's unruffled tone in the face of formidable challenges. DeVoto's assessment also includes his criticism of Herbert Eugene Bolton's translation of the journal; and later scholars have agreed with DeVoto that for this project the great Bolton relied too trustingly on the less-than-perfect work of an assistant.*

*Happily for us a new translation appeared in 1976, as part of the nation's bicentennial celebration. Not only does the translator, Fray Angélico Chavez, come to the text "as a twelfth-generation Hispanic New Mexican with an ear for the language of the times and the locale—and as one thoroughly conversant with ecclesiastical and Franciscan terminology along with the style in which those eighteenth-century friars expressed themselves" (Vélez de Escalante 1976, xi), but writing in English, he also ranks among the most noted of New Mexico's twentieth-century poets. Fray Chavez's translation was edited and annotated by Ted J. Warner, assisted by a team of seventeen other scholars who retraced the route of the Domínguez-Escalante party and attempted "to locate as precisely as possible the actual trail and the campsites of the 1776 expedition" (1976, xix).*

*All that twentieth-century creative and scholarly activity hasn't disturbed the serenity that DeVoto found in* The Domínguez-Escalante Journal, *but it does make the newer translation pleasant and interesting reading. Chavez and Warner even tell us a little about what happened to Domínguez and Escalante after the expedition. Because of a Spanish retrenchment policy made necessary by shrinking funds and limited manpower, the two missionaries could not keep their promises to return and set up missions among the Utes. Instead Domínguez had to go back to Mexico, in order to defend himself against charges lodged by other New Mexican missionaries, who resented his treatment of them when he had earlier undertaken a tour of inspection of their missions. Thirty more years of what Warner characterizes as Domínguez's "selfless service to the Church" did not suffice to restore a reputation tarnished by the spiteful attacks of his churchly brethren. As for Escalante, he died in 1780 in his early thirties, en route to Mexico City for treatment of a health problem that had caused him pain and discomfort for years.*

*When he lay dying, did Escalante wonder whether the shamans whom he and Domínguez had encountered and denounced might have been able to cure him? Probably not, for as you will see in the selections that follow, the Christian faith of Domínguez and Escalante matches their serenity—perhaps it even caused it. Still no amount of faith and serenity could make dealings with other human beings problem-free—and the good fathers describe their difficulties in securing reliable guides, getting good directions, and mak-*

*ing their men follow orders. They devote more space to such problems than they do to descriptions of the wonders they encountered—such as the pictographs they saw in a place they named "El Cañón Pintado" ("Painted Canyon"), rock art that Warner's team of scholars found still there in what is now called Douglas Canyon, south of Rangeley, Colorado. And the priests also describe only in passing some Anasazi ruins. However, so matter-of-factly do they recount all these wonders—and in such clear detail—that a twentieth-century reader who has seen even some of that country can easily slip through the looking glass of the imagination and become part of the adventure. It takes the rude shock of a necessary footnote to remind such a reader that more than two centuries have passed since Domínguez and Escalante dreamed of a quicker route to Monterey, a highway lined with gold-bearing mines and edenic valleys filled with docile natives eager to be converted. Here's the footnote that brings us back to present reality (Vélez de Escalante 1976, 99n.384):*

> Access to the floor of Padre Creek [in the Grand Canyon] was over a steep sandstone slope which a man could negotiate without danger. However, lest the horses lose their footing and tumble to the canyon floor, the expedition hacked out some shallow footholds, or steps, for about ten feet in one of the most dangerous places, making it less hazardous for the animals. This used to be one of Utah's most historic sites. It is now covered with 550 feet of water from Lake Powell.

### Selected Bibliography

DeVoto, Bernard. *The Course of Empire.* Boston: Houghton Mifflin, 1952.

Vélez de Escalante, Silvestre. *The Domínguez-Escalante Journal: Their Expedition through Colorado, Utah, Arizona, and New Mexico in 1776.* Trans. by Fray Angelico Chavez. Ed. by Ted J. Warner. Provo, 1976. Reprint. Salt Lake City: University of Utah Press, 1994.

# Searching for a Shortcut: Fray Silvestre Vélez de Escalante's Journal of the Domínguez-Escalante Expedition (1776)

## Suspicions, Rock Art, and More Suspicions

September 6 . . .

The companions conversant with the Yuta language tried to convince us that Silvestre the guide was leading us by that route either to keep us winding about so as not to proceed further or to hand us over to a Sabuagana ambuscade that could be awaiting us. To make the guide more suspect to us, they assured us of their having heard many Sabuaganas at the encampment telling him to lead us on the trail which went to the lake and, after having kept us needlessly winding around for eight or ten days, to make us turn back. And even though it was not altogether incredible that some could have said this, we never believed that the guide had agreed to it, nor even that it had actually happened, because not one of these companions of ours had told us anything like it up to here—the fact being that, while at the encampment, they did not cease magnifying other less fearsome difficulties, and more likely ones, and that in any ill event they risked only a bit less than we did. . . .

September 9

On the 9th we left El Paraje de Santa Delfina along the same canyon, and having gone half a league northwest we swung north-northwest; then, after having trekked nine leagues in this direction all through the canyon over a well-beaten path—and with only one bad stretch, which can be avoided by crossing the stream a little ahead, and going across a thicket of high sagebrush and willows of the kind they call *latilla*—we got out of it. Halfway in this canyon toward the south there is a quite lofty rock cliff on which we saw, crudely painted, three shields, or "Apache shields," of hide, and a spear head. Farther down on the north side we saw another painting which supposedly represented two men in combat. For this reason we named it El Cañón Pintado, and it is only through it that one can go from the ridge mentioned to the nearest river, for the rest of the terrain in between is very broken and rocky.

On this same side of the canyon, already near its exit, there is an exposed vein of metallic ore, but we were ignorant of its nature or quality, although one companion took one of the rocks fallen off the vein, and Don Bernardo Miera, showing it to us, said it was of the sort which miners call *tepustete* [perhaps iron pyrites or "fool's gold"] and that it is an indication of gold ore. We neither decided nor shall we vouch for this, for not having mining expertise and because a more thorough testing is always required than what we could do at the time. Having passed the canyon, we traveled half a league north-northwest and came to a river which we named San Clemente; we crossed it and halted on its northern edge, where there is a middle-sized meadow of good pasturage. This river is middling and flows west through here, and the terrain adjacent to it offers no prospects for a settlement. Today ten leagues. . . .

September 16

On the 16th we set out for La Vega de Santa Cruz (on El Río de San Buenaventura), went up about a mile to the north, arrived at the ford, and crossed the river. We took to the west and, after going one league along the northern side and meadow of the river, crossed another smaller one which comes down from the northwest, and we entered it. Over the same meadow we turned south-southwest for a league and crossed another rivulet, a little larger than the first, which comes down from the same northwesterly direction and enters the river. From both of them irrigation ditches could be dug for watering the land on this side, which is likewise good for farming even when they could not be conducted from the large river. We continued toward the southwest, getting away from the river, which swings to the south among hills and ravines of finely ground stone in spots. We descended to a dry arroyo down a long and very stony grade, its ascent on the other side being not as bad.

As soon as we reached the top we found a spoor, of one or two days' imprint, of about twelve horses and some people on foot; and after a close study of the surroundings, indications were found that they had been lying in wait or spying for some time on the ridge's highest part, without letting go of the horses. We suspected that they might be some Sabuaganas who could have followed us to deprive us of the animal herd at this place, where we would likely attribute the deed to the Comanches instead of the Yutas, since we were no longer in the latters' country but the formers'.

What is more, Silvestre the guide gave us a strong basis for the suspicion the night before when casually and without being noticed he went off a short distance from the king's camp to sleep. All through the trip he had not worn the blanket we gave him, and today he left the place with it on, without taking it off all day, and we suspected that, for his having had an understanding with the Sabuaganas, he wore it so as to be recognized in case they attacked us. He increased our suspicion all the more when he lagged behind for a while, pensive and confused, before reaching the ridge where we found the spoor—now wanting to go along the river's edge, now to lead us along this route. We gave him no sign whatsoever of our suspicion by dissembling it altogether, but as our journey progressed he gave us convincing proofs of his innocence.

We continued exactly where the spoor led, descended once more to El Río de San Buenaventura, and saw that the ones making the tracks had stayed for a long while in the leafy poplar grove and meadow which it has. We kept on following it over the meadow by the river's edge, naming the site Las Llagas de Nuestro Padre San Francisco—after having gone over the broken hills and slopes, and the meadow mentioned, six leagues to the southwest, and in the whole day's march eight leagues.

As soon as we halted, two companions went southwest along the trail to explore the terrain roundabout and concluded that they had been Comanches.

September 17

On the 17th we set out from the meadow of Las Llagas de Nuestro Padre San Francisco toward the southwest, went up some low hills, and after going a league left the path we were following, the one on which the spoor of horses and people continued. Silvestre told us that they were Comanches who were going in pursuit of the Yutas who, while likely on a bison hunt, had made their presence felt. We convinced ourselves of this, from the direction they were taking as well as from other signs they left. We crossed a dry arroyo, climbed up a hill, and after going west a league and a half over good terrain, almost flat and arid, arrived at a high ridge from which the guide pointed out to us the junction of the rivers San Clemente and San Buenaventura, which now joined together, flowed to the south with respect to where we stood.

We descended to a plain and another river's large meadow, and, after going west another league and a half, arrived at the juncture of two medium-sized rivers which come down from the sierra which lies near here and to the north of El Río de San Buenaventura. The one more to the east before the juncture runs to the southeast, and we named it Río de San Damián; the other to the east, and we named it Río de San Cosme. We continued upstream along the latter, and after going west one league we saw ruins near it of a very ancient pueblo where there were fragments of stones for grinding maize, of jars, and of pots of clay. The pueblo's shape was circular, as indicated by the ruins now almost completely in mounds. We turned southwest over a plain which lies between the two rivers, went up some hills of loose stone, and very troublesome to the already hoofsore mounts; we went down another meadow of El Río de San Cosme, and, having gone southwest for half a league and one-half toward the west over the meadow, we halted on it, naming it La Ribera de San Cosme. Today eight leagues.

A little after we had stopped, we saw wisps of smoke at the sierra's base, and when we asked the guide who in his opinion had sent them up, he said that they could be Comanches or some of the Lagunas who usually came hunting hereabouts. . . .

October 8

On the 8th we set out from San Atenógenes over the plain toward the south. We traveled only three leagues and a half with great difficulty, because it was so soft and miry everywhere that many pack animals and mounts, and even those that were loose, either fell down or became stuck altogether. We stopped about a mile west of the arroyo, naming the place Santa Brígida, where, after having taken a bearing by the north star, we computed 38° 3′ 30″ of latitude. Today three leagues and a half to the south.

Today we suffered greatly from the cold because the north wind did not cease blowing all day, and most acutely. Up to here we had kept our intent of reaching the garrison and new establishments of Monterey. But, figuring that we were still distant from them, although we yet had to descend only one degree and 23½ seconds to this Paraje de Santa Brígida, we had advanced westward only 136½ leagues, according to each day's directions. And as for the conclusion we were making, partly from not having found among all these latter peoples any reports about the Spaniards and padres of the said Monterey, partly because of the great difference in longitude with which this port and La Villa de Santa Fe are shown on the maps, we had many leagues left to us toward the west.

Since winter had already set in most severely, for all the sierras we managed to see in all directions were covered with snow, the weather very unsettled, we therefore feared that long before we got there the passes would be closed to us, so that they would force us to stay two or three months in some sierra where there might not be any people or the wherewithal for our necessary sustenance. For the provisions we had were very low by now, and so we could expose ourselves to perishing from hunger if not from the cold. We also figured that, even granting that we arrived in Monterey this winter, we could not be in La Villa de Santa Fe until the month of June the following year.

This delay, along with others which will arise during the ordinary and necessary pursuit of so interesting an undertaking as the one we have been treating, could be very prejudicial to the souls which, as mentioned before, yearn for their eternal salvation through holy baptism. These, on seeing such a great delay in what we promised, would feel frustrated in their hopes, or they would conclude that we had purposely deceived them. As a result, their conversion and the extension of his majesty's dominions in this direction would become much more difficult in the future. To this could be added the possibility that Joaquín the Laguna, frightened and vexed by so many hardships and want, could wander off or return to his country or to other peoples he might have heard about, as did the other one.

Weighing all this, therefore, and that by continuing south from Santa Brígida we could discover a shorter and better route than that of the Sabuaganas to go from Santa Fe to La Laguna de los Timpanois and to these other full-bearded Indians—and perhaps some other nation heretofore unknown which may always have been living in the region north of El Río Grande—we thereupon decided to continue south for as much as the terrain permitted as far as El Río Colorado, and from here point our way toward Cosnina, Moqui, and Zuñi. . . .

October 18

The three Indians mentioned who came with us were so scared that they did not want to go farther, nor let us come near them, until they questioned Joaquín the Laguna, and they calmed down with what he told them about us. Among other things they asked him, very much impressed by his valor, was how it happened that he had dared to come with us. He, in his desire to take away their fear in order to relieve the privation he was suffering to our sorrow, answered them as best he could at the time. And so he relieved them of much of the fear and suspicion which they still felt, this no doubt being the reason why they did not leave us before we reached the water source mentioned.

As soon as we camped we gave them the woolen stuff that we promised, with which they were greatly pleased. Then, when they learned that we came without food supplies, they told us to have one of our own go over with one of theirs to their humble abodes, which were somewhat distant, and to bring some back—that the others would remain with us in the meantime. We sent one of the mixed-breeds along with Joaquín the Laguna, giving them the wherewithal for buying provisions and a pack horse on which to bring them. They left with the other Indian and returned after midnight, bringing back a small quantity of wild sheep meat, dried cactus prickly pear done into cakes, and seeds from wild plants. They also brought news about one of the two who had gone for water the night before, saying that he had been at the camp. The other had arrived tonight before ten. . . .

October 22

After we had retired to rest, some of the companions, Don Bernardo Miera among them, went to one of the huts to chat with the Indians. They told them that the said Don Bernardo had been sick all along, and one old Indian from among those present, either because our own requested it or on his own accord, set about to cure him with chants and ceremonials which, if not overt idolatries (which they had to be), were wholly superstitious. All of our own gladly permitted them, the sick man included, and they hailed them as indifferent kindly gestures when they should have prevented them for being contrary to the evangelical and divine law which they profess, or at least they should have withdrawn. We heard the Indian's chanting, but did not know what it was all about. As soon as they gave us a detailed account next morning, we were extremely grieved by such harmful carelessness and we reprimanded them, instructing them in doctrine so that they would never again lend their approval to such errors through their willing attendance or in any other manner.

This is one of the main reasons why the infidels who have most dealings with the Spaniards and Christians in these parts show more resistance to the truth of the Gospel, and their conversion becomes more difficult each day. While we were preaching the necessity of holy baptism to the first Sabuaganas we saw, the interpreter, so as not to displease them or else lose the friendship of long standing which they maintain with them through the despicable fur trade (even in the face of just prohibitions by the lord governors of this kingdom, who time and again have decreed that no Indian, mixed-breed Indian, or Hispanic settler may enter infidel country without first having obtained permission for it from his lordship), translated for them in these very words: "The padre says that the Apaches, Navajos, and Comanches who are not baptized cannot enter heaven, and that they go to hell where God punishes them, and they will burn forever like wood in the fire"—and with this the Sabuaganas became overjoyed on hearing themselves excluded, and their foes included, in the unavoidable destiny of either being baptized or of being lost forever. The interpreter was reprimanded, and he changed his conduct on seeing his stupid puny faith exposed.

We could add other examples, heard from those very ones who while among the Yutas have attended and perhaps approved and even participated in many idolatrous practices; but the two just related, to which we bear witness, suffice. For, if in our company, after having heard these idolatries repeatedly being refuted and condemned, they attend them, furnish occasion for them, and applaud them, what will they not do while wandering three or four months among the infidel Yutas and Navajos with no one to correct them or restrain them?

Besides this, they (some of them) have furnished us sufficient reasons during this trip to suspect that, when some go to the Yutas and remain among them in their greed for pelts, others go after the flesh which they find here for their bestial satisfaction. And so, therefore, they blaspheme against Christ's name and impede or, to put it better, oppose the spreading of the faith. Oh, with how much severity should similar evils be attended to! May God in His infinite goodness inspire the most suitable and practical means.

CHAPTER 27

# Don Quixote in the Wilderness: John Ledyard (1779)

*A long list of laurels makes Captain James Cook (1728–79) the eighteenth century's greatest navigator. On three major voyages between 1768 and 1779, Cook mapped much of the Pacific Ocean, charting significant islands of the South Seas and filling in the map of coastal North America from Oregon to the tip of Alaska. He claimed the continent of Australia for Great Britain and sowed grave doubts about the appealing fable of the Northwest Passage. On top of that, Cook found the right blend of care and discipline and won the admiration of his crews.*

*But Cook was no writer. His weighty tomes about his voyages are jam-packed with information about navigation, the weather, and the tides. They make tedious reading. Yet they show Cook to be exactly what he was, a capable and fastidious man. Beyond that the writer seems at times to have ice water running in his veins. J. C. Beaglehole, the foremost scholar on the captain, concedes in his monograph on the topic that Cook ". . . did not have the dramatic mind. . . " (1970, 20), then sighs that many of Cook's pages seem ". . . the writing of a tired man" (1970, 21). Witness Cook's attempt at the Nootka Indians of Vancouver Island: "A remarkable sameness character-ized the countenance of the whole nation. . . " (Cook and King 1969, 198). That is, when confronted by a strange people, the good captain commits the typical tourist's gaffe. These foreigners all look alike, and that's the end of that.*

*For excitement, dramatic build, for suspense, thrills, and what we call "human interest," we must turn from Cook to a member of his crew, a loner so emotionally hyperactive that Thomas Jefferson suspected a lurking genius, but quipped: "Unfortunately he has too much imagination" (1955, 160). Yes, a naive pomposity, a clownishness, a touch of the* luftmensch, *clung to*

*John Ledyard. An international wanderer, he may have mooched off his friends, proving that a man can live on next to nothing by the excellence of his blarney. He may have been unceremoniously thrown out of Russia during a penniless attempt to walk around the world, even while protesting that he was "... a traveler and a friend to mankind..." (Ledyard 1963, 157). And his fellows might chuckle gently behind his back over his not always convincing "... passion for lofty sentiment and description" (Ledyard 1963, xxxi). Yet there was a rightness, even a prophetic rightness, to some of the dreamer's visionary flights, though they kept crashing.*

*John Ledyard was the first person to attempt to organize an American expedition to tap the fur trade of the Pacific Northwest. Better businessmen than he would soon bring it off and profit enormously from the booming trade, while inadvertently strengthening the United States' claims to a large chunk of real estate. If not the first, Ledyard was among the earliest to buck cultural limitations and analyze events from other than the whites' perspective. He tried to see things through Indians' eyes (1963, xliii). He could work himself into ecstasy over nature's panoramas and abundance. He also could make mistakes, such as repeating the myth of Indian cannibalism (Ledyard 1963, 73), and he didn't see the contradiction in his enthusiasm for getting rich on the fur trade and his admiration for traditional Indian life. But his defense of the Indians, his adoration of nature, and his childish faith in nature's goodness struck three loud notes that writers continue to play in western American literature.*

*Mercurial, restless, eccentric, John Ledyard was one of those people who, though he doesn't seem to fit anywhere, nonetheless is so happily absorbed in his own dreams that he doesn't realize it. Born in Groton, Connecticut, young Ledyard trekked north to New Hampshire's Dartmouth College, then a poor-man's cluster of log cabins on the edge of the wilderness, devoted to teaching young men how to be missionaries to the Indians. The Indian part took but the theology didn't. The aspirant kept vanishing into the woods to live with neighboring tribes. After a brief college career marked by practical jokes and petitions written in mock humility to the college's stuffy president, Rev. Eleazar Wheelock—Ledyard wanted the institution to offer dancing classes and fencing lessons and was wont to prance around the rustic campus in Turkish pantaloons—the rebellious Ledyard quit. To this day applauded by undergraduates as the first student to escape Dartmouth, he left Indian style, paddling away in a canoe down the Connecticut River. A hundred and forty miles later, he arrived at an uncle's house in Hartford sporting an immense bear coat.*

*The quixotic pattern held to Ledyard's dying day. He ran off to sea, jumped ship at Gibraltar, and joined the British Army. An irate captain took him by the collar and hauled him back to his vessel. Back in the thirteen colonies that were coming to revolutionary boil, Ledyard proved himself irrefrangible by taking ship again, this time for England, where he had hopes of warming relationships with his long-lost and presumably better-off relatives, the Ledyards of Bristol. But it didn't work out. He fled from ". . . a kind of Police of that city. . . ," he vaguely remarks, once again into the arms of the British Army (Lehmann-Haupt 1939, 88). Whatever the undocumented vicissitudes of his military career, he met the redoubtable Captain Cook and sweet-talked a berth aboard the* Resolution *as a corporal of marines on Cook's last voyage. Still in the military after three years of adventures ranging from the allures of tropical maidens to the forbidding icebergs beyond the Arctic Circle, he was shipped to America to throw his shoulder against his rebel countrymen. In a typical solution, he deserted, then in 1783 published his only book, his memoirs of explorations with the famous Cook.*

*By now Ledyard's mind was a chemical storm of Big Ideas, and thereafter it was hustle, hustle, hustle. In Philadelphia he lived on the advances of investors who had taken fire with the young man's vision of getting rich on the Northwest's furs, then he slipped off to France. In Paris he warmed up to Thomas Jefferson, becoming an avatar in reverse of the future Lewis and Clark, by proposing to walk the length of Siberia, cross the Bering Strait, and from thence hoof it through more thousands of miles of wilderness to arrive in the fledgling United States. None of this came off. But the free-lancer kept talking to men with money in their pockets and a self-indulgence for whim. In 1789 some London gentlemen got up a grubstake and packed him off to explore the source of Africa's Niger River and return with a fortune of gold. Again, and finally, Ledyard didn't make it. He died in Cairo under puzzling circumstances. The man of limitless horizons was still in his thirties.*

*The second selection, Ledyard's first glimpse of the Northwest's riches, takes place on the western coast of Vancouver Island; though the other two pieces treat of events in Hawaii, they nonetheless typify both Ledyard's criticism of white/Indian relations and his transport over the wild nature promoted by his book.*

### Selected Bibliography

Beaglehole, J. C. *Cook the Writer.* Sydney: Sydney University Press, 1970.

Cook, James, and James King. *Seventy North to Fifty South: The Story of Captain Cook's Last Voyage.* [1784]. Ed. by Paul W. Dale. Englewood Cliffs, N.J.: Prentice-Hall, 1969.

Jefferson, Thomas. *The Papers of Thomas Jefferson*. Vol. 12. Ed. Julian P. Boyd. Princeton, N.J.: Princeton University Press, 1955.

Ledyard, John. *John Ledyard's Journal of Captain Cook's Last Voyage*. [1783]. Ed. by James Kenneth Munford. Corvallis: Oregon State University Press, 1963.

Lehmann-Haupt, Hellmut. *The Book in America*. New York: R. R. Bowker, 1939.

Sparks, Jared. *The Life of John Ledyard, the American Traveler*. Cambridge: Hilliard and Brown, 1828.

JOHN LEDYARD

# Don Quixote in the Wilderness: John Ledyard (1779)

## Glimpses of Hawaii and the Northwest

THESE EXHIBITIONS on the part of the natives were considered by us in a kind of dubious light for though they evidently entertained us, we were not certain they were solely intended for that purpose, and if they happened to be numerous on any of those occasions we had always the guard under arms. The spectators on some of those occasions amounted to above ten thousand people. However we never let them know by any superfluity of parade or other means that we were jealous of their numbers or their boldness and skill, though we certainly were, and prudence demanded it. Our only defence was certainly our imaginary greatness, and this would unavoidably decline if not preserved by some studied means. It was therefore determined to preserve and if possible to promote this imaginary superiority; and as nothing could be more condusive to accomplish it than some extraordinary exhibition that would be incomprehensibly great to them, and without any hazard of miscarriage on our part, we were resolved to play off some of our fire-works that were brought from Woolwich for some such occasion; this was made known to the natives at the conclusion of one of their games, on which occasion they expressed great satisfaction, and a night being pitched upon, every thing was prepared for the occasion. The natives expected it would have been an heiva, as they call their games, at least somewhat like their own, and according to our personal appearance anticipated the satisfaction of finding us inferior to them; but in this they were totally mistaken, for when the first sky-racket ascended full one half of several thousand Indians ran off and appeared no more that evening; some of those who remained fell prone upon the earth with their faces downward and some in other attitudes, but all expressive of the most extreme surprize and astonishment. Polahow and Phenow who sat next to Cook and his officers with some other Indian Chiefs and women of distinction, were not less astonished than the multitude, and would instantly have worshiped Cook as a being of much superior order to themselves, and intreated him not to hurt them or their people, adding that they were friends and would always continue such; Cook assured Polahow that he nor any of his people should be hurt, and begged him to speak and pacify the people, and persuade them to stay and see the rest of the heiva. After this were exhibited some flower pots, horrizontal wheels, roses, water-rackets, crackets, serpents, &c. and it is hard to say whether they were upon the whole most terrified or delighted. When the entertainment ended and the assembly began to disperse nothing was heard but cries expressive of the wonders they had seen, the greatness of our heiva, and the poorness of their own; indeed this and the exhibition of our mathematical and philosophical apparatus at our astronomical tents, confirmed them in the fear and admiration of our greatness; and these circumstances received a great addition from an eclipse of the sun which happened during our stay—this we foretold to them, and also acquainted them with the time it would disappear.

These circumstances joined with others secured us indeed from open insults but were ineffectual to prevent those of a more distant kind; thefts, and indeed robberies, when occasion offered, grew daily after the first week to disturb us. At first the interpositions of Polahow and particularly Phenow tended partly to aleviate these inconveniences by restoring our purloined property, or by making compensation for the defaults of their people by presents of hogs and the fruits of the country, which indeed went a great way with Cook, who, as he was purser of the ships, was often influenced more by acquiring a hog from the natives than the fear of losing the friendship of his hospitable allies, or the honor of being always nice in the distribution of impartial justice; but then it must be remembered that the ability of performing the important errand before us depended very much if not entirely upon the precarious supplies we might procure from these and other such islands, and he must of consequence be very anxious and solicitous in the concernment; but perhaps no considerations will excuse the severity which he sometimes used towards the natives on these occasions, and he would perhaps have done better to have considered that the full exertion of extreme power is an argument of extreme weakness, and nature seemed to inform the insulted natives of the truth of this maxim by the manifestation of their subsequent resentments; for before we quit Tongotaboo we could not go any where into the country upon business or pleasure without danger. It will be needless to particularlize the instances of punishment inflicted upon the natives, or the instances of satisfaction made Cook on those occasions; but as one was something more curious and less disgustful than some others I shall mention it. We had two fine fowls, a peacock and hen, that we had brought from home at the expence of much care and trouble; and they had been too long admired and gazed at by the people not to wish them their own, and the opportunities that daily offered to take them, were too favorable not to determine them to make them such: The morning after they were missing, Cook perceived it would be a serious, if not an unfortunate circumstance without the exertions both of policy and dispatch, and therefore sent an officer from the ship to the tents with orders immediately to put poor Polahow under an arrest and the guard under arms, and upon the back of those orders came others to arrest Phenow too....

This inlet proving to be a sound was called George's-Sound. It lies in lat. 49. 33. N. and in 233. 16. E. long. and as it afforded excellent timber we furnished ourselves with a new mizen-mast, spare yards and other spars, besides wood. It also afforded us excellent water, a variety of good fish and the shores with some excellent plants. The country round this sound is generally high and mountainous, though further to the northward and eastward it appears more open and level. It is intirely covered with woods, such as maple, ash, birch, oak, hemlock, but mostly with tall well grown pine. We also found currant bushes, wild raspberry and juniper bushes, and little crabed apple-trees, but could not learn whether they bore any fruit, neither is it probable they do. We saw no plantations or any appearance that exhibited any knowledge of the cultivation of the earth, all seemed to remain in a state of nature; but as our observations did not extend three miles into the country they are imperfect. Neither did we explore the sound higher up than three leagues, as that satisfied us that it was of no great extent beyond. The light in which this country will appear most to advantage respects the variety of its animals, and the richness of their furr. They have foxes, sables, hares, marmosets, ermines, weazles, bears, wolves, deer, moose, dogs, otters, beavers, and a species of weazle called the glutton; the skin of this animal was sold at Kamchalka, a Russian factory on the Asiatic coast for sixty rubles, which is near 12 guineas, and had it been sold in China it would have been worth 30 guineas. We purchased while here about 1500 beaver, besides other skins, but took none but the best, having no thoughts at that time of using them to any other advantage than converting them to the purposes of cloathing, but it afterwards happened that skins which did not cost the purchaser six-pence sterling sold in China for 100 dollars. Neither did we purchase a quarter part of the beaver and other furrskins we might have done, and most certainly should have done had we known of meeting the opportunity of disposing of them to such an astonishing profit. . . .

These enclosed plantations extended about 3 miles from the town, near the back of which they commenced, and were succeeded by what we called the open plantations. Here the land began to rise with a gentle ascent that continued about one mile when it became abruptly steep. These were the plantations that contained the bread-fruit-trees. (What Ceres are thy wheaten sheves, and thy yellow harvests compared with this scene! Have the songs of poets done thee so much honor from a sickly theme, what would they do another deity from beholding this extensive display of spontaneous vegitation. Son of _____ what are thy fields but the sad testimony of toil, and when thy feeble plants hath passed the thousand dangers that attend its progress to a state of perfection in the field, what is it then, are not the subsequent operations necessary for the use of man still more numerous and complicated. Man eateth it by the sweat of his brow. But behold now these bread-fruit-plains thine eye cannot discern their limits, and the trees are like the cedars of Lebanon in number and in stature—can the groveling swine trample them under his feet, or are they destroyed by a gust of rain. Here is neither toil or care, man stretcheth forth his hand and eateth without parsimony or anticipated want.)

After leaving the bread-fruit-forests we continued up the ascent to the distance of a mile and an half further, and found the land thick covered with wild fern, among which our botanist found a new species. It was now near sun-down, and being upon the skirts of those woods that so remarkably surrounded this island at a uniform distance of 4 and 5 miles from the shore, we concluded to halt, especially as there was a hut hard by that would afford us a better retreat during night than what we might expect if we proceeded. When we reached the hut we found it inhabited by an elderly man, his wife and daughter the emblem of innocent uninstructed beauty. They were somewhat discomposed at our appearance and equipment, and would have left their house through fear had not the Indians who accompanied us persuaded them otherwise, and at last reconciled them to us. We sat down together before the door, and from the height of the situation we had a complete retrospective view of our rout, of the town, of part of the bay and one of our ships, besides an extensive prospect on the ocean, and a distant view of three of the neighbouring islands.

It was exquisitly entertaining. Nature had bestowed her graces with her usual negligent sublimity. The town of Kireekakooa and our ship in the bay created the contrast of art as well as the cultivated ground below, and as every object was partly a novelty it transported as well as convinced.

As we had proposed remaining at this hut the night, and being willing to preserve what provisions we had ready dressed, we purchased a little pig and had him dressed by our host who finding his account in his visitants bestired himself and soon had it ready. After supper we had some of our brandy dilated with the mountain water, and we had so long been confined to the poor brakish water at the bay below that it was a kind of nectar to us.

# CHAPTER 28

# Cartographer of the Human Heart: David Thompson (1784)

*One of the problems with stereotypes—the troglodytic marine sergeant, the absentminded professor—is that enough of them exist in flesh and blood to lend credence to the misleading conventions. As for the West, it's easy to dismiss fur traders as brutish louts, wrecking harmonious native cultures for their own greed. Furthermore if one of the frontiersmen also happens to be a surveyor and mapmaker, a man devoted to sextants and telescopes, to poring over bloodless calculations and endless tables of numbers, we immediately pile on another misconception, that of the scientist as cold fish, unperceptive beyond the scope of his shiny instruments.*

*That such a man could be one of the greatest explorers of the West and also possess the combined insights of the anthropologist and the poet's delicacy defies our cliché-bound expectations. Yet here he is, pausing in the midst of exploring the source of the Mississippi River to describe a beautiful illusion produced by an Indian fisherman standing alert in his canoe while floating through an early morning fog (Thompson 1916, 286–87): "On the Lake, especially in the fore part of the day, a low fog [rises] on the surface of the water, caused by the coldness of the water and the higher temperature of the air; which hides the Canoe; and only the Indian Man, with his poised spear ready to strike is seen, like a ghost gliding slowly over the water." That the writer also was a devout yet tolerant man who practiced his beliefs while striving to look beyond the limits of his Puritanism and understand other cultures, who when an adult married a teenage Indian girl and could talk easily with the Indians almost as if one of them, makes him sound like yet another stereotype, one of those wilderness saints created by maundering Hollywood scriptwriters.*

*At the age of fourteen, David Thompson stood on the shore of Hudson*

*Bay, already homesick as he watched the ship that had brought him from England recede into the distance. He'd been apprenticed to the Hudson's Bay Company, hardly a happy escape from the poverty of his widowed mother. Besides the pluck that overcame his pangs as he adjusted to life at a bleak outpost, he was fortunate to have a solid grounding in mathematics, learned at a London charity school. Fortunate, too, to bump into Philip Turnor. The first master surveyor of the Canadian West taught the boy his trade. Surveying on his own as he traveled the continent for his employer, Thompson later transferred to the North West Company, a more enlightened rival of his first firm, which encouraged Thompson's explorations. Maps of the time left much of the West blank. Between 1784 and 1812, Thompson crisscrossed the unknown lands by foot, horse, and canoe, covering tens of thousands of miles and eventually reaching the Pacific Ocean. Over the years he blazed new routes through the American and Canadian wilderness and opened Montana, Idaho, Washington, Oregon, and British Columbia to the fur trade. Most notably he was the first white man to travel the full length of the Columbia River. All the while he was drawing maps of what he'd seen, maps so precise that a century later a member of the Geological Survey of Canada, checking the accuracy of the lone man's calculations, declared them ". . . of the very highest order. . . " (Thompson 1916, xix).*

*And all the while, too, whether fighting off hordes of mosquitoes in the north woods or trying to stay alive in subzero weather, Thompson was writing in his journals. They have a subtle virtue beyond their eminence among the earliest records of the region and its native peoples. Thompson's journals show ". . . how vigorous and interesting factual prose can be" (Thompson 1971, 22), as in the example of the ghostly fisherman. Beyond the surprising grace of a literary flight that can happen at any turn in Thompson's pages, beyond his humor and charm, are the psychological insights dear to modern novelists. Sometimes, as in the first selection, they reveal an unintentional irony as, despite efforts to overcome his prejudices, Thompson falls prey to his own snare. More typically, however, when self-righteous white men saw only the surface, exaggerating rumors and rare instances of Indian cannibalism into hideous practices, Thompson understood the dynamics and pathos of fellow humans struggling the best they could to survive. No glib fan of the cult of the Noble Savage, in the disastrous greed of the Indians for white civilization's goods he also recognized the tragedy of the Indians' rush into the slaughter of beaver, recognizing frailties in others because he first saw them so clearly in himself.*

### Selected Bibliography

Garrod, Stan. *David Thompson.* Toronto: Grolier, 1988.

Thompson, David. *David Thompson's Narrative of His Explorations in Western America, 1784–1812.* Ed. by J. B. Tyrrell. Toronto: Champlain Society, 1916.

———. *Travels in Western North America, 1784–1812.* Ed. by Victor G. Hopwood. Toronto: Macmillan, 1971.

DAVID THOMPSON

# Cartographer of the Human Heart: David Thompson (1784)

## The Manito and Instinct

DURING THE TIME we were waiting [for] the wind to calm, I had an opportunity of seeing the Indian superstition on the polar bear; on one of these days we noticed a polar bear prowling about in the ebb tide; the Indians set off to kill it as the skin could be taken to the factory in the canoe; when the bear was shot, before they could skin him and cut off his head, the tide was coming in, which put them in danger; they left the skin to float ashore, and seizing the head, each man having hold of an ear, with their utmost speed in the mud brought the head to land; the tide was up to their knees when they reached the shore. On the first grass they laid down the head, with the nose to the sea, which [nose] they made red with ochre; they made a speech to the manito of the bears, that he would be kind to them as they had performed all his orders, had brought the head of the bear ashore, and placed it with its nose to the sea, begging him to make the skin float ashore, which, at the factory, would sell for three pints of brandy; the manito had no intention that they should get drunk; the skin did not float ashore and was lost.

In the afternoon of the third day the wind calmed, the Indians told me at noon that we had stayed there too long, that they would now sing and calm the wind, for their song had great power; they sang for about half an hour, and then said to me, "You see the wind is calming, such is the power of our song."

I was hurt at their pretensions and replied, "You see the ducks, the plover and other birds follow the ebb tide; they know the wind is calming without your song. If you possess such power why did you not sing on the first day of our being here?" They gave no answer; it is a sad weakness of the human character... which is constantly found, more or less, in the lower orders of thinly populated countries; they all possess, if we may credit them, some superhuman power.

The ebb tide had now retired about one and a half miles from us. Near sunset, each of us cut a bundle of small willows, and with the canoe and paddles, carried them about a mile, when we laid the canoe down, spread the willows on the mud, and laid down to await the return of the tide; as soon as it reached us we got into the canoe and proceeded up the Kisiskatchewan River for several miles, then crossed to the south shore and landed at a path of four miles in length, through woods of small pines, on low wet marshy ground, to York Factory, thank good Providence. . . .

In the latter end of the month of May, 1792, the ice had broken up. Mr Cooke and myself in a canoe proceeded about twenty miles up the [Nelson] River [from York Factory] to shoot the reindeer, as they crossed the river; we passed two days, in which time we had killed ten deer. On the third morning, the weather cold and uncomfortable, we were sitting by our fire when we heard a noise as of distant thunder, and, somewhat alarmed, put our four guns and blankets into the canoe, and sat quietly in it, waiting what it could be. With surprise we heard the sound increasing and rushing towards us, but we were not long in suspense.

About forty yards below us, a vast herd of reindeer, of about one hundred yards of front, [came] rushing through the woods, headlong descended the steep bank, and swam across the river; in the same manner ascended the opposite bank and continued full speed through the woods. We waited to see this vast herd pass, expecting to see it followed by a number of wolves, but not one appeared, and in this manner the herd continued to pass the whole day to near sunset, when a cessation took place. On each hand were small herds of ten to twenty deer, all rushing forward with the same speed. The great herd were so closely packed together that not one more, if dropped among them, could find a place.

The next day, a while after sunrise, the same sound and rushing noise was heard, and a dense herd of the same front, with the same headlong haste, came down the bank and crossed the river, and continued to about two in the afternoon, attended by small herds on either side, after which small herds passed, but not with the same speed, and by sunset finally ceased.

We attempted to estimate the number of deer that passed in this great herd, but the natives pointed out their method, which we thought the best; this was to allow the deer a full hour and a half (by the sun) in the morning to feed, and the same before sunset. This would give ten full hours of running, at what we thought twenty miles an hour, which they reduced to twelve miles, observing that large herds appear to run faster than they really do. By this means they extended the herd of the first day to 120 miles in length and the herd of the second day to half as much more, making the whole length of the herd to be 180 miles in length, by 100 yards in breadth. The natives do not understand high numbers, but they readily comprehend space, though they cannot define it by miles and acres, and their clock is the path of the sun. By the above space, allowing to each deer ten feet by eight feet, an area of eighty square feet, the number of reindeer that passed was 3,564,000, an immense number, without including the many small herds. Thus what we learn by numbers, they learn by space.

Then, applying themselves to me, they said, "You that look at the stars, tell us the cause of the regular march of this herd of deer." I replied, "Instinct." "What do you mean by that word?" "Its meaning is the free and voluntary actions of an animal for its self-preservation." "Oh, oh, then you think this herd of deer rushed forward over deep swamps, in which some perished [while] the others ran over them, down steep banks to break their necks, swam across large rivers where the strong drowned the weak, went a long way through the woods where they had nothing to eat, merely to take care of themselves. You white people, you look like wise men and talk like fools. The deer feeds quietly, and lays down when left to itself. Do you not perceive this great herd was under the direct order of their manito and that he was with them? He had gathered them together, made them take a regular line, and drove them on to where they are to go." "And where is that place?" "We don't know, but when he gets them there, they will disperse, none of them will ever come back." And I had to give up my doctrine of instinct to that of their manito. I have sometimes thought instinct to be a word invented by the learned to cover their ignorance of the ways and doings of animals for their self-preservation; it is a learned word and shuts up all the reasoning powers. . . .

Both [French] Canadians and Indians often enquired of me why I observed the sun and sometimes the moon in the daytime, and passed whole nights with my instruments looking at the moon and stars. I told them it was to determine the distance and direction from the place I observed to other places; neither the Canadians nor the Indians believed me, for both argued that, if what I said was truth, I ought to look to the ground, and over it, and not to the stars. Their opinions were that I was looking into futurity and seeing everybody, and what they were doing, [and] how to raise the wind. But [they] did not believe [that] I could calm it; this they argued from seeing me obliged to wait the calming of the wind on the great lakes, to which the Indians added that I knew where the deer were and other superstitious opinions.

During my life I have always been careful not to pretend to any knowledge of futurity, and [said] that I knew nothing beyond the present hour; neither argument nor ridicule had any effect, and I had to leave them to their own opinions, and yet, inadvertently on my part, several things happened to confirm their opinions.

One fine evening in February two Indians came to the house to trade; the moon rose bright and clear with the planet Jupiter a few degrees on its east side, and the Canadians as usual predicted that Indians would come to trade in the direction of this star. To show them the folly of such prediction, I told them the same bright star, the next night, would be as far from the moon on its west side; this of course took place from the moon's motion in her orbit, and is the common occurrence of almost every month, yet all parties were persuaded I had done it by some occult power to falsify the prediction of the Canadians. . . .

I had always admired the tact of the Indian in being able to guide himself through the darkest pine forests to exactly the place he intended to go, his keen constant attention on everything: the removal of the smallest stone, the bent or broken twig, a slight mark on the ground, all spoke plain language to him. I was anxious to acquire this knowledge, and often being in company with them, sometimes for several months, I paid attention to what they pointed out to me, and became almost equal to some of them, which became of great use to me. . . .

Wisk-a-hoo was naturally a cheerful, good-natured, careless man, but hard times had changed him; he was a good beaver-worker and trapper, but an indifferent moose-hunter; now and then, he killed one by chance. He had been twice so reduced by hunger as to be twice on the point of eating one of his children to save the others, when he was fortunately found and relieved by the other natives; these sufferings had, at times, unhinged his mind and made him dread being alone. He had for about a month been working beaver and had now joined Tapahpahtum, and their tents were together; he came to trade, and brought some meat the other had sent. It was usual when the natives come to trade to give them a pint of grog, a liquor which I always used very sparingly; it was a bad custom, but could not be broken off. Wiskahoo, as soon as he got it, and while drinking of it, used to say in a thoughtful mood, "Nee weet to go—I must be a man eater." This word seemed to imply, "I am possessed of an evil spirit to eat human flesh." "Wee-tee-go" is the evil spirit, that devours humankind.

When he had said this a few times, one of the men used to tie him slightly, and he soon became quiet; these sad thoughts at times came upon him, from the dreadful distress he had suffered; and at times took him in his tent, when he always allowed himself to be tied during his sad mood, which did not last long. Three years afterwards, this sad mood came upon him so often that the natives got alarmed. They shot him, and burnt his body to ashes, to prevent his ghost remaining in this world.

A-pist-a-wah-shish (the dwarf) was of low stature, but strongly made and very active, a good beaver-worker, and a second-rate hunter of moose deer; he was careful and industrious. When the leaves of the trees had fallen and winter was coming on, he had parted with the others to work beaver. At first he was successful, but the third house he attacked, the beaver had worked [so] many stones into it that he broke his ice chisel and blunted one of his axes useless; the other was all they had to cut firewood. The edges of the lakes were frozen over and canoes could not be used; distressing times came, and they were reduced to use as food the youngest child to save the others.

They were so weak they could barely get a little wood for the fire, sitting in sorrow and despair, looking at the child next to lose its life. A reindeer came and stood a few yards from the tent door; he shot it, and [it] became the means of saving them, and recovering their strength, and for the [rest of the] winter he was a fortunate hunter. Both himself, his family, and the natives believed that this deer was sent by the manito in pity to himself and family. He kept the skin, which I saw.

The Indians did not hold him culpable; they felt they were all liable to the same sad affliction, and the manito sending him a deer showed a mark of favour. As the strong affections of an Indian [are] centred in his children, for they may be said to be all he has to depend upon, they believe the dreadful distressed state of mind which necessity forces on them to take the life of one of their children to preserve the others, leaves such sad indelible impressions that the parents are never again the same [as] they were before, and are liable to aberrations of mind.

It is only on this region and the lakes westward to near the great plains (where there are horses), that the natives are subject to this distress of hunger; [here] their dogs are starved and do them very little good. If the country contained but half the deer and other animals some writers speak of, the natives would not suffer as they do. Notwithstanding the hardships the natives sometimes suffer, they are strongly attached to their country of rivers, lakes, and forests. . . .

Whether fish or meat, whatever is not required is carefully put by for [the] next meal. They carefully collect every article that can be of use to them; and when they remove, which they very often do, from place to place, the women are very heavily loaded; the men with little else [to carry] than their gun and their fishing tackle; even a girl of eight years will have her share to carry, while the boys have some trifle or only their bows and arrows. This hard usage makes women scarce among them, and by the time a girl is twelve years of age, for the young men cannot readily obtain a wife, she is given as a wife to a man of twice her age, and on this account polygamy is rare among them.

The hardships the women suffer induces them too often to let the female infants die as soon as born, and [they] look upon it as an act of kindness to them, and when any of us spoke to a woman who had thus acted, the common answer was, she "wished her mother had done the same to herself".

Upon reasoning with the men, on the severe laborious life of the women, and the early deaths it occasioned, and that it was a disgrace to them, and how very different the Nahathaways treated their women, they always intimated [women] were an inferior order of mankind, made for the use and service of the men; the Nahathaways were a different people from [them], and they were not guided by them; and I found [women] were too often regarded as the property of the strongest man, until they have one or more children. I have been alone with them for months, and always found them a kind good people, but their treatment of the women always made me regard them as an unmanly race of men. . . .

He invited us to pass the night at his tent which was close by; the sun was low, and we accepted the offer. In the tent was an old man almost his equal age, along with women and children. We preferred the open air, and made a good fire to which both of the old men came, and after smoking awhile, conversation came on, as I had always conversed with the natives as one Indian with another, and been attentive to learn their traditions on the animals, on mankind, and on other matters in ancient times, and the present occasion appeared favourable for this purpose.

Setting aside questions and answers which would be tiresome, they said, by ancient tradition of which they did not know the origin, the beavers had been an ancient people, and then lived on the dry land. "They were always beavers, not men; they were wise and powerful, and neither man nor any animal made war on them. They were well clothed as at present, and, as they did not eat meat, they made no use of fire, and did not want it. How long they lived this way we cannot tell, but we must suppose they did not live well, for the Great Spirit became angry with them, and ordered Weesaukejauk to drive them all into the water and there let them live, still to be wise, but without power, to be food and clothing for man, and the prey of other animals, against all which his defence shall be his dams, his house, and his burrows. You see how strong he makes his dams; those that we make for fishing weirs are often destroyed by the water, but his always stand. His house is not made of sand, or loose stones, but of strong earth with wood and sometimes small stones, and he makes burrows to escape from his enemies, and he always has his winter stock of provisions secured in good time. When he cuts down a tree, you see how he watches it, and takes care that it shall not fall on him."

"But if so wise, for what purpose does the beaver cut down large trees of which he makes no use whatever?" [I asked.] We do not know, perhaps an itching of his teeth and gums.

Here the old Indian paused, became silent, and then in a low tone [they] talked with each other, after which he continued his discourse. "I have told you that we believe that in years long passed away, the Great Spirit was angry with the beaver, and ordered Weesaukejauk (the Flatterer) to drive them all from the dry land into the water, and they became and continued very numerous, but the Great Spirit has been, and now is, very angry with them, and they are now all to be destroyed. About two winters ago Weesaukejauk showed to our brethren, the Nipissings and Algonquins, the secret of their destruction: that all of them were infatuated with the love of the castorum of their own species and more fond of it than we are of fire water. We are now killing the beaver without any labour, we are now rich, but shall soon be poor, for when the beaver are destroyed we have nothing to depend on to purchase what we want for our families. Strangers now overrun our country with their iron traps, and we and they will soon be poor. . . . "

Some three years [earlier] (1797) the Indians of Canada and New Brunswick, on seeing the steel trap so successful in catching foxes and other animals, thought of applying it to the beaver, instead of the awkward wooden traps they made, which often failed. At first they were set in the landing paths of the beaver, with about four inches of water on them, and a piece of green aspen for a bait, and in this manner more were caught than by the common way, but the beaver paths made their use too limited, and their ingenuity was employed to find a bait that would allure the beaver to the place of the trap. Various things and mixtures of ingredients were tried without success, but chance made some try if the male could not be caught by adding the castorum of the female; a mixture of this castorum beat up with the green buds of the aspen was made. A piece of dry willow of about eight inches in length, beat and bruised fine, was dipped in this mixture; it was placed at the water edge about a foot from the steel trap, so that the beaver should pass direct over it and be caught; this bait proved successful, but, to the surprise of the Indians, the females were caught as well as the males. The secret of this bait was soon spread; every Indian procured from the traders four to six steel traps; the weight of one was about six to eight pounds. All labour was now at an end; the hunter moved about at pleasure with his traps and infallible bait of castorum.

Of the infatuation of this animal for castorum I saw several instances. A trap was negligently fastened by its small chain to the stake to prevent the beaver taking away the trap when caught; it slipped, and the beaver swam away with the trap, and it was looked upon as lost. Two nights after, he was taken in a trap with the other trap fast to his thigh. Another time, a beaver passing over a trap to get the castorum had his hind leg broke; with his teeth he cut his broken leg off and went away; we concluded he would not come again, but two nights afterwards, he was found fast in a trap. In every case the castorum is taken away. The stick with this was always licked or sucked clean. It seemed to act as a soporific, as they remained more than a day without coming out of their houses.

The Nipissings, the Algonquins and Iroquois Indians, having exhausted their own countries, now spread themselves over these countries, and as they destroyed the beaver moved forwards to the northward and westward. The natives, the Nahathaways, did not in the least molest them; the Chippewas and other tribes made use of traps of steel and of the castorum. For several years all these Indians were very rich; the women and children, as well as the men, were covered with silver broaches, ear rings, wampum, beads, and other trinkets. Their mantles were of fine scarlet cloth, and all was finery and dress. The canoes of the fur traders were loaded with packs of beaver, the abundance of the article lowered the London prices. Every intelligent man saw the poverty that would follow the destruction of the beaver, but there were no chiefs to control it; all was perfect liberty and equality. Four years after (1797), almost the whole of these extensive countries were denuded of beaver, the natives became poor, and with difficulty procured the first necessaries of life, and in this state they remain, and probably forever. A worn out field may be manured and again made fertile, but the beaver, once destroyed, cannot be replaced; they were the gold coin of the country, with which the necessaries of life were purchased. . . .

# CHAPTER 29

# "An Irreparable Loss":
# The Diaries of Frances Hornby
# Barkley (1787)

*Although no European women accompanied Cabeza de Vaca and his com-
panions when they journeyed across the Southwest, later Spanish expeditions
did include women. Accorded only passing mention in the men's diaries and
reports (as, for example, when an expedition had to halt for a day while a
woman gave birth), these women probably felt about their husbands' wan-
derlust in pursuit of dreams of golden cities something similar to the feelings
of wives of nineteenth-century Anglo pioneers with dreams of westering: that
is, a resentment at being dragged away from family and friends to look for
pie in the sky in some godforsaken wilderness. We do not know for sure what
they felt, however, because to date nothing written by women about pre–
Lewis and Clark explorations has been published—with the one exception
that follows.*

*Does this absence from the published record indicate that women did not
write about their experiences on these expeditions? Possibly, since the patri-
archal societies of the sixteenth, seventeenth, and eighteenth centuries usually
provided advanced schooling only for male children. But it's also possible that
nineteenth- and early twentieth-century historians turning over hundreds of
pages in musty old archives simply passed by any writing that did not (in
their eyes) have historical significance. When new generations of scholars re-
examine the archives, we may find at least some interesting and illuminating
unpublished texts by women.*

*For now we can offer from published records only fragments from diaries
kept by Frances Hornby Barkley, the wife of Captain Charles William Barkley. Just married, the Barkleys sailed to the Northwest Coast in 1787, and*

*they returned in 1792. The historian W. Kaye Lamb has concluded that the fragments are probably from Mrs. Barkley's diaries—but we can't be entirely sure, because while they were still in manuscript, the diaries burned to ashes in a 1909 fire that also consumed Mrs. Barkley's grandson, Captain Edward Barkley, at Westholme, Vancouver Island. The fragments that survived were not salvaged from the ashes of the fire, for it left nothing legible. Rather they came from notes taken years earlier by Captain John T. Walbran, when he had borrowed the manuscripts for information to use in his British Columbia Coast Names, 1592–1906 (1909). Comparing Walbran's notes from the diaries with Mrs. Barkley's more general "Reminiscences" (which survived the fire), Lamb concluded that Walbran's transcription probably approximates what was in the diaries.*

*Yet Walbran himself called the burning of the diaries "an irreparable loss" (Lamb 1942, 35). Having seen numerous examples of what a difference in effect paraphrasing of exploration narratives can cause, the editors of this anthology join Walbran in lamenting the loss. His transcription gives us only a tantalizing glimpse of a pre–Lewis-and-Clark western narrative from a woman's point of view.*

*Before we share that glimpse, you should know that on each of their two voyages, the Barkleys had embarked on "a poaching expedition" (Lamb 1942, 38). Only two British corporations—the East India Company and the South Sea Company—had legal authority to trade with natives on the Northwest Coast. Since Captain Barkley had been employed by the East India Company and since those who helped finance his first voyage were still employed by it, he obviously knew that he was about to engage in poaching.*

*In pursuing their dream of quick riches, Barkley and his associates covered their poachers' tracks by changing their ship's name from the* Loudoun *to the* Imperial Eagle *and sailing under the Austrian flag. The ruse failed to fool another Englishman, Captain James Colnett, who encountered the* Imperial Eagle *in Nootka Sound in July of 1787. In his journal Colnett speaks of the "Illegality" of Barkley's trading and says (Lamb 1942, 43):*

> On the Eighteenth I sent a letter to Captain Berkley [sic], by my chief mate, requesting he would shew him his Authority for trading in the Southsea Company's limits; my right for so doing carried with him, it was refus'd but several letters & Messages pass'd, but it being in a language my chief mate could not understand we remain'd as much uninform'd as ever, but himself & Crew being mostly Englishmen which is contrary to act of Parliament it remains to be settled on our return to England.

*Apparently the poaching charge never came to court in England. After sailing on down the coast and losing four crewmen who were apparently killed by natives, Barkley sailed for China with the furs he had already collected. He sold the furs for $30,000 and then sailed for Mauritius and thence to Calcutta. Word of his adventures had reached the East India Company, however; to avoid trouble, Barkley's associates sold the ship, breaking their contract with him. He sued them for the breach of contract and was awarded 5,000 pounds. The Barkleys' 1792 voyage to the Northwest Coast had an ending even less fortunate than that of their 1787 voyage, for in 1793 the French on Mauritius confiscated Barkley's ship and all his cargo. Although he eventually managed to regain control of the ship, his later years were not "overly prosperous" (Lamb 1942, 47).*

*When her husband died in 1832, Mrs. Barkley kept his two logbooks, and from these and two of her diaries and some letters, she began writing her reminiscences. At her death in 1845, all the Barkley papers became the property of her eldest son, who loaned the logbooks "to Lord Aberdeen in 1846, in the hope that they might furnish evidence of value to Great Britain in the settlement of the Oregon boundary dispute" (Lamb 1942, 32). Mrs. Barkley's diaries remained with her heirs and were destroyed by the fire that consumed her grandson Edward in 1909.*

*The footnotes in Lamb's edition of the diary fragments alert readers to changes in place names. What the Barkleys called King George's Sound is now Nootka Sound. Wickaninnish's Sound is now Clayoquot Sound; Village Island is Effingham Island; Admiralty Bay is Yakutat Bay; Norfolk Sound is Sitka Sound. Of places named by Captain Barkley—Barkley Sound, Frances Island, Hornby Peak, Cape Beale, Williams Point—only Barkley Sound and Cape Beale appear on modern maps. "Mr. Mackey" was Dr. John McKay, who had been left at Nootka Sound in July 1786 by another British ship, so that he could convince the natives to gather and save a large number of furs for trading with the ship when it returned. According to Walbran, Dr. McKay informed the Barkleys "that he had been living at Nootka amongst the Indians for the previous twelve months, during which time he had completely conformed himself to their habits and customs, which Mrs. Barkley in her diary emphatically states were disgusting" (Lamb 1942, 41).*

### Selected Bibliography

Lamb, W. Kaye. "The Mystery of Mrs. Barkley's Diary: Notes on the Voyage of the 'Imperial Eagle,' 1786–87." *British Columbia Historical Quarterly* 6 (January 1942):31–75.

## On the coast of Alaska in the brig *Halcyon,* August, 1792.

On the 16th of August 1792 we made the coast of America again in two places at once, the northern and southern extreme of Behring's Bay, with Mount St. Elias and Mount Fairweather both in view. They are very high mountains and their heads are covered with snow. The weather at this time was tolerably warm, but misty and like the weather we met with on the coast of Asia, very changeable and at times chilly. The coast was entirely unknown. We did not reach a port of safety until the 18th, owing to unfavourable winds, and then further to the north than Captain Barkley originally intended. The land formed a deep bay, called Admiralty bay, a bay of large extent with many harbors in it. The one in which we cast anchor was called Lord Mulgrave's harbor. The country looked green and pleasant to the eye, the anchorage safe and snug. Several canoes came alongside and some had women on board. They appeared most disgusting objects covered with dirty sea-otter skins, with the fur to the skin, the leather tanned red and filthy beyond description. It was here we first saw women with those pieces of shaped wooden lip ornaments, which are described in Captain Cook's voyages—if such a frightful appendage can be called ornamental, a thing that distorts the mouth and gives the whole features a new and most unpleasant character. The piece of wood is inserted into a slit made in the under lip when the females are about 14 years old, and it is replaced from year to year, larger and larger, until in middle age it is as large as the bowl of a table spoon and nearly the same shape, being concave on the inside of the lip, which it presses out from the gum, thereby showing the whole of the teeth and gums,—a frightful sight at best, but still worse when the teeth are black and dirty, which was invariably the case, also generally uneven and decayed. This odious mouthpiece so completely disfigured them, that it was impossible to tell what they would have been without it, for even their complexions could not be ascertained, their skins being besmeared with soot and red ochre. Their hair is dark and shiny and appeared to be kept in good order, parted in the middle and kept smooth on each side behind the ears and tied behind the top in a knot. The men, on the contrary, have their hair matted and daubed with oil and ochre. The dresses of both sexes are made with the skins of animals, sometimes with the fur on and sometimes without. The women seldom wear any valuable furs, the men sometimes wear sea-otter skin of which they well know the value, and will strip themselves whenever they can make a good bargain. The women have sometimes a kind of rug thrown over their shoulders, a manufacture of their own. They wear it over their skin dresses, the men in like manner wear two or more sea-otter skins, which they throw over themselves. The people we saw did not seem settled. They had come on a fishing expedition, we conjectured, and they hastily built up huts, with boards, with which each canoe was furnished, upon the small island, and when they had sold the few furs they had with them, and had got all they could out of the ship, the most of them went off, leaving a few fishermen who were very diligent in catching fish, which we bought, and the women frequently supplied us with very nice berries of different kinds, such as wild strawberries of excellent flavor, and, considering the difficulty of picking them in such a wild country, plentiful. The men brought an indifferent kind of salmon with a long snout, it might have been out of season, the flesh looked very pale; they likewise, brought a few river trout. These were large, but the flesh quite white, not the pale pink color of our English trout. The only weapon that we saw them with was spears, with large sharp iron barbs. These iron barbs were at least 18 inches long, and they seemed to possess a great number of them. The men had also daggers, suspended from their necks.

I was allowed to land here often, and Capt. Barkley and myself explored the island, which sheltered and made the harbour we lay in, and was astonished to see on this island the traces of cultivation. The ground was covered with coarse grass and oats amongst it. Peas, one crop apparently just out of bearing and another in bloom, and plenty of strawberry plants not of the wild sort, but evidently planted ones. These plants were also stripped of their fruit, no doubt by our Indian friends who had brought them on board for sale.

The ship having now been put in order and the water butts filled, we prepared for our departure on the 25th August, when we were surprised by the appearance of a brig which hove in sight in the offing. We were much pleased by the idea of seeing some of our countrymen when we saw a boat approaching and entering the sound. Capt. Barkley rowed off in order to conduct them into port or render them any assistance they might require, and was astonished and disappointed at finding there was no officer in the boat, only four sailors, who said they were dispatched on seeing a sail in the sound to get relief, they being very short of provisions. They said that their vessel was an American brig, commanded by Capt. Hancock, last from China, that they were going to try their fortune on the coast, and were on their way to Prince William Sound. The brig was to remain at the entrance to the bay until they returned to report their success.

The four men were taken on board and given refreshment, being very much exhausted, and when they had rested, they got into their boat again in order to join their own vessel, but no vessel was to be seen, so after pretending to have been rowing all night, they returned in the morning, saying the brig must have been blown off the coast, but as it was a very fine night, Capt. Barkley began to suspect that all was not right, but, as the men appeared able-bodied seamen, he took them on board the *Halcyon* and promised them a passage to China. They were extremely thankful for this offer, not, as they said, much relishing being left to winter on this coast with savages. They had no stores or clothes with them in the boat, except what they had on, and it had altogether a very odd appearance.

We remained three days to give the vessel an opportunity of returning, but as they did not, we left Mulgrave harbor with this addition to our crew. That these men had been turned adrift, and deserted there could be no doubt, but for what reason we could not find out. We had scarcely got an offing when on the 29th a violent gale arose, so that we were obliged to stand out to sea, and when we had weathered the gale, Capt. Barkley looked for a harbor, but was unsuccessful, the wind continuing to blow off the shore. He was obliged to give up his intention of visiting Portlock's harbor, the weather being so unfavorable. But when the weather became more mild my husband made for Norfolk sound, where the *Halcyon* anchored in a cove at the bottom of the bay, the surrounding country looking very green and pleasant. The day after our arrival we had a number of visitors who were in large well-appointed canoes. They soon fixed their habitations on the beach opposite the vessel, and displayed several fine sea-otter skins for sale, but they set such a high value on them that it was very difficult to do any trade, there being no end to their demands. Powder and shot was always the first thing they wanted, two or three musskets being in every canoe, then blankets, cooking utensils, and tools or other iron weapons. Indeed they seemed the most dangerous and most mischievous set we had ever seen, being very expert with their iron weapons, and so dilatory in their traffic that although there seemed no difficulty in getting a fresh supply of furs, they kept haggling about the price for what they had at such length that much time was lost, yet Capt. Barkley purchased a good lot of furs.

The inhabitants increased daily, and they got so bold and troublesome at last that it became difficult to avoid disputes, they stealing every article that they could lay their hands upon, stripping them when they went on shore, and upon the slightest offence presenting their fire arms at us, the use of which they perfectly knew, but we conjectured had never felt the effect of, and certainly not of our great guns. Capt. Barkley, on one or two occasions, had our great guns fired off to astonish them, but they only seemed to think him in play. Thank God, we left them in ignorance of their deadly effect, but as they saw the trees shivered and broken by the cannon shot, they must have been aware of what mischief they could do. Once in particular, Capt. Barkley saw several war canoes with his night glass stealing along under the shadow of the land on a fine moonlight night, and as we were very indifferently manned, he was suspicious of their intentions. We therefore had the whole broad-side fired off over their heads, which made a tremendous noise among the trees. Every canoe scuttled off, but we kept perfect silence on board that they might not think we were alarmed. Early next morning they came alongside again, dressed in their war dresses and singing their war songs and keeping time with their paddles. When they had paddled three times around the vessel they set up a great shout, they pulled off their masks, resumed their usual habits, and exhibited their sea-otter skins for trade, giving us to understand that they had been on a war expedition and had taken these skins from their enemies. They never alluded to the firing but went on trading as if nothing had passed.

They are a very savage race, and their women are still more frightful than the women of Admiralty bay, the disgusting mouthpiece being still larger than theirs, in fact, the mouthpieces of the old women were so large that the lip could not support them, so that they were obliged to hold it up with their hands and to close their mouths with great effort. When shut, the under lip entirely hid the upper one and reached up to the nose. This gave them a most extraordinary appearance, but when they opened it to eat, no description can be given of what it is like, for they are obliged to support the lip whilst they opened their mouths, and then they throw the food into their mouths, throwing back their heads with a jerk to prevent the food lodging in the artificial lip or saucer, which is concave, and when let down receives whatever escapes the right channel. How any rational creature could invent such an inconvenient machine I am at a loss even to guess, as there is no stage of it that has the most distant appearance of ornament even in the young women. It looks like a second mouth as long as the lip will bear its weight. The women supplied us here regularly with a vast quantity of fresh plucked berries and wild flowers. There was one sort of berry different to any one I have ever seen. It was of a pale transparent red, the size of a currant, but grows separately, like the black currant on the slender twigs of a very elegant bush as tall as a barberry and much such a plant. They brought boughs with the fruit hanging to them. The fruit was rather tart but of a delicious flavor. I made preserve of it which proved very grateful to us all when we were at sea, and we regaled ourselves with all in our reach whilst it was fresh. The strawberries were done, but the other berries brought to us for sale were often covered with the leaves of that plant, so strawberries must be wild in the woods, although those we met with in Admiralty bay had been cultivated. The men would not perform any work. They seemed idle, now and then bringing us a few fish and that is all we could obtain from them in the way of food. They seemed to think of nothing but their arms, being very proud of their spears, which are very formidable weapons, being similar to those used by the natives of Admiralty bay, and they are very expert in the use of them, and informed us they liked them better than muskets, because they were sure to hit with them, whereas the fire arms made a great noise but did not always do execution. We conversed with them through the vocabularies annexed to Capt. Cook's narrative, the aptitude Capt. Barkley showed in learning languages being of an extraordinary nature, to which was joined great perserverance. The language of the natives of Nootka sound he soon understood, having on our visit to that part of the coast on the previous voyage of the *Imperial Eagle* regularly studied it. I have no memorandum of the time we remained at Norfolk sound, but the long boat was despatched from thence to Portlock's harbor, and was absent sixteen days, and returned with only one skin, Mr. Nowell, the mate, who commanded her having experienced very bad weather. He reported that the sound in which Portlock's harbor is situated of such vast extent that he did not attempt to explore it. This is a part of the coast my husband was most desirous of visiting, but as I have before observed, we were blown off it, which appeared not to be favored with pleasant weather when we consider this was the month of August.

[Captain Walbran states that the diary concluded at this point.]

# CHAPTER 30

# The Roads to Santa Fe: Pedro Vial and Francisco Amangual

## (1792)

*Linked to Mexico City by the Camino Real (Royal Road), Santa Fe suffered the fate of a frontier outpost hundreds of miles from its source of supplies. The conductas (caravans) that took goods 1,600 miles from Mexico City to Santa Fe could not bring enough to satisfy demand, and the prices they charged left the Santa Fe merchants constantly in debt. In 1786 the Spanish began a series of explorations to find new trade routes to Santa Fe and to improve travel and communication between the settlements of their northeastern border, in order to forestall incursions into the area by other powers, including the French, the British, and the Americans.*

*The leader of most of the Spanish expeditions was Pedro Vial, born sometime between 1746 and 1755 in Lyons, France. He said he came to the Missouri River before the American Revolution; and he must have spent some time on the frontier, for in 1786 the Spaniards picked him to find a route from San Antonio to Santa Fe. Among other frontier skills, Vial had learned how to communicate with and travel among tribes as fierce and varied as the Apaches, Utes, Kiowas, Comanches, Kansas, Osages, Otos, Missouris, Iowas, Sioux, Arapahos, and Pawnees. Surviving such contact with his scalp intact, Vial led another expedition in 1788–89, and in 1792–93 his 2,279-mile round-trip journey from Santa Fe to St. Louis was accomplished with such speed (except for six weeks as a captive of the Kansas Indians) that Spanish authorities at last awoke to the proximity of the still-infant United States.*

*In 1797 Vial went to live among the Comanches, and two years later, according to the historians Noel M. Loomis and Abraham P. Nasatir, "he was a resident of Portage des Sioux, just north of St. Louis." In 1803, however,*

*Vial was back in Santa Fe, and two years later the Spanish sent him on expeditions ostensibly only to visit with various Indian tribes, but actually to incite the natives to stop the imminent Lewis and Clark expedition. Ironically, five years later, Clark would issue Vial a license to trap on the Missouri. Some time after that, Vial returned to Santa Fe, where he died in 1814.*

*That his biographers can tell us little more of him seems understandable, given his laconic journal entries. Here, for example, are some typical entries from the diary (Loomis and Nasatir 1967, 273) Vial kept on his expedition from Béxar to Santa Fe in 1786–87 (the numbers at the end of each entry indicate the number of leagues traveled that day):*

[December] 15 I set out to the north, going right along the Brazos River until I stopped for the night on the same river. 5

16 I set out from this place in the same direction, and slept without any mishap by the same river. 5

17 I went in the same direction from this place until I arrived at an arroyo with water. 8

18 I set out from this place in the same direction until I came to a lagoon with water. 7

19 I set out from this place in the same direction until I returned to the same river for the night. 5

20 I set out from this place in the same direction, until I came to a forest, where I found water. 5

*In the selections that follow, Vial fortunately provides a fuller account of his captivity among the Kansas during his trip to St. Louis in 1792. An entry from the diary of Vial's return journey shows how the fluid boundaries of the early frontier could lead to cases of mistaken identity, and how such mistakes placed lives in jeopardy.*

*Perhaps Vial's captivity convinced the Spanish that future expeditions should be larger and better armed. In any case, in 1808, when William Clark was issuing a license to Vial, the Spanish sent a force of two hundred men with eight hundred animals and wheeled vehicles in their train to find a new route from San Antonio to Santa Fe. They followed one of the roughest routes across the Llano Estacado, and they were led by Francisco Amangual, a soldier who had been born at Majorca in 1739. Like Vial, Amangual had years of experience on the frontier, having been stationed in the Southwest since the 1760s. Besides his many military assignments, he served as superintendent of the first hospital in Texas. He retired after the expedition of 1808 and died four years later.*

*Although not as richly detailed as the Lewis and Clark journals,* this area. We wanted to find them because I knew that they were well disposed toward the government of the province of Louisiana. And at about 4 o'clock in the afternoon we found them in their hunting-camp on the shore of the same Arkansas River. They approached us, and with the river between us, we fired some shots into the wind so that they would hear and see us. They immediately began to move, and came across to us. The first who met us, greeted us affectionately, shaking hands. I asked them what tribe they were, and they told me they were Kansas. At the same moment they took possession of our horses and equipment, cutting our clothes with knives, leaving us entirely naked. They wanted to kill us, at which one of them cried to the others [Seville copy: some of them shouted to those who were going to do it], telling them they should not do it with rifles or arrows but with hatchet-blows or lances, because they had us surrounded and they might cause some unfortunate accident to themselves. In this conflict, one of them took our part, begging and supplicating the others not to take our lives. At that time I was approached by another whom I had known among the Frenchmen, and, taking me by the hand, he made me mount his own horse with him. Then another one came up behind and hurled a spear at me, but my good friend guarded me, dismounting from the horse, leaving me on it, and grabbed the evil-intentioned one. When they saw that, many of them rushed up and tried to kill me from behind, but a brother of the one who had just protected me, seated himself on the croup of the horse with the same intention [of protecting me]. That had hardly happened when I was approached by another Indian who had been a servant [criado] in the village of St. Louis of Illinois, who spoke very good French, and he, recognizing me, began to shout, "Don't kill him! Don't kill him! We shall find out from where he comes, because I know him." And, taking the reins of the horse, he took me to his lodge and said, "Friend, how your Excellency must hurry if you want to save your life, because among us it is the custom and the law that, after having eaten, no one can be killed." I did it with the promptness that the case required, after which they left me alone. After a moment, some of the chiefs came to me and asked me from where I came, to which I answered that I had come from Santa Fe, sent by the great chief, their Spanish father, to open a road from Illinois—to which Spanish chief [in Illinois] I carried letters. Thereupon they left me alone until the following day, when they reunited me with my two companions, who had suffered violence equal to mine and had been freed by other Indians of good heart, although Vicente Villanueba came out with his head cut and a daggerthrust in the belly that would have been fatal if, at the moment of receiving it, he had not pulled away, and had [he not had] the good services of another Indian who saved him, receiving the force of the blow on one arm, which left him seriously wounded. They kept us naked in that encampment until the 16th of August, we having traveled that day 4.

September 16—We set out from the village of the Kansas in search of the Missouri River, embarking in a pirogue belonging to the traders from St. Louis, traveling by the Kansas River to its junction with the Missouri, which distance is 120 leagues [312 miles], uninhabited on either shore. After eight days of navigation, we entered the Missouri. On this river the masters of the pirogue frequently stopped to hunt deers and bears, which abound on the shores—for which reason we did not arrive at St. Louis, Illinois, until October 3, at night, notwithstanding the fact that that place is not more than 140 leagues from the confluence of the Kansas and the Missouri. On the shores of the latter, I had formerly [*antiguamente*] been acquainted with two villages [of Indians], one of Osages and the other of Missouris, but now they are deserted because of [the inhabitants'] having been driven away by the Sioux [or Sacs] and Iowas.

As soon as I arrived at the town of St. Louis, I presented myself to the commandant and delivered to him the letter and the instructions that I was carrying from the governor of New Mexico, and also the diary of my trip.

I made my residence in St. Louis from the said third day of October, 1792, to June 14 following, 1793, which delay was unavoidable, as much because of the season as from fear of the Osages, who frequently interrupt navigation and travel on the Missouri River.

{October 19}—We set out at 6 o'clock in the morning on said course, and slept on the banks of the same river. At midnight we were attacked by 56 warriors armed with 22 muskets, a blunderbuss, and the rest of them [with] lances and arrows. They beat my boys with cudgels, thinking we were Comanches, and for a little while did not fire their rifles. They recognized our horses and made an outcry, and we awoke and seized our arms. Then the Indians with me told me not to fire at them, that they were their own people. There were two chiefs who then joined us and shook hands with me. One of them was displeased with the blows they had given my boys, and took a cudgel and beat those who had done it. Then, seating himself at my side, he told me it was fortunate they had discovered our horses, for if they had not, they would have killed us, thinking we were Comanches. I then took out four twists of tobacco and gave them to the chiefs to distribute to their people. The whole night was spent smoking and talking. The two chiefs who had come with me were displeased with the others because those others were going on campaign against the Comanches while the chiefs with me were going to make peace with them and to see their Spanish father. But the new chiefs answered that the Comanches had already killed their relatives.

At 8 o'clock in the morning of the 20th, those who had come with me, without saying a word, returned to their village, and left me with the new chiefs with whom they were displeased. These latter told me that my life was safe, that they would not kill us, and they asked me for powder, balls, and other goods, and when they received those, they left, leaving me alone with my two young men and one [Indian] who remained because he was eager to see his Spanish father and the Comanches, and even though they would kill him, he had to come. We left on the 21st, hiding ourselves in the cañadas, camping without wood or water. We traveled 8

22—On the same course and same river, we traveled 7

23—Along the said river and course, we traveled 6

24—Our course to the southwest, we encountered a medium-sized river, which we followed, and stopped on its bank, having made 6

At midnight, Vicente Villanueva awoke me, telling me, "Look, here is a horse saddled; perhaps it is a Comanche coming to attack." At once I took my arms and, going out, recognized that it was one of mine. I reprimanded him for not having unsaddled it, but the young man told me, "I think the Indian may have saddled it to steal it." The Indian, pretending to sleep, simulated fear on awakening, asking, "What has happened?" To which I answered that I had found a horse of mine saddled, and he told me that he did not think so, that we were camped in a stopping place [burial ground] of the Comanches; that some of the dead must have saddled the horse; that in his dreams he had heard their whistling. He asked me for tobacco, and, raising his arm, said he was going to bury it to quiet the dead. We passed the rest of the night without sleep, taking care that our horses should not be run off, and at daybreak I sent him [the Indian] back to his village, giving him some small presents.

## Mistaken Identity Almost Proves Fatal for Amangual

April 19— This day dawned with no unusual incident, and we set out. At sunrise there arrived the corporal and five [they started with six] soldiers, and reported that they had not found the six missing animals. Our course has been along a little valley with small plateaus until we crossed the creek formed by the spring, and after traveling a short distance, we entered a rocky, hilly country [and traveled over it] until we reached a beautiful plain with good grass, several low hills, and some evergreen oaks. A long distance to the north there is an extended range of hills, and to the south there can be seen a grove of trees along the Colorado River. To the north was a hill with two peaks which the Indians said was called the Eagle's nest [La Casa de la Aguila]. We traveled in that direction until we climbed a range of extensive hills, and from there we saw a great plain with much grass, where there is a river which descends to join the Colorado. Having arrived at its bank, [we found the river] delightful both for its beautiful location as well as for its groves of very tall walnut trees; it seems like a paradise, had abundant water with much fish, and nearby there are extensive plains covered with grass. The Indians say that at about 9 or 10 leagues, the water comes gushing out of a rock. It [the river] flows north northwest and east east south [!]. In our course we found many buffaloes [in this day's march]. The Indians killed several, and the troops carried the meat to camp to cure it. Night fell without any other unusual incident. [Bexar copy only: 8 leagues]

April 20— This day dawned without incident except that the *cavallada* of the Colony stampeded, and part of it was found with the *cavallada* of the New Kingdom of León. After the horses were cut out, there were 18 animals missing, and some troops have gone in search of them. We did not set out on the march, for the need of resting the *cavallada*, which is run down, and because this place is suited to condition them, and [also because] the troops can provide themselves with meat, and should not reach a state of want as long as there is a remedy. Five soldiers and one corporal have gone out together to hunt meat; night fell without their having returned. At 8 o'clock in the evening, the Comanche Indian who had come from San Antonio as guide with the expedition, complained that he had lost an iron chain that he kept in a stable [or mounted on a quirt] because of which the adjutant was ordered to question the sentries, where was found the guilty soldier from the company of Don Matías Cantu, which is attached to the company of Don José Agabo de Ayala, called Faustino Lozano. When this fact was proved, I ordered assembly to be sounded, and the soldiers formed a circle. The soldier was brought in by a corporal and two privates as guards, placed in the center and his case recited. [Then] he was given twenty-five blows with a slender stick by the same corporal for his punishment and an example for the troops. He was then placed in the guardhouse until further orders [should be given].

April 25— On this day there was no departure because we had to parley with the Indians who gathered in this village, and to appoint the guides who are to go with our expedition. Night fell without incident. This day we gave a small gift to the Indians, as had been done with Cordero, which also was delivered to Cordero in order that it be distributed through him, and there was a drill by the companies. In the afternoon we went to the village of Chief Chiojas, where assembled all the chiefs and the rest of their *bolos* and Chief Cordero, and by means of our interpreter I made to them a long and clear speech that our arrival was with the object of inviting them to visit us, to let them know the love of our king and father toward them, the loyalty and fidelity that we bear him; that they should observe the same, that they should not trade with any other nation that may come to induce them, for their [any other nation's] object is none other than that of afterward turning them from their loyalty to us; [I asked them] if they knew if any Americans from other nations have entered their lands and if they knew if they had a trading post; to which they responded, first, that they were satisfactorily informed of everything, for they considered themselves Spaniards and believe everything that comes from us, and without accepting anything from other nations; and, second, that they know nothing about what was asked them. It caused a great parley to take place; they spoke of all that we imposed on them, and that they were faithful to everything, likewise to us, that just like the defenders against the enemies, they would do the same. Afterward there was a discussion of the guides for our trip, which was left for them to discuss among themselves. And on the following day they decided those who should be most useful for the places in which we had to travel, and at the same time of good conduct and loyal to their nation—the best qualities required for this task—to which we agreed. Upon completion of everything expressed, we withdrew to our encampment, accompanied by Cordero, with no incident other than that upon our arrival we found one of the sick men from the company of Lieut. Luciano Garcia, named Rafael Mansilla, very ill with pain in the side, for which reason the chaplain immediately went to confess him. No other incident occurred, and night fell.

April 26— Today we remained in camp in the same place awaiting what was mentioned yesterday. During the night, nothing unusual occurred except that the sick man, mentioned before, continued very ill, and because of that, the chaplain went to hear his dying confession and grant him absolution according to the papal bull. At night of this day, Captain Agabo de Ayala went out with an escort of 8 men and a corporal to reconnoiter the pasture lands, and three hours later he returned with nothing unusual, after having found it to be very good pasture as far as the Colorado, which he reconnoitered. This day [also] 7 soldiers went to hunt, and [Bexar copy picks up here again] they returned with meat, with no unusual incident. At sundown a very ominous thundercloud appeared in the northwest, which *al esclarecerse* turned into a norther so violent that it seemed to be a hurricane of the worst kind ever experienced [with] lightning and thunder. Night fell without unusual incident.

April 27— Today we remained in camp in the same place to wait for the guides [to tell us] where we should spend the night. It continued to rain, and there was a norther so violent that it tore some of the tents to shreds; it blew until midnight, when it abated completely. The day dawned clear. The aforesaid soldier died at 9 o'clock, and was buried in the afternoon. At sundown a storm [*frolundada*] commenced to blow towards the southeast and to the northeast, and it started lightening and thundering, but it did not amount to a great deal. At midnight, however, it changed to the north, and then returned to the southeast, and [finally] blew from all directions. Such was the fury of it that the tents were of no value, and all the troops were swimming in it, and at that hour the weather became calm, but very cloudy. Without anything further occurring, today we all wrote to Bexar to report our situation. . . .

May 13— Today dawned with nothing unusual having occurred. We continued to travel over a high and level country, covered with red sand and some clumps of mesquite trees that were high and thickly wooded; there were several *cañadas* formed by the beginning and ending of elevations. [Bexar copy: After traveling a short distance, we crossed said elevations and reached an extensive plain, with many small lakes and pools of rain water. There were some clumps of mesquite trees and small cottonwoods; the place is a delightful valley, about 1 league in extent in every direction; its length was cut short by an elevation, very large and level, which we climbed. We again descended to another level, very delightful, that had similar *cañadas* and much water and grass, and a few mesquite trees toward the edges. As the Indian guides reported that if water should be found farther on, it would be merely by chance, as there were no water holes, we decided to camp on an elevated plain with a commanding view near a] *cañada* that held much rain water, and they run from the north to the west. [Immediately] an Indian guide went out in search of a water hole for the following day. He returned and reported that he had found plenty of water a long distance away. Night came with no unusual incident except that a soldier of the New Kingdom of León, who was attached to the company of Don José Agabo de Ayala, was seriously ill with syphilis. After he was treated with some medicine, he was confessed today. [Bexar copy: As soon as he reported to me, I sent him to his captain, who should give him some kind of medicine. He gave his confession today.] 5½ leagues. . . .

May 22— Dawn came today with no unusual incident having occurred. We stayed in camp until noon in order to set out in the afternoon and spend the night at a point from which we could reach a water hole tomorrow. We set out at 12 o'clock, and, although it was late, we traveled toward the north. Leaving behind the rims that form the canyon, we began to travel over plains so immense that the eye could not see their end. There was nothing but grass and a few small pools of rain water, with very little water, and some dry holes, on these plains; where we camped, it was necessary to drive stakes for the horses of the guard and for precaution. No unusual incident occurred other than the fact that I became sick in one eye; therefore, the expedition started, [while] I remained at the place with an escort of ten men and one sergeant, to wait for the sunset so that I could continue on our route. Night fell, and we were without water, but at 8 o'clock I arrived at the camp, no unusual incident having occurred. 8½ leagues. . . .

May 25— Dawn came today with no unusual incident. Consequently we continued on our way, traveling over plains so extensive that the horizon was tiring to the eye. We traveled all day over this kind of land, and found some dry lakes that showed signs of accumulating much water in time of rain. It could be seen that there is usually much grass during the rainy season, but at this time it had been trampled by a large number of buffaloes, which, in time, have exhausted [eaten up all] the grass. Furthermore, there has been such a severe drouth that today the plains are so burned up and clean that we have not found in all our route the least blade of dry grass or weed. This condition was so noticeable that it caused great astonishment. We continued traveling until about sundown, when we reached some small hills where, *a la hora que señala la tabla,* we pitched camp. At that place there were buffaloes as far as the eye could see. Night came without incident. 18 leagues. . . .

May 30— Dawn came today with the unusual incident that the *cavallada* of the First Company of the Colony had stampeded, and half of them were missing. Consequently, steps were taken to find them. We remained in camp, waiting for the return of the *cavallada* and in order to give time for the ground and the clothes of the troops to get dry, since it had rained all night. As the *cavallada* was found at noon, we started out toward the river, traveling over very difficult terrain with many hills, *cañadas*, creeks, bluffs, cliffs, and precipices, with a great many impossible conditions. It was necessary for the unassigned troops to use crowbars and pickaxes to make a path up and down for the train, which was traveling with extreme difficulty; it was almost necessary for the muleteers to take the baggage in their arms and to make an infinite number of turns looking for the best terrain for us to travel over, until we reached the banks of the Red River [Canadian]. At that point, where we camped, the river flows as far as the eye can see from west to east. It is narrow, shallow, and close to the surface of the ground, with low banks, the highest being about one *vara*. There were very level, grassy plains on both sides. The water, as well as the ground around there, is red. Two parties of troops were sent out to patrol and reconnoiter the ground on both sides of the river. At sundown they returned and reported that nothing unusual had been found. In this manner, night came. 6 leagues. . . .

June 1— Dawn today came without unusual incident. We continued to travel a short distance from the river; we could not travel along its banks because we could not find a way for the mule train and the troops. We traveled near the river until 9:30 o'clock over low hills until we again reached the river at a point where steep bluffs made it necessary for us to open a road by means of crowbars, axes, and pickaxes. We continued to travel over hills, and after we had traveled a short distance, three men on horseback were sighted running away on the other side of the river to the north. Therefore, a detachment from the vanguard went out to reconnoiter, and found them to be settlers from the jurisdiction of Santa Fe who were hunting. When the detachment learned that they were not suspicious, it returned and joined the squadron. We passed a small elevation that forms a grassy plain near the river; soon thereafter, five men and one Frenchman who said his name was Don Pedro, arrived. They said they were settlers of the town of Santa Fe and that they had come out with permission from the governor of that capital to look for buffaloes for meat. In the afternoon the five men withdrew to their camp, which was near ours, [but] the Frenchman remained to spend the night with us. He stated that this territory is very peaceful; that this river is the Colorado, which is otherwise known as the Red River, but that it does not flow by Natchitoches; and that a long distance from here it joins the Napestle, and both of them join the Mississippi; and that the river we passed on the twenty-second of May was the Natchitoches [Red] River, and that we had reached its source. Thus night came without unusual incident. 2½ leagues

June 2— Dawn came today without incident, and we continued on our way, traveling along the river over terrain with creeks and low hills and the river's watershed. After we had traveled a short distance, some men were sighted, who were found to belong to the same party we met yesterday. We were informed that troops were traveling along the river to meet us. Among these men there was one named Manuel Martínez, who said he was interpreter to the Indian tribes, and that he was hunting with the Indians of the San Miguel del Bado missions. They told us that by crossing the river to the north side where it was flat, we would find a road over which we could travel, and that it was impossible to travel the way we were going without great difficulties with our train because of the creek and bluffs. Consequently, at 8 o'clock in the morning we crossed the river and traveled along its banks in the direction of the plateau; the river runs in the same direction. Thus we traveled until we reached the place where the aforesaid Indians and soldiers were camped, and, since there was much grass there, and a spring of water, we camped there. No other unusual incident occurred on the route. The aforesaid soldier told us that he had explored the river together with Lieutenant Don Facundo [Melgares], and that the water of this [river] exhausted itself in the sand, and that the bed was dry; and that it was not the one that flows to Natchitoches; that the source of this [river] was in the Sierra Blanca, but that two days' journey away it was impossible to travel on horseback; and that [even] on foot it was not possible to go down to the river to get a drink; that the small amount of water in it was rain water; that farther on, the river was formed by several creeks that enter it, and all of them have their source in the aforesaid Sierra Blanca, which is four days' journey from this place; and that its route lay over mountains that cause it to have an impassable depth. Thus night came without further incident. 6 leagues

June 3— Dawn came today without unusual incident. Therefore, we continue to travel on our way along the river on a level, sandy plain and many sand banks that form elevations and depressions. To the south there are some hills and bluffs that run in the direction of the river bed, which has many turns and a deep and narrow channel with high bluffs. We went down an open road or grassy plain where we found some clumps of cottonwood, and from there we could see many hills to the west; we camped in a meadow covered with grass. A short while later, a settler of the province of New Mexico arrived and said that he was at the head of 120 men who had come hunting with permission from the governor of the province. He reported that it [the party] had had no unusual incident on its route. They remained in our camp all afternoon and gave us information about the route. Late that afternoon they returned to their camp. Thus night came without further incident. 5½ leagues

# CHAPTER 31

# The Mists Drawn Back:
# Alexander Mackenzie (1793)

*One man did yeoman's service in building on the work of others to help shape the maps of the West now in the geography books. It should come as no surprise that he was a fur trader eager to increase his company's profits by finding a more efficient way to tap the wealth of pelts waiting in the wilderness. For economics almost always is one of the huge wheels driving exploration, and the fur trade was a central motive for opening up western Canada. If Scottish-born Alexander Mackenzie could find the fabled northern sea passage, then Britain could seize the route and capture the lucrative trade with China. And if he could find the Great River of the West, he might similarly open up communication with the Pacific Ocean and thus more easily exploit the riches in between.*

*Yet motives rarely are simple. Mackenzie hardly was a rapacious villain blinded by greed. He was curious to find what the unknown held, and if as a leader he had the necessary inner strength to discipline the little band of rowdy frontiersmen he led into the teeth of the wilderness, he also could be more than fair with his men. On this score, while praising Mackenzie's courage, the eminent historian Bernard DeVoto (1952, 309) may be a bit too harsh in describing the adventurer as ". . . a hard man to like. . ." On one occasion, for instance, Mackenzie showed his mettle by refusing to abandon a sick Indian guide who couldn't keep up with the pace of the party. Patriotism should be factored in, along with vision, for Mackenzie wanted his country to establish the new trading posts rather than the rival nations then groping along the Pacific coast. Add to that Mackenzie's youth. On both his 1789 trip north up what is now called the Mackenzie River to the Arctic Ocean—thus proving that the Northwest Passage was an impractical route because of the ice—and on his 1793 foray west by canoe over the divide of the Canadian Rockies and down to the Pacific Ocean—which indicated no easy water ac-*

*cess to the coast—he was still in his twenties. In one sense the young hero of Canada was a failure; Mackenzie didn't find what he wanted. But he expanded knowledge and brought geographic reality into play to rein in sometimes outlandish speculations. And the fact, too, that he didn't immediately succeed in opening the Pacific coast to trade doesn't abrogate his vision, for others who came after him eventually implemented his plan.*

*The following presents two scenes from Mackenzie's account of his 1793 journey to the Pacific. It should be kept in mind that his small party was in constant danger from cold and starvation, from the crazed, chilling rivers the men followed by canoe, and from Indians frowning on the passing intruders. The prolonged stress kept the men—hungry, lost, not knowing what horror might lie around the next bend—in a state of jitters. And when in the first passage below their single canoe wrecks in the middle of the wilderness, the young leader has to marshal all the psychology he can to keep his bedraggled men from losing their courage and giving up on their venture. As one historian describes the leader of this forlorn hope: ". . . Mackenzie kept his terrified, near-mutinous men moving westward for weeks on his own reserves of will power and courage" (Smith 1973, 93).*

*The second selection shows Mackenzie at a dramatic moment some weeks later. After twelve hundred miles of strenuous travel, including several difficult portages through the mountains, his canoe glides down the Bella Coola River in present-day British Columbia and out into an arm of the Pacific. The lack of exhilaration in his account at the final achievement is due to more than Mackenzie's Scottish reserve. His men were too weary for hilarity, and they feared troubles from coastal Indians already disgruntled by their contact with "Macubah"—an Indian version of George Vancouver's last name—who had visited the area by sea early in the previous month. The dicey situation and Mackenzie's skill in keeping it from blowing up into violence foreshadow the touchy problems ahead in the relationships between the two cultures.*

*Mackenzie began with a crew of ten—two Indians and eight whites, along with a dog. Though the size of the group varied according to the number of Indian guides picked up and dropped off along the way, how the men traveled is more revealing than their precise number. They ran the wild, frothing rivers of the Canadian Rockies in one huge freight canoe, typical of those used in the fur trade. Mackenzie's probably was well over thirty feet long and nearly a yard deep at the center. It carried in the vicinity of three thousand pounds of provisions, ammunition, and goods for barter. Yet constructed of birch bark and light wooden struts, it was easily carried by two men on the rugged, mountain portages (Smith 1973, 90). This sacrifice of strength to decrease the canoe's weight came with a penalty. The fragility of the birch canoe and the men's dependence on this one craft illustrate the critical nature of the adventurers' situation. A spill in any one of the hundreds of rapids the men roared through might have meant the loss of the canoe and its contents, both crucial to the party's survival in the wilderness. No wonder the men were constantly on edge.*

*To swing from a specific to a more general context, two other continental crossings bracket Mackenzie's feat. A book could be written comparing and contrasting the three journeys. As regards Cabeza de Vaca's trek two hundred and fifty years before Mackenzie's, one might ponder the following. Both men had a grasp of geopolitics far ahead of their time, and both possessed the diplomatic wit (Cabeza de Vaca being aided by miraculous intervention) to talk their ways out of crises. The Spaniard's style is highly literary, manipulating words to justify his actions and nudge his king toward a kindlier treatment of the Indians. Far less emotional in his approach, Mackenzie's text is calculated in a different way. Mackenzie lets drama emerge from his reserved recitation of events and, hoping to convince and move both his cautious government and hardheaded businessmen into action, allows his factual description of the lucrative potential for trading to speak for itself. That leaves Cabeza de Vaca's account far more sophisticated in another respect. At the heart of the matter, both Cabeza de Vaca and Mackenzie willingly entered the unknown with commercial gain in mind. Yet the foundering of his expedition in Florida forced the desperate Cabeza de Vaca to cross the continent. Along the way he changed. His trek became more than a journey of survival. As would become true of much American literature, from Melville to Hemingway to Edward Abbey, Cabeza de Vaca's physical travel also entailed an inner, spiritual journey.*

*The comparison of Mackenzie's trip with the later transcontinental crossing of Lewis and Clark (1804–6) has an ironic twist in it. Scholars have no end of debating which of the two forays was the superior accomplishment. Whatever one's position, one essential fact shouldn't be overlooked in the feud. Upon reading an edition of Mackenzie's* Voyages *(1801), the American president Thomas Jefferson saw the need for firming up the United States' claim to the Pacific Northwest. As a result he rushed Lewis and Clark into action in order to counter the claims of the rival British in the area (Smith 1973, 167 n).*

### Selected Bibliography

DeVoto, Bernard. *The Course of Empire.* Boston: Houghton Mifflin, 1952.

Mackenzie, Alexander. *The Journals and Letters of Sir Alexander Mackenzie.*

Ed. by W. Kaye Lamb. Cambridge: Cambridge University Press, 1970.
Smith, James K. *Alexander Mackenzie, Explorer: The Hero Who Failed*. Toronto: McGraw-Hill Ryerson, 1973.

ALEXANDER MACKENZIE

# The Mists Drawn Back:
# Alexander Mackenzie (1793)

## Journal of a Voyage to the Pacific Ocean

THURSDAY, JUNE 13. At an early hour of this morning the men began to cut a road, in order to carry the canoe and lading beyond the rapid; and by seven they were ready. That business was soon effected, and the canoe reladen, to proceed with the current which ran with great rapidity. In order to lighten her, it was my intention to walk with some of the people; but those in the boat with great earnestness requested me to embark, declaring, at the same time, that, if they perished, I should perish with them. I did not then imagine in how short a period their apprehension would be justified. We accordingly pushed off, and had proceeded but a very short way when the canoe struck, and notwithstanding all our exertions, the violence of the current was so great as to drive her sideways down the river, and break her by the first bar, when I instantly jumped into the water, and the men followed my example; but before we could set her straight, or stop her, we came to deeper water, so that we were obliged to re-embark with the utmost precipitation. One of the men who was not sufficiently active, was left to get on shore in the best manner in his power. We had hardly regained our situations when we drove against a rock which shattered the stern of the canoe in such a manner, that it held only by the gunwales, so that the steersman could no longer keep his place. The violence of this stroke drove us to the opposite side of the river, which is but narrow, when the bow met with the same fate as the stern. At this moment the foreman seized on some branches of a small tree in the hope of bringing up the canoe, but such was their elasticity that, in a manner not easily described, he was jerked on shore in an instant, and with a degree of violence that threatened his destruction. But we had no time to turn from our own situation to inquire what had befallen him; for, in a few moments, we came across a cascade which broke several large holes in the bottom of the canoe, and started all the bars, except one behind the scooping seat. If this accident, however, had not happened, the vessel must have been irretrievably overset. The wreck becoming flat on the water, we all jumped out, while the steersman, who had been compelled to abandon his place, and had not recovered from his fright, called out to his companions to save themselves. My peremptory commands superseded the effects of his fear, and they all held fast to the wreck; to which fortunate resolution we owed our safety, as we should otherwise have been dashed against the rocks by the force of the water, or driven over the cascades. In this condition we were forced several hundred yards, and every yard on the verge of destruction; but, at length, we most fortunately arrived in shallow water and a small eddy, where we were enabled to make a stand, from the weight of the canoe resting on the stones, rather than from any exertions of our exhausted strength. For though our efforts were short, they were pushed to the utmost, as life or death depended on them. This alarming scene, with all its terrors and dangers, occupied only a few minutes; and in the present suspension of it, we called to the people on shore to come to our assistance, and they immediately obeyed the summons. The foreman, however, was the first with us; he had escaped unhurt from the extraordinary jerk with which he was thrown out of the boat, and just as we were beginning to take our effects out of the water, he appeared to give his assistance. The Indians, when they saw our deplorable situation, instead of making the least effort to help us, sat down and gave vent to their tears. I was on the outside of the canoe, where I remained till every thing was got on shore, in a state of great pain from the extreme cold of the water; so that at length, it was with difficulty I could stand, from the benumbed state of my limbs.

The loss was considerable and important, for it consisted of our whole stock of balls, and some of our furniture; but these considerations were forgotten in the impressions of our miraculous escape. Our first inquiry was after the absent man, whom in the first moment of danger, we had left to get on shore, and in a short time his appearance removed our anxiety. We had, however, sustained no personal injury of consequence, and my bruises seemed to be in the greater proportion.

All the different articles were now spread out to dry. The powder had fortunately received no damage, and all my instruments had escaped. Indeed, when my people began to recover from their alarm, and to enjoy a sense of safety, some of them, if not all, were by no means sorry for our late misfortune, from the hope that it must put a period to our voyage, particularly as we were without a canoe, and all the bullets sunk in the river. It did not, indeed, seem possible to them that we could proceed under these circumstances. I listened, however, to the observations that were made on the occasion without replying to them, till their panic was dispelled, and they had got themselves warm and comfortable, with an hearty meal, and rum enough to raise their spirits.

I then addressed them, by recommending them all to be thankful for their late very narrow escape. I also stated, that the navigation was not impracticable in itself, but from our ignorance of its course; and that our late experience would enable us to pursue our voyage with greater security. I brought to their recollection, that I did not deceive them, and that they were made acquainted with the difficulties and dangers they must expect to encounter, before they engaged to accompany me. I also urged the honour of conquering disasters, and the disgrace that would attend them on their return home, without having attained the object of the expedition. Nor did I fail to mention the courage and resolution which was the peculiar boast of the North men; and that I depended on them, at that moment, for the maintenance of their character. I quieted their apprehension as to the loss of the bullets, by bringing to their recollection that we still had shot from which they might be manufactured. I at the same time acknowledged the difficulty of restoring the wreck of the canoe, but confided in our skill and exertion to put it in such a state as would carry us on to where we might procure bark, and build a new one. In short, my harangue produced the desired effect, and a very general assent appeared to go wherever I should lead the way.

Various opinions were offered in the present posture of affairs, and it was rather a general wish that the wreck should be abandoned, and all the lading carried to the river, which our guide informed us was at no great distance, and in the vicinity of woods where he believed there was plenty of bark. This project seemed not to promise that certainty to which I looked in my present operations; besides, I had my doubts respecting the views of my guide, and consequently could not confide in the representation he made to me. I therefore dispatched two of the men at nine in the morning, with one of the young Indians, for I did not venture to trust the guide out of my sight, in search of bark, and to endeavour, if it were possible, in the course of the day, to penetrate to the great river, into which that before us discharges itself in the direction which the guide had communicated. I now joined my people in order to repair, as well as circumstances would admit, our wreck of a canoe, and I began to set them the example.

At noon I had an altitude, which gave 54.23 North latitude. At four in the afternoon I took time, with the hope that in the night I might obtain an observation of Jupiter, and his satellites, but I had not a sufficient horizon, from the propinquity of the mountains. The result of my calculation for time was 1.38.28 slow apparent time.

It now grew late, and the people who had been sent on the excursion already mentioned, were not yet returned; about ten o'clock, however, I heard a man halloo, and I very gladly returned the signal. In a short time our young Indian arrived with a small roll of indifferent bark: he was oppressed with fatigue and hunger, and his clothes torn to rags; he had parted with the other two men at sun-set, who had walked the whole day, in a dreadful country, without procuring any good bark, or being able to get to the large river. His account of the river, on whose banks we were, could not be more unfavourable or discouraging; it had appeared to him to be little more than a succession of falls and rapids, with occasional interruptions of fallen trees.

Our guide became so dissatisfied and troubled in mind, that we could not obtain from him any regular account of the country before us. All we could collect from him was, that the river into which this empties itself is but a branch of a large river, the great fork being at no great distance from the confluence of this; and that he knew of no lake, or large body of still water, in the vicinity of these rivers. To this account of the country, he added some strange, fanciful, but terrifying descriptions of the natives, similar to those which were mentioned in the former voyage.

We had an escape this day, which I must add to the many instances of good fortune which I experienced in this perilous expedition. The powder had been spread out, to the amount of eighty pounds weight, to receive the air; and, in this situation, one of the men carelessly and composedly walked across it with a lighted pipe in his mouth, but without any ill consequence resulting from such an act of criminal negligence. I need not add that one spark might have put a period to all my anxiety and ambition.

I observed several trees and plants on the banks of this river, which I had not seen to the North of the latitude 52 such as the cedar, maple, hemlock, &c. At this time the water rose fast, and passed on with the rapidity of an arrow shot from a bow.

Friday, June 14. The weather was fine, clear, and warm, and at an early hour of the morning we resumed our repair of the canoe. At half past seven our two men returned hungry and cold, not having tasted food, or enjoyed the least repose for twenty-four hours, with their clothes torn into tatters, and their skin lacerated, in passing through the woods. Their account was the same as that brought by the Indian, with this exception, that they had reason to think they saw the river, or branch which our guide had mentioned; but they were of opinion that from the frequent obstructions in this river, we should have to carry the whole way to it, through a dreadful country, where much time and labour would be required to open a passage through it.

Discouraging as these accounts were, they did not, however, interrupt for a moment the task in which we were engaged, of repairing the canoe; and this work we contrived to complete by the conclusion of the day. The bark which was brought by the Indian, with some pieces of oilcloth, and plenty of gum, enabled us to put our shattered vessel in a condition to answer our present purposes. The guide, who has been mentioned as manifesting continual signs of dissatisfaction, now assumed an air of contentment, which I attributed to a smoke that was visible in the direction of the river; as he naturally expected, if we should fall in with any natives, which was now very probable, from such a circumstance, that he should be released from a service which he had found so irksome and full of danger. I had an observation at noon, which made our latitude 54.23.43 North. I also took time, and found it slow apparent time 1.38.44.

Saturday, June 15. The weather continued the same as the preceding day, and according to the directions which I had previously given, my people began at a very early hour to open a road, through which we might carry a part of our lading; as I was fearful of risquing the whole of it in the canoe, in its present weak state, and in a part of the river which is full of shoals and rapids. Four men were employed to conduct her, lightened as she was of twelve packages. They passed several dangerous places, and met with various obstructions, the current of the river being frequently stopped by rafts of drift wood, and fallen trees, so that after fourteen hours hard labour we had not made more than three miles. Our course was South-East by East, and as we had not met with any accident, the men appeared to feel a renewed courage to continue their voyage. In the morning, however, one of the crew, whose name was Beauchamp, peremptorily refused to embark in the canoe. This being the first example of absolute disobedience which had yet appeared during the course of our expedition, I should not have passed it over without taking some very severe means to prevent a repetition of it; but as he had the general character of a simple fellow, among his companions, and had been frightened out of what little sense he possessed, by our late dangers, I rather preferred to consider him as unworthy of accompanying us, and to represent him as an object of ridicule and contempt for his pusillanimous behaviour; though, in fact, he was a very useful, active, and laborious man.

At the close of the day we assembled round a blazing fire; and the whole party, being enlivened with the usual beverage which I supplied on these occasions, forgot their fatigues and apprehensions; nor did they fail to anticipate the pleasure they should enjoy in getting clear of their present difficulties and gliding onwards with a strong and steady stream, which our guide had described as the characteristic of the large river we soon expected to enter. . . .

Saturday, July 20. We rose at a very early hour this morning, when I proposed to the Indians to run down our canoe, or procure another at this place. To both these proposals they turned a deaf ear, as they imagined that I should be satisfied with having come in sight of the sea. Two of them peremptorily refused to proceed; but the other two having consented to continue with us, we obtained a larger canoe than our former one, and though it was in a leaky state we were glad to possess it.

At about eight we got out of the river, which discharges itself by various channels into an arm of the sea. The tide was out, and had left a large space covered with sea-weed. The surrounding hills were involved in fog. The wind was at West, which was a-head of us, and very strong; the bay appearing to be from one to three miles in breadth. As we advanced along the land we saw a great number of sea-otters. We fired several shots at them, but without any success from the rapidity with which they plunge under the water. We also saw many small porpoises or divers. The white-headed eagle, which is common in the interior parts; some small gulls, a dark bird which is inferior in size to the gull, and a few small ducks, were all the birds which presented themselves to our view.

At two in the afternoon the swell was so high, and the wind, which was against us, so boisterous, that we could not proceed with our leaky vessel, we therefore landed in a small cove on the right side of the bay. Opposite to us appeared another small bay, in the mouth of which is an island, and where, according to the information of the Indians, a river discharges itself that abounds in salmon.

Our young Indians now discovered a very evident disposition to leave us; and, in the evening, one of them made his escape. Mr. Mackay, however, with the other, pursued and brought him back; but as it was by no means necessary to detain him, particularly as provisions did not abound with us, I gave him a small portion, with a pair of shoes, which were necessary for his journey, and a silk handkerchief, telling him at the same time, that he might go and inform his friends, that we should also return in three nights. He accordingly left us, and his companion, the young chief, went with him.

When we landed, the tide was going out, and at a quarter past four it was ebb, the water having fallen in that short period eleven feet and an half. Since we left the river, not a quarter of an hour had passed in which we did not see porpoises and sea-otters. Soon after ten it was high water, which rendered it necessary that our baggage should be shifted several times, though not till some of the things had been wetted.

We were now reduced to the necessity of looking out for fresh water, with which we were plentifully supplied by the rills that ran down from the mountains.

When it was dark the young chief returned to us, bearing a large porcupine on his back. He first cut the animal open, and having disencumbered it of the entrails, threw them into the sea; he then singed its skin, and boiled it in separate pieces, as our kettle was not sufficiently capacious to contain the whole: nor did he go to rest, till, with the assistance of two of my people who happened to be awake, every morsel of it was devoured.

I had flattered myself with the hope of getting a distance of the moon and stars, but the cloudy weather continually disappointed me, and I began to fear that I should fail in this important object; particularly as our provisions were at a very low ebb, and we had, as yet, no reason to expect any assistance from the natives. Our stock was, at this time, reduced to twenty pounds of pemmican, fifteen pounds of rice, and six pounds of flour, among ten half-starved men, in a leaky vessel, and on a barbarous coast. Our course from the river was about West-South-West, distance ten miles.

Sunday, July 21. At forty minutes past four this morning it was low water, which made fifteen feet perpendicular height below the high-water mark of last night. Mr. Mackay collected a quantity of small muscles which we boiled. Our people did not partake of this regale, as they are wholly unacquainted with sea shell-fish. Our young chief being missing, we imagined that he had taken his flight, but, as we were preparing to depart, he fortunately made his appearance from the woods, where he had been to take his rest after his feast of last night. At six we were upon the water, when we cleared the small bay, which we named Porcupine

Cove, and steered West-South-West for seven miles, we then opened a channel about two miles and an half wide at South-South-West, and had a view of ten or twelve miles into it. As I could not ascertain the distance from the open sea, and being uncertain whether we were in a bay or among inlets and channels of islands, I confined my search to a proper place for taking an observation. We steered, therefore, along the land on the left, West-North-West a mile and an half; then North-West one fourth of a mile, and North three miles to an island; the land continuing to run North-North-West, then along the island, South-South-West half a mile, West a mile and an half, and from thence directly across to the land on the left, (where I had an altitude,) South-West three miles. From this position a channel, of which the island we left appeared to make a cheek, bears North by East.

Under the land we met with three canoes, with fifteen men in them, and laden with their moveables, as if proceeding to a new situation, or returning to a former one. They manifested no kind of mistrust or fear of us, but entered into conversation with our young man, as I supposed, to obtain some information concerning us. It did not appear that they were the same people as those we had lately seen, as they spoke the language of our young chief, with a different accent. They then examined every thing we had in our canoe, with an air of indifference and disdain. One of them in particular made me understand, with an air of insolence, that a large canoe had lately been in this bay, with people in her like me, and that one of them, whom he called *Macubah,* had fired on him and his friends, and that *Bensins* had struck him on the back, with the flat part of his sword. He also mentioned another name, the articulation of which I could not determine. At the same time he illustrated these circumstances by the assistance of my gun and sword; and I do not doubt but he well deserved the treatment which he described. He also produced several European articles, which could not have been long in his possession. From his conduct and appearance, I wished very much to be rid of him, and flattered myself that he would prosecute his voyage, which appeared to be in an opposite direction to our course. However, when I prepared to part from them, they turned their canoes about, and persuaded my young man to leave me, which I could not prevent.

We coasted along the land at about West-South-West for six miles, and met a canoe with two boys in it, who were dispatched to summon the people on that part of the coast to join them. The troublesome fellow now forced himself into my canoe, and pointed out a narrow channel on the opposite shore, that led to his village, and requested us to steer towards it, which I accordingly ordered. His importunities now became very irksome, and he wanted to see every thing we had, particularly my instruments, concerning which he must have received information from my young man. He asked for my hat, my handkerchief, and, in short, every thing that he saw about me. At the same time he frequently repeated the unpleasant intelligence that he had been shot at by people of my colour. At some distance from the land a channel opened to us, at South-West by West, and pointing that way, he made me understand that *Macubah* came here with his large canoe. When we were in mid-channel, I perceived some sheds, or the remains of old buildings, on the shore; and as, from that circumstance, I thought it probable that some Europeans might have been there, I directed my steersman to make for that spot. The traverse is upwards of three miles North-West.

We landed, and found the ruins of a village, in a situation calculated for defence. The place itself was over grown with weeds, and in the centre of the houses there was a temple, of the same form and construction as that which I described at the large village. We were soon followed by ten canoes, each of which contained from three to six men. They informed us that we were expected at the village, where we should see many of them. From their general deportment I was very apprehensive that some hostile design was meditated against us, and for the first time I acknowledged my apprehensions to my people. I accordingly desired them to be very much upon their guard, and to be prepared if any violence was offered to defend themselves to the last.

We had no sooner landed, than we took possession of a rock, where there was not space for more than twice our number, and which admitted of our defending ourselves with advantage, in case we should be attacked. The people in the three first canoes, were the most troublesome, but, after doing their utmost to irritate us, they went away. They were, however, no sooner gone, than an hat, an handkerchief, and several other articles, were missing. The rest of our visitors continued their pressing invitations to accompany them to their village, but finding our resolution to decline them was not to be shaken, they, about sun-set relieved us from all further importunities, by their departure.

Another canoe, however, soon arrived, with seven stout, well-looking men. They brought a box, which contained a very fine sea-otter skin, and a goat skin, that was beautifully white. For the former they demanded my hanger, which, as may well be supposed, could not be spared in our present situation, and they actually refused to take a yard and an half of common broad cloth, with some other articles, for the skin, which proves the unreflecting improvidence of our European traders. The goat-skin was so bulky that I did not offer to purchase it. These men also told me that *Macubah* had been there, and left his ship behind a point of land in the channel, South-West from us: from whence he had come to their village in boats, which these people represented by imitating our manner of rowing. When I offered them what they did not choose to accept for the otter-skin, they shook their heads, and very distinctly answered 'No, no.' And to mark their refusal of any thing we asked from them, they emphatically employed the same British monosyllable. In one of the canoes which had left us, there was a seal, that I wished to purchase, but could not persuade the natives to part with it. They had also a fish, which I now saw for the first time. It was about eighteen inches in length, of the shape and appearance of a trout, with strong, sharp teeth. We saw great numbers of the animals which we had taken for sea otters, but I was now disposed to think that a great part of them, at least, must have been seals.

The natives having left us, we made a fire to warm ourselves, and as for supper, there was but little of that, for our whole daily allowance did not amount to what was sufficient for a single meal. The weather was clear throughout the day, which was succeeded by a fine moon-light night. I directed the people to keep watch by two in turn, and laid myself down in my cloak.

# CHAPTER 32

# "Thus Ended a Very Unpleasant Affair, with the Ruin of a Pretty Face": Alexander Henry (1799)

*If predicting the future is an enticement the prudent avoid, reconstructing the past comes with its own set of difficulties. At its best history is an assemblage of what might have been, its conclusions impermanent, shrouded by perennial doubts. The problem becomes ever more complex when we're dealing with other cultures.*

*What were the Indians "really like" at first contact with Europeans? It seems a simple question, but it's one that probably will never yield to a satisfactory answer. For starters, contrary to popular romantic imaginings, Indians were not all of a kind. They were incredibly diverse in languages, customs, and mores. Some native peoples ate fish, a tabooed diet in the eyes of their horrified neighbors. Some tribes were powerful and aggressive, preying on docile bands and driving them from their homelands. Indian cultures, along with all others, were in a state of flux, adapting to circumstances, changing their ways and their territories over the centuries. On top of that, add the lack of written Indian records and the misunderstandings that result when one culture views another through a distorted glass of prejudices, and some scholars might simply throw up their hands at the impossibility of the task.*

*Yet if we did that, we'd have no history, and demanding a whole loaf or nothing at all, absolutists would retreat into the pleasurable alternative of substituting myth for factual approximations. Instead, learning to live with doubts, we find some accounts that are telling despite their gross imperfections. Outstanding among them is the journal of the fur trader Alexander Henry. His is one of the best and most detailed stories of life among the Indians, yet this ironically, for Henry was a businessman rather than a* littérateur, *had little sympathy for his human subjects, and apparently wrote down the events of his daily experiences in the wilderness without any view of publication.*

*Compounding the ironies, we know almost nothing about the early life of Alexander Henry—not to be confused with an elder, fur-trader relative of the same name—not even the younger Henry's birth date. Most of what we do know emerges from his extensive journals, kept between 1799 and 1814. Here Henry records the life of a trader who traveled extensively over the years, manning posts from Lake Superior to the mouth of the Columbia River. There he drowned when his boat capsized while Henry sailed out to reach a company ship.*

*Alexander Henry wrote of many things—of prairie fires, attacks by wild animals, of packs made up and scouts sent out, recording the minutiae of wilderness life. In this, however, Indians played the essential role, for they were at once the source of Henry's furs and the trader's potential enemies, and he's constantly looking over his shoulder, evaluating the tensions around him. Thus few journal pages go by without a mention of Indians and what they're up to. Readers may well be shocked at the violence, and the acceptance of violence, in Henry's journal. For instance, this chilling blend of strayed horses, brutality, and gardening (Henry 1897, 243): "We found our strayed horses, Indians having asked for liquor, and promised to decamp and hunt well all summer, I gave them some. Grande Gueule stabbed Capot Rouge, Le Boeuf stabbed his young wife in the arm, Little Shell almost beat his old mother's brains out with a club, and there was terrible fighting among them. I sowed garden seeds" (243).*

*One almost can be sure that the prime cause of the continuing turmoil Henry describes was the alcohol that Henry provided. He himself recognizes its effect, calling liquor "the root of all evil" (1897, 209) among the Indians, yet as a businessman he provided it anyway, as almost all traders did if they wished to trade. What we see in the following pages is aberrant behavior among the Indians, brought on by a new variable in their lives that they couldn't handle.*

*Yet if the violence is shocking, it also was commonplace on the frontier, and Henry, no man of literary artistry, dutifully sets it all down, as part of the scenes around him, until his journal takes on its own straightforward literary qualities, combining the authenticity of the diarist Samuel Pepys with the clinical detachment of the novelist Émile Zola.*

*A note to avoid confusion about the text in which the following was first published. Editor Coues's subtitle to Henry's journals might lead readers to believe that the journals of the explorer David Thompson also appear in this*

She requested a dram, although she was sober. I offered her a little mixed liquor, which she refused, telling me she wanted "augumaucbane." I was obliged to open my case and give her a glass of French brandy, which I made her swallow at one draught; but whether it actually choked her or she was feigning, she fell down as if senseless and lay like a corpse. I was anxious to get her away, but my endeavors were in vain; it was totally dark and I began to believe her dead. I thought to draw her to the tent door, and woke up my servant, whom I desired to assist me. I sent him for a kettle of water, which I poured over her head while he held her up; a second was applied in the same manner, but to no purpose. I became uneasy about her, and sent for a third kettle, the contents of which I dashed in her face with all my strength. She groaned, and began to speak. I lost no time before sending the man to conduct her to her canoe. In a half an hour she returned, having shifted her clothes and dressed very fine; her husband being an excellent hunter and without children, she had always plenty of finery. She told me in plain terms that she had left her husband and come to live with me. This was news I neither expected nor desired. I represented to her the impropriety of her doing so, her husband being fond of her and extremely jealous. Her answer was, that she did not care for him or any other Indian, and was determined to stay with me at the risk of her life. Just then we heard a great bustle across the river, and the Indians bawling out "take care!" We were going to be fired on. We saw the flash of a gun, but it appeared to miss fire. I had no doubt the woman was the cause of this, and I insisted on her returning to her husband; but she would not. Observing that the men had made a fire, I called my servant and desired him to take her to the fire and keep her from troubling me again. This he did much against her inclination, being compelled to use main strength, and by good luck got her on board a canoe that was crossing. The noise we had heard on the other side was made by the husband, who, knowing of his wife's intention, had determined to shoot at my tent; but his gun only flashed, and his brothers took it from him. On his wife's return he asked her where she had been. She made no secret of the matter, but said she was determined to go with me. "Well, then," said the Indian, "if you are determined to leave me, I will at least have the satisfaction of spoiling your pretty face." He caught up a large fire-brand, threw her on her back, and rubbed it in her face with all his might, until the fire was extinguished. Then letting her up, "Now," says he, "go and see your beloved, and ask him if he likes you as well as he did before." Her face was in a horrid condition. I was sorry for it; she was really the handsomest woman on the river, and not more than 18 years of age. Still,

I can say I never had connection with her, as she always told me if I did that she would publish it and live with me in spite of everybody. This I did not wish, as I was well aware of the consequences. Thus ended a very unpleasant affair, with the ruin of a pretty face. . . .

Crooked Legs and his family arrived from below. His young wife is now perfectly recovered, and enjoys a glass. All who had any skins to trade held a drinking match, during which the lady gave her old husband a cruel beating with a stick, and then, throwing him on his back, applied a fire brand to his privates, and rubbed it in, until somebody interfered and took her away. She left him in a shocking condition, with the parts nearly roasted. I believe she would have killed him, had she not been prevented; if he recovers, it will be extraordinary. This was done in revenge for his having stabbed her some time ago. . . .

Thursday, Dec. 25th—Christmas. Treated my people with high wine, flour, and sugar. *26th.* Crow came in with his brother Charlo on a travaille, at the point of death. *28th.* Sent two men to make salt, near the entrance of the little river. I was informed of a cruel affair which happened two years ago at Red lake. The woman is here to whom the affair happened. It seems her husband was a young Indian by whom she had one child, but who thought proper to have two wives. Not liking this, she joined another camp, where she took a new husband. Soon after this second marriage, the two camps met and had a drinking match. The first husband went to his rival, and insisted upon taking the child, telling him he might keep the woman, as he did not want her. They were both scoundrels; the child was not many months old. The father caught hold of one leg of the child, saying he would have him; the husband caught hold of the other leg, saying the father should not take him away. They began to pull and haul; on a sudden the father gave a jerk; and the other resisting, the child was torn asunder. Charlo lies here very sick; he is troubled with an ugly cough, and can scarcely move. His brothers have only been once to see him; they have no more feeling than brutes, and have left him to care for his two young children, one five and the other seven years of age. In a drinking match a few days ago one of the women bit an Indian's finger off. She came to me for salve to cure it as best I could. On the 31st an Indian woman arrived, who is a near relation of Charlo's deceased wife. She sat down by him, screaming and howling in a terrible manner, calling on the deceased by name, and frequently sobbing, "Oh, my relation! my relation!" I began to feel for the poor woman, but she soon after dried her tears, and was the merriest one we had in the house. This is real Indian grief, but does not affect the heart. This evening I was offered a bed-fellow, but refused. The Indians are very officious in wishing to provide me with a wife, but my inclination does not agree with theirs in the least.

Sunday, Jan. 1st, 1801. The new year was ushered in by several volleys, which alarmed a camp of Indians near by. The men came running in armed, having ordered the women to hide themselves. But they were agreeably deceived, and got a share of what was going—some sherub and cakes. Every woman and child was soon at the fort; all was bustle and confusion. I gave my men some high wine, flour, and sugar; the Indians purchased liquor, and by sunrise every soul of them was raving drunk—even the children. Buffalo in great abundance; some within gunshot of the fort. The plains were entirely covered; all were moving in a body from N. to S.

An Indian who pretended to be a medicine man was employed by Maymiutch to cure his sick brother. The fellow came accordingly with his drum and medicine bag, half drunk, and began to make a terrible noise, beating the drum, singing and dancing, tumbling and tossing, and blowing upon the sick man, until he worked himself into a foam; when, redoubling his exertions, with one heavy stroke he burst his drum, trampled it to pieces, and went away quite exhausted, leaving his patient almost worried to death. However, this affair got him two blankets, a large kettle, and Charlo's gun. I saw a curious farce during the night between my men and some old women about 70 years of age [details omitted]. Liard's daughter took possession of my room, and the devil could not have got her out.

Jan. 2d. At daybreak I heard a crash in my kitchen, and found the chimney had fallen from top to bottom; it was lying on the floor, and the fire was blazing on. The cold was severe; weather cloudy and calm. The oaks made a continual cracking noise as they split with the frost, sometimes like the report of a gun. Buffaloes came within gunshot of the stockades, but the dogs drove them away. I was tempted to go hunting for two reasons. One was, to give the men time to repair the chimney, and the other, to get rid of the encumbrance who occupied my room. I soon came near the buffaloes, and found an Indian who had killed a cow, and was cutting her up. But the cold was so intense that it obliged him to give it up and return to his tent. I fired many shots, but killed only three; it was impossible to cut them up. I contented myself with raising the fat and tongues, and returned at dusk with a heavy load on my back. I was vexed to find my room still occupied, and no sign of her budging. . . .

Mar. 14th. In a drinking match at the Hills yesterday, Gros Bras [Thick Arms] in a fit of jealousy stabbed Aupusoi to death with a handdague [dagger]; the first stroke opened his left side, the second his belly, and the third his breast; he never stirred, although he had a knife in his belt, and died instantly. Soon after this Aupusoi's brother, a boy about 10 years of age, took the deceased's gun, loaded it with two balls, and approached Gros Bras' tent. Putting the muzzle of the gun through the door the boy fired the two balls into his breast and killed him dead, just as he was reproaching his wife for her affection for Aupusoi, and boasting of the revenge he had taken. The little fellow ran into the woods and hid. Little Shell [Petite Coquille] found the old woman, Aupusoi's mother, in her tent; he instantly stabbed her. Ondainoiache then came in, took the knife, and gave her a second stab. Little Shell, in his turn taking the knife, gave a third blow. In this manner did these two rascals continue to murder the old woman, as long as there was any life in her. The boy escaped into Langlois' house, and was kept hid until they were all sober. . . .

Feb. 15th. Indians drinking at the fort. Tabashaw stabbed a near relation of his own, Missistaygouine, in six different places in the breast and sides; every stab went up to the handle; the poor fellow lingered an hour and died. Water Hen [Poule d'Eau], in fighting with another Indian, was thrown into the fire and roasted terribly from his neck to his rump. Both these affairs proceeded from jealousy. 25th. In the evening we were surprised by hearing three reports of a gun. Old Fallewine [Vieux Folle Avoine, Old Wild Rice], soon arrived, and bawled out at a distance, as soon as he thought we could hear him, that five Indians had been murdered near Portage la Prairie since I passed there, relations of himself and some others camped here. This firing was the usual signal of death in carrying news from one camp to another. But the Indians totally neglect their ancient customs; and to what can this degeneracy be ascribed but to their intercourse with us, particularly as they are so unfortunate as to have a continual succession of opposition parties to teach them roguery and destroy both mind and body with that pernicious article, rum? What a different set of people they would be, were there not a drop of liquor in the country! If a murder is committed among the Saulteurs, it is always in a drinking match. We may truly say that liquor is the root of all evil in the North West. Great bawling and lamentation went on, and I was troubled most of the night for liquor to wash away grief. . . .

Oct. 30th. My Assiniboine chief arrived with a young Saulteur, Nawicquaicoubeau, who, having been long married to an Assiniboine woman, was perfectly well acquainted with their language. They wanted me to send people to the hills to trade, which I would not do, giving them many plausible reasons; they were soon satisfied and promised to bring in their hunt themselves. After the gates were closed, I gave them a quart of rum; they drank very quietly. I sat up with them in the hall until ten, when, desiring Langlois to take care of them, I went to bed. About two I awoke at the report of a gun in the hall, and William Henry rushed in to tell me that Nawic. had shot Duford. I sent him to detain the Indian, and desired Langlois to come to me. I wished to be informed of the particulars before going to see the Indian, as I determined he should pay for it with his life. But Langlois related the following story: He sat up with them until midnight, when he went to bed, leaving them quietly enjoying their liquor. He did not go to sleep, wishing to overhear their private conversation, and thus learn their real intentions, as we still doubted whether they would bring their hunt here or to Rivière la Souris. They conversed first about hunting and then in what manner they would bring in their provisions, etc.; then on their war excursion of last fall, and Nawic. accused the party in general of cowardice, whilst he boasted of his own bravery and former exploits, saying the Sioux were only brave in great numbers, and that man to man they were cowards and old women, who never dared face a Saulteur. During this discourse they sang their war songs, recounted their exploits, and performed the manoeuvres usual in battle. These repeated exertions so agitated their minds, and the fumes of liquor had taken such effect, that they were transported to a degree of frenzy. They could not remain seated on their epishemaunts on the floor, but attempted to rise up, and, as they supposed, to fight their battles over again in pantomime. The chief reeled about for a few moments and then fell dead drunk, but the other fellow staggered about the hall for some time. His gun and bow and arrows were lying near him, but he performed all his antics with his pipe-stem instead of his weapons. The candle having burned down, and the fire nearly gone out, the room became dark. Langlois went outdoors while the Indian was still tumbling about, scarcely able to stand.

Langlois soon returned, and on entering the room heard the Indian uttering hideous yells and bawling out: "The bad dogs! I see them— there they are—come on, friends—don't flinch—take courage—revenge the death of our relations; come on, I say—have at them—fire!" Langlois was passing him, when suddenly the gun went off so near his face as to singe his hair; he heard the Indian fall, but the darkness prevented his seeing anything. At the same moment he heard Duford fall in his cabin, calling out, "Oh! Mr. Michel, I am killed." The Indian as soon exclaimed, "What have I done? What is the matter?" When the candle was lighted, Duford was found lying in his room, by his bedside, weltering in blood; the Indian was seated with his head between his legs; and one of our own guns was lying upon the floor. It was a fine gun, with extremely weak springs, and had been known repeatedly to go off in handling it carelessly. One of my people had been out shooting pheasants the day before, and returned late in the evening, after the Indians had begun to drink; he had placed this gun inside Duford's cabin, close to the door. The Indian, although very drunk, on seeing the mischief he had done fell a-crying and lamenting, assuring the bystanders that he did not do it intentionally, and that, if they were of a different opinion, they were welcome to kill him—he was ready to die—they might strike, as he knew he deserved death. I then went to Duford and inquired the particulars; he related nearly the same story, with this addition, that the Indian, in tumbling about the hall, had fallen near his room and pulled down a blanket which Duford had hung up to serve instead of a door. It was supposed his hand closed upon the gun by accident, as Duford said the Indian fell backward into the room. When the latter had recovered himself and was staggering about in the dark, Duford got up to fasten the blanket, not a word having passed between them; he secured one corner with an awl, spread out the blanket, and was fastening the other corner with an awl also, when suddenly the shot was fired through the blanket. On mature deliberation, I felt that I could not punish the fellow with death, as it appeared to me that it was plainly an accident; for had he been maliciously inclined, he naturally would have used his own gun, that stood near, primed and loaded with ball.

# "The Most Horrid Sight . . . That Ever my Eyes Witnessed": John R. Jewitt (1803)

*Feeble from an ax blow, the sailor is led to a hideous sight. Staggering with pain, he beholds the heads of his shipmates lined up, surrounded by Indians dripping with the blood of their victims and busily ransacking the* Boston. *John R. Jewitt was lucky, however. He was the ship's blacksmith, and the Indians needed his skills to repair their muskets and fashion implements from the metal recently acquired from white traders. Jewitt, then, along with John Thompson, a sailmaker also of use to the tribe, were spared the bludgeoning of the other whites.*

*But the two men paid dearly for survival, spending the next twenty-eight months as slaves of the Indians. Among the Nootkas this state obliged the captive to work and fight for his owner, yet though the slave had certain property rights—including the right to own other slaves—the slave none-theless lived at the pleasure of his master. Jewitt's bizarre tale of surviving such intricacies in an alien culture is one of the most fantastic "true stories" in the captivity literature of the American West.*

*Born in England, Jewitt learned his trade from his blacksmith father. Eager for adventure, at the age of nineteen the youth signed aboard the American ship* Boston, *bound for the Pacific Northwest. Rounding Cape Horn and heading north, some months later the ship glided into Nootka Bay, on the west coast of Vancouver Island, and began to trade for furs. Yet misunder-standings and human perversity had come into play since the opening of the fur trade on the coast in the late 1700s. Bad blood developed, with occasional violence between the Indians and visiting whites. In March of 1803, a band of Nootkas pretending peace came aboard the* Boston *bearing gifts, but at a signal from their chief, Maquina, the warriors fell on the unsuspecting crew and began their slaughter with daggers and clubs. Before the ship accidentally caught fire, the Indians reveled in their prize, offloading a bonanza: hundreds of muskets, ammunition, cloth, and other such booty.*

*Prospects for rescue didn't look good for the two slaves. Hearing of the bloodshed and not wishing to risk a similar fate, sea captains avoided the bay. For their part the Indians began having second thoughts about the takeover. They feared reprisals from the big ships plying the coast and often wondered if the best way to get themselves off the hook wouldn't be to kill their two white slaves and thereby get rid of the evidence. Thus besides the severity of their labors, cutting firewood and grubbing for food while suffering abuses from the haughty Indians, the two men were also constantly on edge about their lives.*

*Yet Jewitt proved himself a wily captive. He spirited letters out via rival local chiefs, and in July of 1805 a sympathetic captain responded, sailing into Nootka Bay with guns at the ready. After some tricky negotiations and deft double-dealing, with "... feelings of joy impossible to be described...," the two white men found themselves stepping aboard the deck of the liberating* Lydia *(Jewitt 1975, 84).*

*Jewitt's narrative rates a high place among the many tales of captivity that inevitably follow people on the move into forbidding territories. Concise yet rich with detail, the account offers reliable pictures both of the Nootka Indian culture and of the tensions arising from early contact with the Europeans. Its literary calculations also set the tale apart. At first glance this presents something of a puzzle. For Jewitt's* Journal, *originally published in 1807, is rather dull fare. When appearing in 1815 and in subsequent editions as his* Narrative, *the tale takes on a new life. It creates devices, using cranky, pugnacious Thompson, for instance, as a foil to the cool-headed, manipulating Jewitt. It moves with literary pace and balance, setting off the scheming of the Indians prior to the attack with the equally swift scheming of Jewitt after the massacre to save Thompson's life. Under the guise of factual reporting, the new version stays just this side of propriety, while occasionally tempting with salacious excitements. As when the oppressive Chief Maquina forces his unwilling bondsman into the marriage bed with a beautiful Indian princess. Or the writer observes that the Nootkas keep any number of other slaves, taken during battles with neighboring tribes, then adds of the women captives (1975, 39):*

> The females are employed principally in manufacturing cloth, in cooking, collecting berries, etc. and with regard to food and living in general have not a much harder lot than their mistresses,

the principal difference consisting, in these poor unfortunate creatures being considered as free to any one, their masters prostituting them whenever they think proper for the purpose of gain. In this way many of them are brought on board the ships and offered to the crews. . . .

*That must have made puritanical Americans suck in their breaths, as their imaginations stretched to picture the deviltry.*

*In a word, the new version knows how to work an audience.*

*Overall the* Narrative *keeps the reader reading on by keeping its pages crackling with action and colorful people, as the story makes its way through labyrinths of suspense to the ultimate rescue. Much of the credit for this no doubt lies with Richard Alsop. A Hartford merchant belonging to a group of authors known as the Connecticut Wits, Alsop interviewed Jewitt in depth, then added literary salt and pepper in his rewriting of the story for the 1815 edition (Meany 1940, 145–46). This version stirs the human psyche by expertly working with one of the basic fears, the horror of abandonment.*

*One last and factual touch. After the rescue, the* Lydia *with its two former slaves safely aboard skirted up and down the coast, spending about a year trading furs. On her way home, she just missed Lewis and Clark, who about this time left their fort, where they'd wintered near the mouth of the Columbia River, for their long return trip across the continent.*

### Selected Bibliography

Jewitt, John R. *A Journal Kept at Nootka Sound by John R. Jewitt, One of the Survivors of the Ship* Boston *During a Captivity Among the Indians from March, 1803, to July, 1805.* [1807]. Ed. by Norman L. Dodge. Boston: Goodspeed's Book Shop, 1931.

———. *Narrative of the Adventures and Sufferings of John R. Jewitt While Held as a Captive of the Nootka Indians of Vancouver Island, 1803 to 1805.* [1815]. Ed. by Robert F. Heizer. Ramona: Ballena Press, 1975.

Meany, Edmond S., Jr. "The Later Life of John R. Jewitt." *British Columbia Historical Quarterly.* 4(3) (1940):143–61.

JOHN R. JEWITT

# "The Most Horrid Sight . . . That Ever My Eyes Witnessed": John R. Jewitt (1803)

## The Most Horrid Sight

ON THE MORNING of the 22d, the natives came off to us as usual with salmon, and remained on board; when about noon Maquina came along side, with a considerable number of his chiefs and men in their canoes, who after going through the customary examination, were admitted into the ship. He had a whistle in his hand, and over his face a very ugly mask of wood, representing the head of some wild beast, appeared to be remarkably good humoured and gay, and whilst his people sung and capered about the deck, entertaining us with a variety of antic trick and gestures, he blew his whistle to a kind of tune which seemed to regulate their motions. As Captain Salter was walking on the quarter deck, amusing himself with their dancing, the king came up to him, and inquired when he intended to go to sea? He answered tomorrow. Maquina then said, 'you love salmon—much in Friendly Cove, why not go then and catch some?' The Captain thought that it would be very desirable to have a good supply of these fish for the voyage, and on consulting with Mr. Delouisa, it was agreed to send part of the crew on shore after dinner with the seine, in order to procure a quantity. Maquina and his chiefs staid and dined on board, and after dinner the chief mate went off with nine men in the jolly-boat and yawl, to fish at Friendly Cove, having set the steward on shore at our watering place, to wash the Captain's clothes.

Shortly after the departure of the boats, I went down to my vice bench in the steerage, where I was employed in cleaning muskets, I had not been there more than an hour, when I heard the men hoisting in the long boat, which, in a few minutes after, was succeeded by a great bustle and confusion on deck. I immediately ran up the steerage stairs, but scarcely was my head above deck, when I was caught by the hair by one of the savages, and lifted from my feet; fortunately for me, my hair being short, and the ribbon with which it was tied slipping, I fell from his hold into the steerage. As I was falling, he struck me with an axe, which cut a deep gash in my forehead, and penetrated the skull, but in consequence of his losing his hold, I luckily escaped the full force of the blow; which, otherwise, would have cleft my head in two. I fell, stunned and senseless, upon the floor—how long I continued in this situation I know not, but on recovering my senses, the first thing that I did, was to try to get up, but so weak was I, from the loss of blood, that I fainted and fell. I was, however, soon recalled to my recollection by three loud shouts or yells from the savages, which convinced me that they had got possession of the ship. It is impossible for me to describe my feelings at this terrific sound. Some faint idea may be formed of them by those who have known what it is to half waken from a hideous dream and still think it real. Never, no, never shall I lose from my mind the impression of that dreadful moment. I expected every instant to share the wretched fate of my unfortunate companions, and when I heard the song of triumph, by which these infernal yells was succeeded, my blood ran cold in my veins.

Having at length sufficiently recovered my senses to look around me, after wiping the blood from my eyes, I saw that the hatch of the steerage was shut. This was done as I afterwards discovered, by order of Maquina, who on seeing the savage strike at me with the axe, told him not to hurt me, for that I was the armourer, and would be useful to them in repairing their arms: while at the same time to prevent any of his men from injuring me, he had the hatch closed. But to me this circumstance wore a very different appearance, for I thought that these barbarians had only prolonged my life in order to deprive me of it by the most cruel tortures.

I remained in this horrid state of suspense for a very long time, when at length the hatch was opened, and Maquina, calling me by name, ordered me to come up. I groped my way up as well as I was able being almost blinded with the blood that flowed from my wound, and so weak as with difficulty to walk. The king, on perceiving my situation, ordered one of his men to bring a pot of water to wash the blood from my face, which having done, I was able to see distinctly with one of my eyes, but the other was so swollen from my wound, that it was closed. But what a terrific spectacle met my eyes: six naked savages, standing in a circle around me, covered with the blood of my murdered comrades, with their daggers uplifted in their hands, prepared to strike. I now thought my last moment had come, and recommended my soul to my Maker.

The king who, as I have already observed, knew enough of English to make himself understood, entered the circle, and placing himself before me, addressed me nearly in the following words—"John—I speak—you no say no—You say no—daggers come!" He then asked me if I would be his slave during my life—If I would fight for him in his battles—If I would repair his muskets and make daggers and knives for him—with several other questions, to all of which I was careful to answer, yes. He then told me that he would spare my life, and ordered me to kiss his hands and feet to show my submission to him, which I did.— In the mean time his people were very clamorous to have me put to death, so that there should be none of us left to tell our story to our countrymen, and prevent them from coming to trade with them; but the king, in the most determined manner, opposed their wishes, and to his favour am I wholly indebted for my being yet among the living.

As I was busy at work at the time of the attack, I was without my coat, and what with the coldness of the weather, my feebleness from loss of blood, the pain of my wound and the extreme agitation and terror that I still felt, I shook like a leaf, which the king observing, went into the cabin, and bringing up a great coat that belonged to the captain, threw it over my shoulders, telling me to drink some rum from a bottle which he handed me, at the same time giving me to understand that it would be good for me, and keep me from trembling as I did. I took a draught of it, after which, taking me by the hand, he led me to the quarter deck, where the most horrid sight presented itself that ever my eyes witnessed—the heads of our unfortunate captain and his crew, to the number of twenty-five, were all arranged in a line, and Maquina ordering one of his people to bring a head, asked me whose it was: I answered, the captain's; in like manner the others were shewed me, and I told him the names, excepting a few that were so horribly mangled that I was not able to recognize them.

I now discovered that all our unfortunate crew had been massacred, and learned, that after getting possession of the ship, the savages had broke open the arm chest and magazine, and supplying themselves with ammunition and arms, sent a party on shore to attack our men, who had gone thither to fish, and being joined by numbers from the village, without difficulty overpowered and murdered them, and cutting off their heads, brought them on board, after throwing their bodies into the sea: On looking upon the deck, I saw it entirely covered with the blood of my poor comrades, whose throats had been cut with their own jack-knives, the savages having seized the opportunity while they were busy in hoisting in the boat, to grapple with them, and overpower them by their numbers; in the scuffle the captain was thrown overboard, and dispatched by those in the canoes, who immediately cut off his head. . . .

Not satisfied with his first refusal to deliver me up to them, the people again became clamorous that Maquina should consent to my being killed, saying that not one of us ought to be left alive to give information to others of our countrymen, and prevent them from coming to trade, or induce them to revenge the destruction of our ship, and they at length became so boisterous, that he caught up a large club in a passion, and drove them all out of the house. During this scene, a son of the king, about eleven years old, attracted no doubt by the singularity of my appearance, came up to me: I caressed him; he returned my attentions with much apparent pleasure, and considering this as a fortunate opportunity to gain the good will of the father, I took the child on my knee, and cutting the metal buttons from off the coat I had on, I tied them around his neck. At this he was highly delighted, and became so much attached to me, that he would not quit me.

The king appeared much pleased with my attention to his son, and telling me that it was time to go to sleep directed me to lie with his son next to him, as he was afraid lest some of his people would come while he was asleep and kill me with their daggers. I lay down as he ordered me, but neither the state of my mind nor the pain I felt would allow me to sleep.

About midnight I was greatly alarmed by the approach of one of the natives, who came to give information to the king that there was one of the white men alive, who had knocked him down as he went on board the ship at night. This Maquina communicated to me, giving me to understand that as soon as the sun rose he should kill him. I endeavoured to persuade him to spare his life, but he bade me be silent and go to sleep. I said nothing more but lay revolving in my mind what method I could devise to save the life of this man. What a consolation thought I, what a happiness would it prove to me in my forlorn state among these heathens, to have a Christian and one of my own countrymen for a companion, and how greatly it would alleviate and lighten the burden of my slavery.

As I was thinking of some plan for his preservation, it all at once came into my mind that this man was probably the sail maker of the ship, named Thompson, as I had not seen his head among those on deck and knew that he was below at work upon sails not long before the attack. The more I thought of it the more probable it appeared to me, and as Thompson was a man of nearly forty years of age, and had an old look, I conceived it would be easy to make him pass for my father, and by this means prevail on Maquina to spare his life. Towards morning I fell into a doze, but was awakened with the first beams of the sun by the king, who told me he was going to kill the man who was on board the ship, and ordered me to accompany him. I rose and followed him, leading with me the young prince, his son.

On coming to the beach I found the men of the tribe assembled. The king addressed them, saying that one of the white men had been found alive on board the ship, and requested their opinion as to saving his life or putting him to death. They were unanimously for the latter: This determination he made known to me. Having arranged my plan, I asked him, pointing to the boy, whom I still held by the hand, if he loved his son, he answered that he did; I then asked the child if he loved his father, and on his replying in the affirmative, I said, and "I also love mine. I then threw myself on my knees at Maquina's feet, and implored him, with tears in my eyes, to spare my father's life, if the man on board should prove to be him, telling him that if he killed my father, it was my wish that he should kill me too, and that if he did not, I would kill myself,— and that he would thus lose my services; whereas, by sparing my father's life, he would preserve mine, which would be of great advantage to him, by my repairing and making arms for him.

Maquina, appeared moved by my entreaties, and promised not to put the man to death if he should be my father. He then explained to this people what I had said, and ordered me to go on board, and tell the man to come on shore. To my unspeakable joy, on going into the hold, I found that my conjecture was true. Thompson was there, he had escaped without any injury, excepting a slight wound in the nose, given him by one of the savages with a knife, as he attempted to come on deck, during the scuffle. Finding the savages in possession of the ship, as he afterwards informed me, he secreted himself in the hold, hoping for some chance to make his escape—but that the Indian who came on board in the night, approaching the place where he was, he supposed himself discovered, and being determined to sell his life as dearly as possible, as soon as he came within his reach, he knocked him down, but the Indian immediately springing up ran off at full speed.

I informed him, in a few words, that all our men had been killed; that the king had preserved my life, and had consented to spare his on the supposition that he was my father, an opinion which he must be careful not to undeceive them in, as it was his only safety. After giving him his cue, I went on shore with him, and presented him to Maquina, who immediately knew him to be the sailmaker, and was much pleased, observing that he could make sails for his canoe. He then took us to his house, and ordered something for us to eat. . . .

Maquina, who was very proud of his new acquisition, was desirous of welcoming these visitors in the European manner. He accordingly ordered his men, as the canoes approached, to assemble on the beach with loaded muskets and blunderbusses, placing Thompson at the cannon which had been brought from the ship and laid upon two long sticks of timber in front of the village, then taking a speaking trumpet in his hand, he ascended with me, the roof of his house, and began drumming or beating upon the boards with a stick most violently.

Nothing could be more ludicrous than the appearance of this motley group of savages collected on the shore, dressed as they were, with their ill-gotten finery, in the most fantastic manner, some in women's smocks, taken from our cargo, others in Kotsacks, (or cloaks) of blue, red or yellow broadcloth, with stockings drawn over their heads, and their necks hung round with numbers of powderhorns, shot-bags, and cartouch-boxes, some of them having no less than ten muskets a piece on their shoulders, and five or six daggers in their girdles. Diverting indeed was it to see them all squatted upon the beach, holding their muskets perpendicularly, with the butt pressed upon the sand, instead of against their shoulders, and in this position awaiting the order to fire. Maquina, at last, called to them with his trumpet to fire, which they did in the most awkward and timid manner, with their muskets hard pressed upon the ground as above-mentioned. At the same moment the cannon was fired by Thompson, immediately on which they threw themselves back and began to roll and tumble over the sand as if they had been shot, when suddenly springing up, they began a song of triumph and running backward and forward upon the shore, with the wildest gesticulations, boasted of their exploits, and exhibited as trophies, what they had taken from us. Notwithstanding the unpleasantness of my situation, and the feelings that this display of our spoils excited, I could not avoid laughing at the strange appearance of these savages, their awkward movements, and the singular contrast of their dress and arms. . . .

The manner in which they paint themselves frequently varies, according to the occasion, but it oftener is the mere dictate of whim. The most usual method is to paint the eye-brows black, in form of a half moon, and the face red in small squares, with the arms and legs and part of the body red; sometimes one half of the face is painted red in squares, and the other black; at others, dotted with spots, of red and black instead of squares, with a variety of other devices, such as painting one half of the face and body red, and the other black. But a method of painting which they sometimes employed, and which they were much more particular in, was by laying on the face a quantity of bear's grease of about one eighth of an inch thick; this they raised up into ridges resembling a small bead in joiner's work, with a stick prepared for the purpose, and then painted them red, which gave the face a very singular appearance. On extraordinary occasions, the king and principal chiefs used to strew over their faces, after painting, a fine black shining powder, produced from some mineral, as Maquina told me it was got from the rocks. This they call pelpelt and value it highly, as, in their opinion, it serves to set off their looks to great advantage, glittering especially in the sun, like silver.—This article is brought them in bags by the Newchemass, a very savage nation who live a long way to the North, from whom they likewise receive a superior kind of red paint, a species of very fine and rich ochre, which they hold in much estimation.

Notwithstanding this custom of painting themselves, they make it an invariable practice, both in summer and winter, to bathe once a day, and sometimes oftener; but as the paint is put on with oil, it is not much discomposed thereby, and whenever they wish to wash it off, they repair to some piece of fresh water and scour themselves with sand or rushes.

In dressing their heads on occasion of a festival or a visit, they are full as particular, and almost as long, as in painting. The hair, after being well oiled, is carefully gathered upon the top of the head, and secured by a piece of pine or spruce bough, with the green leaves upon it. After having it properly fixed in this manner, the king and principal chiefs used to strew all over it the white down obtained from a species of large brown eagle, which abounds on this coast, and which they are very particular in arranging so as not to have a single feather out of place, occasionally wetting the hair to make it adhere. This, together with the bough, which is sometimes of considerable size, and stuck over with feathers by means of turpentine, gives them a very singular and grotesque appearance, which they, however, think very becoming, and the first thing they do on learning the arrival of strangers, is to go and decorate themselves in this manner. . . .

The expedition consisted of forty canoes, carrying from ten to twenty men each. Thompson and myself armed ourselves with cutlasses and pistols, but the natives, although they had plenty of European arms, took with them only their daggers and cheetoolths, with a few bows and arrows, the latter being about a yard in length, and pointed with copper, muscle shell, or bone: the bows are four feet and a half long, with strings made of whale sinew.

To go to A-y-chart, we ascended from twenty to thirty miles, a river about the size of that of Tashees, the banks of which are high and covered with wood. At midnight, we came in sight of the village, which was situated on the west bank, near the shore, on a steep hill difficult of access, and well calculated for defense. It consisted of fifteen or sixteen houses, smaller than those at Nootka, and built in the same style, but compactly placed. By Maquina's directions the fight was deferred until the first appearance of dawn, as he said that was the time when the men slept the soundest.

At length all being ready for the attack, we landed with the greatest silence, and going around so as to come upon the foe in the rear, clambered up the hill, and while the natives, as is their custom, entered the several huts, creeping on all fours, my comrade and myself stationed ourselves without, to intercept those who should attempt to escape, or come to the aid of their friends. I wished if possible, not to stain my hands in the blood of any fellow creature, and though Thompson would gladly have put to death all the country, he was too brave to think of attacking a sleeping enemy.

Having entered the house, on the war-whoop being given by Maquina, as he seized the head of the chief, and gave him the fatal blow, all proceded to the work of death. The A-y-charts being thus surprised, were unable to make resistance, and with the exception of a very few, who were so fortunate as to make their escape, were all killed or taken prisoners on condition of becoming slaves to their captors. I had the good fortune to take four captives, whom Maquina, as a favor, permitted me to consider as mine, and occasionally employ them in fishing for me; as for Thompson, who thirsted for revenge, he had no wish to take any prisoners, but with his cutlass, the only weapon he would employ against them, succeeded in killing seven stout fellows, who came to attack him, an act which obtained him great credit with Maquina and the chiefs, who after this, held him in much higher estimation, and gave him the appelation of Chehiel-suma-har, it being the name of a very celebrated warrior of their nation in ancient times, whose exploits were the constant theme of their praise.

After having put to death all the old and infirm of either sex, as is the barbarous practice of these people, and destroyed the buildings, we reembarked with our booty in our canoes, for Nootka, where we were received with great demonstrations of joy, by the women and children, accompanying our war song with a most furious drumming on the houses. The next day a great feast was given by Maquina, in celebration of his victory, which was terminated as usual with a dance by Sat-sat-sak-sis. . . .

It was now past mid-summer, and the hopes we had indulged of our release became daily more faint, for though we had heard of no less than seven vessels on the coast, yet none appeared inclined to venture to Nootka. The destruction of the Boston, the largest, strongest, and best equipped ship, with the most valuable cargo of any that had ever been fitted for the North west trade, had inspired the commanders of others with a general dread of coming thither, lest they should share the same fate; and though in the letters I wrote (imploring those who should receive them to come to the relief of two unfortunate Christians who were suffering among heathen) I stated the cause of the Boston's capture, and that there was not the least danger in coming to Nootka, provided they would follow the directions I laid down, still I felt very little encouragement that any of these letters would come to hand, when on the morning of the nineteenth of July, a day that will ever be held by me in grateful remembrance, of the mercies of God, while I was employed with Thompson in forging daggers for the king, my ears were saluted with the joyful sound of three cannon, and the cried of the inhabitants, exclaiming, Weena, weena—Mamethlee—that is, strangers—white men.

Soon after several of our people came running into the house, to inform me that a vessel under full sail was coming into the harbour. Though my heart bounded with joy, I repressed my feelings, and affecting to pay no attention to what he said, told Thompson to be on his guard, and not betray any joy, as our release, and perhaps our lives, depended on our conducting ourselves so as to induce the natives to suppose we were not very anxious to leave them. We continued our work as if nothing had happened, when in a few minutes after, Maquina came in, and seeing us at work, appeared much surprised, and asked me if I did not know that a vessel had come. I answered in a careless manner, that it was nothing to me. How, John, said he, you no glad go board. I replied that I cared very little about it, as I had become reconciled to their manner of living, and had no wish to go away. He then told me, that he had called a council of his people respecting us, and that we must leave off work and be present at it.

The men having assembled at Maquina's house, he asked them what was their opinion should be done with Thompson and myself, now a vessel had arrived, and whether he had better go on board himself, to make a trade, and procure such articles as were wanted. Each one of the tribe who wished, gave his opinion. Some were for putting us to death, and pretending to the strangers, that a different nation had cut off the Boston, while others, less barbarous, were for sending us fifteen or twenty miles back into the country, until the departure of the vessel. These, however, were the sentiments of the common people, the chiefs opposing our being put to death, or injured, and several of them, among the most forward of whom were Yealthlower and the younger chief, Toowinnakinnish, were for immediately releasing us; but this, if he could avoid it, by no means appeared to accord with Maquina's wishes.

Having mentioned Toowinnakinnish, I shall briefly observe, that he was a young man of about twenty-three years old, the only son of Toopeeshottee, the oldest and most respected chief of the tribe. His son had always been remarkably kind and friendly to me, and I had in return frequently made for him daggers, cheetoolths, and other things, in my best manner. He was one of the handsomest men among them, very amiable, and much milder in his manners than any of the others, as well as neater both in his person and house, at least his apartment, without even excepting Maquina.

With regard, however, to Maquina's going on board the vessel, which he discovered a strong inclination to do, there was but one opinion, all remonstrating against it, telling him that the captain would kill him or keep him prisoner, in consequence of his having destroyed our ship. When Maquina heard their opinions, he told them that he was not afraid of being hurt from going on board the vessel, but that he would, however, as it respected that, be guided by John, whom he had always found true. He then turned to me, and asked if I thought there would be any danger in his going on board. I answered, that I was not surprised at the advice his people had given him, unacquainted as they were with the manners of the white men, and judging by their own, but if they had been with them as much as I had, or even himself, they would think very different. That he had almost always experienced good and civil treatment from them, nor had he any reason to fear the contrary now, as they never attempted to harm those who did not injure them, and if he wished to go on board, he might do it, in my opinion with security.

After reflecting a few moments, he said, with much apparent satisfaction, that if I would write a letter to the captain, telling him good of him, that he had treated Thompson and myself kindly since we had been with him, and to use him well, he would go. It may easily be supposed that I felt much joy at this determination, but knowing that the least incaution might annihilate all my hopes of escape, was careful not to manifest it, and to treat his going or staying as a matter perfectly indifferent to me. I told him that if he wished to write such a letter, I had no objection, as it was the truth, otherwise I could not have done it.

I then proceeded to write the recommendatory letter, which the reader will naturally imagine was of a somewhat different tenor from the one he had required; for if deception is in any case warrantable, it was certainly so in a situation like ours, where the only chance of regaining that freedom of which we had been so unjustly deprived, depended upon it; and I trust that few, even of the most rigid, will condemn me with severity for making use of it, on an occasion which afforded me the only hope of ever more beholding a Christian country, and preserving myself, if not from death, at least from a life of continued suffering.

The letter which I wrote, was nearly in the following terms:—

To Captain _____
of the Brig _____
Nootka, July 19, 1805.

Sir

The bearer of this letter is the Indian king by the name of Maquina. He was the instigator of the capture of the ship Boston, of Boston, in North America, John Salter captain, and of the murder of twenty five men of her crew, the only two survivors being now on shore—Wherefore I hope you will take care to confine him according to his merits, putting in your dead-lights, and keeping so good a watch over him, that he cannot escape from you. By so doing we shall be able to obtain our release in the course of a few hours.

John R. Jewitt, Armourer of
the Boston, for himself and
John Thompson, Sail-maker of
the said ship.

I have been asked how I dared to write in this manner, my answer is, that from my long residence among these people, I knew that I had little to apprehend from their anger upon hearing of their king being confined, while they knew his life depended upon my release, and that they would sooner have given up five hundred white men, than have had him injured. This will serve to explain the little apprehension I felt at their menaces afterwards, for otherwise, sweet as liberty was to me, I should hardly have ventured on so hazardous an experiment.

On my giving the letter to Maquina, he asked me to explain it to him. This I did line by line, as he pointed them out with his finger, but in a sense very different from the real, giving him to understand that I had written to the captain, that as he had been kind to me since I had been taken by him, that it was my wish that the captain should treat him accordingly, and give what molasses, biscuit and rum he wanted. When I had finished, placing his finger in a significant manner on my name at the bottom, and eyeing me with a look that seemed to read my inmost thoughts, he said to me, "John you no lie?" Never did I undergo such a scrutiny, or ever experience greater apprehension than I felt at that moment, when my destiny was suspended on the slightest thread, and the least mark of embarrassment on mine, or suspicion of treachery on his part, would probably have rendered my life the sacrifice.

# Epilogue

In 1795 a man with $1.75 in his pocket, a rank tenderfoot with no wilderness experience, started up the Missouri River into the wild unknown. A group of English romantics had sent John Evans across the sea to find the Welsh Indians, a fabled "lost tribe" that flickered in Europeans' imaginations as the terra incognita receded west.

That Evans, along with others who tried to make contact with the mythical, blue-eyed band, came back disappointed hardly surprises us. In a few years Lewis and Clark would do further damage to the West as dreamscape. They discovered that, contrary to the common hope of Easterners panting after a lucrative trade with China, no easy water route existed between the Mississippi River and the Pacific Ocean. In the next decades, the geography of the West came clear, and in many ways it was a disappointing geography. In all the huge expanse of the West there were no bearded, redheaded Indians, no tribes of dwarfs, no trumpeting mammoths or eerie mountains that glowed through the night. Instead the dream-inspiring region was, like any other on the earth, a place with its own unique set of mountain systems and water drainages, flora, fauna, and mineral deposits—some of them breathtaking in their vastness and richness but none of them preternatural. True the dream lived on long after it had been debunked, and the hearts of some people still skip beats when they think of the West as a fantastic treasure trove of resources and adventure in the modes that gave us the witless clearcutting of forests and the romances of Zane Grey. But slowly it's been seeping into the national consciousness: the laws of physics apply west of the Mississippi River as they do everywhere else on the planet.

That comes as bad news to creators of literature. Only a few decades ago, as sagacious a western novelist as Wallace Stegner referred to his homeland as "the geography of hope." Its open spaces, resources, and scenic landscapes set the region apart, made the region unique, made it a focus for hearts yearning for renewal. Yet in the short time since, we've learned that the West is not immune from the overpopulation, erosion, and race riots plaguing the rest of the nation. A talented writer in the generation after Stegner bears this out. All his writing life, the Pennsylvania-born Edward Abbey tried to convince himself and his readers that the West was different, a place of freedom derived from spacious natural beauty, but despite his soaring, descriptive prose, Abbey's vision was more wish than reality, as he himself grudgingly shows. In his disillusioned novels, hope-filled, outdoor-loving heroes are ground up beneath the wheels of a technological civilization asphalting the earth as it triumphs over nature.

As reality crowds in on us, it seems that we've passed through the stage in which either the fantasy West or the West as special, physical place can serve as a valid underpinning of western American literature. That would appear to leave few options. Traditional western novels of cowboy-and-Indian travails may continue to have their following, but they can be read only by the willfully unsophisticated without continuing smirks. On the other hand, a writer of Abbey's sophistication seems doomed from the start, because the modern reality of the West falls short of his expectations.

Still, people who write about literature can be a depressive lot, moaning that the age of fine literary wine has passed and taking perverse comfort that they now must content themselves with the dregs. But maybe they're shortchanging the West with their convenient melancholia. It is true that there are no more alluring blank spaces on the West's maps. The region's motels, freeways, and pizza parlors mark it as homogenized, along with the rest of the nation. One must now pay a fee to enter what should be the wild, challenging grandeur—our last untamed places—of the national parks, as if one were buying a ticket to a movie, to a show.

However, though such features are painfully evident, they also may be more superficial than we think. If anything the West remains a place of unsettled spaces, differences, and tensions, a place with subtleties not fully explored. Tucson, Arizona, and Missoula, Montana, are nearly twelve hundred miles apart, and they differ radically in climate, landscape, and ethnic makeup. To step off the airplane from one city into the other is to step from one subculture into another, each with its own discrete mix of economic factors and hopes for the future. The June drizzle falling on Missoula's lush greenness and onto the surrounding snow-capped peaks is hardly Tucson's July thunderburst that snaps lightning across the bare mountains above the city and has the bone-dry desert canyons roaring with boulder-filled torrents. The differences are deep, and they show in the ways people live and how they think. By necessity the novelist who grew up in San Francisco's Chinatown will tell a different story than the writer from Albuquerque's barrio. The West's continuing settlement, perennial water crises, and the rub of racial groups all go into the mix of what the West is about, and they all provide the conflicts and hopes that are the raw stuff from which literature, a ruderal plant in the West, continues to spring.

Finally the specific link between the fantasies of John Evans and our own dreams. In recent years the West's literature has often found its best expression in nature writing, a genre linearly descended, in part, from exploration narratives such as those collected in this volume. Disillusioned contemporary writers look more closely at the reality that scaled the illusions from our perceptions. And what we see now is far different from the visions that pulled John Evans and other dreamers ever farther westward into the wilderness. We see a ravaged landscape, a biotic holocaust, as we seem to be spinning out of control and heading toward ecocide. The good news—if a note of optimism can be sounded in the face of such a dire prospect—the good news is that at least some people have recognized the danger of our exploding population and our industrialized lifestyle. Besides offering a varied selection of fine writing, what this anthology can add to the awakening perception of our common peril is a picture of what our world was like before the destruction began, as well as the realization that ecocidal dreams die hard. The visions of streets paved with gold, visions that sent Europeans to their ships and forty-niners across the mountains and plains, still live on in our belief that we can all have palatial and gadget-filled homes with three-car garages and children to fill all the cars and then some—all that the cornucopia of our dreams promises and all without paying any price for what we must do to the world around us if we are to fulfill our fantasies. Clearly humans of all races and creeds must somehow overcome the dazzlement with technology that is becoming our fatal addiction. We would be wise to quit living the dream of King Midas, before we suffer his fate. To begin living what is, paradoxically, the newest and oldest of all dreams: the dream of the earth.

## Selected Bibliography

Lyon, Thomas J., ed. *This Incomperable Lande: A Book of American Nature Writing*. Boston: Houghton Mifflin, 1989.

Thanks are due to the following for permission to reprint extracts from material copyrighted or controlled by them:

*British Columbia Historical Quarterly* for "Extracts from the Diaries of Frances Hornby Barkley" (1942).

Cambridge University Press for *The Journals and Letters of Sir Alexander Mackenzie,* ed. W. Kaye Lamb, ©1970.

Victor G. Hopwood for *Travels in Western North America, 1784–1812* by David Thompson, ed. Victor G. Hopwood, ©1971.

Macmillan Publishing Company for *Cabeza de Vaca's Adventures in the Unknown Interior of America,* ed. and trans. Cyclone Covey, ©1961.

Minnesota Historical Society for *Five Fur Traders of the Northwest,* ed. Charles M. Gates, ©1933, 1965.

The New Mexico Historical Society for *Discovery of the Seven Cities of Cíbola by Marco da Niza,* ed. and trans. Percy M. Baldwin (1926); and for *The Gallegos Relations of the Rodriguez Expedition to New Mexico by Hernán Lamero Gallegos,* eds. George P. Hammond and Agapito Rey (1927).

Ross & Haines for *The Explorations of Pierre Esprit Radisson,* ed. Arthur T. Adams, ©1961.

Stanford University Press for *Journal of a Voyage with Bering, 1741–1742 by George Wilhelm Steller,* ed. O. W. Frost, ©1988.

The University of California Press for *Font's Complete Diary of the Second Anza Expedition,* ed. Herbert E. Bolton (1931).

The University of New Mexico Press for *Historia de la Nueva Mexico, 1610: A Critical and Annotated Spanish/English Edition* by Gaspar Perez de Villagra, ed. and trans. Miguel Encinias, Alfred Rodríguez, and Joseph P. Sánchez, ©1992; and for *The Rediscovery of New Mexico, 1580–1594,* eds. George P. Hammond and Agapito Rey, ©1966.

The University of Oklahoma Press for *After Coronado: Spanish Exploration Northeast of New Mexico, 1696–1727* by Alfred Barnaby Thomas, (1934); for *Pedro Vial and the Roads to Santa Fe* by Noel M. Loomis and Abraham P. Nasatir, ©1967; and for *The California Coast: A Bilingual Edition of Documents from the Sutro Collection,* ed. Donald C. Cutter, ©1969.

The Utah State Historical Society for *The Domínguez-Escalante Journal: Their*

*Expedition through Colorado, Utah, Arizona, and New Mexico in 1776*, ed. Ted. J. Warner, trans. Fray Angelico Chavez, ©1976.

# Index

# About the Editors

Donald A. Barclay is Reference Librarian at New Mexico State University. Originally from Idaho, he is a graduate of Boise State University and earned graduate degrees at the University of California—Berkeley.

James H. Maguire is Professor of English at Boise State University, where he has also served as an editor of the Western Writers Series since 1972. He is the author of *Mary Hallock Foote* (1972) and the editor of *The Literature of Idaho: An Anthology* (1986). He is also a contributing editor to *A Literary History of the American West* (1987).

Peter Wild is Professor of English at the University of Arizona. An award-winning poet, he recently edited the autobiography of early desert traveler John C. Van Dyke (Utah 1993).